Hello, I'm Amélie.
The old man at my house just got
through a deadline, so today I took
him out to see cherry blossoms.
He's a completely hopeless case
though. He's been staying indoors
all the time lately, so his legs and
back have gotten really weak. Look
at me! The petals! Every time I
run, they fly up into the air!

—*Yūki Tabata's dog, 2016*

YŪKI TABATA

was born in Fukuoka Prefecture
and got his big break in the 2011
Shonen Jump Golden Future Cup
with his winning entry, *Hungry
Joker*. He started the magical fantasy
series *Black Clover* in 2015.

BLACK CLOVER
VOLUME 6
SHONEN JUMP Manga Edition

Story and Art by YŪKI TABATA

Translation ● TAYLOR ENGEL, HC LANGUAGE SOLUTIONS, INC.
Touch-Up Art & Lettering ● ANNALIESE CHRISTMAN
Design ● SHAWN CARRICO
Editor ● ALEXIS KIRSCH

Printed in the U.S.A.

Published by VIZ Media, LLC
P.O. Box 77010
San Francisco, CA 94107

10 9 8 7 6 5 4 3 2 1
First printing, April 2017

SHONEN JUMP
VIZ media
www.shonenjump.com www.viz.com

SHONENJUMP MANGA

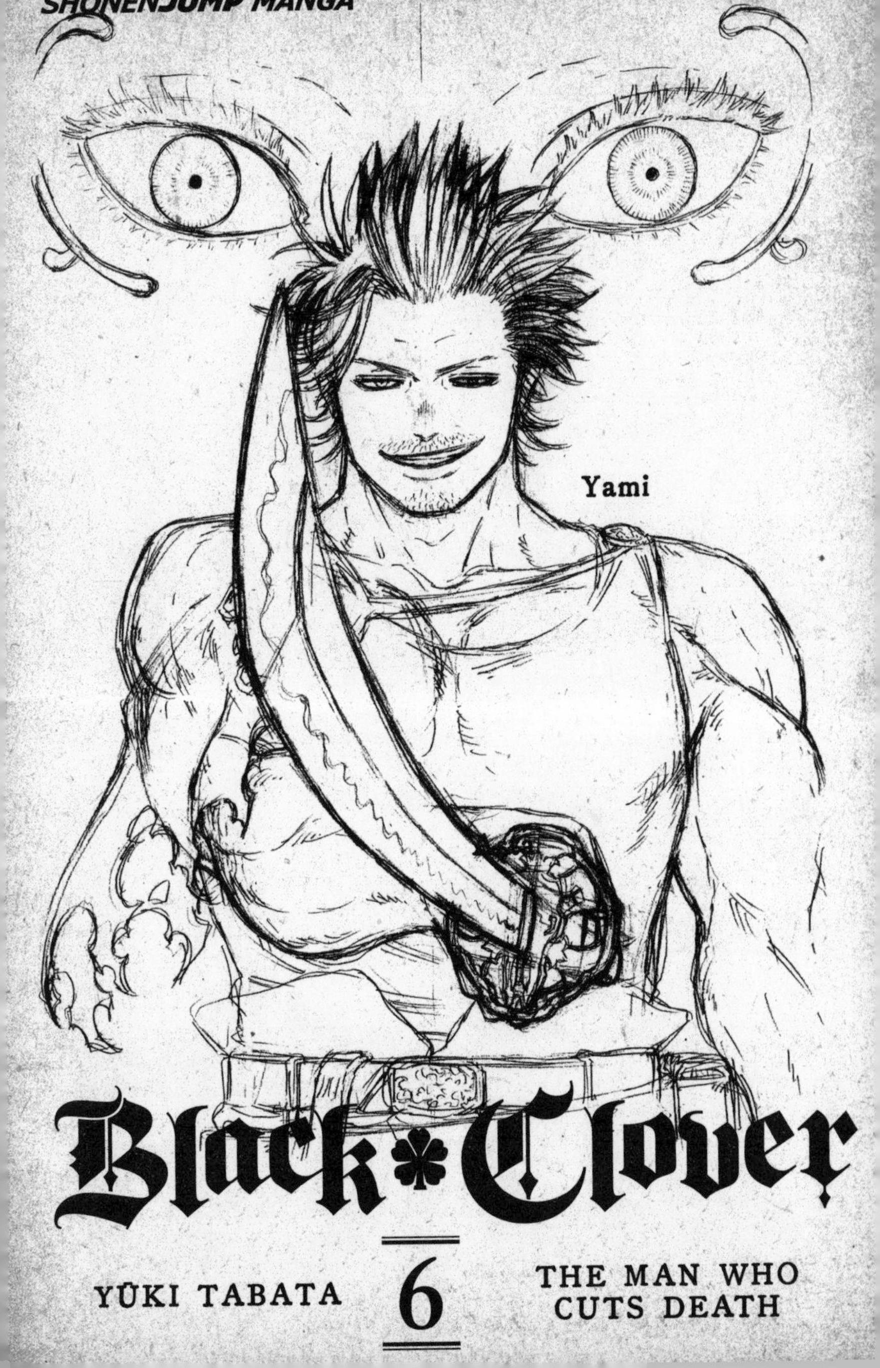
Yami

Black Clover

6

YŪKI TABATA

THE MAN WHO CUTS DEATH

Characters

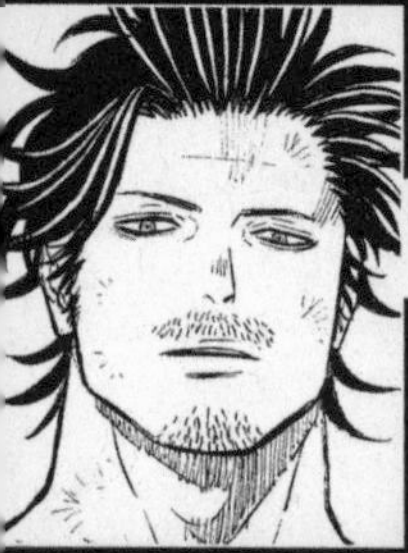

Yami Sukehiro

Member of:
The Black Bulls
Magic: ?

A captain who looks fierce and has a hot temper, but is very popular with his brigade.

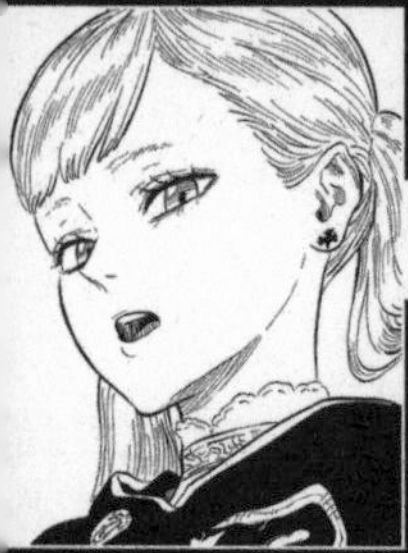

Noelle Silva

Member of:
The Black Bulls
Magic: Water

A royal. She's really impudent, but can be kind too.

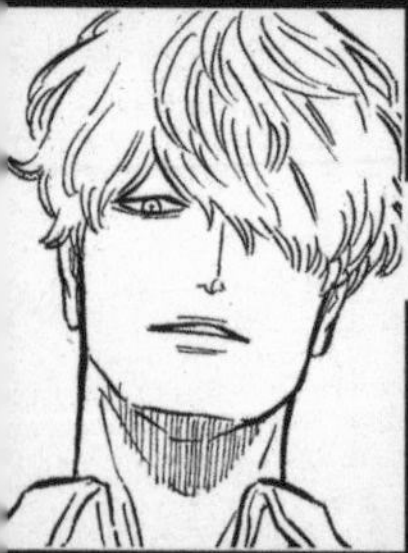

Gauche Adlai

Member of:
The Black Bulls
Magic: Mirror

A former convict with a blind, pathological love for his little sister.

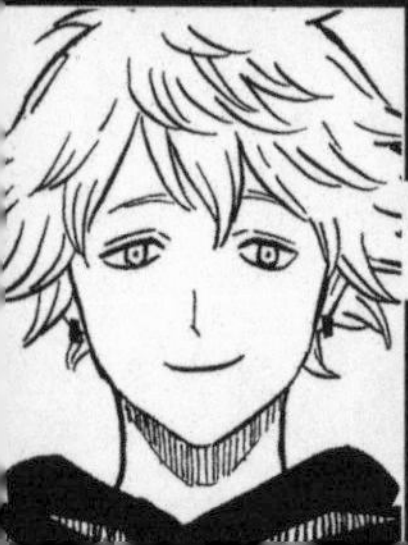

Finral Roulacase

Member of:
The Black Bulls
Magic: Spatial

A flirt who likes girls so much it gets in the way of his missions.

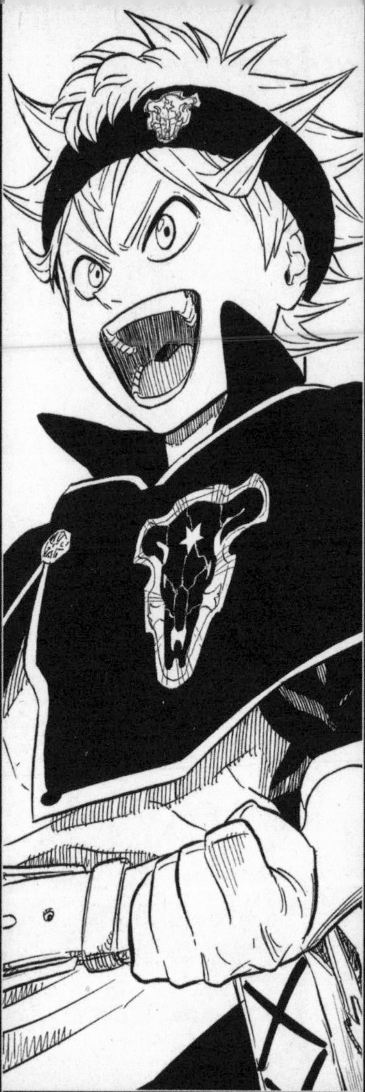

Asta

Squad: The Black Bulls
Magic: None (Anti-Magic)

He has no magic, but he's working to become the Wizard King through sheer guts and his well-trained body.

Theresa

Member of: Formerly "The Crimson She-Leopard"
Magic: Flame

A nun from the church. She used to be a Magic Knight.

Marie Adlai

Gauche's younger sister. A little girl who's full of kindness and consideration for others.

Neige

Magic: Snow

He helped his brother kidnap lots of children in order to extract their magic.

Rebecca Scarlet

A sensible oldest daughter who works in a restaurant to support her brothers and sisters.

Valtos

Member of: The Eye of the Midnight Sun
Magic: Spatial

A cool, collected guy who worships his leader.

Sally

Member of: The Eye of the Midnight Sun
Magic: Gel

A mad magic scientist. She uses dark magic items.

STORY

In a world where magic is everything, Asta and Yuno are both found abandoned on the same day at a church in the remote village of Hage. Both dream of becoming the Wizard King, the highest of all mages, and they spend their days working toward that dream.

The year they turn 15, both receive grimoires, magic books that amplify their bearer's magic. They take the entrance exam for the Magic Knights, nine groups of mages under the direct control of the Wizard King. Yuno, whose magic is strong, joins the Golden Dawn, an elite group, while Asta, who has no magic at all, joins the Black Bulls, a group of misfits. With this, the two finally take their first step toward becoming the Wizard King...

During a vacation, Asta runs into a pair of brothers who have been kidnapping children and stealing their magic. Asta thinks he's rescued the children, but Sally from the Eye of the Midnight Sun abruptly appears. She then uses a dark magic item to amplify the magic of one of the kidnappers, turning him into a huge, mindless monster! Asta will give anything to protect the children, but will it be enough...?!

CONTENTS

BLACK 🍀 CLOVER

6

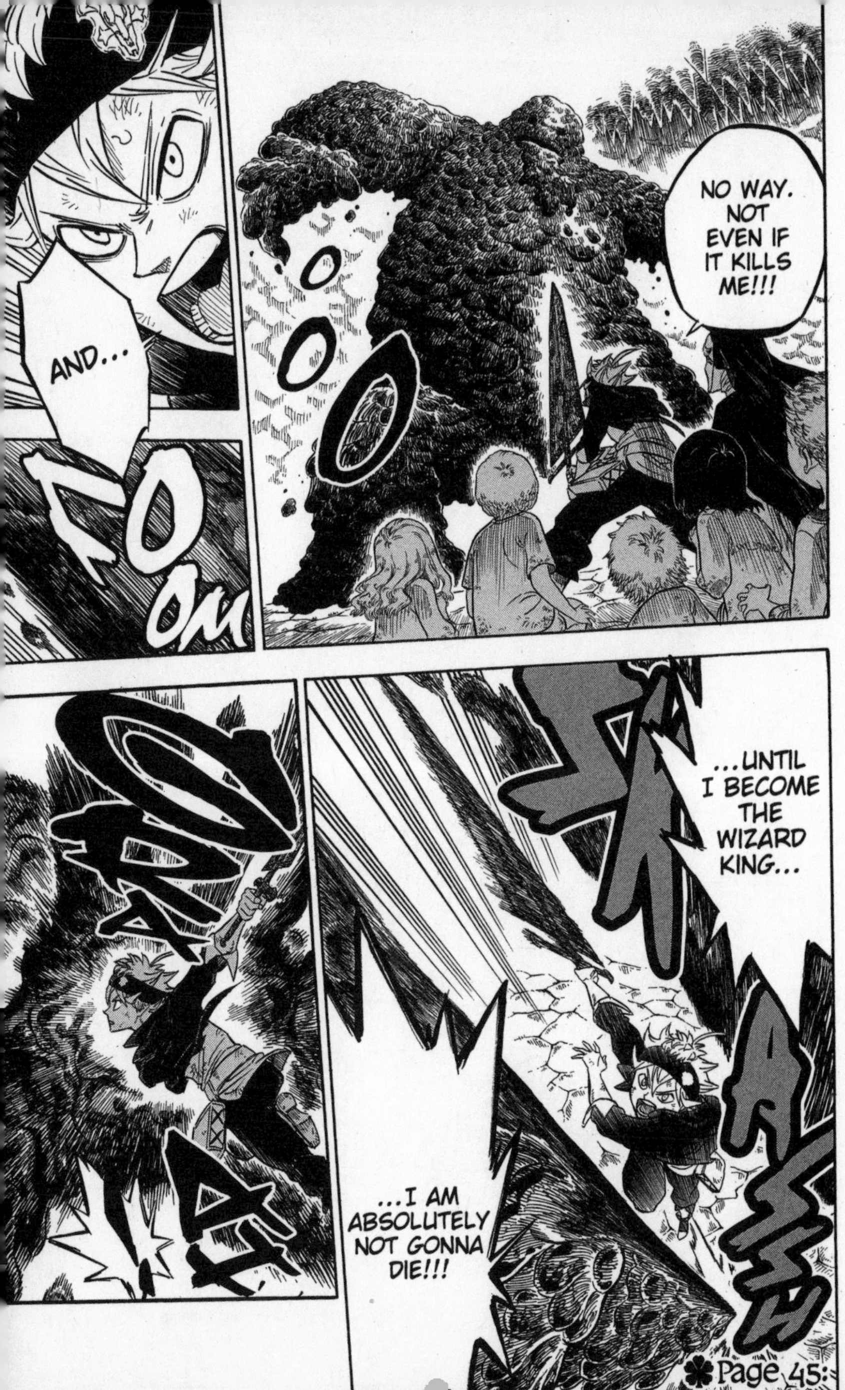
NO WAY. NOT EVEN IF IT KILLS ME!!!
AND...
...UNTIL I BECOME THE WIZARD KING...
...I AM ABSOLUTELY NOT GONNA DIE!!!

Page 45: To Help Somebody Someday

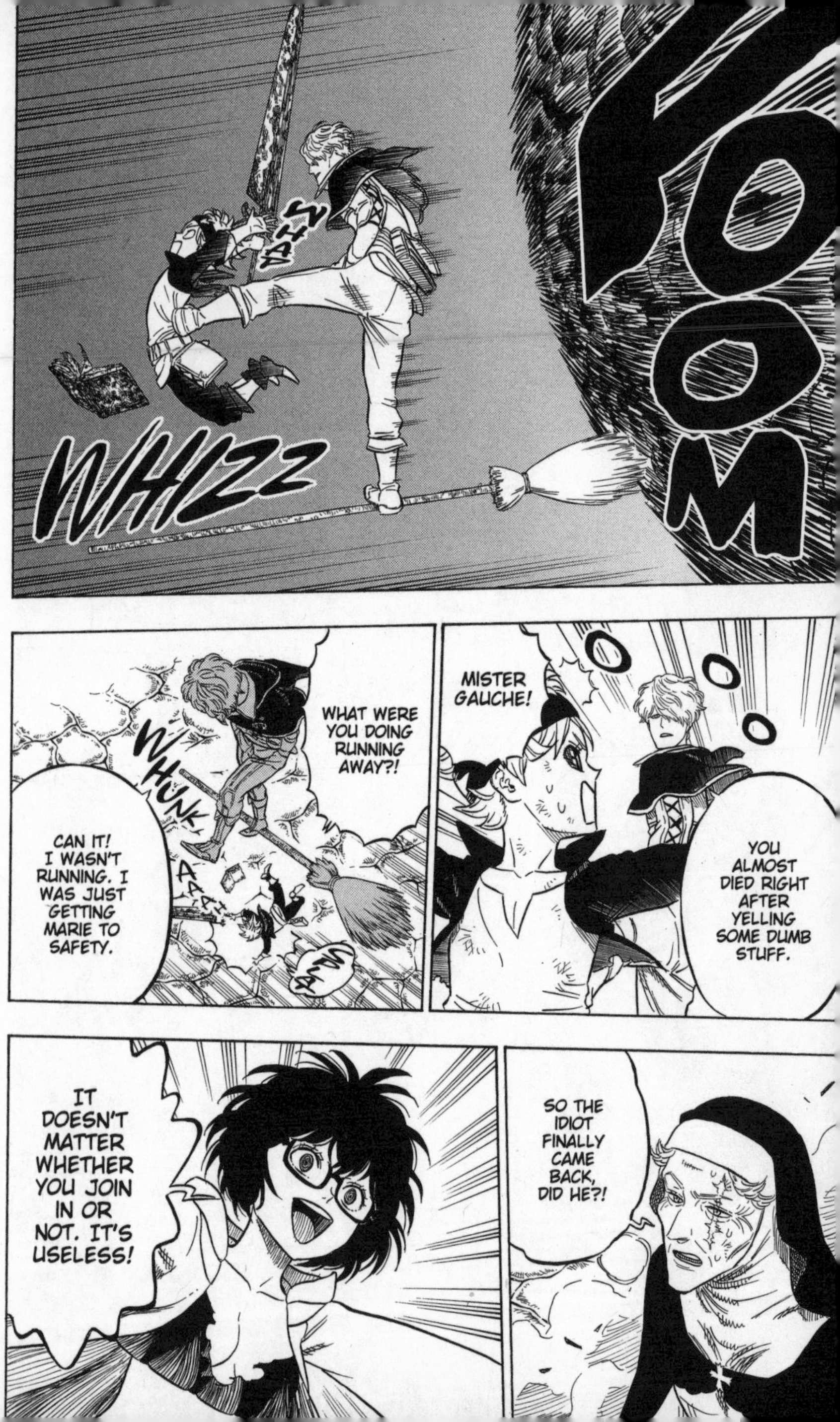
VOOM
WHAP
WHIZZ
MISTER GAUCHE!
YOU ALMOST DIED RIGHT AFTER YELLING SOME DUMB STUFF.
WHAT WERE YOU DOING RUNNING AWAY?!
WHUNK
CAN IT! I WASN'T RUNNING. I WAS JUST GETTING MARIE TO SAFETY.
SO THE IDIOT FINALLY CAME BACK, DID HE?!
IT DOESN'T MATTER WHETHER YOU JOIN IN OR NOT. IT'S USELESS!

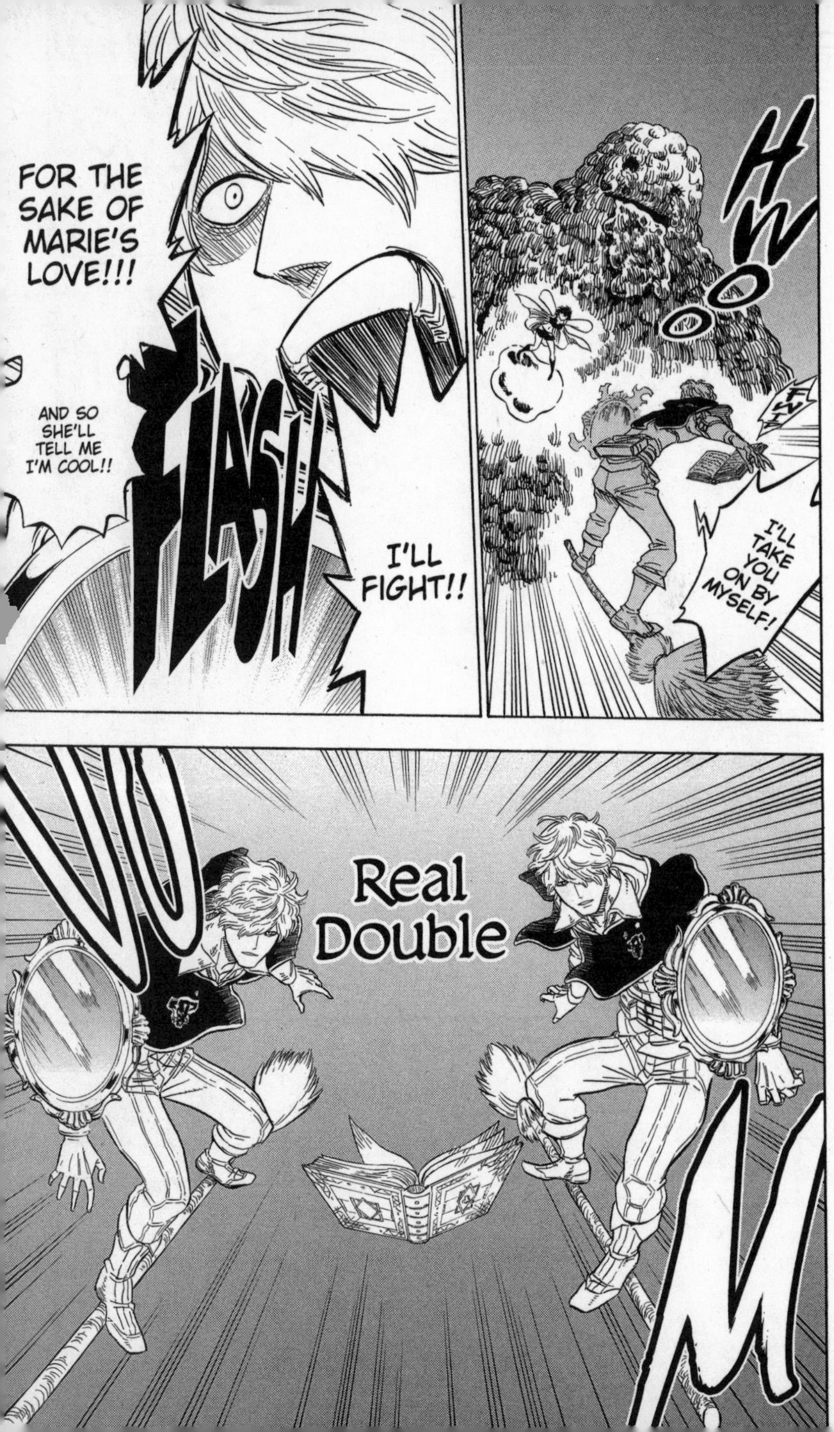
HWOOO
I'LL TAKE YOU ON BY MYSELF!
FOR THE SAKE OF MARIE'S LOVE!!!
AND SO SHE'LL TELL ME I'M COOL!!
FLASH
I'LL FIGHT!!
Real Double

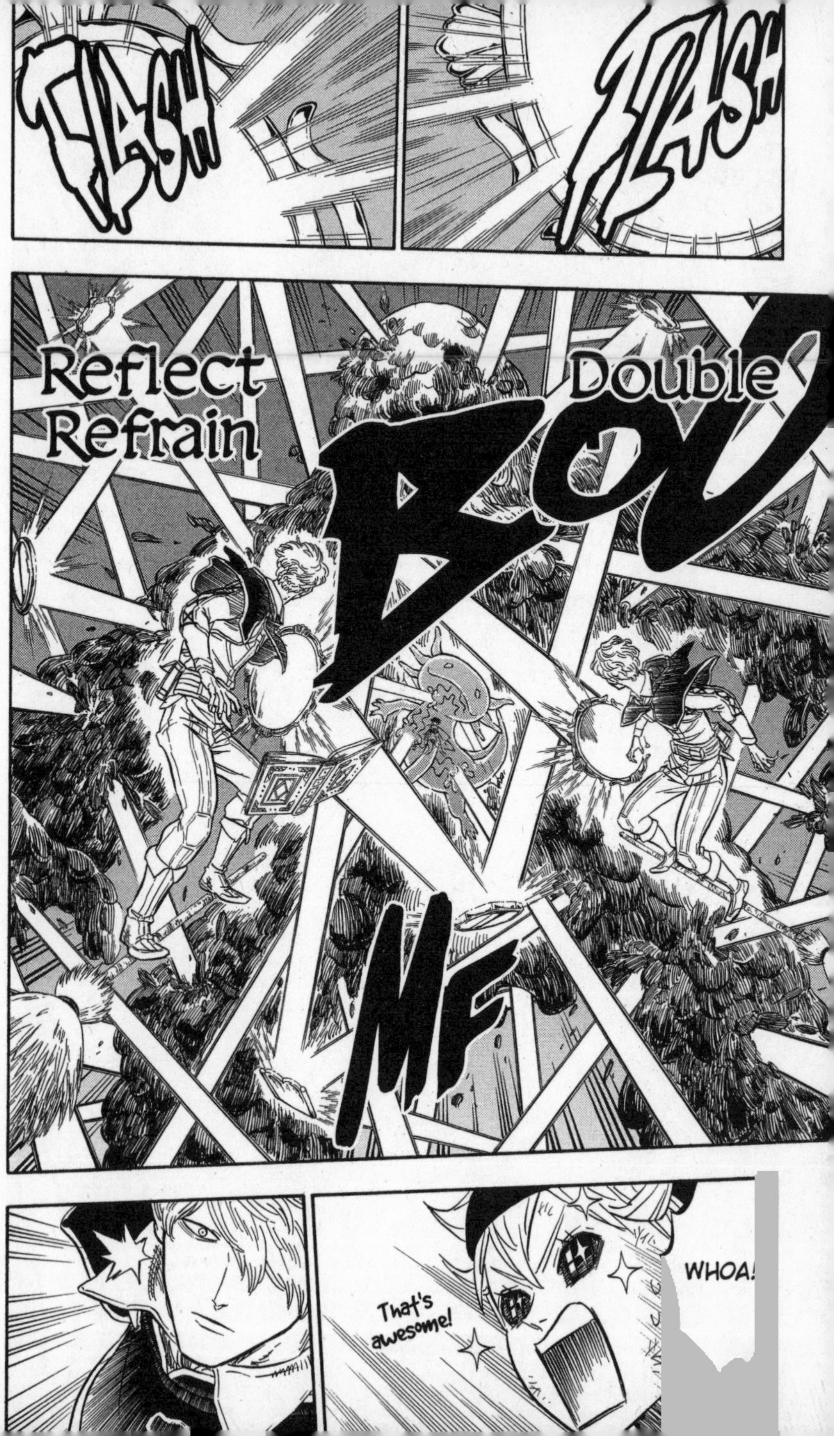
FLASH
FLASH
Double
Reflect Refrain
BOOMF
WHOA!
That's awesome!

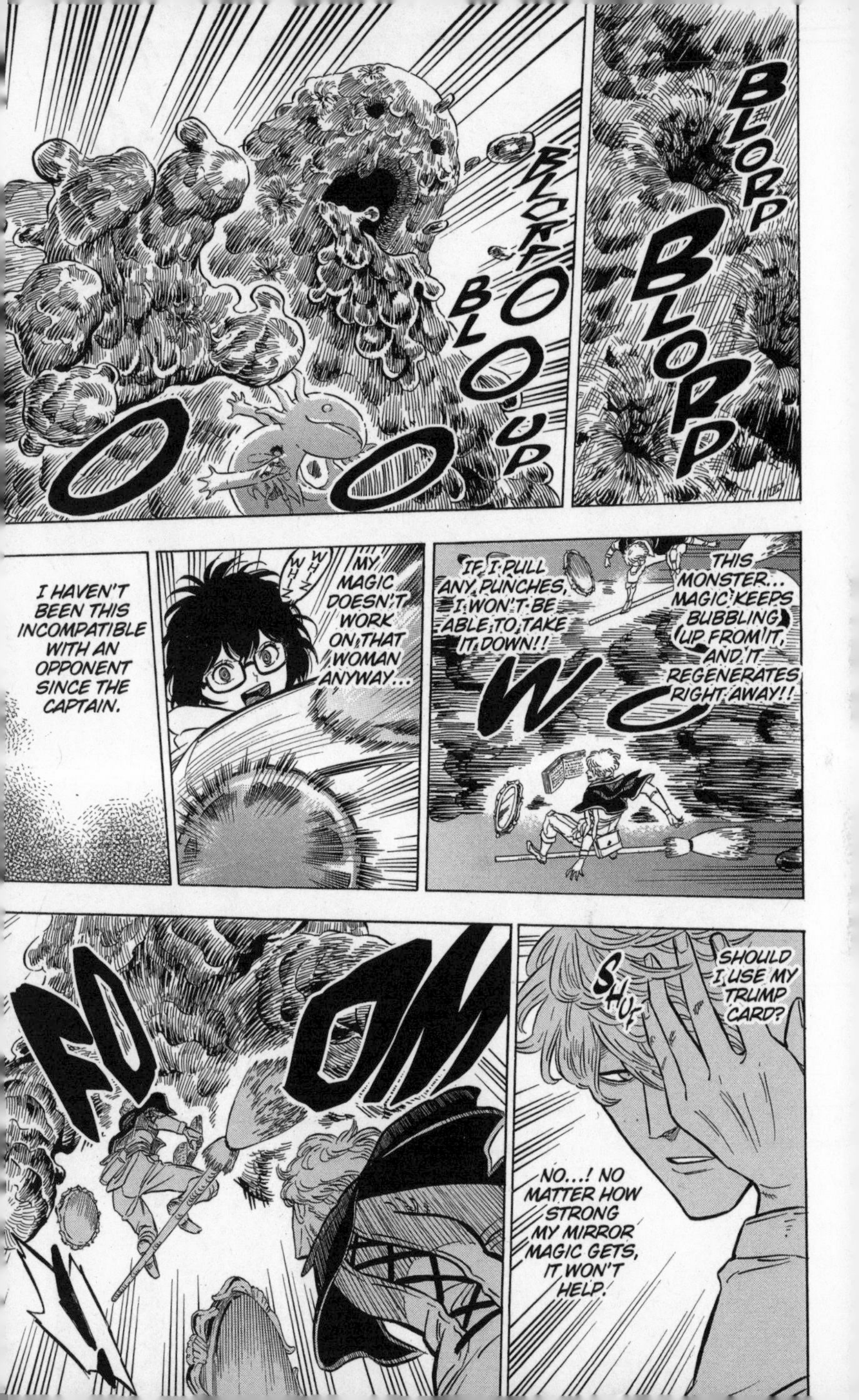
BLORP
BLORP
BLORP
BLORP
BLOOOOUP
THIS MONSTER... MAGIC KEEPS BUBBLING UP FROM IT, AND IT REGENERATES RIGHT AWAY!!
IF I PULL ANY PUNCHES, I WON'T BE ABLE TO TAKE IT DOWN!!
WOO
MY MAGIC DOESN'T WORK ON THAT WOMAN ANYWAY...
WHIZ
WHIZ
I HAVEN'T BEEN THIS INCOMPATIBLE WITH AN OPPONENT SINCE THE CAPTAIN.
SHOULD I USE MY TRUMP CARD?
SHU
NO...! NO MATTER HOW STRONG MY MIRROR MAGIC GETS, IT WON'T HELP.
FOOM

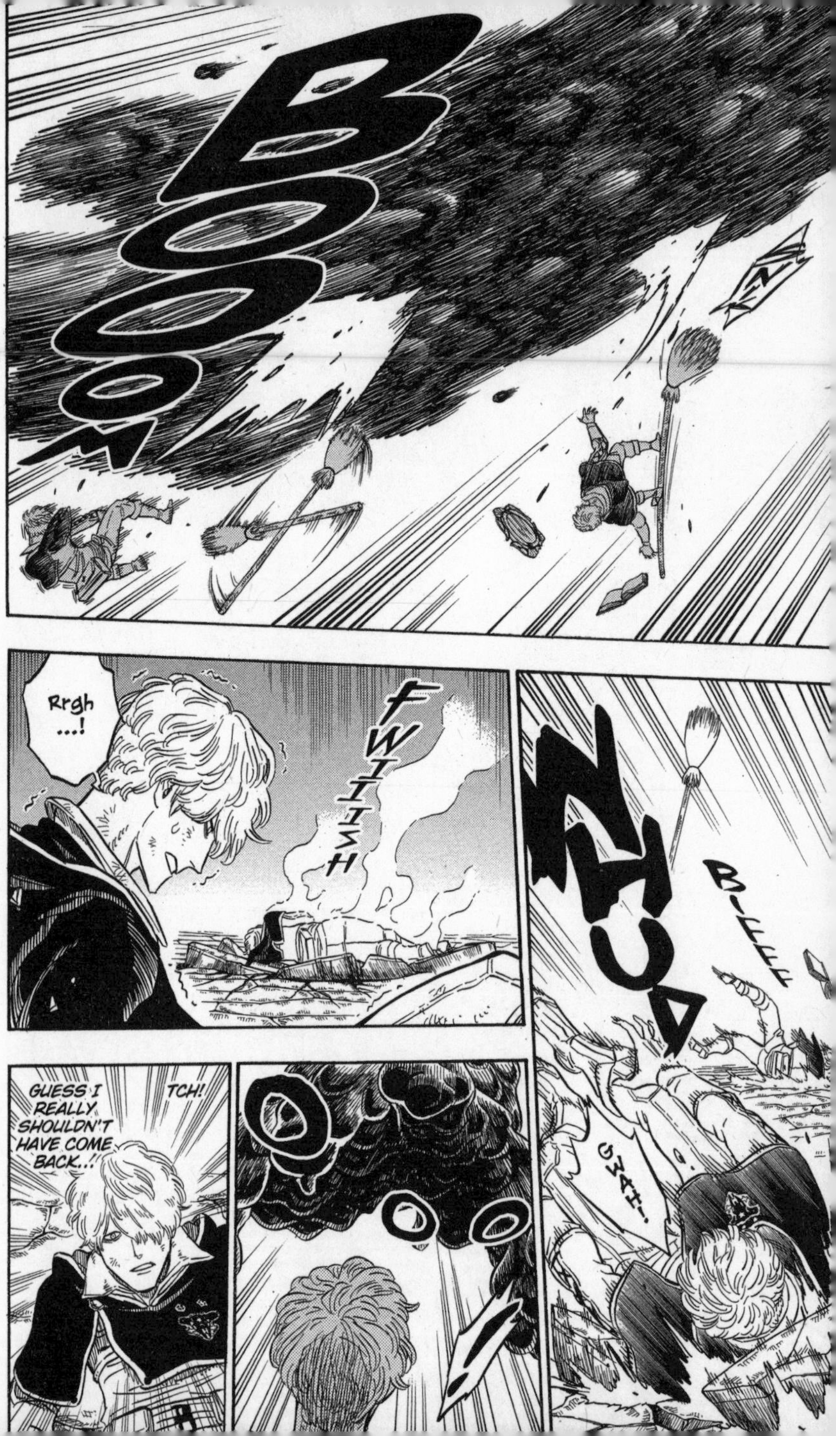
BOOOOM
THUD
GWAH!
Rrgh ...!
FWIIISH
TCH!
GUESS I REALLY SHOULDN'T HAVE COME BACK..!

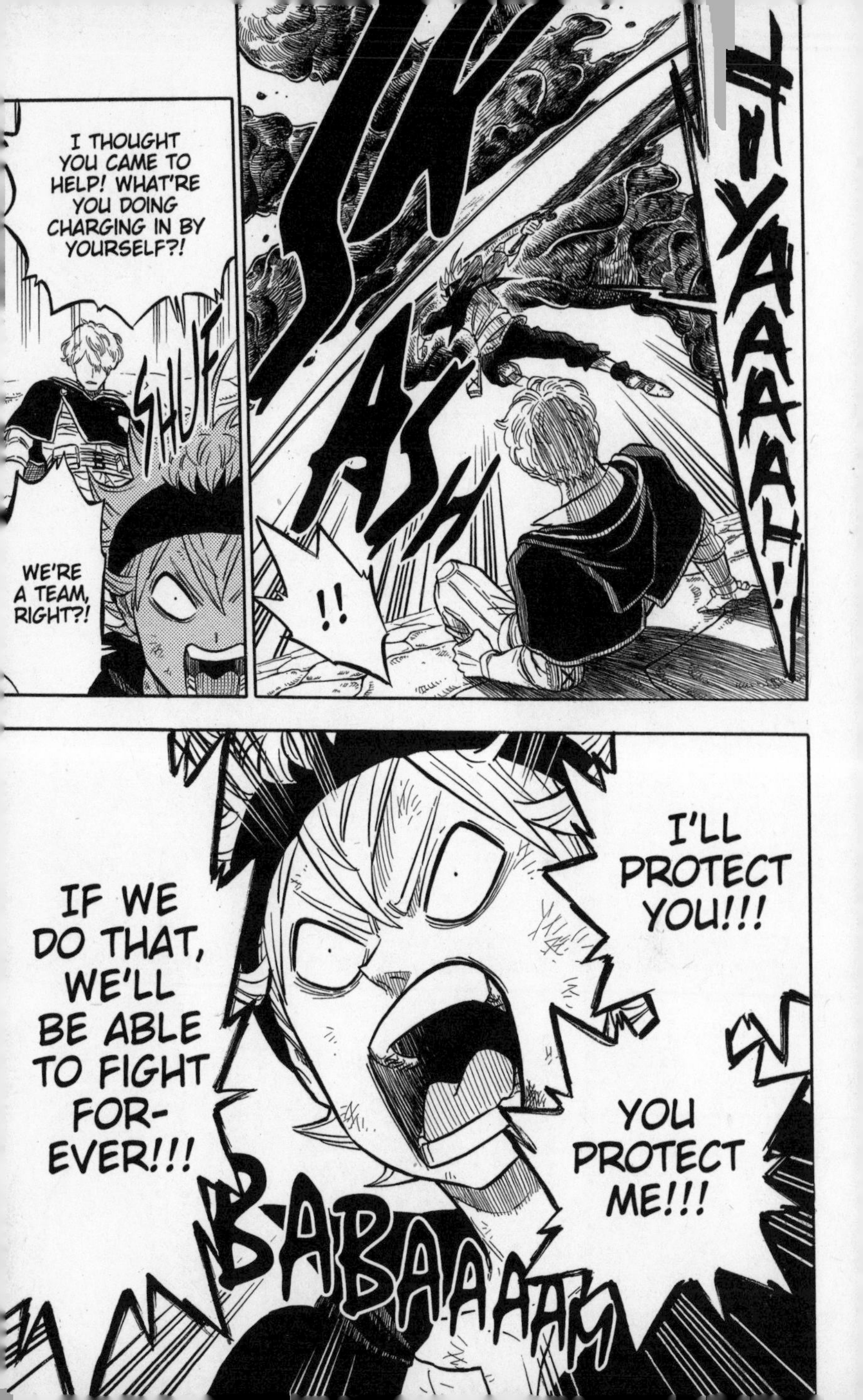
HIYAAAAH!!
SLASH
!!
I THOUGHT YOU CAME TO HELP! WHAT'RE YOU DOING CHARGING IN BY YOURSELF?!
SHUF
WE'RE A TEAM, RIGHT?!
I'LL PROTECT YOU!!!
YOU PROTECT ME!!!
IF WE DO THAT, WE'LL BE ABLE TO FIGHT FOR-EVER!!!
BABAAAAM

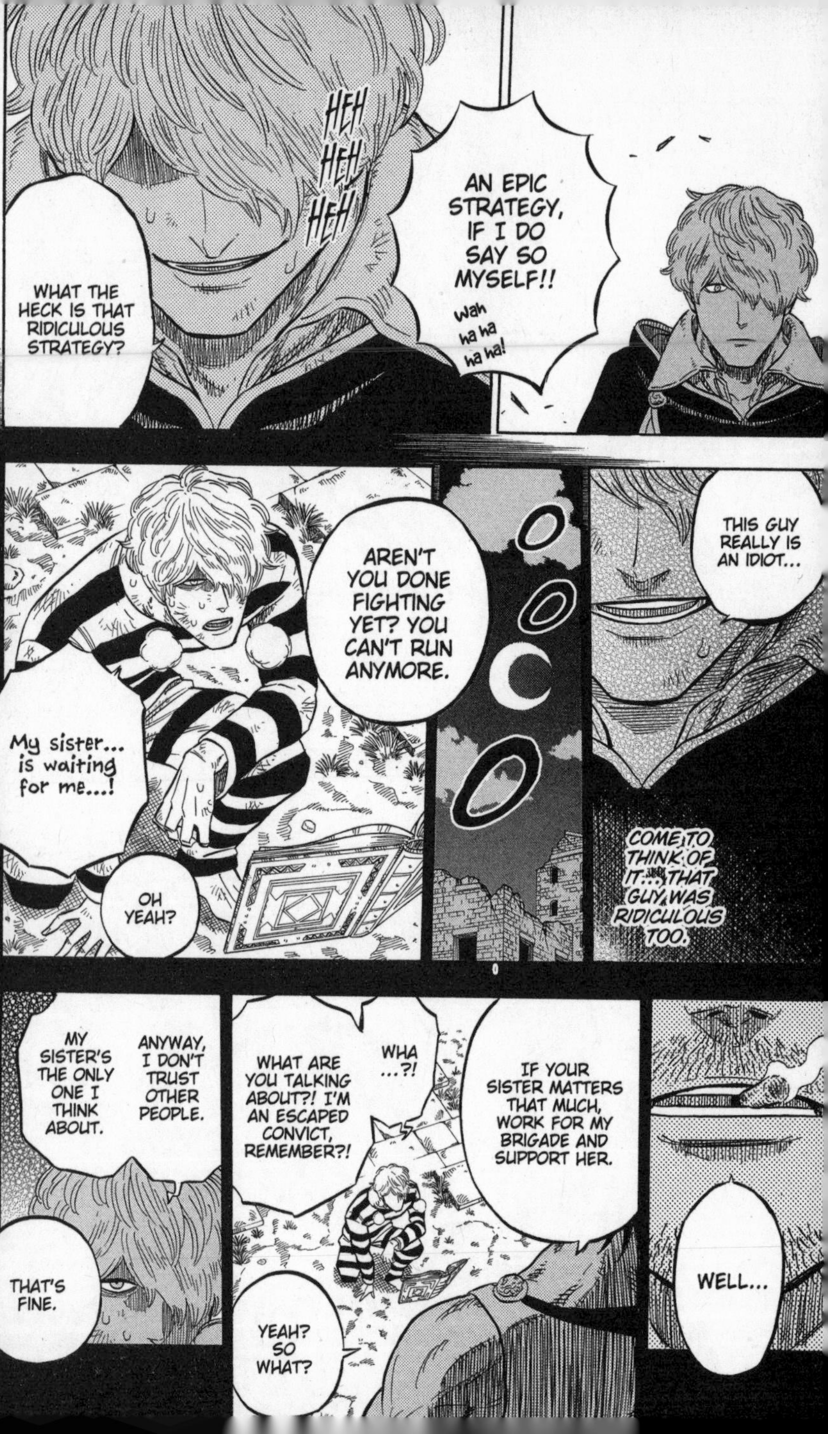
AN EPIC STRATEGY, IF I DO SAY SO MYSELF!!
wah ha ha ha ha!
HEH HEH HEH
WHAT THE HECK IS THAT RIDICULOUS STRATEGY?
THIS GUY REALLY IS AN IDIOT...
COME TO THINK OF IT... THAT GUY WAS RIDICULOUS TOO.
AREN'T YOU DONE FIGHTING YET? YOU CAN'T RUN ANYMORE.
My sister... is waiting for me...!
OH YEAH?
WELL...
IF YOUR SISTER MATTERS THAT MUCH, WORK FOR MY BRIGADE AND SUPPORT HER.
WHA ...?!
WHAT ARE YOU TALKING ABOUT?! I'M AN ESCAPED CONVICT, REMEMBER?!
YEAH? SO WHAT?
ANYWAY, I DON'T TRUST OTHER PEOPLE.
MY SISTER'S THE ONLY ONE I THINK ABOUT.
THAT'S FINE.

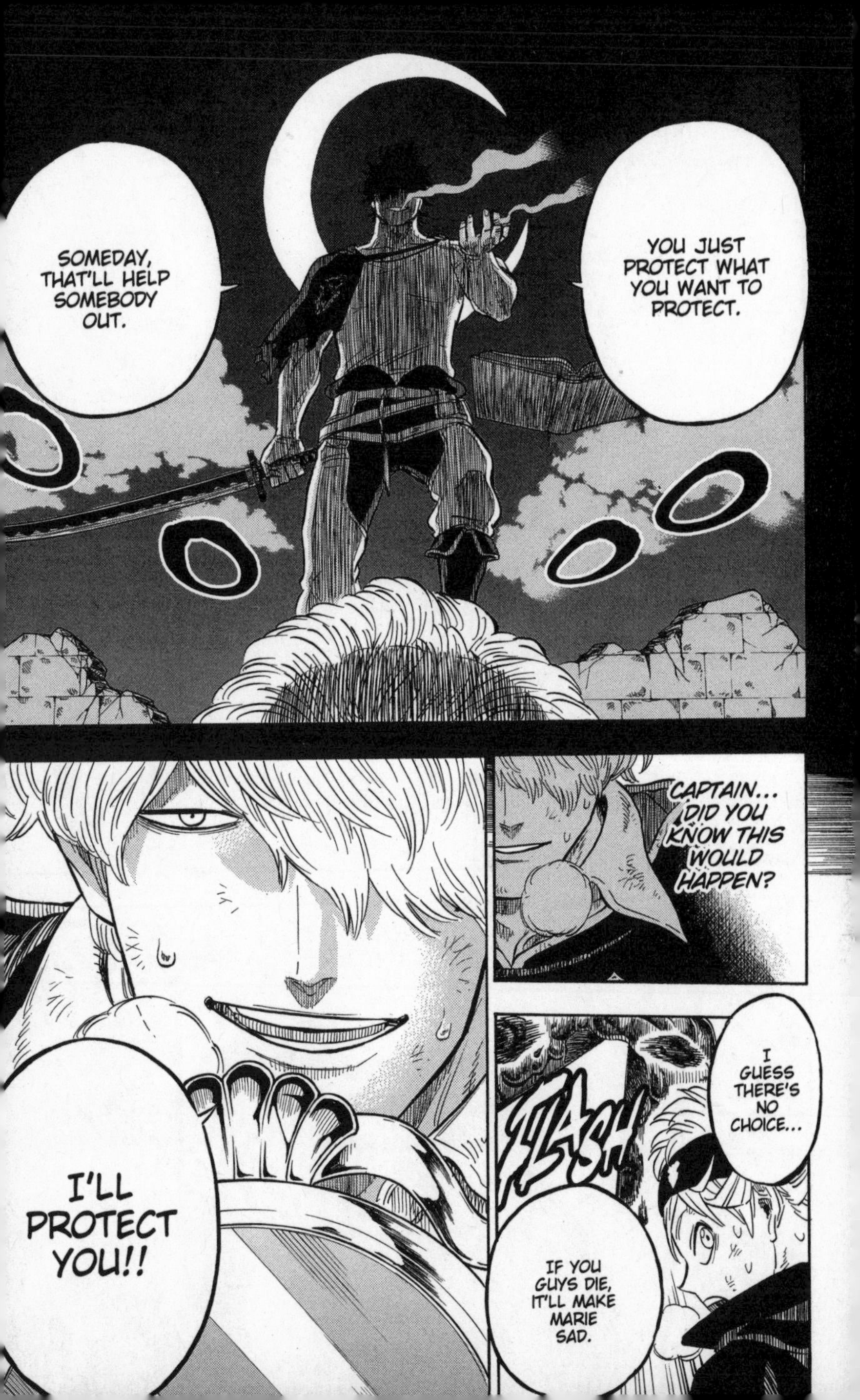
YOU JUST PROTECT WHAT YOU WANT TO PROTECT.
SOMEDAY, THAT'LL HELP SOMEBODY OUT.
CAPTAIN... DID YOU KNOW THIS WOULD HAPPEN?
I GUESS THERE'S NO CHOICE...
FLASH
IF YOU GUYS DIE, IT'LL MAKE MARIE SAD.
I'LL PROTECT YOU!!

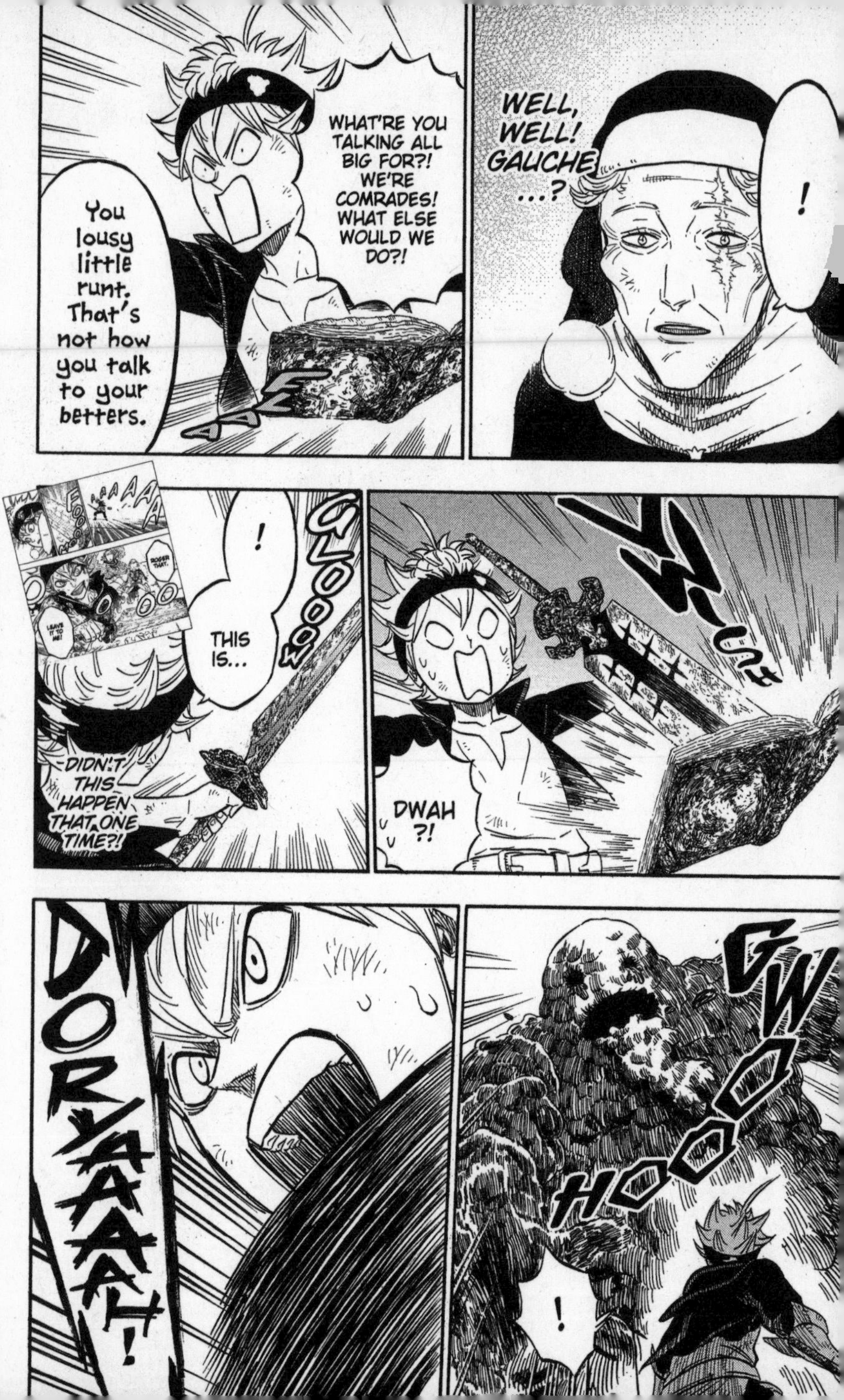
WELL, WELL! GAUCHE ...?
!
WHAT'RE YOU TALKING ALL BIG FOR?! WE'RE COMRADES! WHAT ELSE WOULD WE DO?!
You lousy little runt. That's not how you talk to your betters.
DWAH ?!
!
THIS IS...
ROGER THAT.
LEAVE IT TO ME!
DIDN'T THIS HAPPEN THAT ONE TIME?!
GWOOOOH
!
DORYAAAAAH!

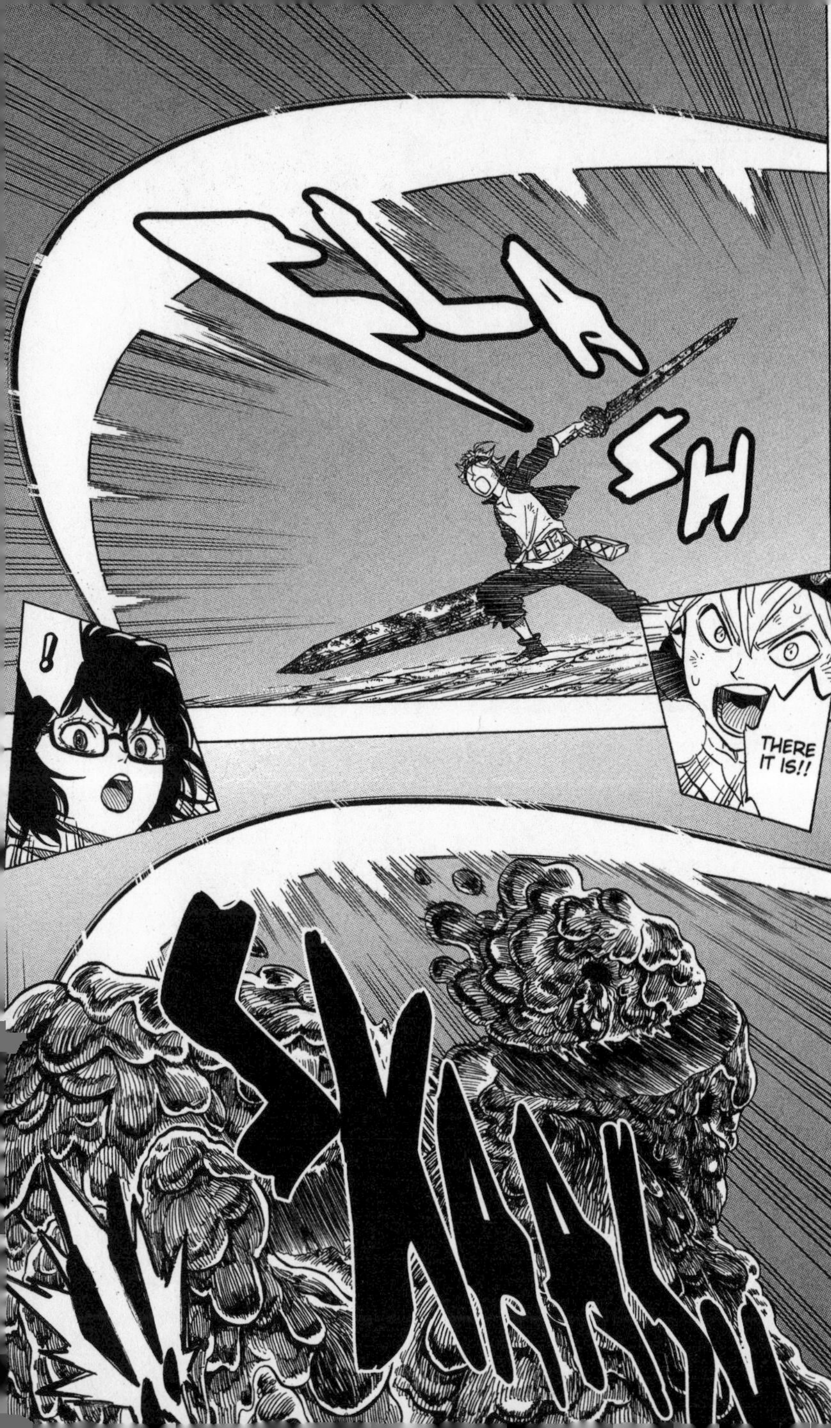
SLASH
THERE IT IS!!
!

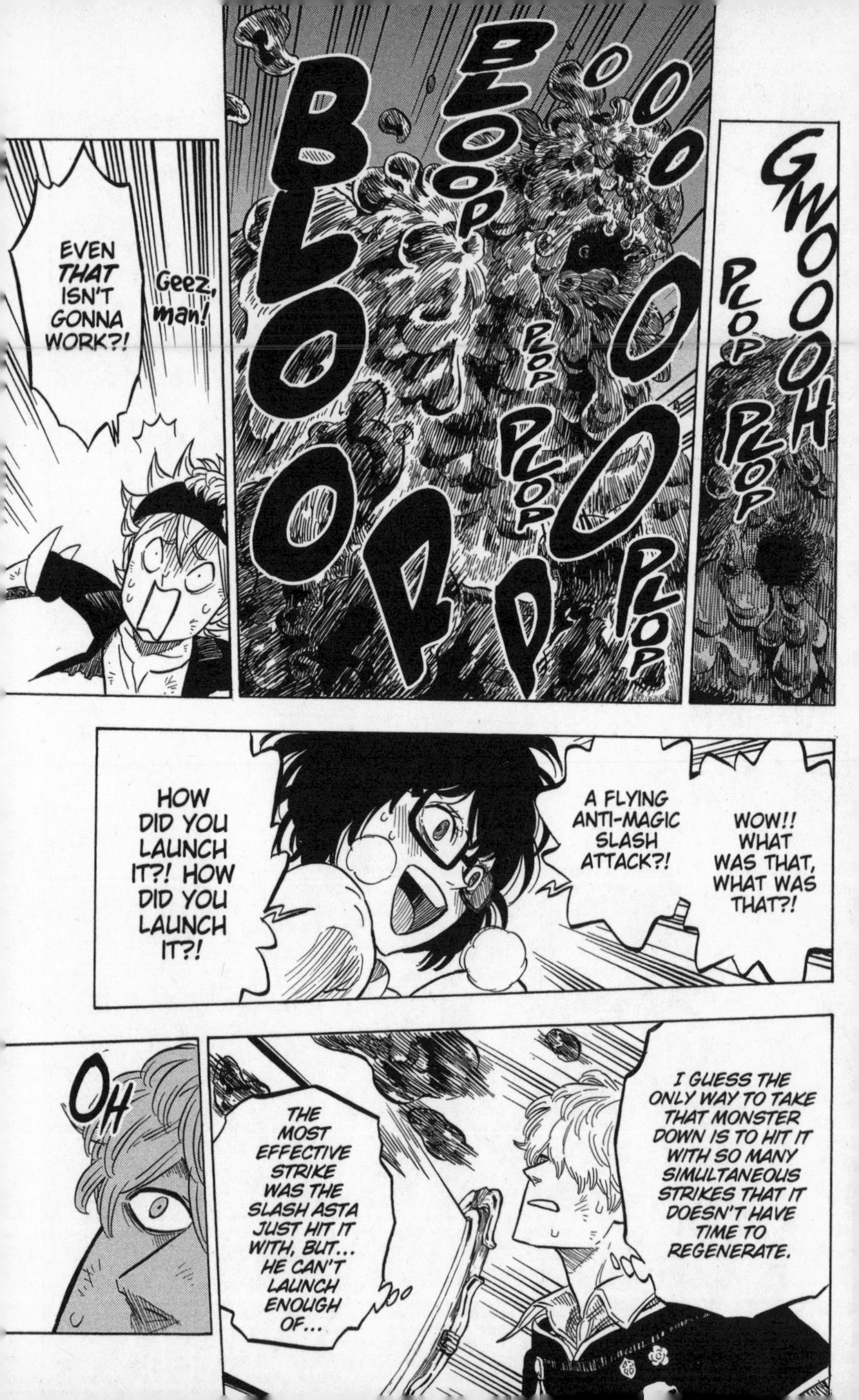

GWOOOOH
PLOP PLOP PLOP
BLOOP
BLOOOOOOOOP
PLOP PLOP PLOP
PLOP PLOP
Geez, man!
EVEN THAT ISN'T GONNA WORK?!
WOW!! WHAT WAS THAT, WHAT WAS THAT?!
A FLYING ANTI-MAGIC SLASH ATTACK?!
HOW DID YOU LAUNCH IT?! HOW DID YOU LAUNCH IT?!
I GUESS THE ONLY WAY TO TAKE THAT MONSTER DOWN IS TO HIT IT WITH SO MANY SIMULTANEOUS STRIKES THAT IT DOESN'T HAVE TIME TO REGENERATE.
THE MOST EFFECTIVE STRIKE WAS THE SLASH ASTA JUST HIT IT WITH, BUT... HE CAN'T LAUNCH ENOUGH OF...
OH

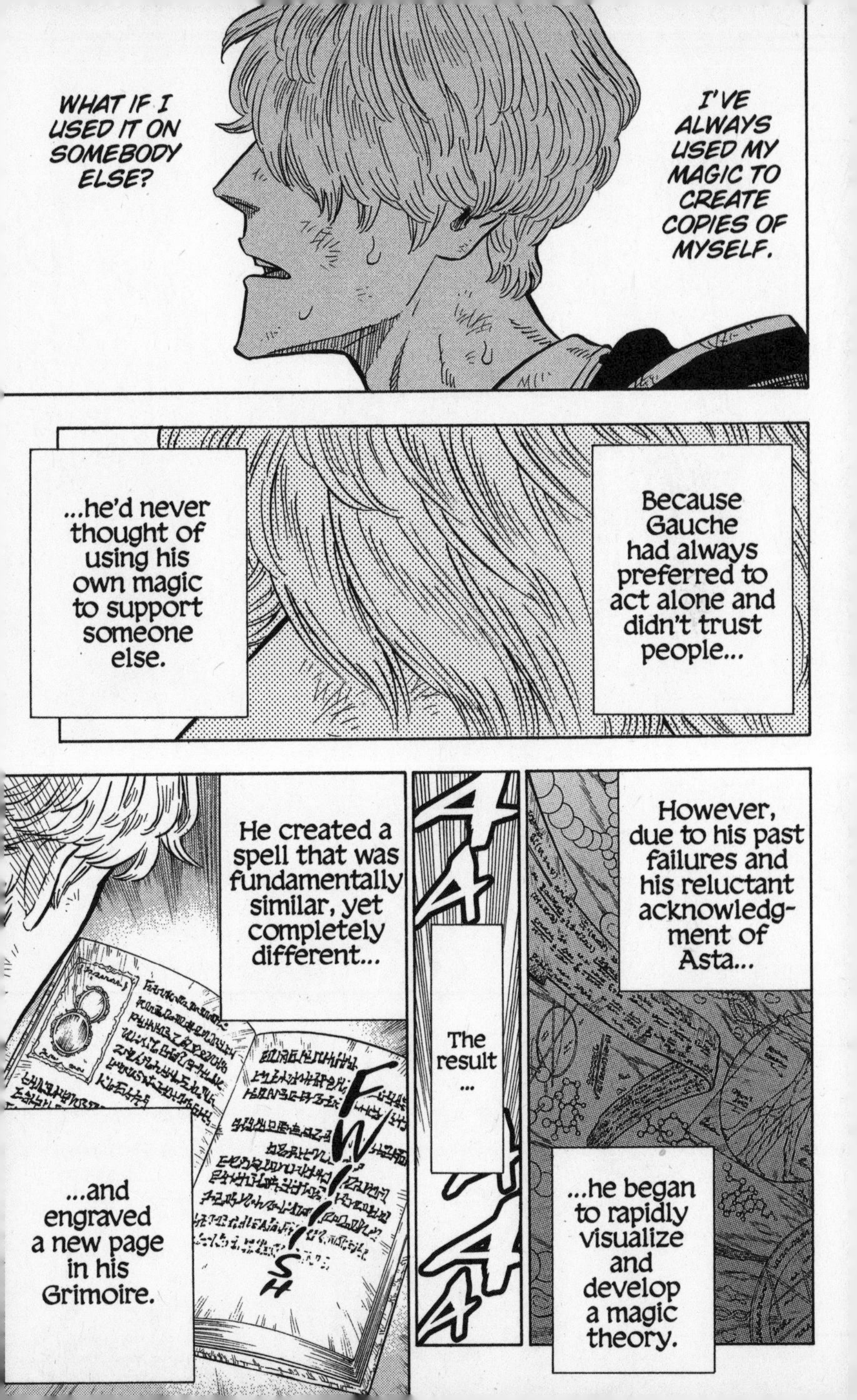
I'VE ALWAYS USED MY MAGIC TO CREATE COPIES OF MYSELF.
WHAT IF I USED IT ON SOMEBODY ELSE?
Because Gauche had always preferred to act alone and didn't trust people...
...he'd never thought of using his own magic to support someone else.
However, due to his past failures and his reluctant acknowledgment of Asta...
...he began to rapidly visualize and develop a magic theory.
The result...
He created a spell that was fundamentally similar, yet completely different...
...and engraved a new page in his Grimoire.
FWISH

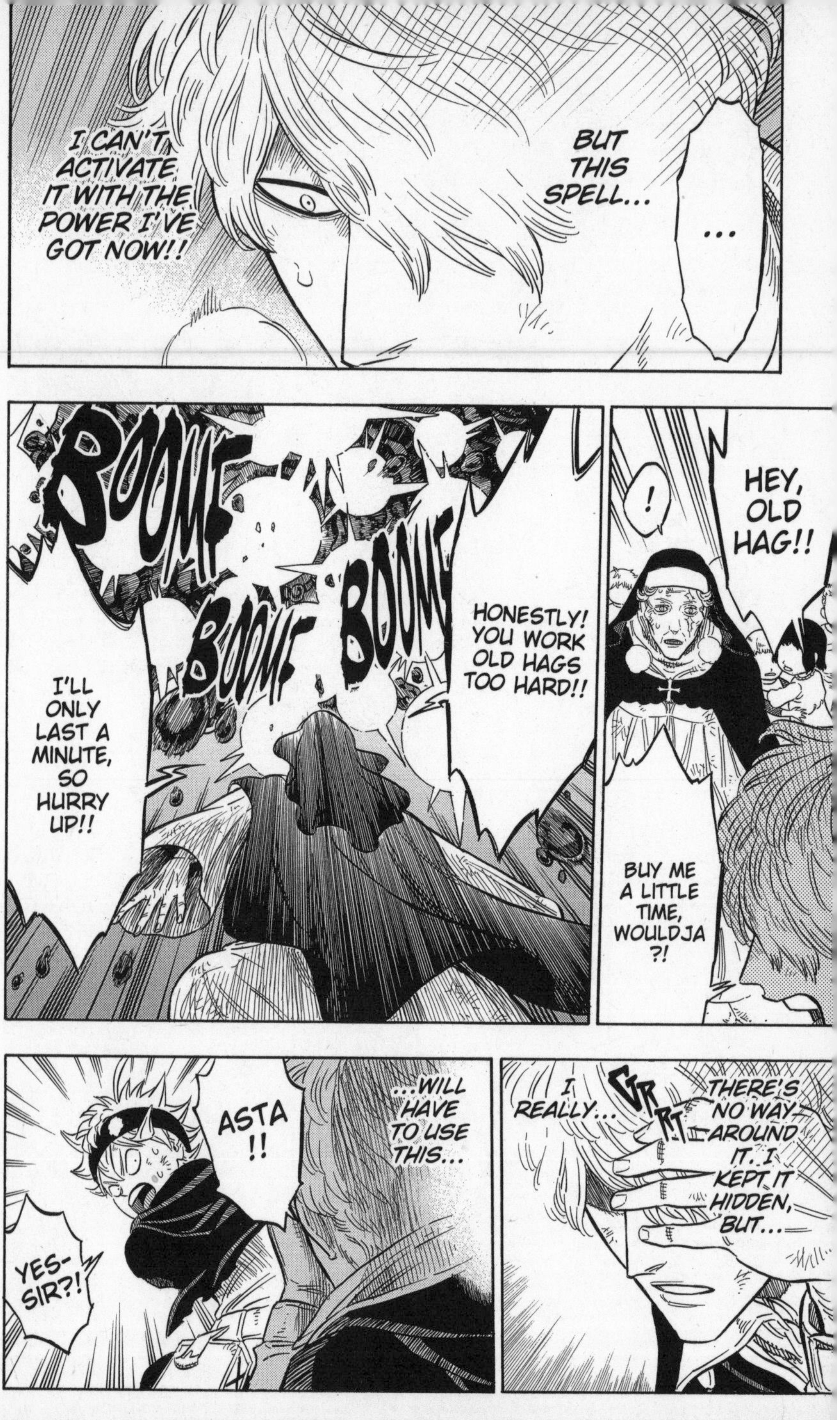
...
BUT THIS SPELL...
I CAN'T ACTIVATE IT WITH THE POWER I'VE GOT NOW!!
!
HEY, OLD HAG!!
BUY ME A LITTLE TIME, WOULDJA?!
BOOM
BOOM
BOOM
HONESTLY! YOU WORK OLD HAGS TOO HARD!!
I'LL ONLY LAST A MINUTE, SO HURRY UP!!
THERE'S NO WAY AROUND IT. I KEPT IT HIDDEN, BUT...
GRRT
I REALLY...
...WILL HAVE TO USE THIS...
ASTA!!
YES-SIR?!

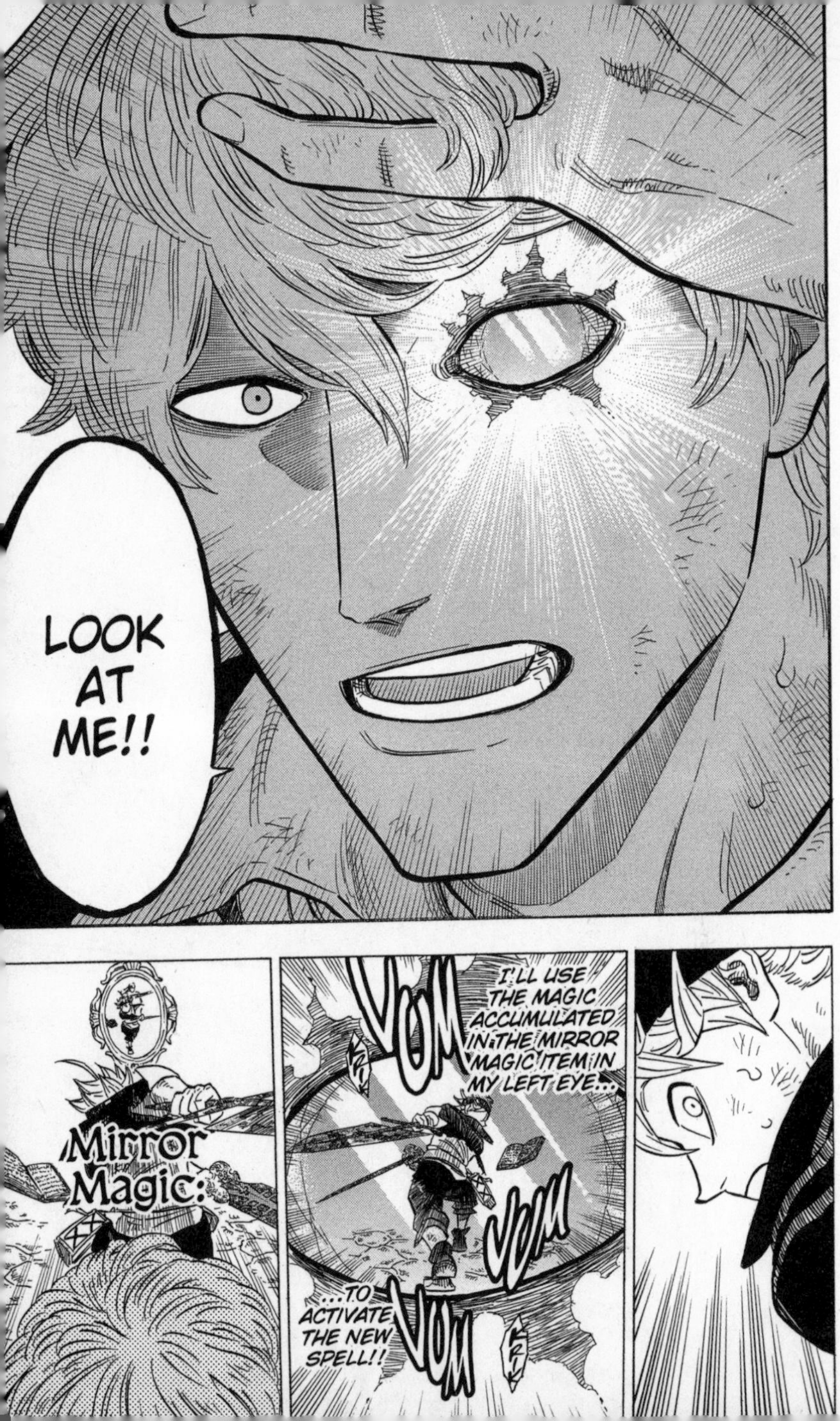
LOOK AT ME!!
VOM
KRI
I'LL USE THE MAGIC ACCUMULATED IN THE MIRROR MAGIC ITEM IN MY LEFT EYE...
VOM
...TO ACTIVATE THE NEW SPELL!!
VOM
KRIK
Mirror Magic:

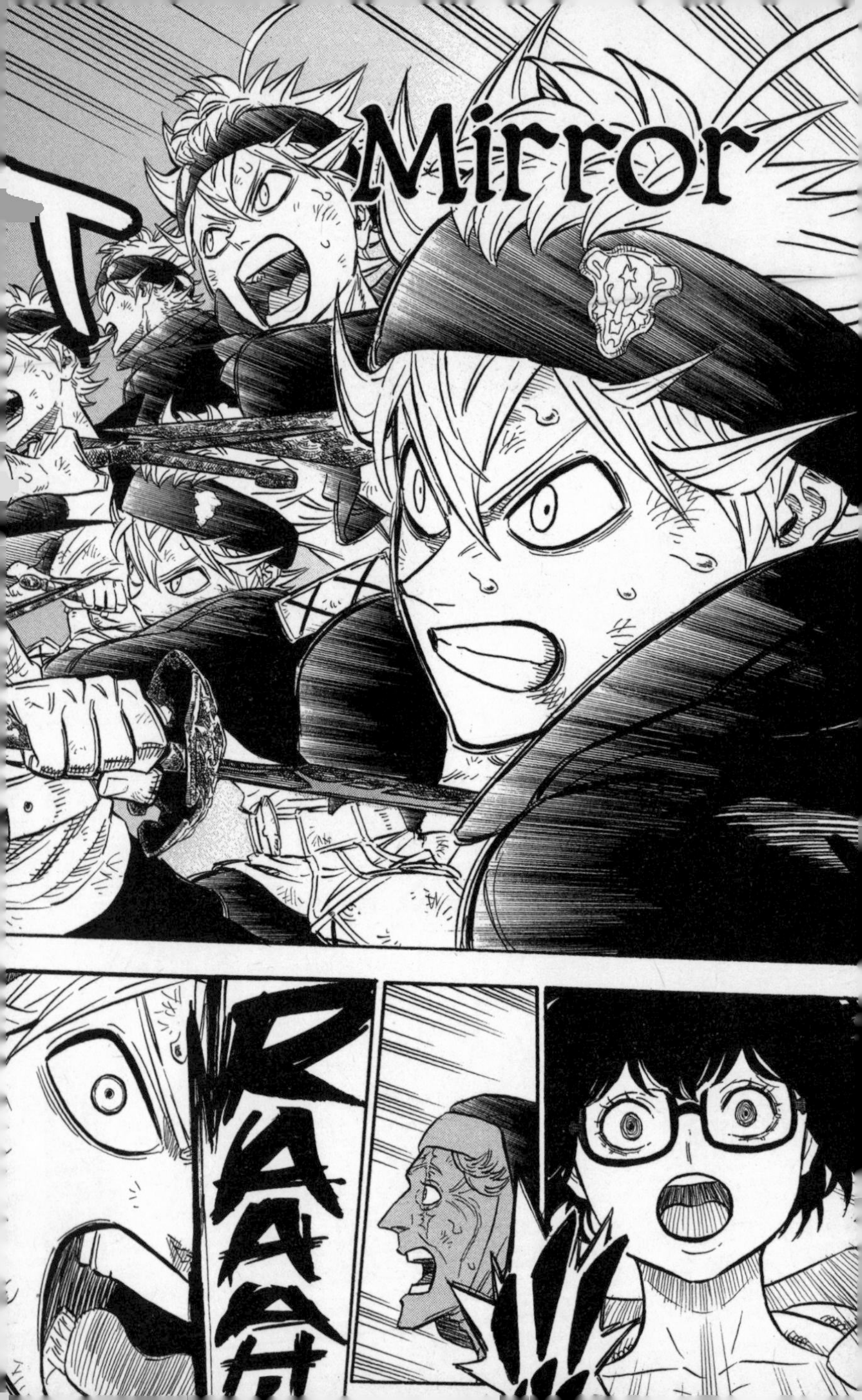
Mirror
!!
KAAAH

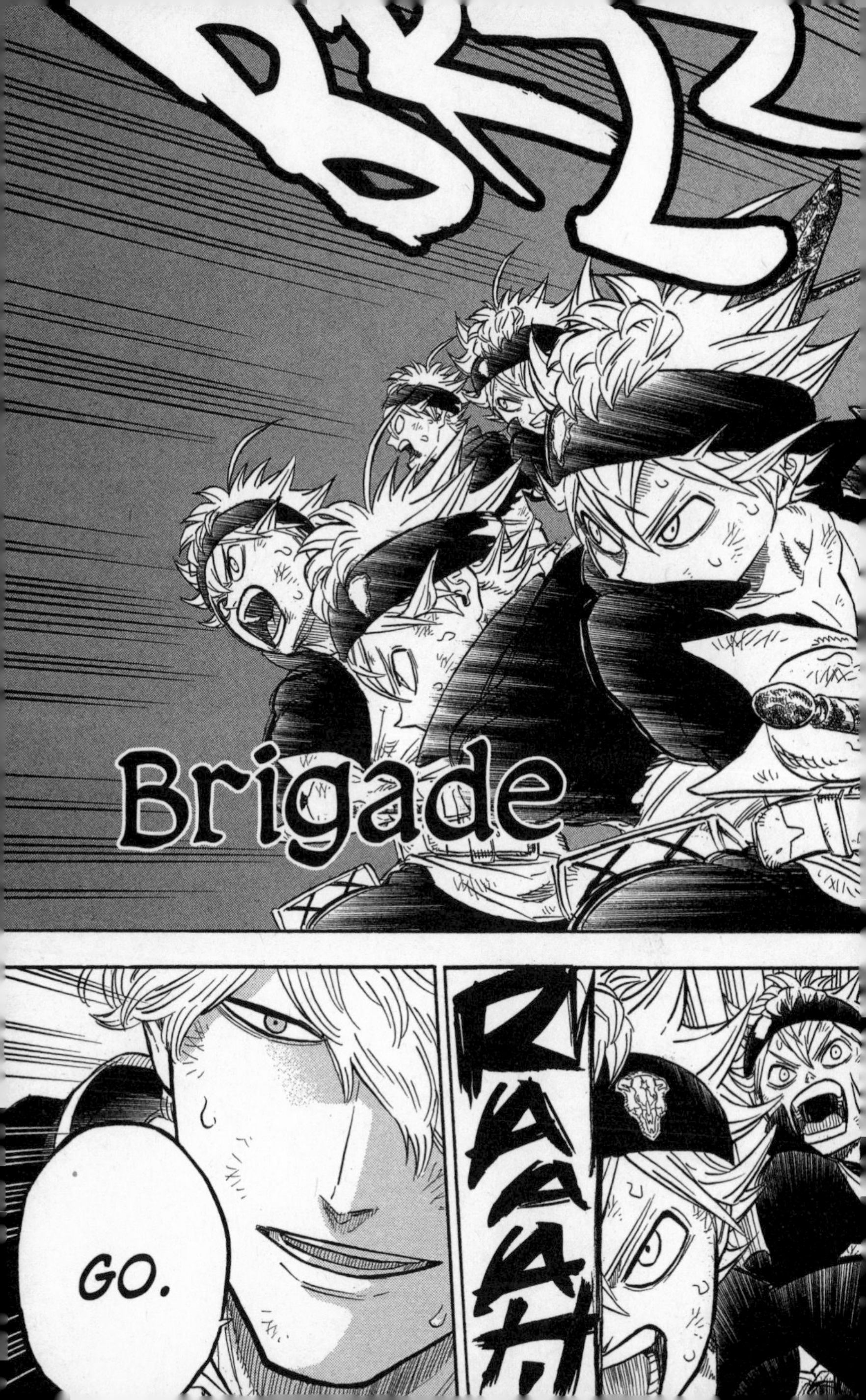
Brigade
RAAAAH
GO.

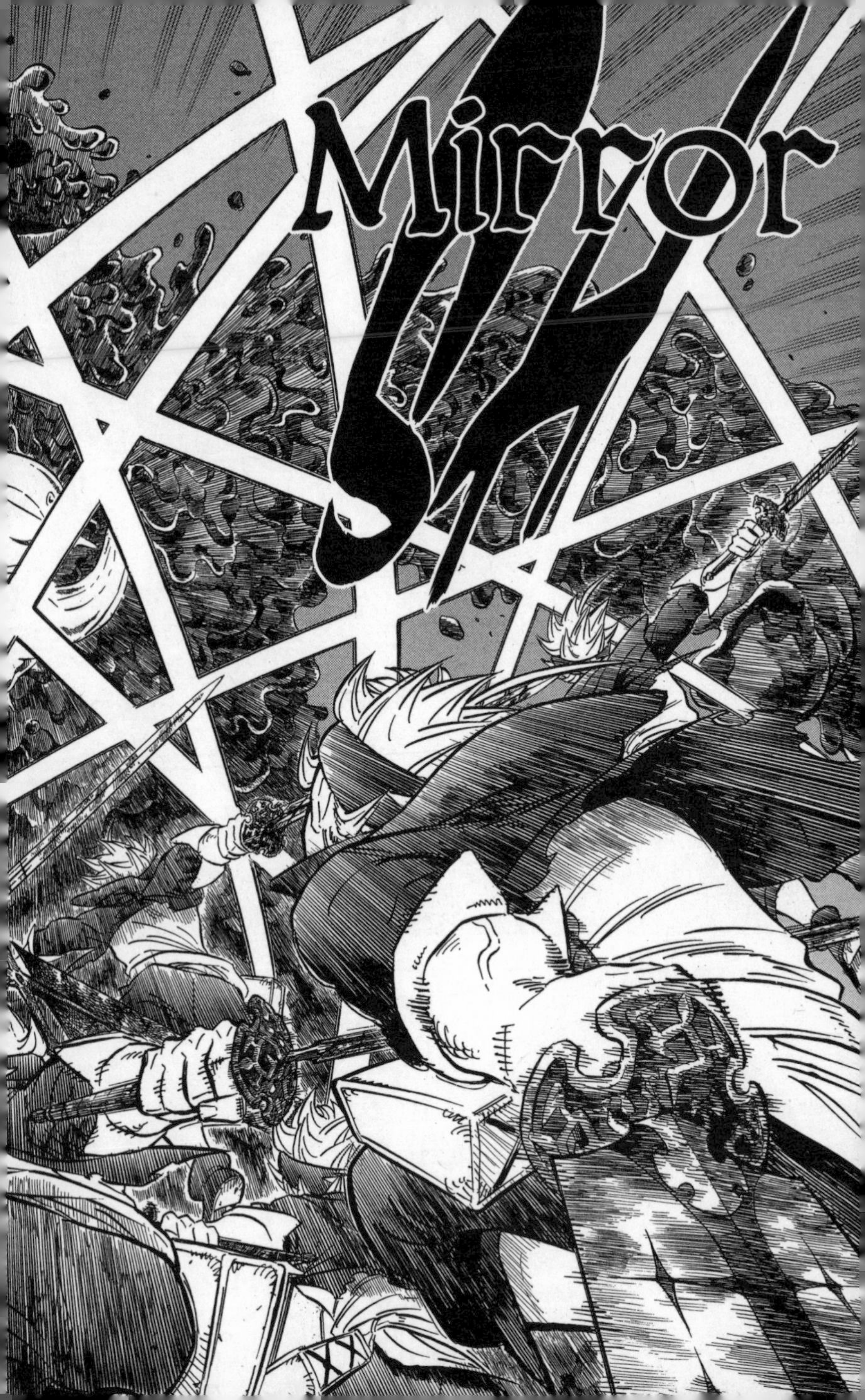
Mirror

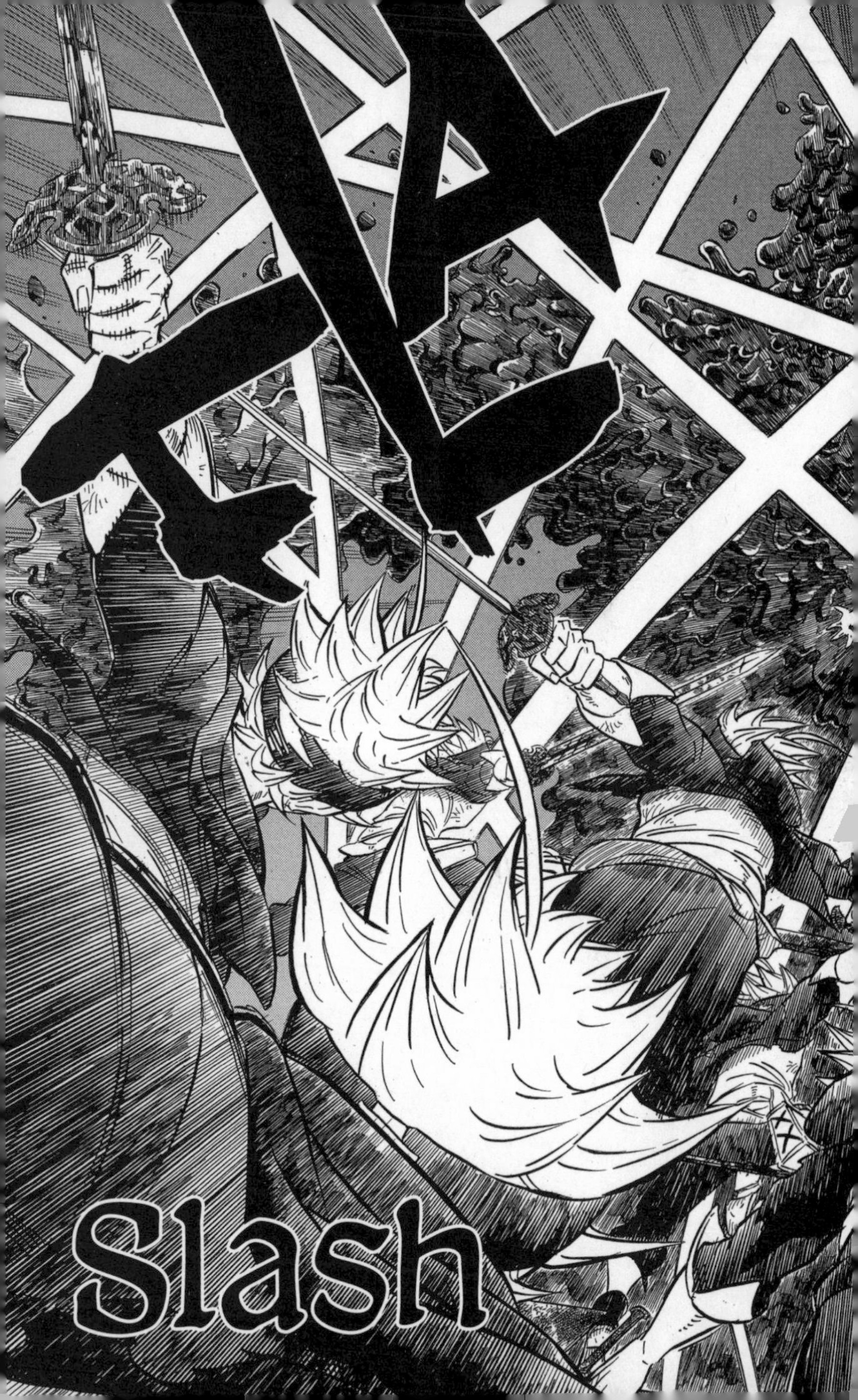
Slash

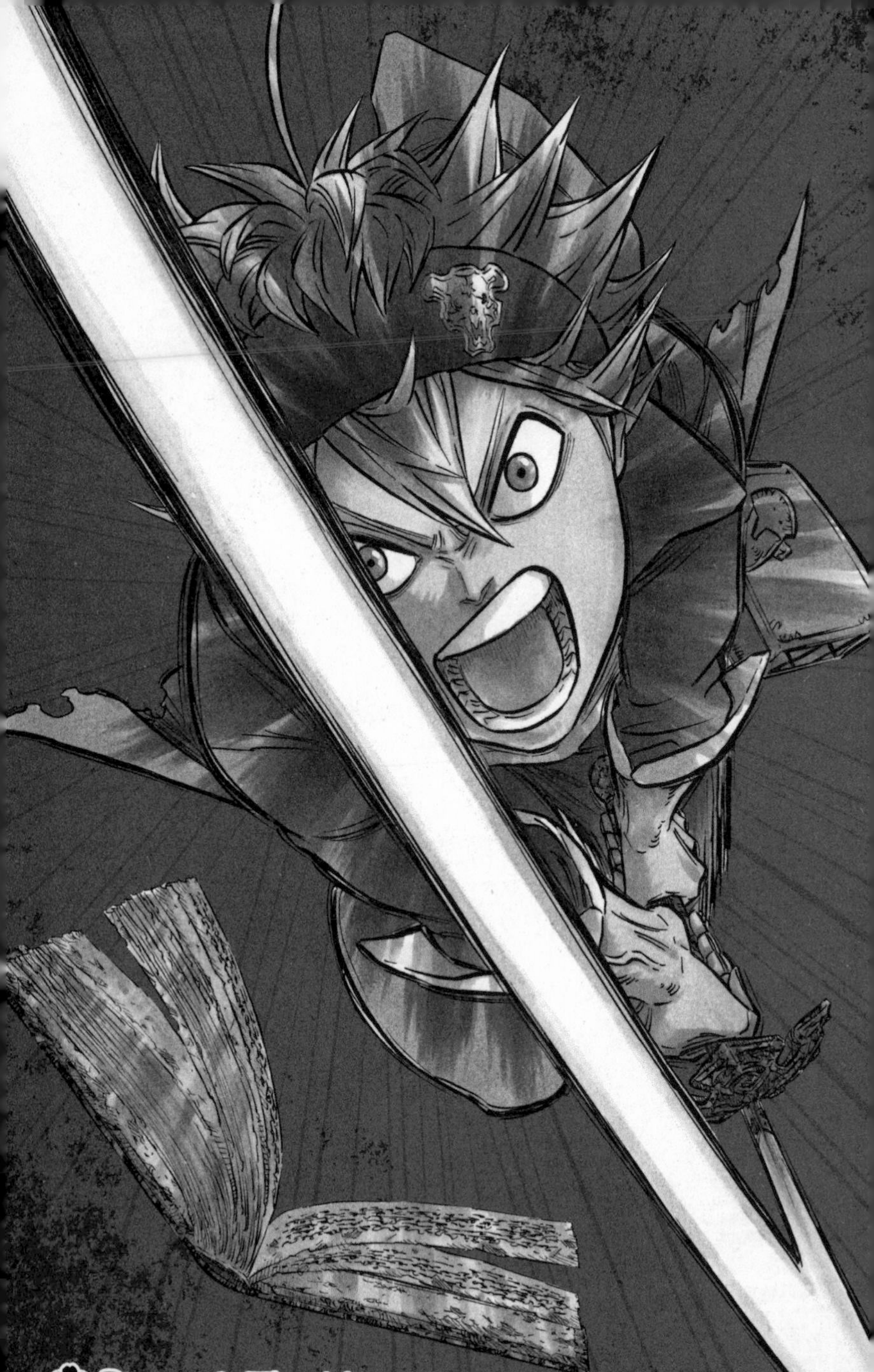

Page 46: The Man Who Cuts Death

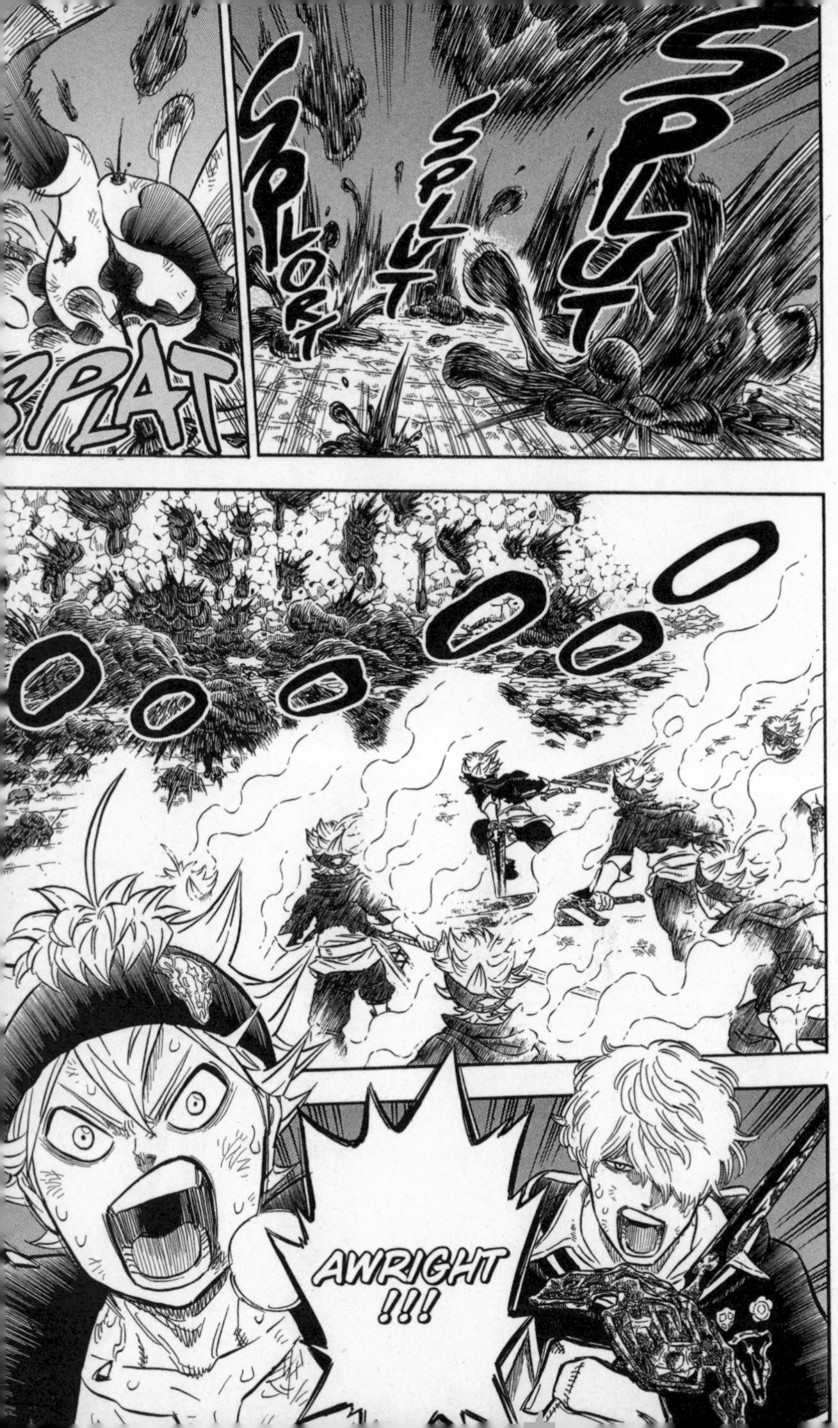
SPLUT
SPLUT
SPLORT
SPLAT
OOOOOO
AWRIGHT!!!

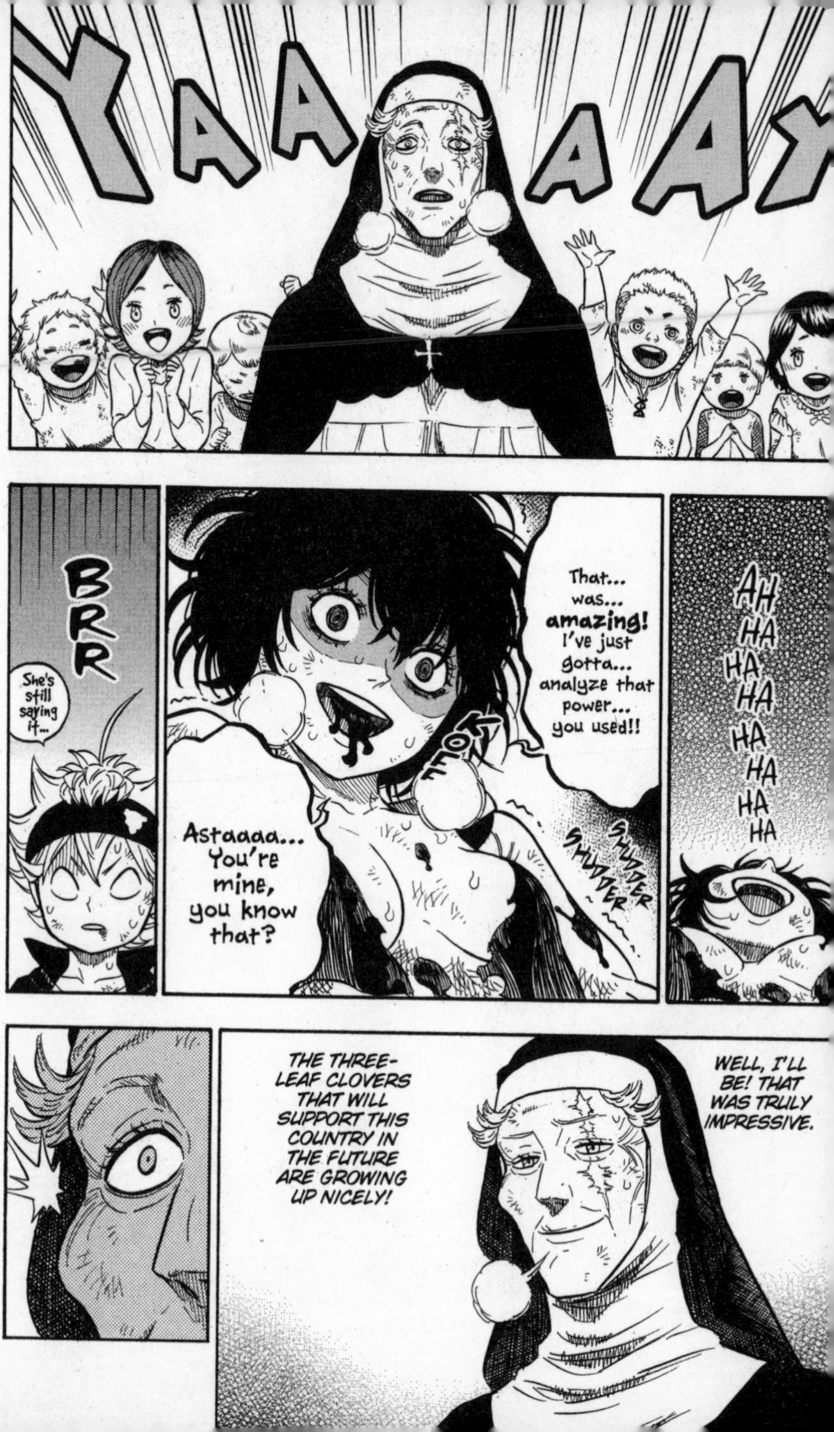
YAAAAAY
AH HA HA HA HA HA HA HA HA
That... was... amazing! I've just gotta... analyze that power... you used!!
KOFF
SHUDDER SHUDDER
Astaaaa... You're mine, you know that?
BRR
She's still saying it...
WELL, I'LL BE! THAT WAS TRULY IMPRESSIVE.
THE THREE-LEAF CLOVERS THAT WILL SUPPORT THIS COUNTRY IN THE FUTURE ARE GROWING UP NICELY!

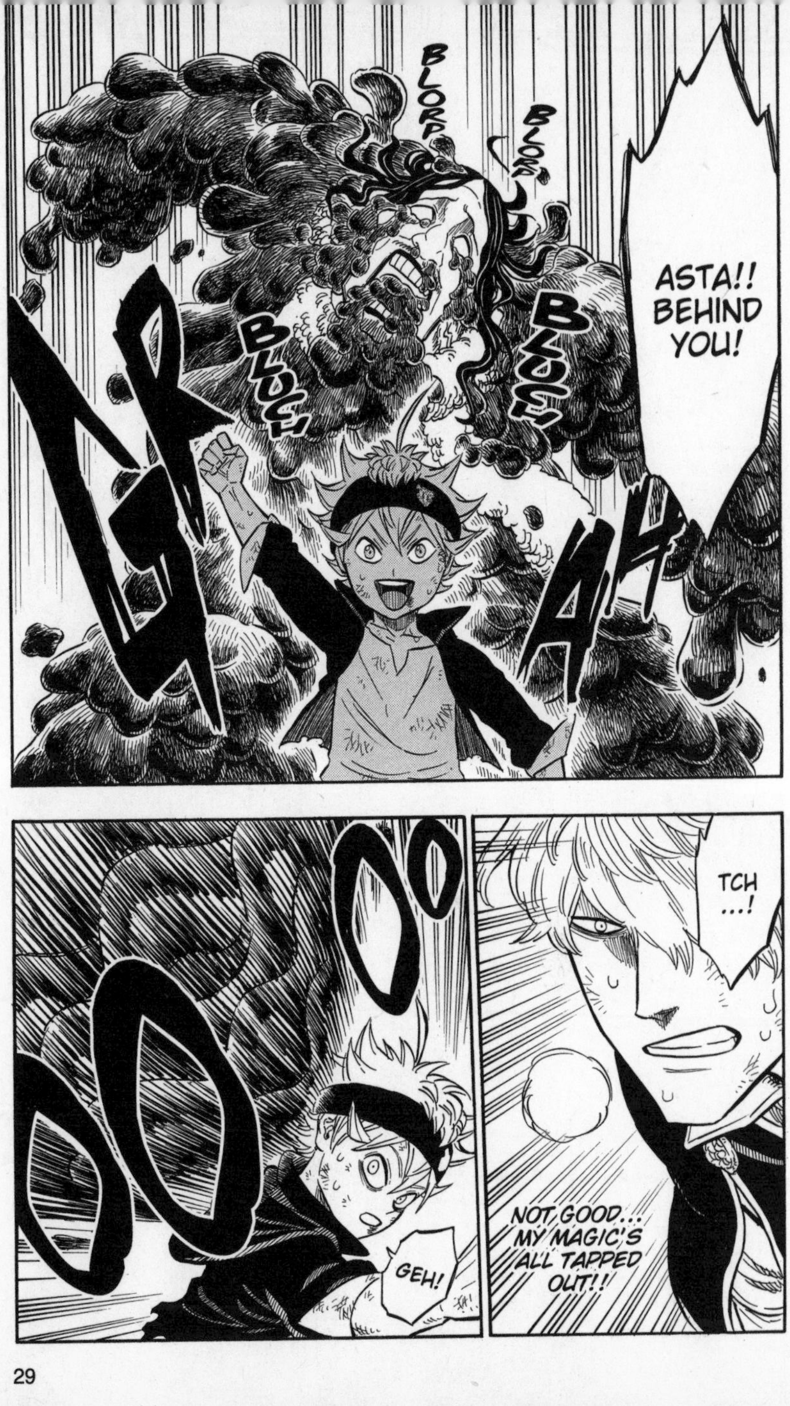
ASTA!! BEHIND YOU!
BLORP
BLORP
BLUCH
BLUCH
TCH ...!
NOT GOOD... MY MAGIC'S ALL TAPPED OUT!!
GEH!

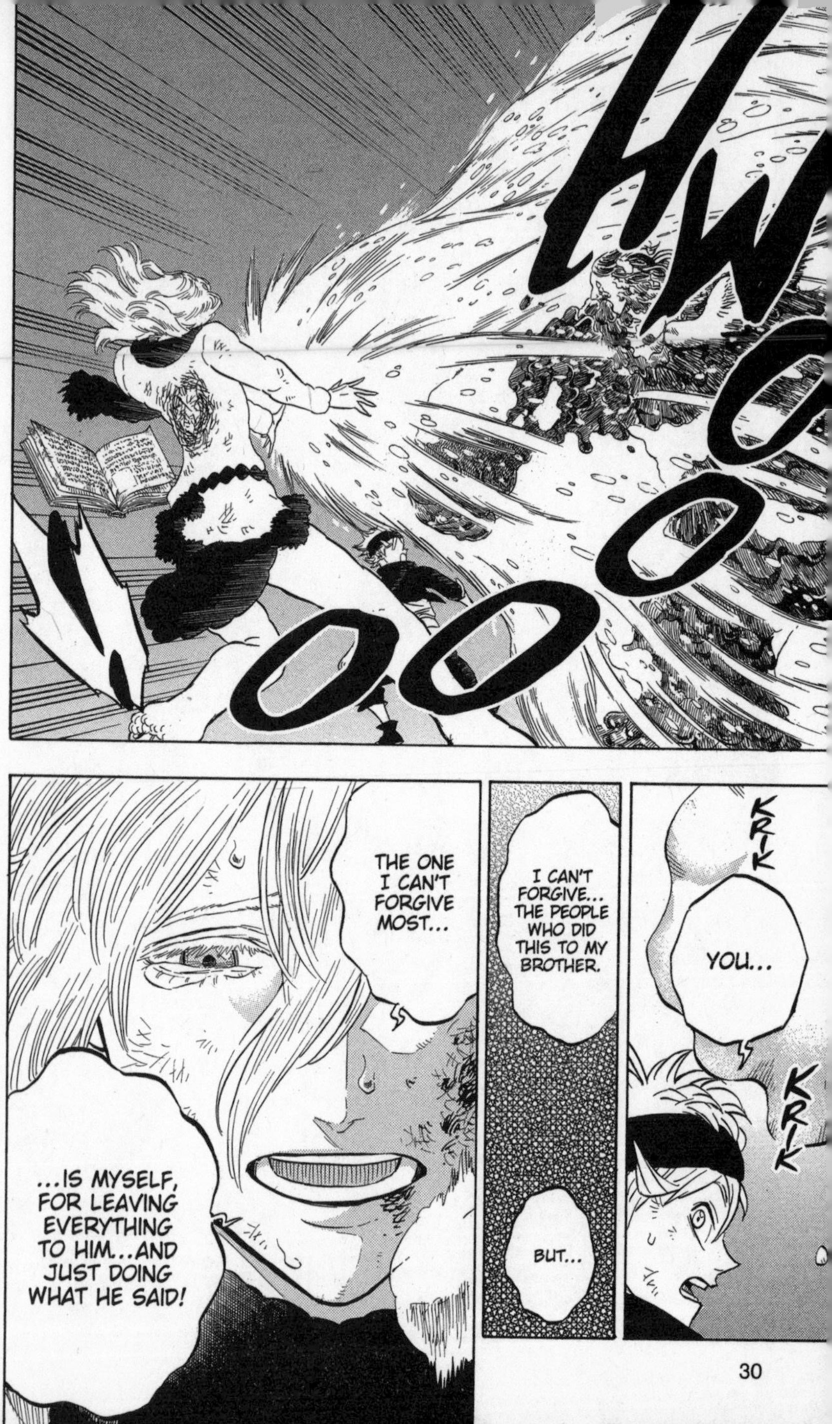
HWOOOOO
KRIK
YOU...
KRIK
I CAN'T FORGIVE... THE PEOPLE WHO DID THIS TO MY BROTHER.
BUT...
THE ONE I CAN'T FORGIVE MOST...
...IS MYSELF, FOR LEAVING EVERYTHING TO HIM...AND JUST DOING WHAT HE SAID!

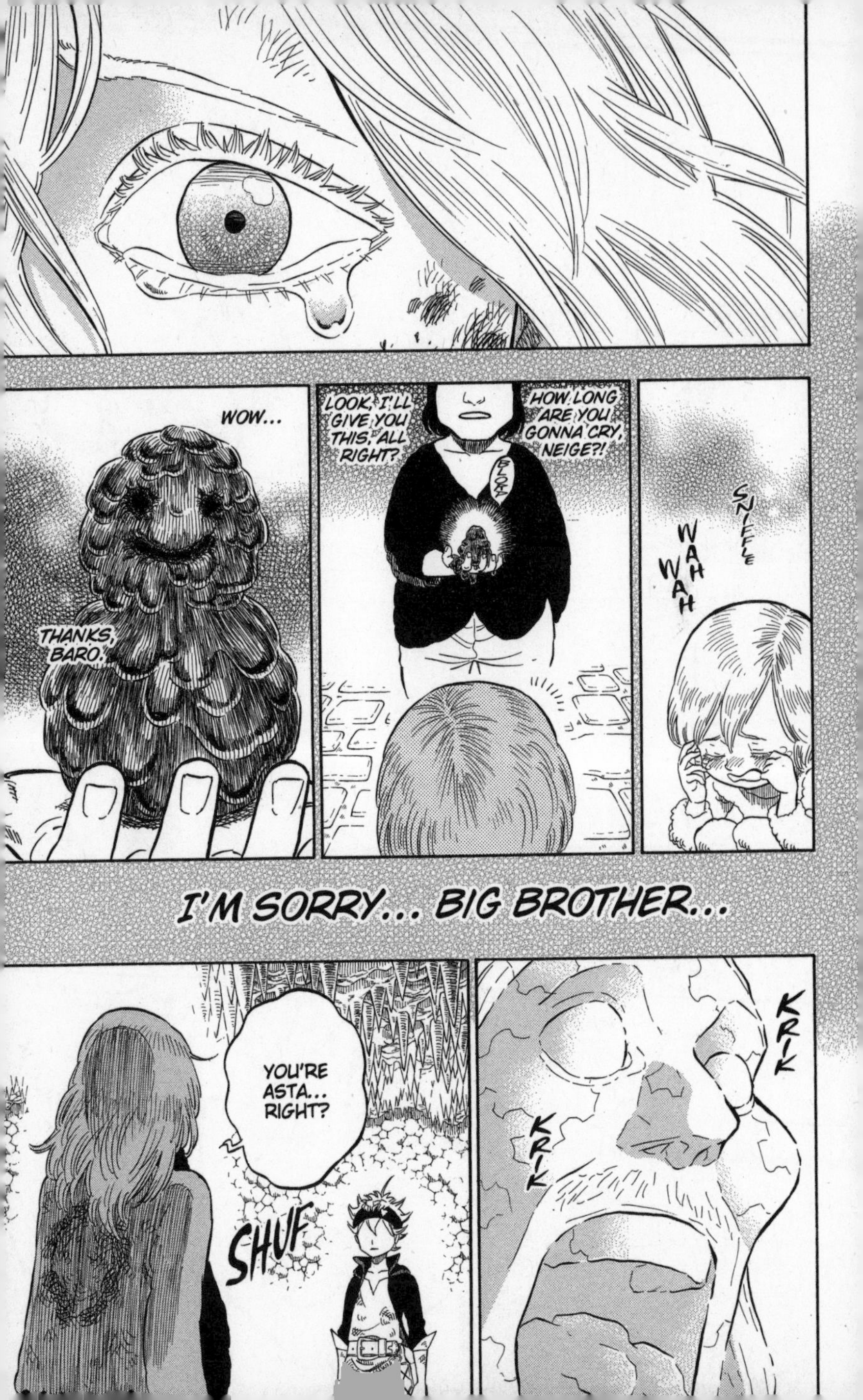
SNIFFLE
WAH WAH
HOW LONG ARE YOU GONNA CRY, NEIGE?!
LOOK, I'LL GIVE YOU THIS, ALL RIGHT?
BLORP
WOW...
THANKS, BARO.
I'M SORRY... BIG BROTHER...
KRIK
KRIK
YOU'RE ASTA... RIGHT?
SHUF

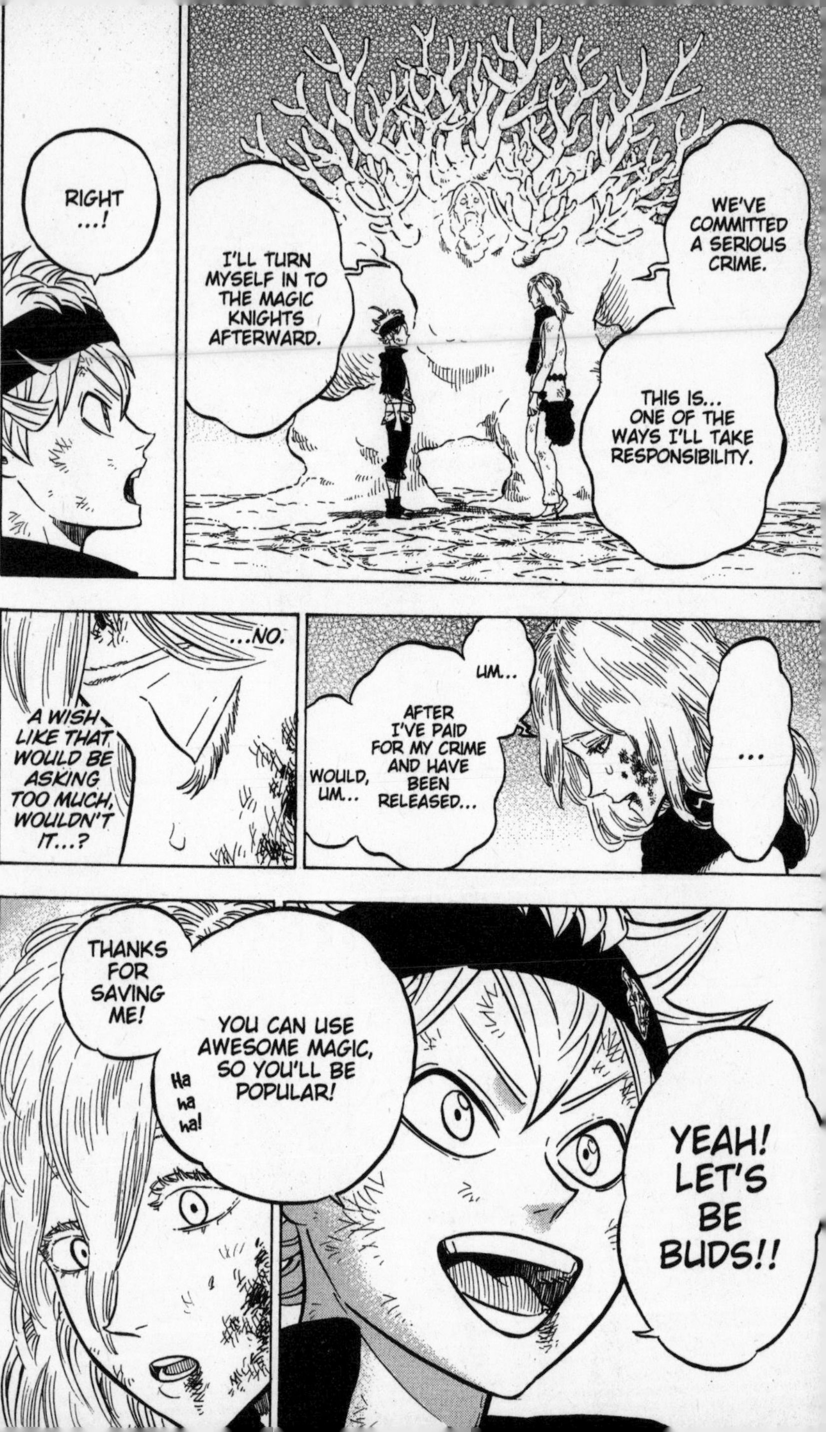
WE'VE COMMITTED A SERIOUS CRIME.
THIS IS... ONE OF THE WAYS I'LL TAKE RESPONSIBILITY.
I'LL TURN MYSELF IN TO THE MAGIC KNIGHTS AFTERWARD.
RIGHT ...!
...
UM...
AFTER I'VE PAID FOR MY CRIME AND HAVE BEEN RELEASED...
WOULD, UM...
...NO.
A WISH LIKE THAT WOULD BE ASKING TOO MUCH, WOULDN'T IT...?
YEAH! LET'S BE BUDS!!
YOU CAN USE AWESOME MAGIC, SO YOU'LL BE POPULAR!
Ha ha ha!
THANKS FOR SAVING ME!

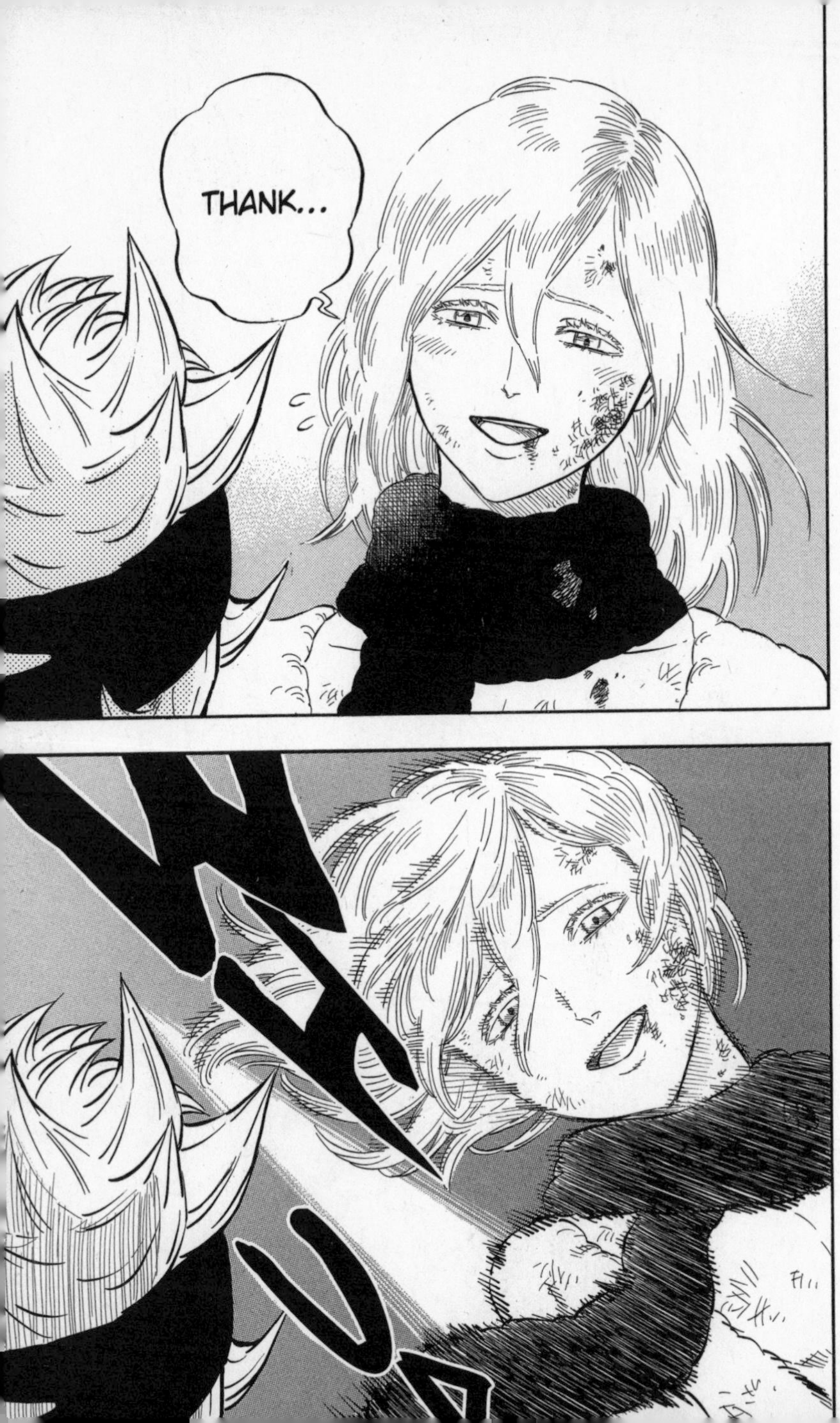
THANK...

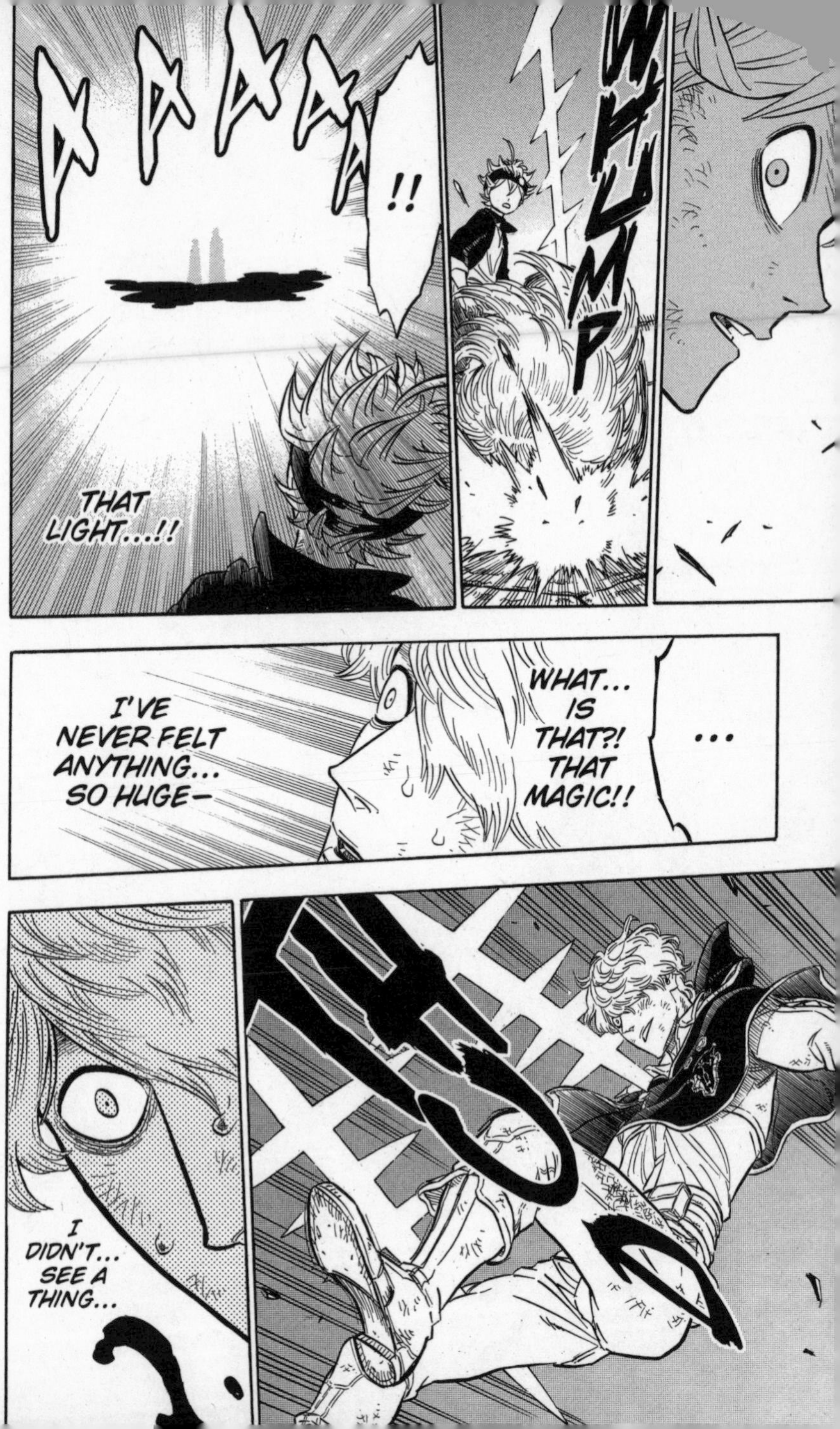
WHUMP
!!
THAT LIGHT...!!
...
WHAT... IS THAT?! THAT MAGIC!!
I'VE NEVER FELT ANYTHING... SO HUGE—
I DIDN'T... SEE A THING...

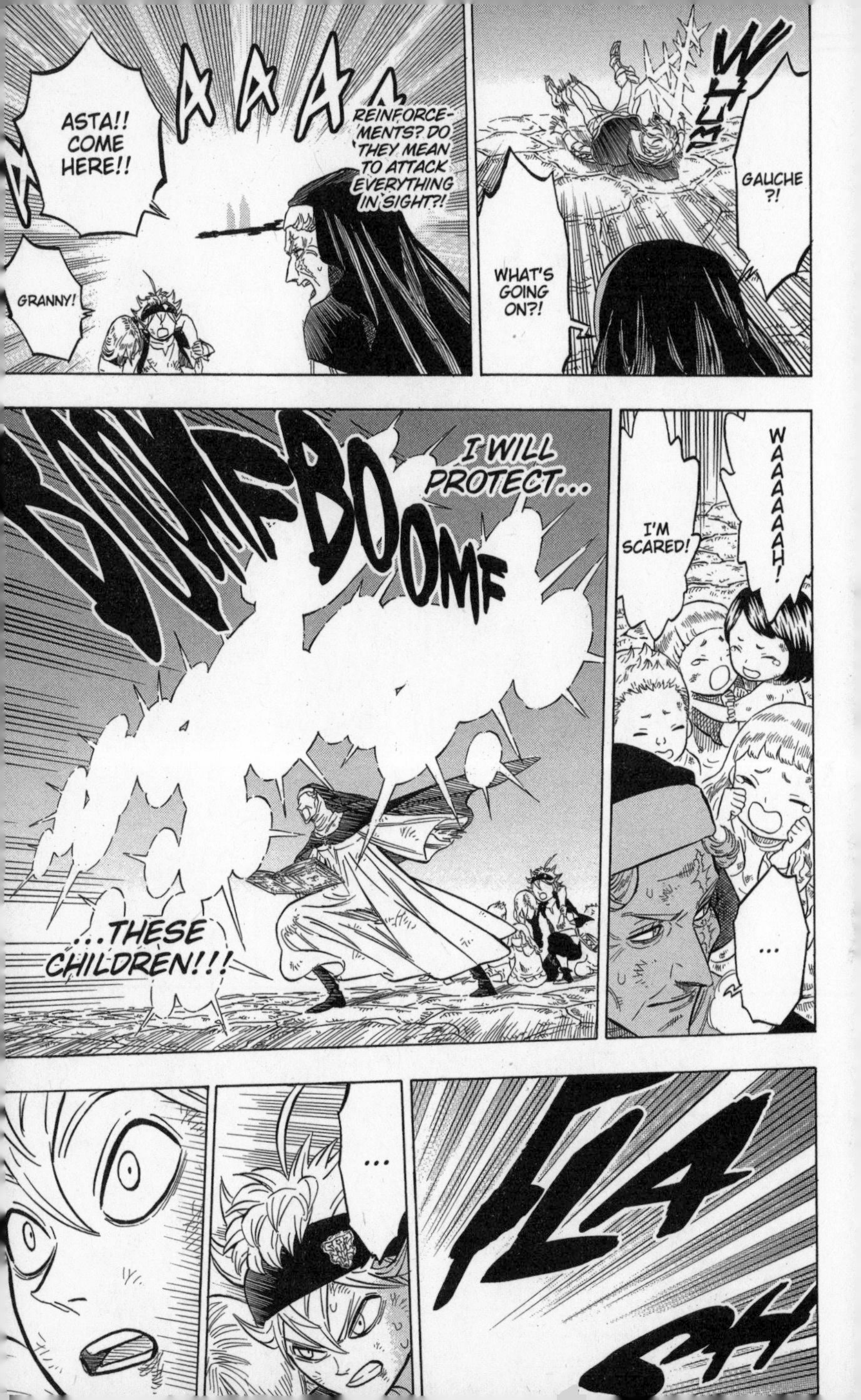
WHUMP
GAUCHE?!
WHAT'S GOING ON?!
AAAA
REINFORCE-MENTS? DO THEY MEAN TO ATTACK EVERYTHING IN SIGHT?!
ASTA!! COME HERE!!
GRANNY!
WAAAAAAH!
I'M SCARED!
...
I WILL PROTECT...
BOOMF
...THESE CHILDREN!!!
...

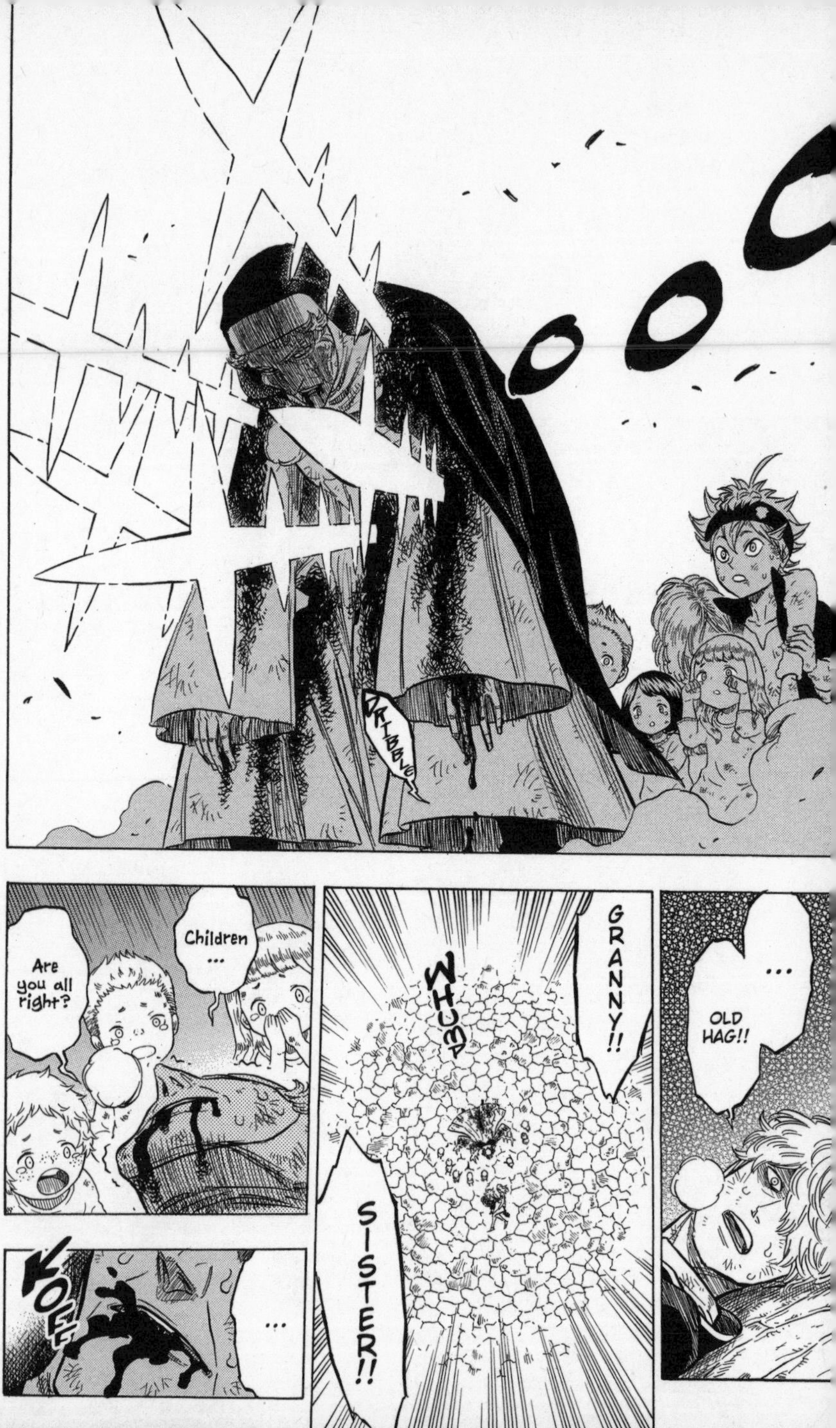
DRIBBLE
...
OLD HAG!!
GRANNY!!
WHUMP
SISTER!!
Children ...
Are you all right?
KOFF
...

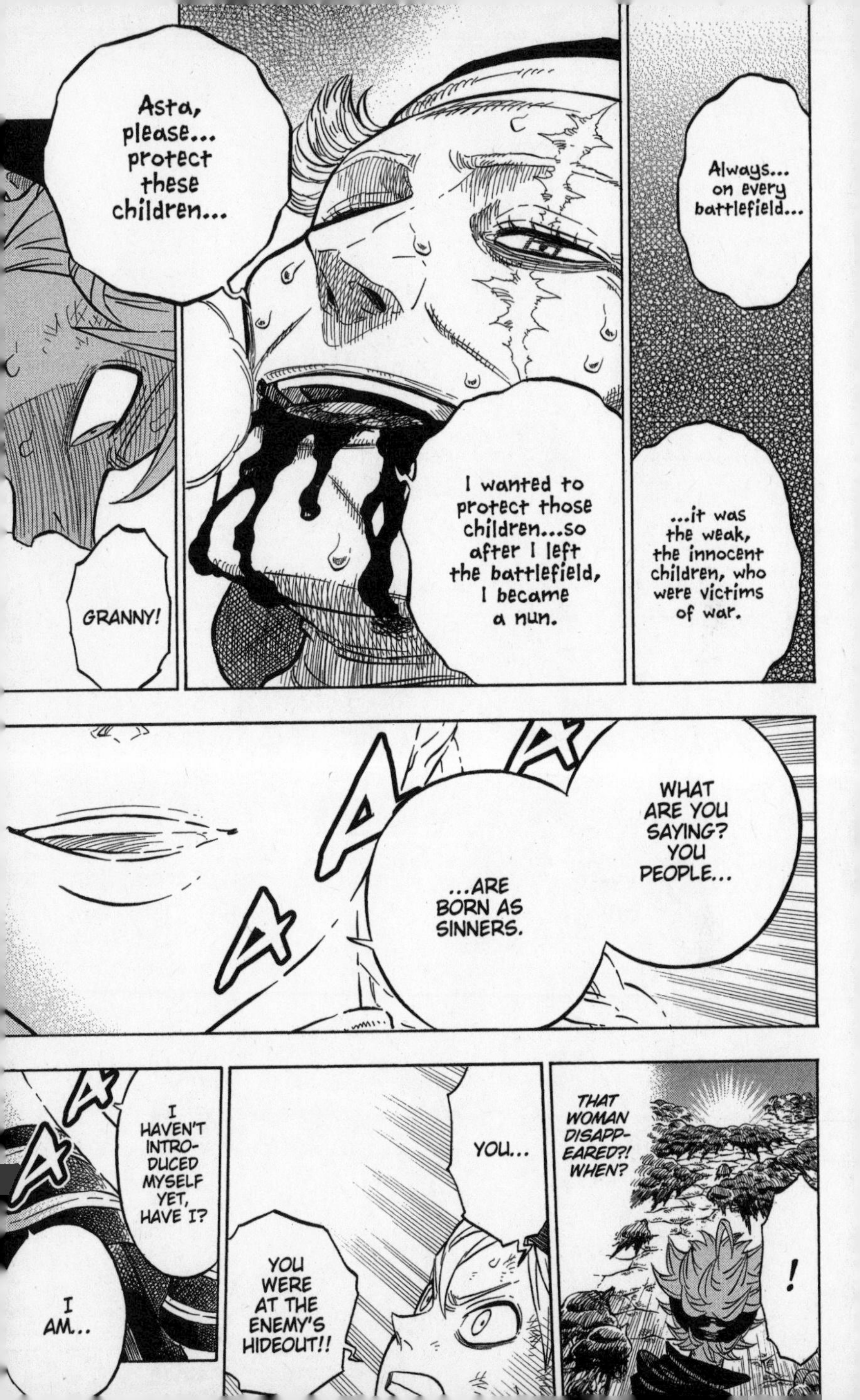
Always... on every battlefield...
...it was the weak, the innocent children, who were victims of war.
I wanted to protect those children...so after I left the battlefield, I became a nun.
Asta, please... protect these children...
GRANNY!
WHAT ARE YOU SAYING? YOU PEOPLE...
...ARE BORN AS SINNERS.
THAT WOMAN DISAPP-EARED?! WHEN?
!
YOU...
YOU WERE AT THE ENEMY'S HIDEOUT!!
I HAVEN'T INTRO-DUCED MYSELF YET, HAVE I?
I AM..

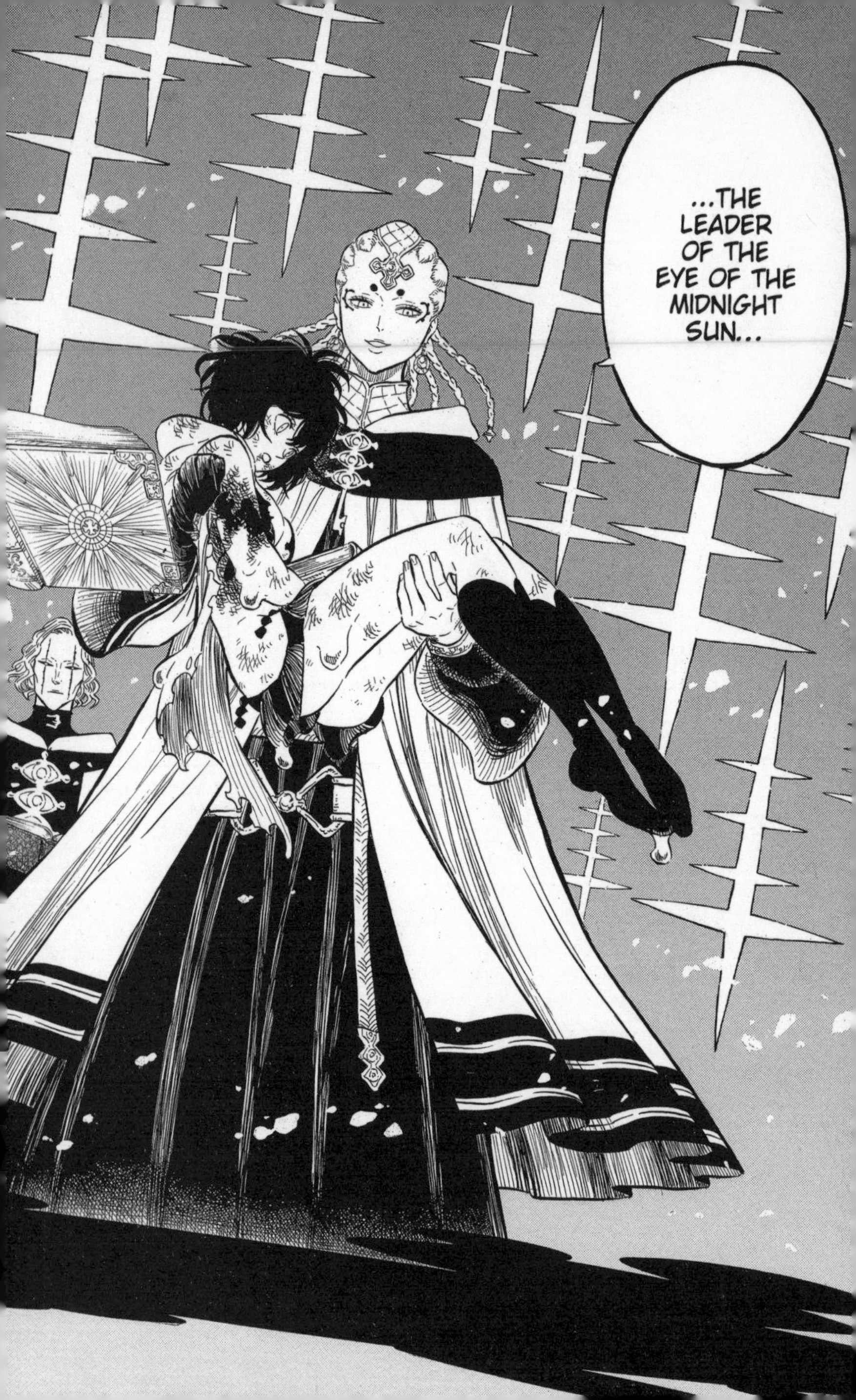
...THE LEADER OF THE EYE OF THE MIDNIGHT SUN...

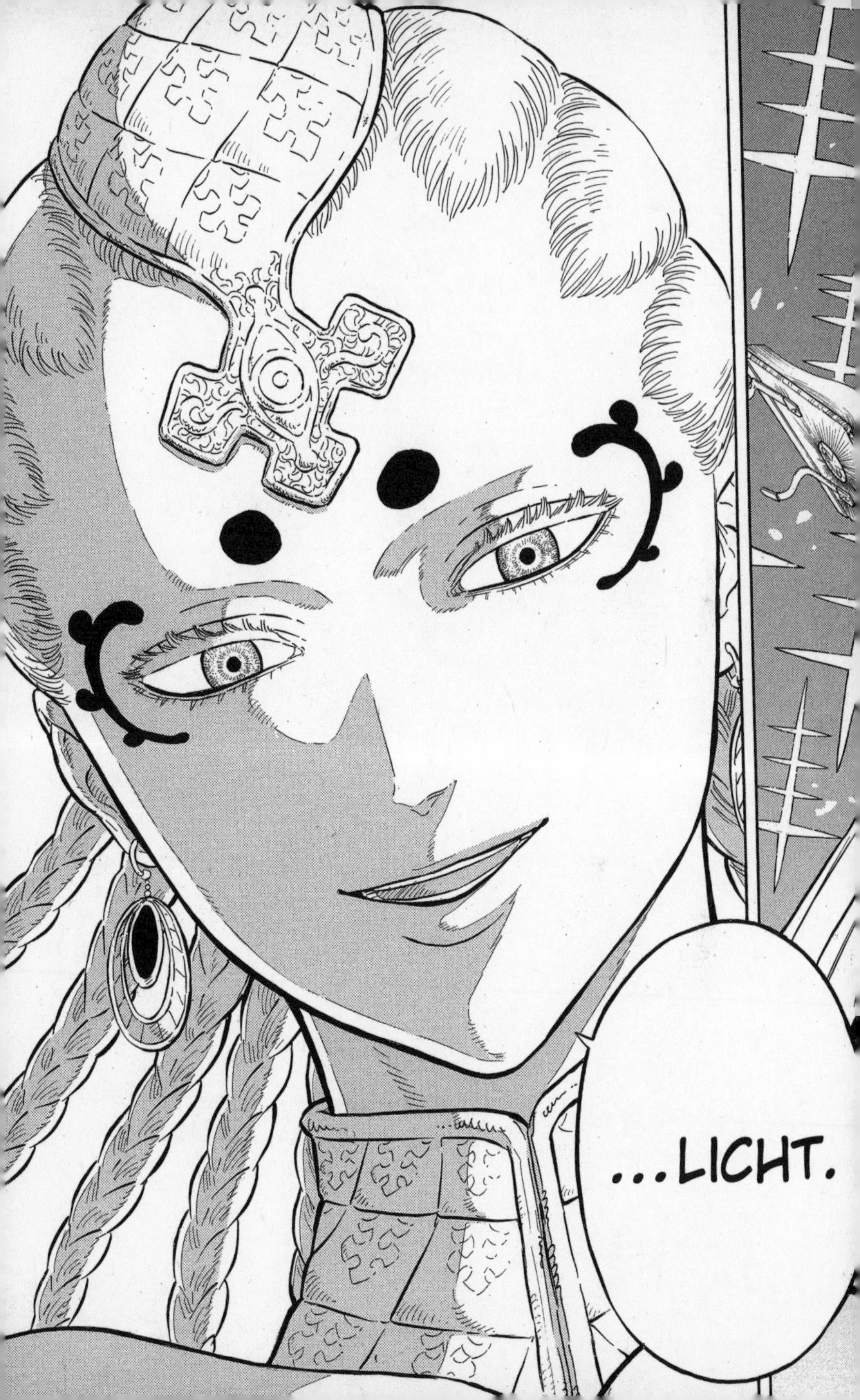
...LICHT.

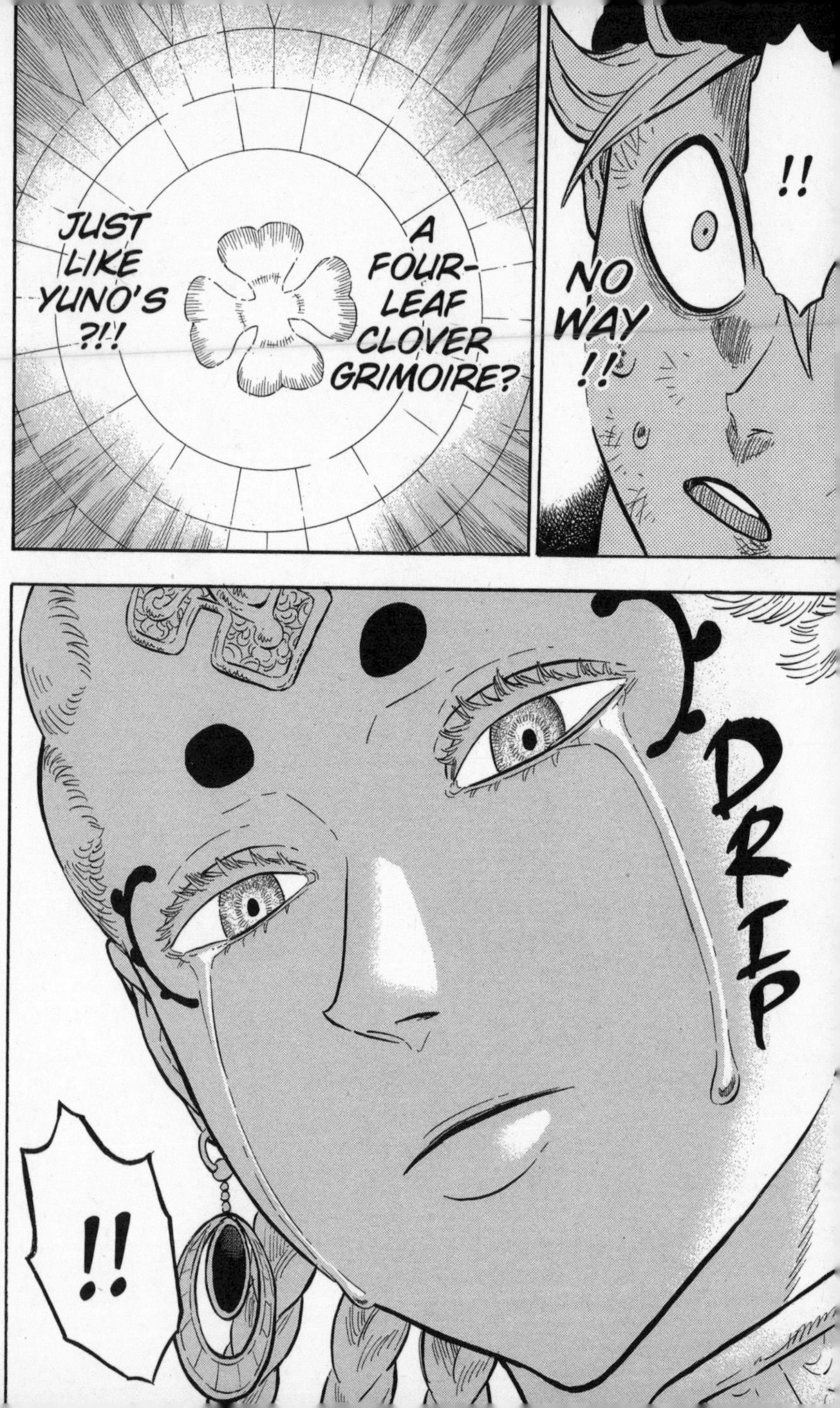
!!
NO WAY!!
A FOUR-LEAF CLOVER GRIMOIRE?
JUST LIKE YUNO'S?!!
DRIP
!!

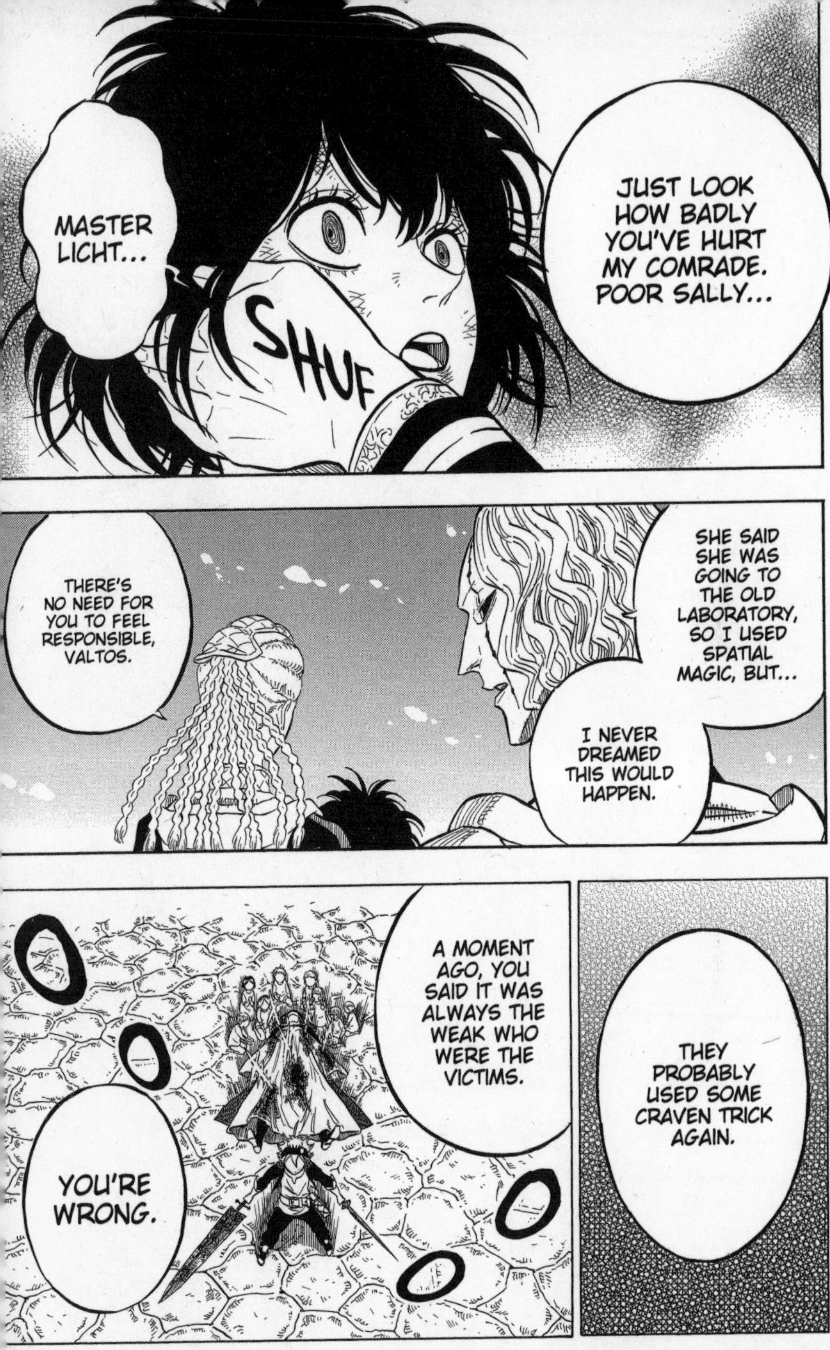
JUST LOOK HOW BADLY YOU'VE HURT MY COMRADE. POOR SALLY...
MASTER LICHT...
SHUF
SHE SAID SHE WAS GOING TO THE OLD LABORATORY, SO I USED SPATIAL MAGIC, BUT...
I NEVER DREAMED THIS WOULD HAPPEN.
THERE'S NO NEED FOR YOU TO FEEL RESPONSIBLE, VALTOS.
THEY PROBABLY USED SOME CRAVEN TRICK AGAIN.
A MOMENT AGO, YOU SAID IT WAS ALWAYS THE WEAK WHO WERE THE VICTIMS.
YOU'RE WRONG.

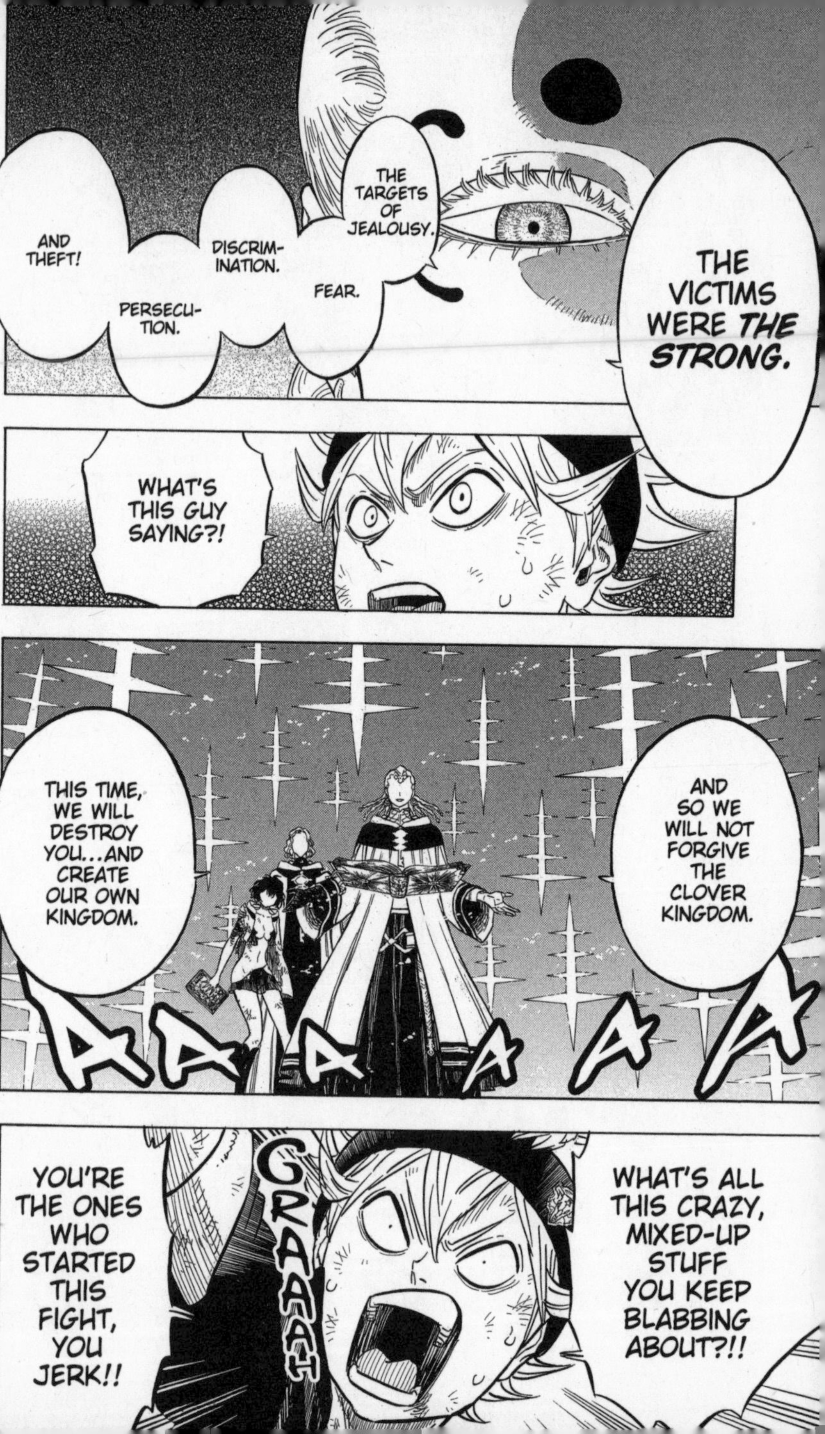

THE VICTIMS WERE THE STRONG.
THE TARGETS OF JEALOUSY.
DISCRIMINATION.
FEAR.
PERSECUTION.
AND THEFT!
WHAT'S THIS GUY SAYING?!
AND SO WE WILL NOT FORGIVE THE CLOVER KINGDOM.
THIS TIME, WE WILL DESTROY YOU...AND CREATE OUR OWN KINGDOM.
AAAAAA
WHAT'S ALL THIS CRAZY, MIXED-UP STUFF YOU KEEP BLABBING ABOUT?!!
GRAAAAH
YOU'RE THE ONES WHO STARTED THIS FIGHT, YOU JERK!!

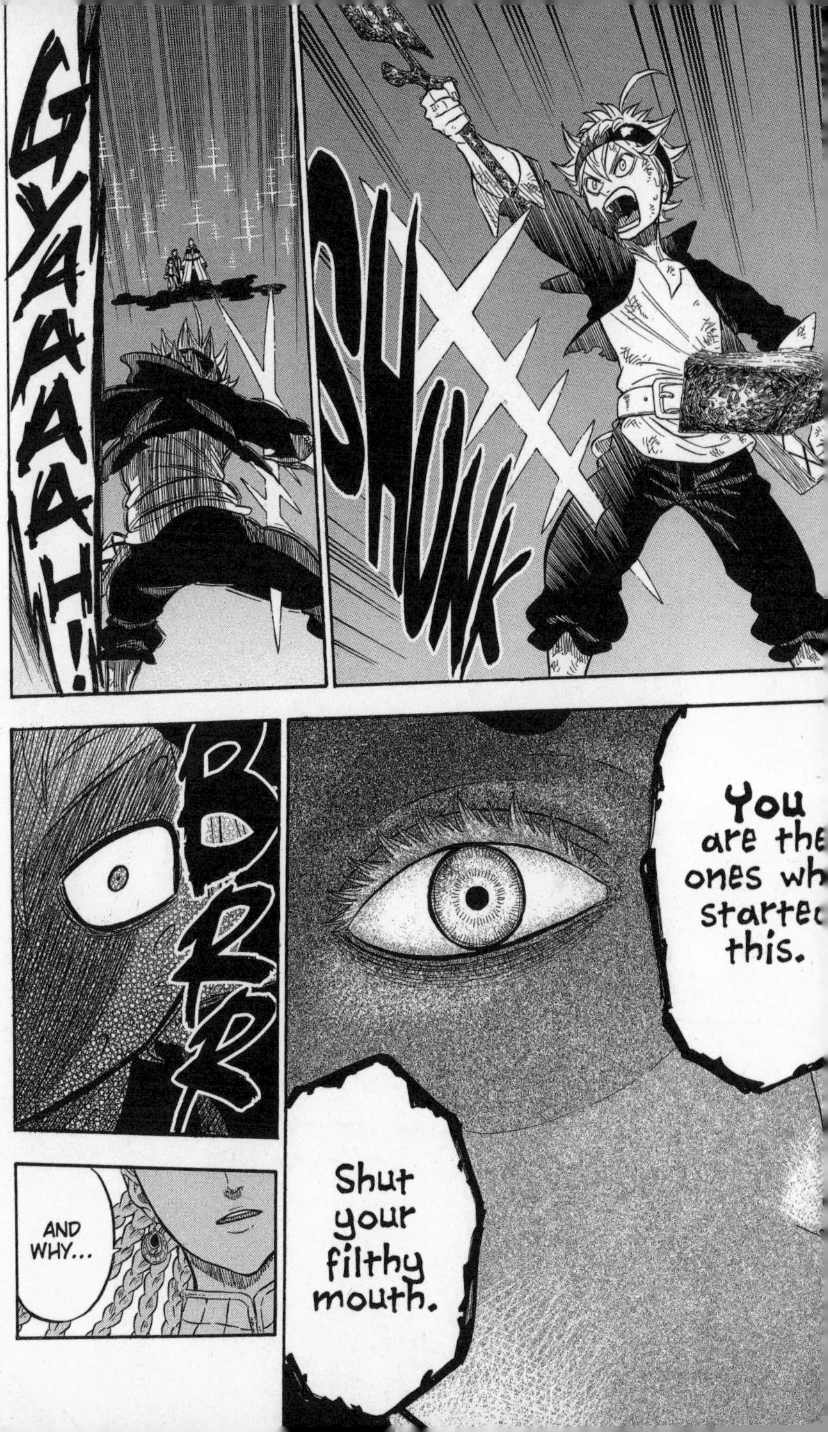
SHUNK
GYAAAH!!
You are the ones wh starte this.
Shut your filthy mouth.
BRRR
AND WHY...

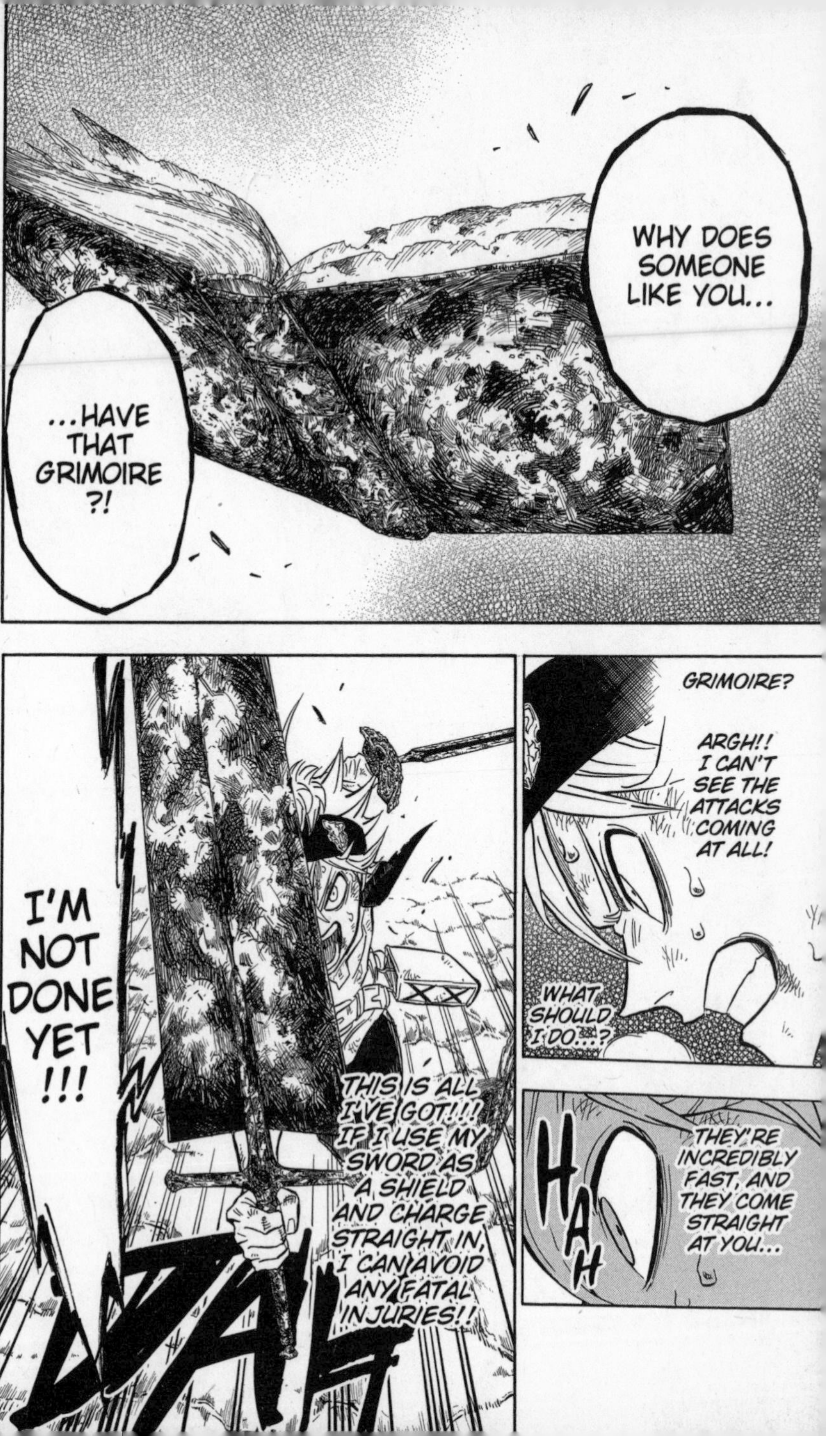
WHY DOES SOMEONE LIKE YOU...
...HAVE THAT GRIMOIRE ?!
GRIMOIRE?
ARGH!! I CAN'T SEE THE ATTACKS COMING AT ALL!
WHAT SHOULD I DO...?
HAH HAH
THEY'RE INCREDIBLY FAST, AND THEY COME STRAIGHT AT YOU...
THIS IS ALL I'VE GOT!!! IF I USE MY SWORD AS A SHIELD AND CHARGE STRAIGHT IN, I CAN AVOID ANY FATAL INJURIES!!
I'M NOT DONE YET !!!

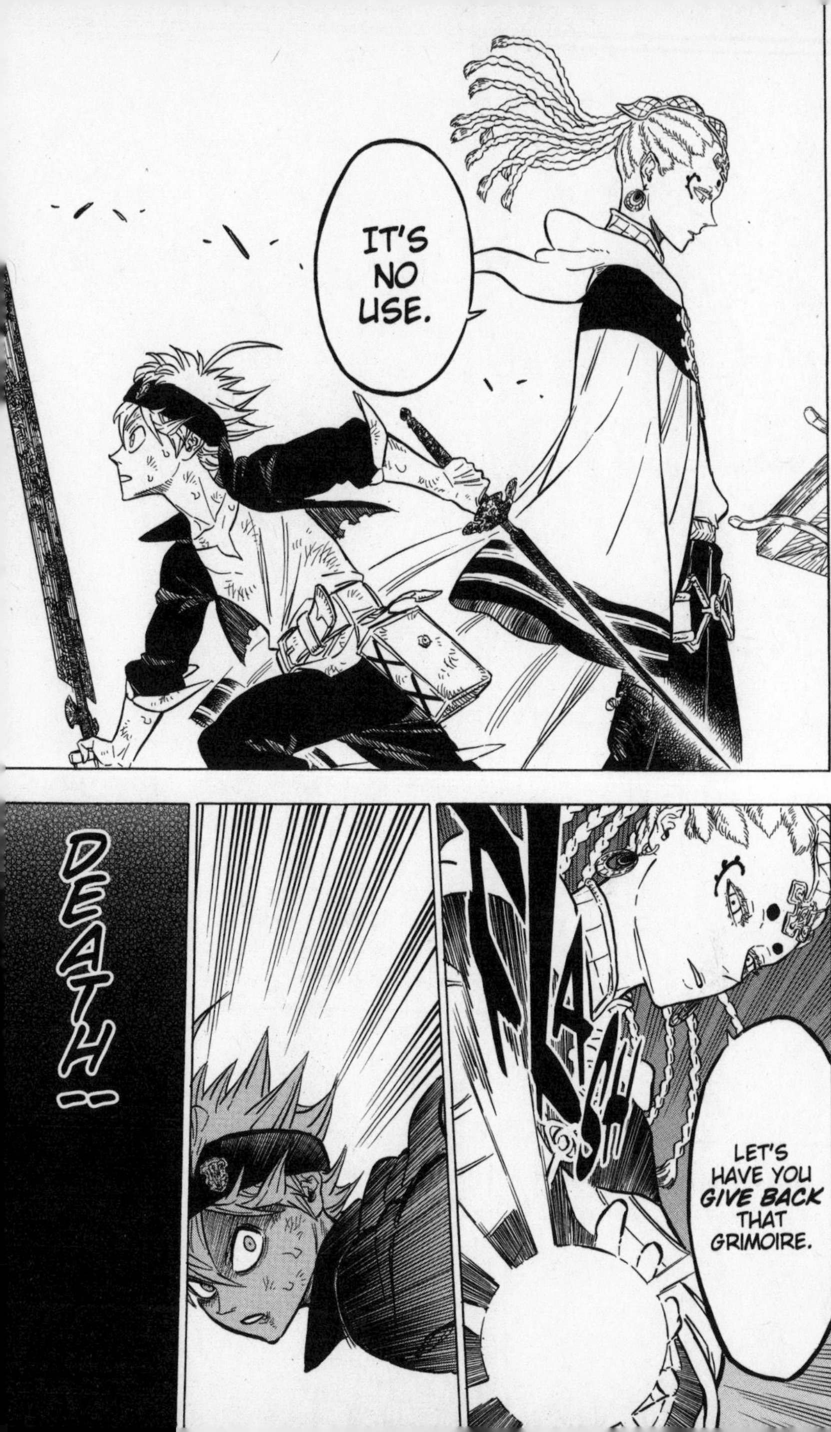
IT'S NO USE.
LET'S HAVE YOU *GIVE BACK* THAT GRIMOIRE.
DEATH!!

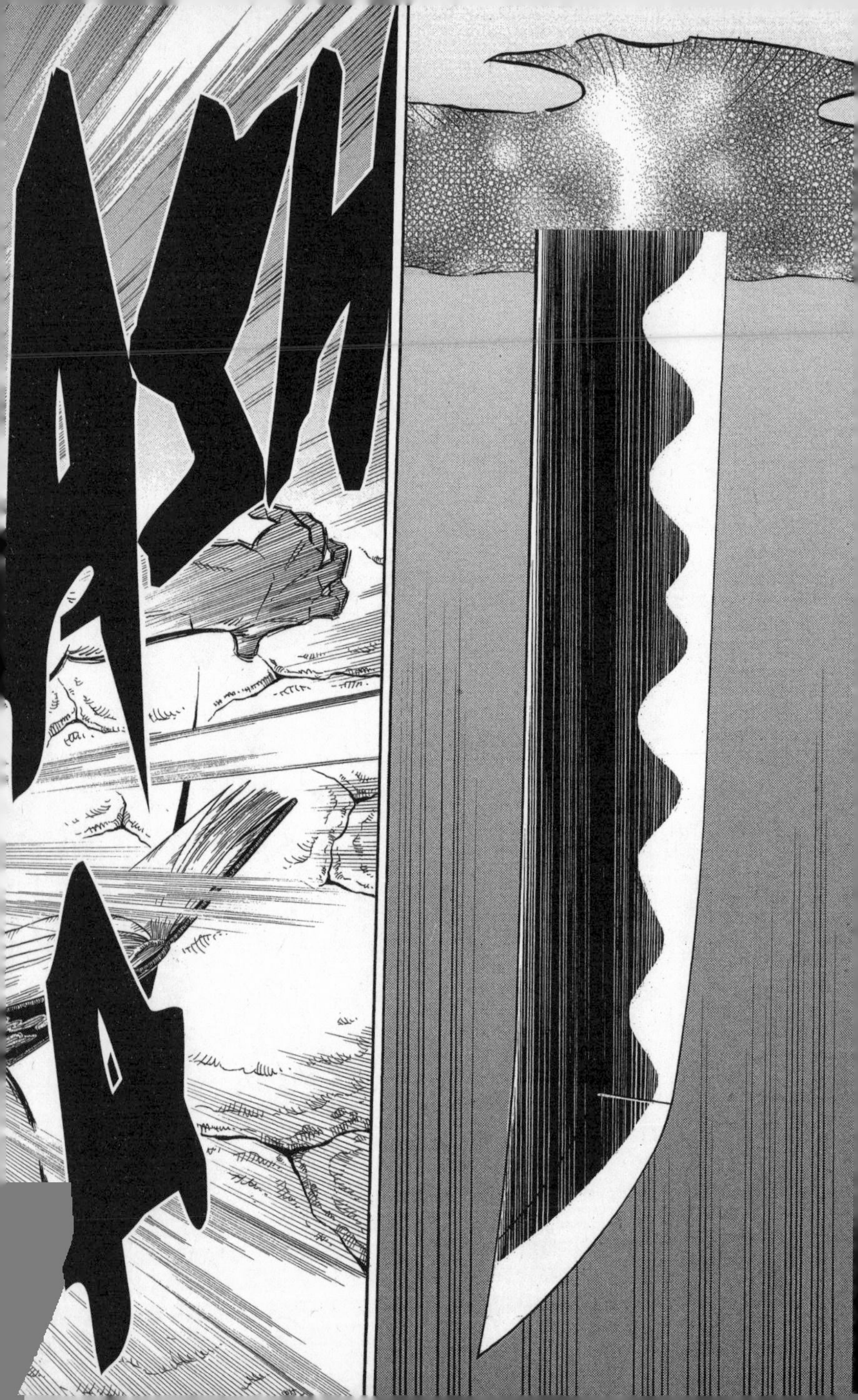

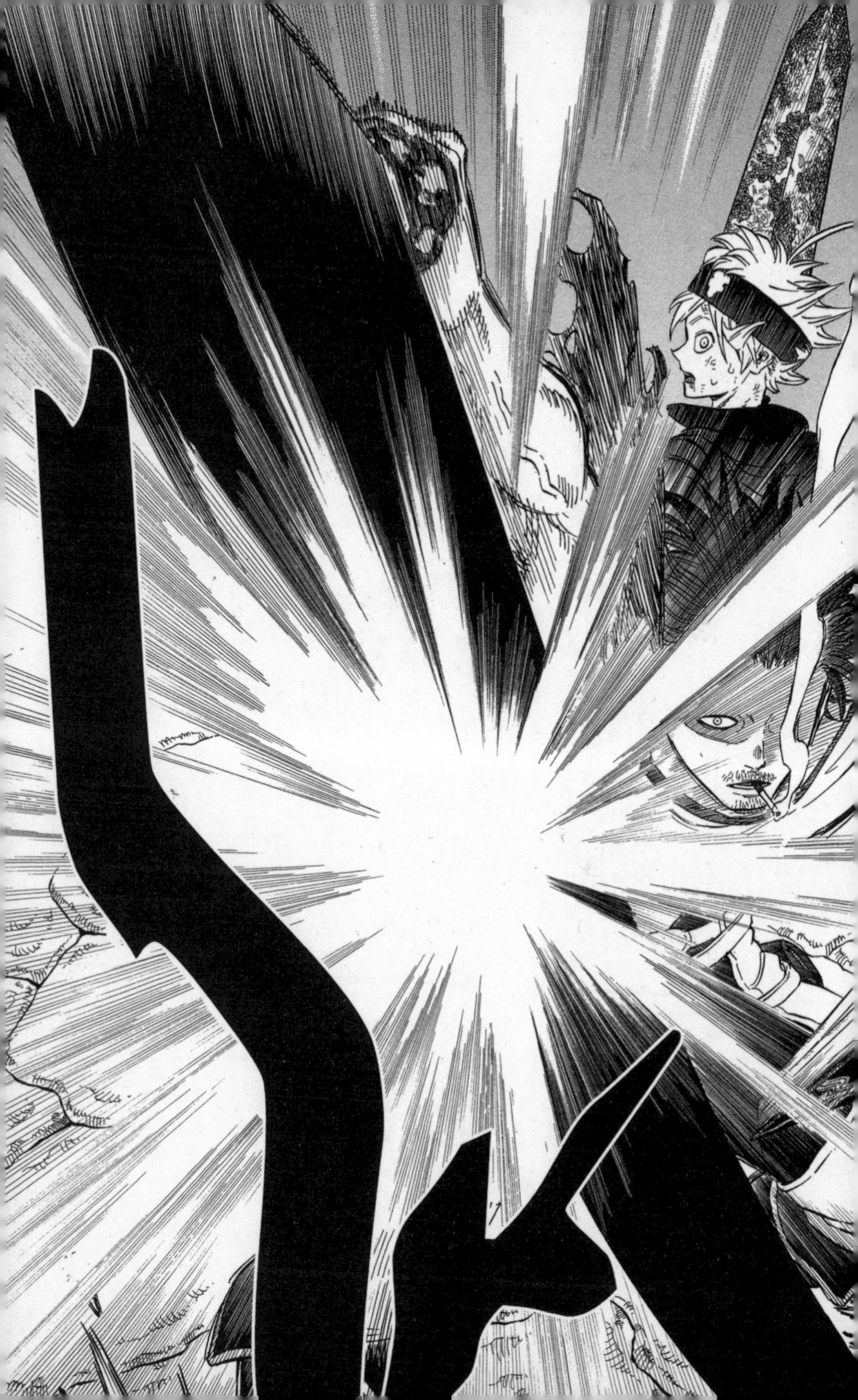

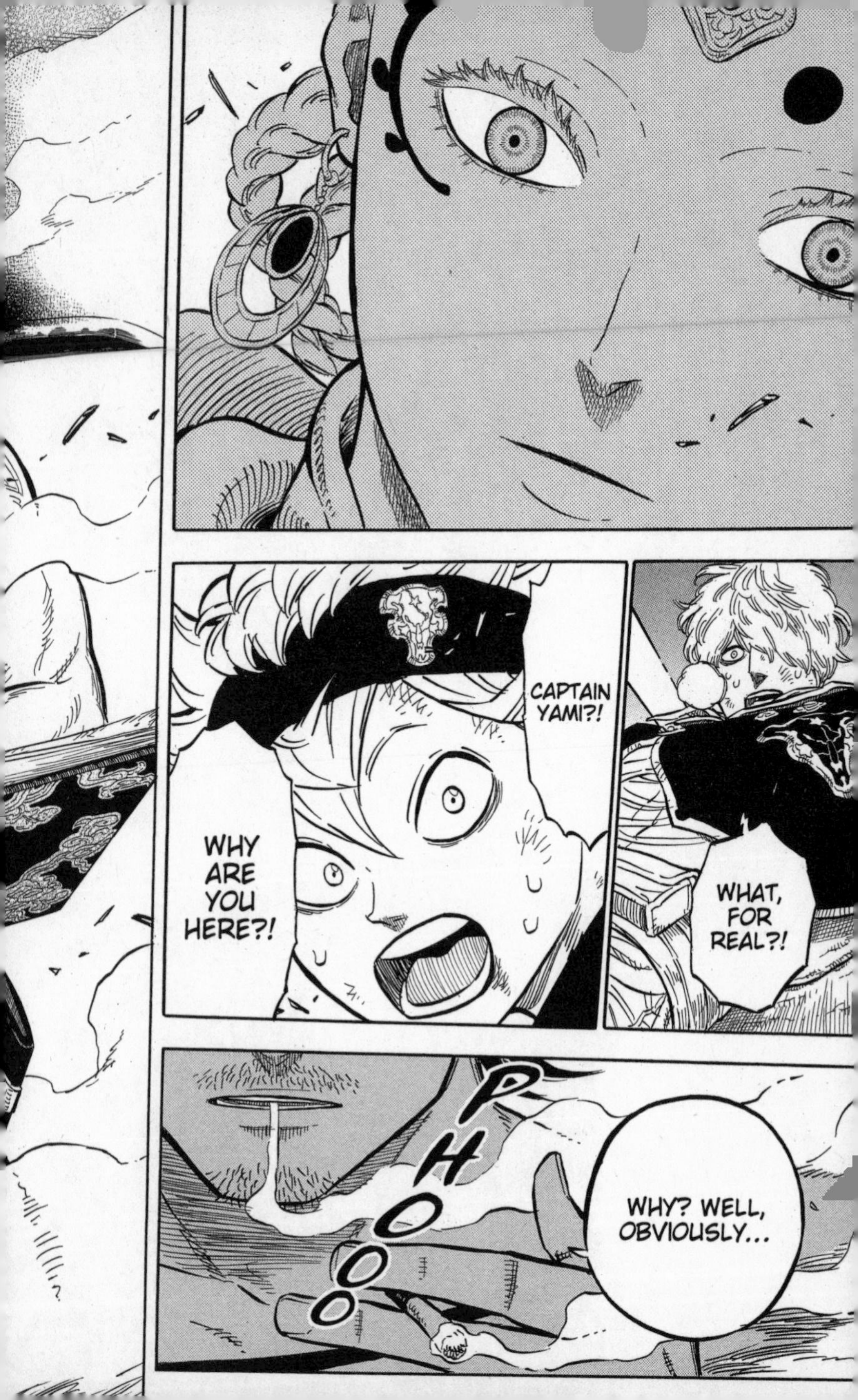
WHAT, FOR REAL?!
CAPTAIN YAMI?!
WHY ARE YOU HERE?!
PHOOOO
WHY? WELL, OBVIOUSLY...

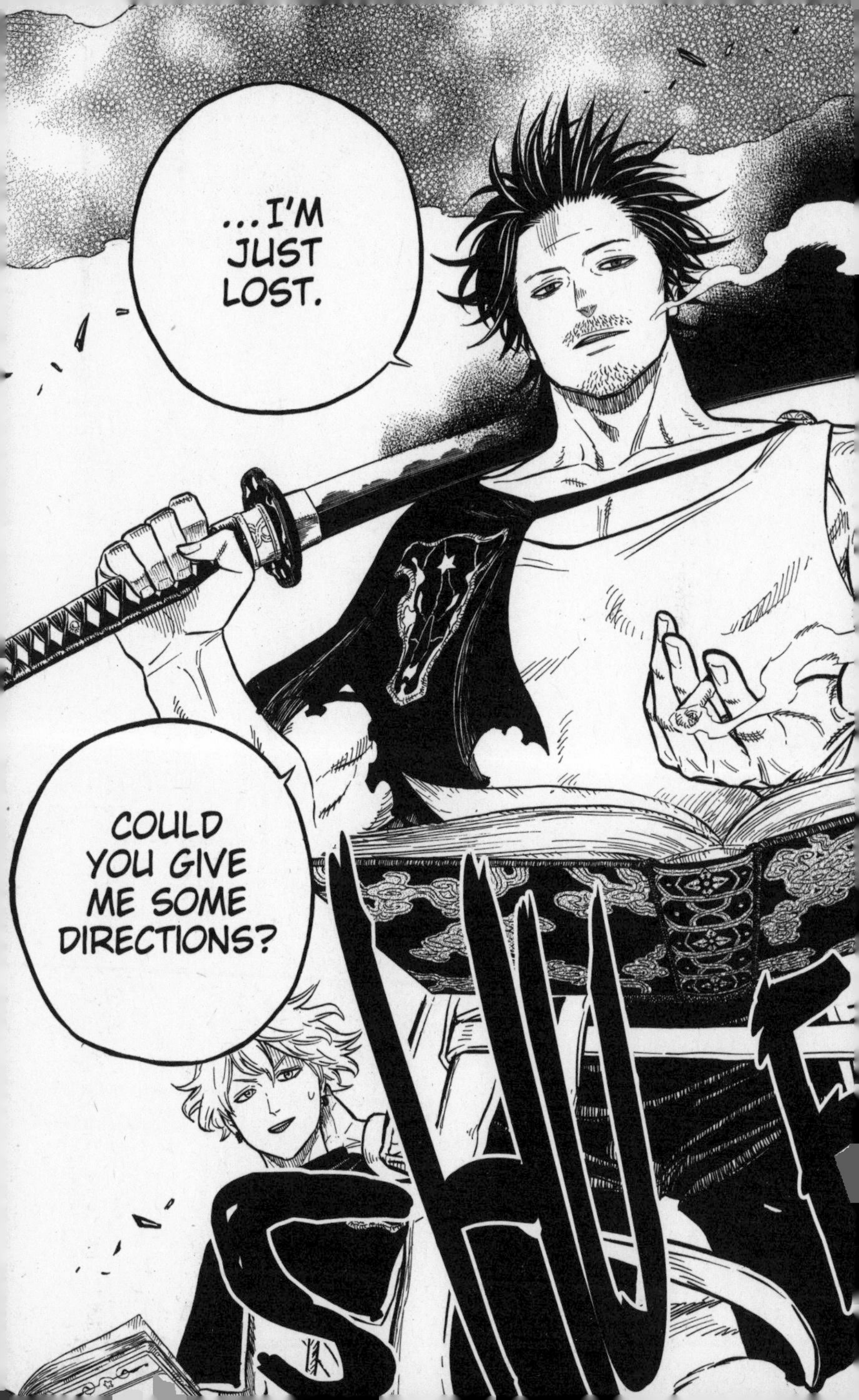
...I'M JUST LOST.
COULD YOU GIVE ME SOME DIRECTIONS?

Sally

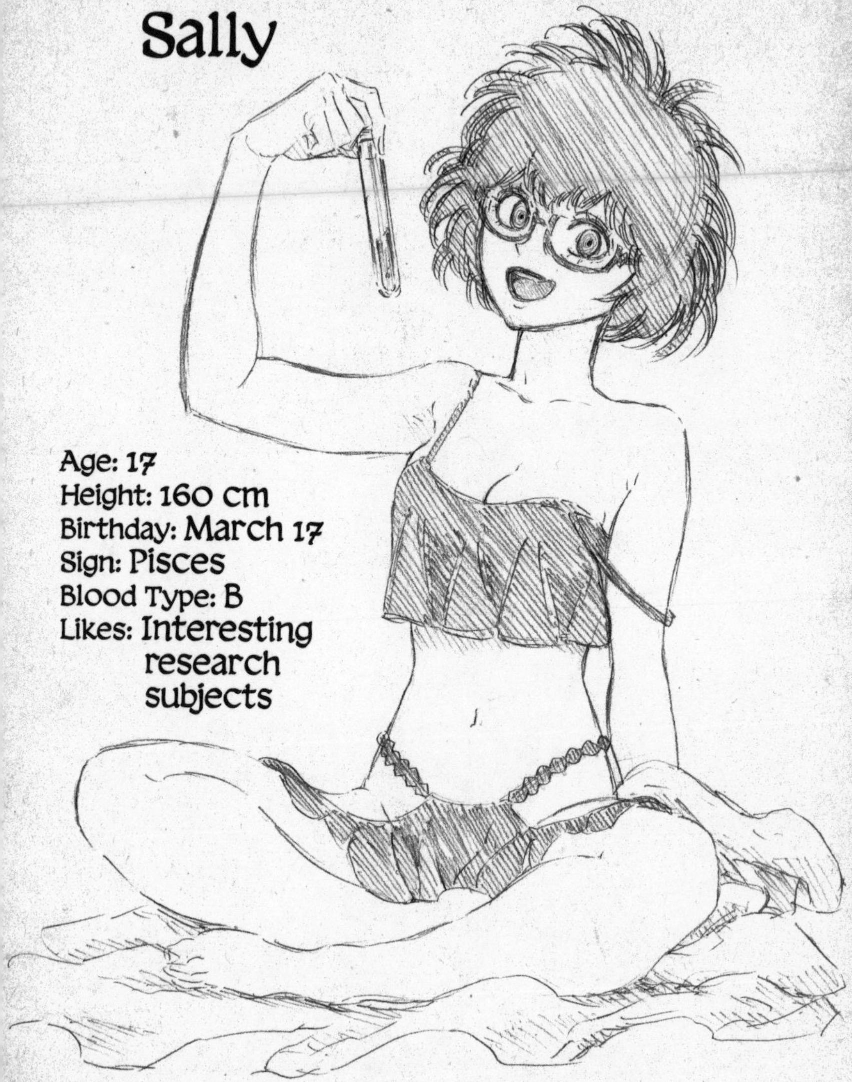

Age: 17
Height: 160 cm
Birthday: March 17
Sign: Pisces
Blood Type: B
Likes: Interesting research subjects

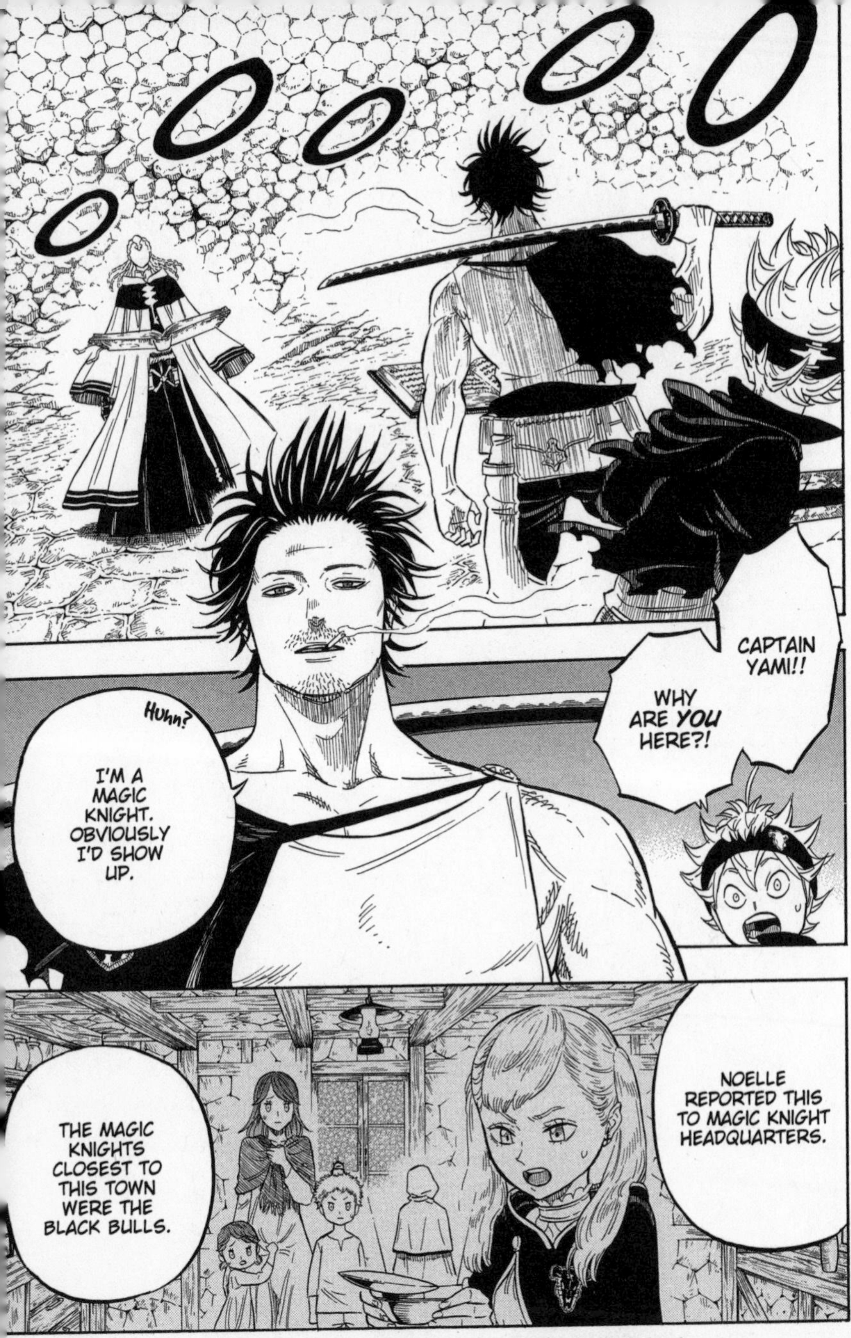
CAPTAIN YAMI!!
WHY ARE YOU HERE?!
Huhn?
I'M A MAGIC KNIGHT. OBVIOUSLY I'D SHOW UP.
NOELLE REPORTED THIS TO MAGIC KNIGHT HEADQUARTERS.
THE MAGIC KNIGHTS CLOSEST TO THIS TOWN WERE THE BLACK BULLS.

Page 47: Light Magic vs. Dark Magic

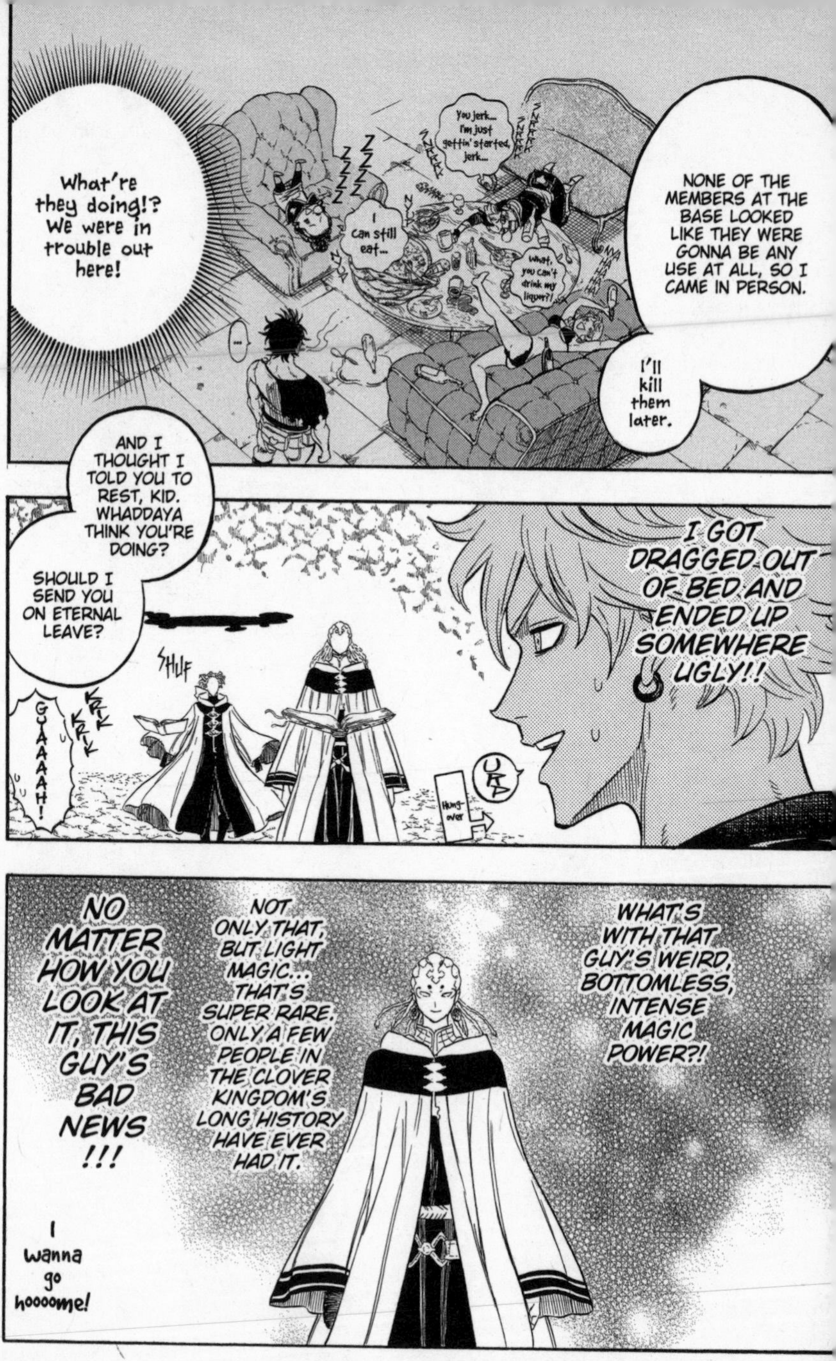
NONE OF THE MEMBERS AT THE BASE LOOKED LIKE THEY WERE GONNA BE ANY USE AT ALL, SO I CAME IN PERSON.
I'll kill them later.
SNRRRK
You jerk... I'm just gettin' started, jerk...
what, you can't drink my liquor?!
ZZZZZ
I can still eat...
What're they doing!? We were in trouble out here!
...
I GOT DRAGGED OUT OF BED AND ENDED UP SOMEWHERE UGLY!!
URP
Hung-over
AND I THOUGHT I TOLD YOU TO REST, KID. WHADDAYA THINK YOU'RE DOING?
SHOULD I SEND YOU ON ETERNAL LEAVE?
SHUF
KRIK KRIK
GUAAAAAH!
WHAT'S WITH THAT GUY'S WEIRD, BOTTOMLESS, INTENSE MAGIC POWER?!
NOT ONLY THAT, BUT LIGHT MAGIC... THAT'S SUPER RARE. ONLY A FEW PEOPLE IN THE CLOVER KINGDOM'S LONG HISTORY HAVE EVER HAD IT.
NO MATTER HOW YOU LOOK AT IT, THIS GUY'S BAD NEWS!!!
I wanna go hoooome!

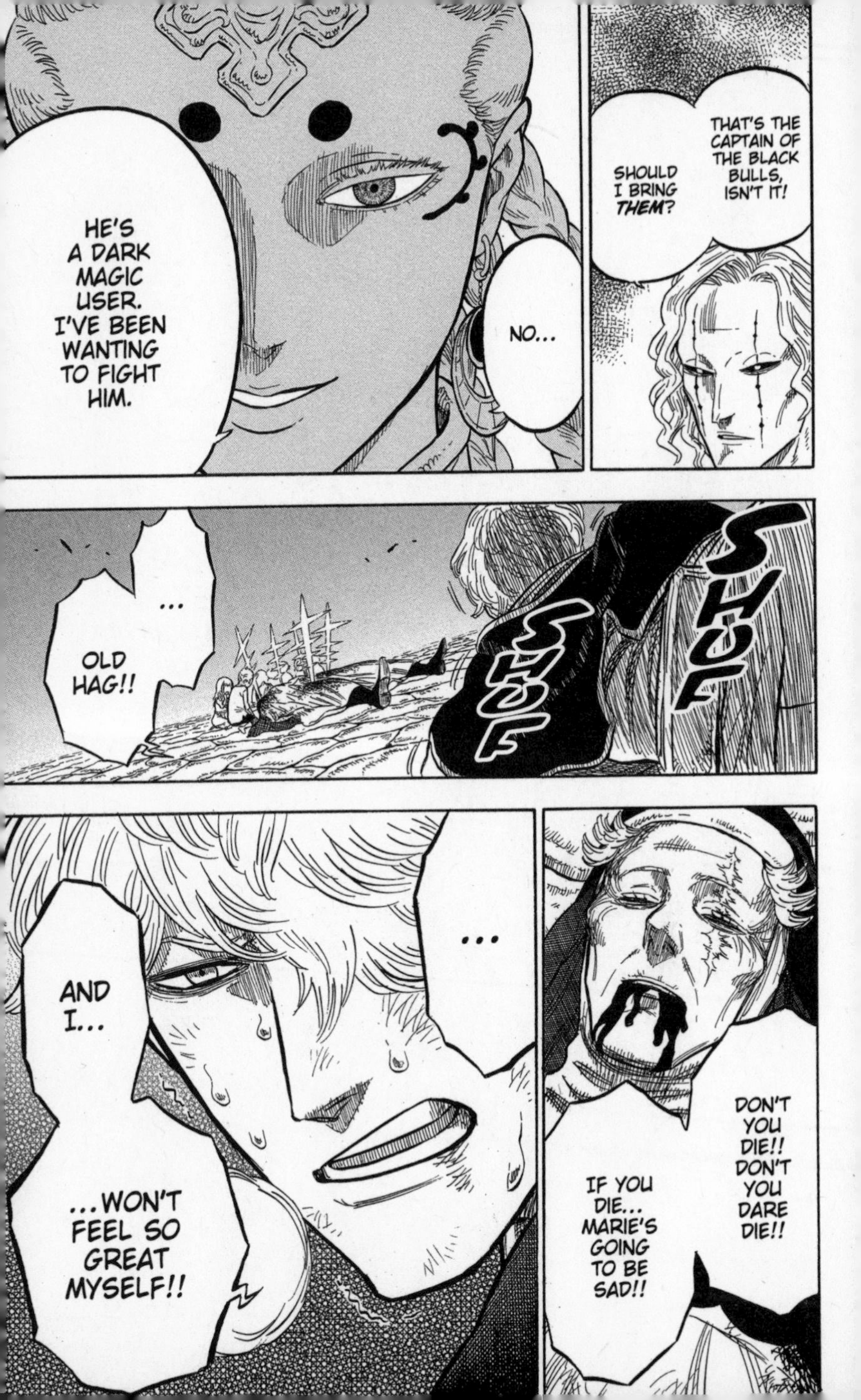
THAT'S THE CAPTAIN OF THE BLACK BULLS, ISN'T IT!
SHOULD I BRING *THEM*?
NO...
HE'S A DARK MAGIC USER. I'VE BEEN WANTING TO FIGHT HIM.
SHUF
SHUF
... OLD HAG!!
DON'T YOU DIE!! DON'T YOU DARE DIE!!
IF YOU DIE... MARIE'S GOING TO BE SAD!!
...
AND I...
...WON'T FEEL SO GREAT MYSELF!!

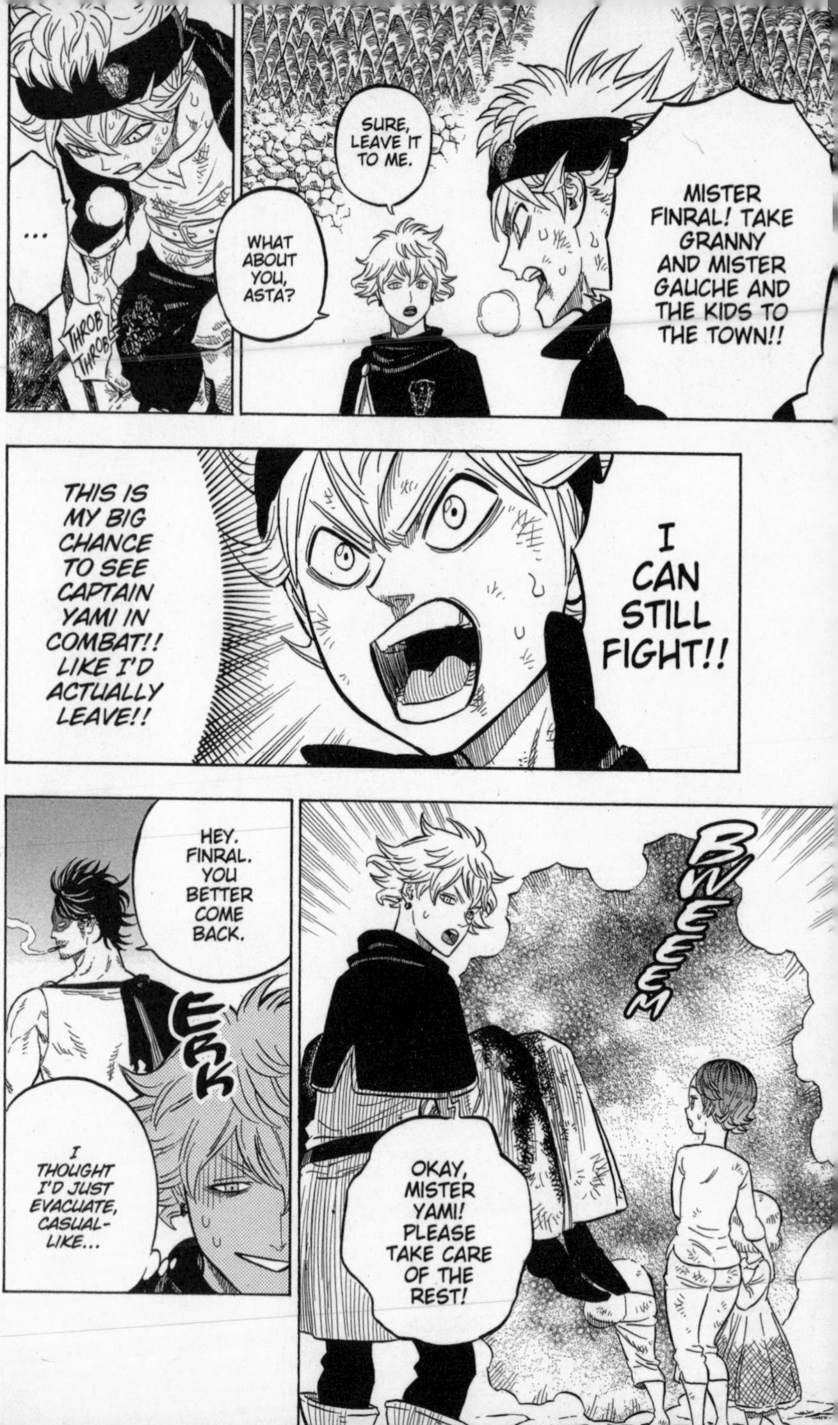
MISTER FINRAL! TAKE GRANNY AND MISTER GAUCHE AND THE KIDS TO THE TOWN!!
SURE, LEAVE IT TO ME.
WHAT ABOUT YOU, ASTA?
THROB THROB
...
I CAN STILL FIGHT!!
THIS IS MY BIG CHANCE TO SEE CAPTAIN YAMI IN COMBAT!! LIKE I'D ACTUALLY LEAVE!!
BWEEEM
OKAY, MISTER YAMI! PLEASE TAKE CARE OF THE REST!
HEY. FINRAL. YOU BETTER COME BACK.
ERK
I THOUGHT I'D JUST EVACUATE, CASUAL-LIKE...

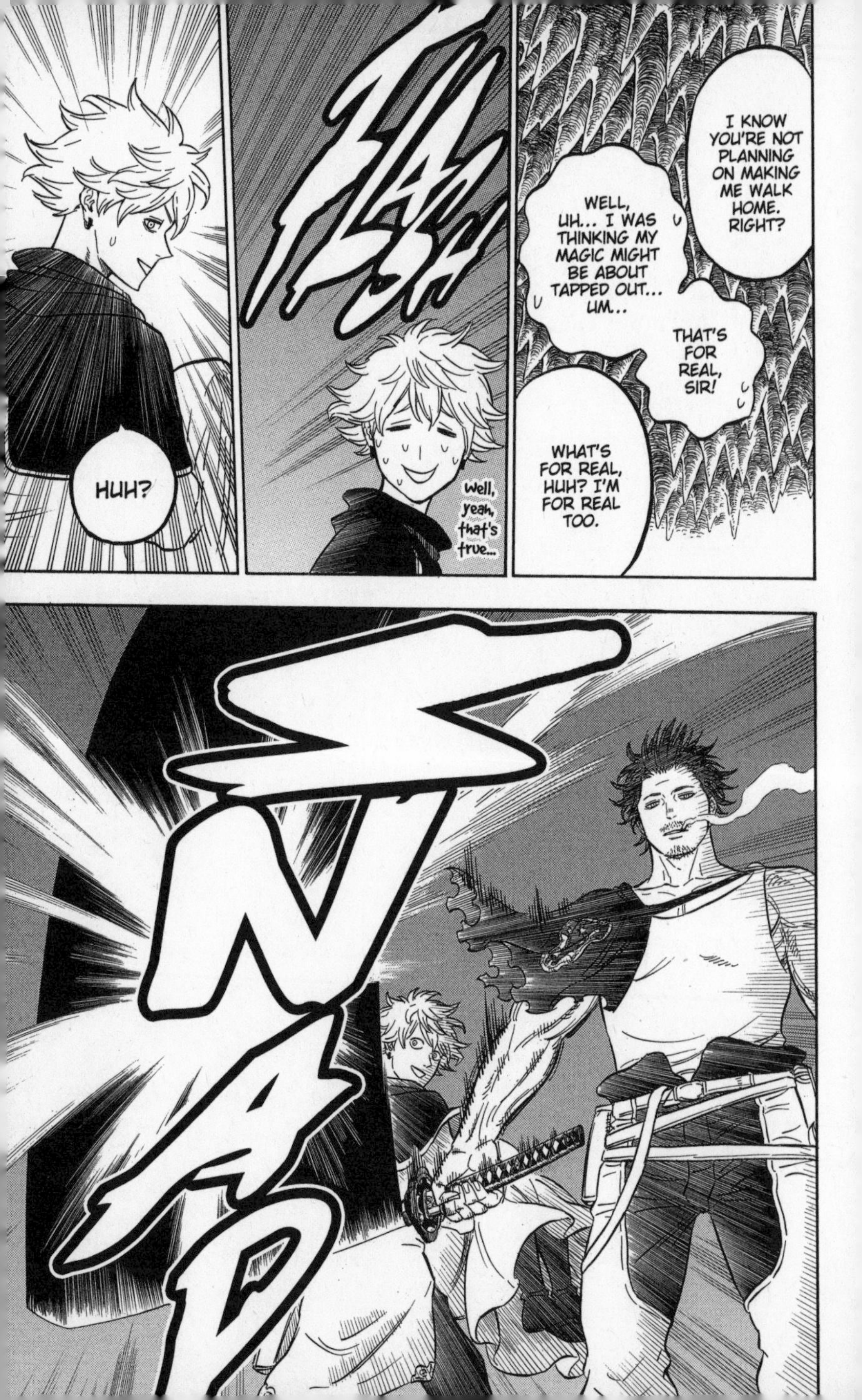
I KNOW YOU'RE NOT PLANNING ON MAKING ME WALK HOME. RIGHT?
WELL, UH... I WAS THINKING MY MAGIC MIGHT BE ABOUT TAPPED OUT... UM...
THAT'S FOR REAL, SIR!
WHAT'S FOR REAL, HUH? I'M FOR REAL TOO.
Well, yeah, that's true...
HUH?

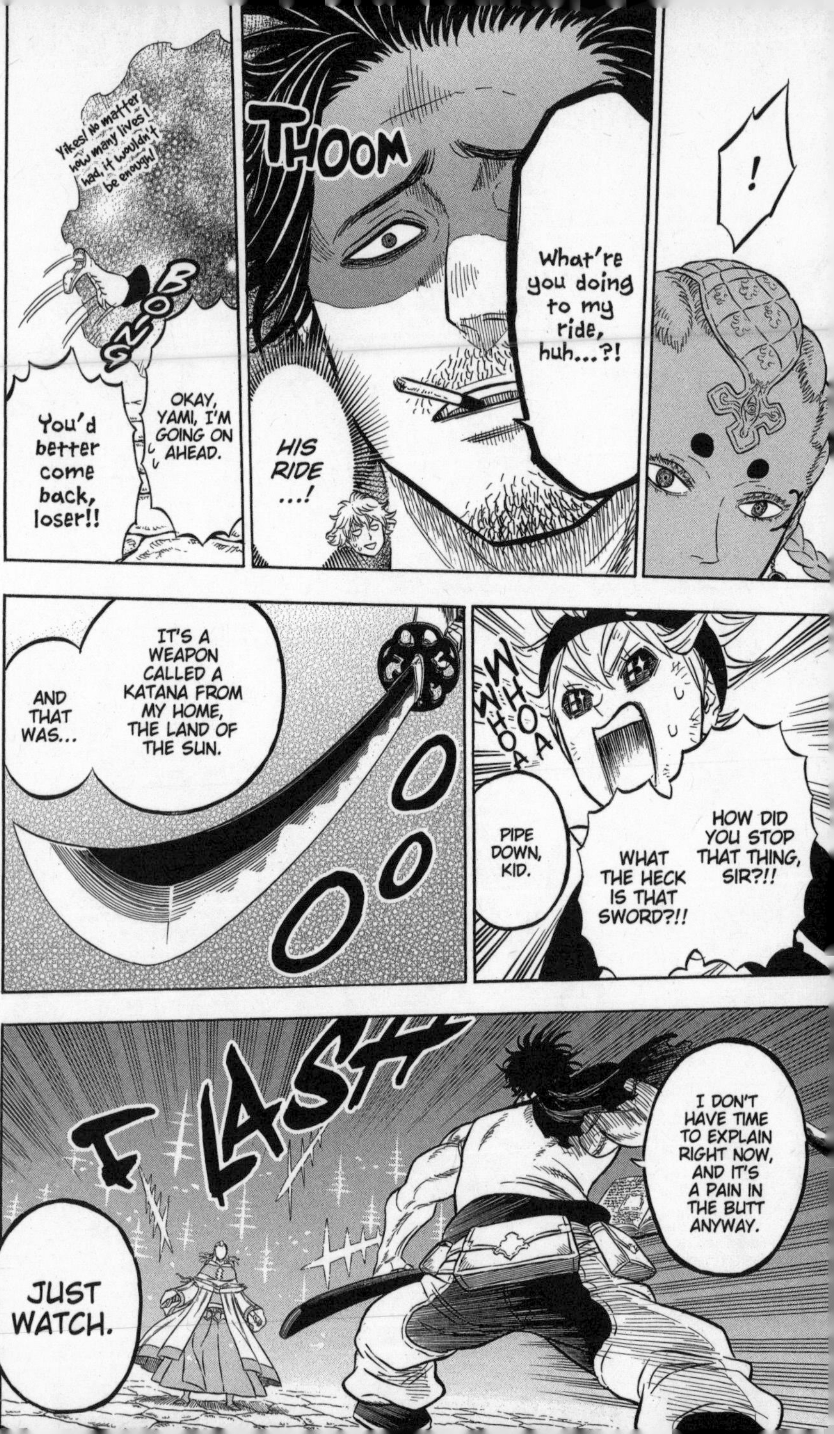
!
THOOM
What're you doing to my ride, huh...?!
HIS RIDE ...!
BONG
Yikes! No matter how many lives I had, it wouldn't be enough!
OKAY, YAMI, I'M GOING ON AHEAD.
You'd better come back, loser!!
WHOA WHOA
HOW DID YOU STOP THAT THING, SIR?!!
WHAT THE HECK IS THAT SWORD?!!
PIPE DOWN, KID.
AND THAT WAS...
IT'S A WEAPON CALLED A KATANA FROM MY HOME, THE LAND OF THE SUN.
OOO
I DON'T HAVE TIME TO EXPLAIN RIGHT NOW, AND IT'S A PAIN IN THE BUTT ANYWAY.
FLASH
JUST WATCH.

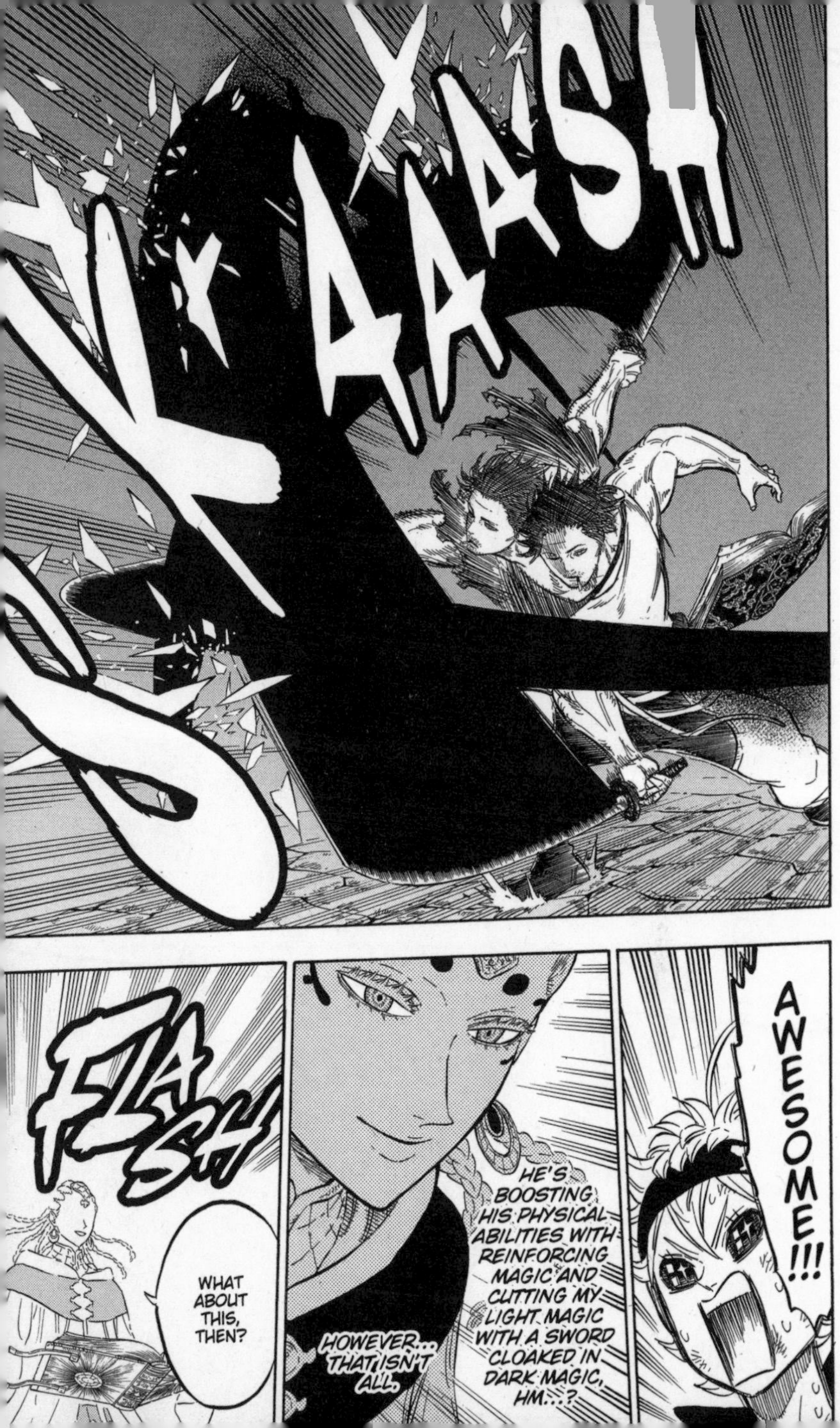
AAASH!!
AWESOME!!!
HE'S BOOSTING HIS PHYSICAL ABILITIES WITH REINFORCING MAGIC AND CUTTING MY LIGHT MAGIC WITH A SWORD CLOAKED IN DARK MAGIC, HM...?
HOWEVER... THAT ISN'T ALL.
FLASH
WHAT ABOUT THIS, THEN?

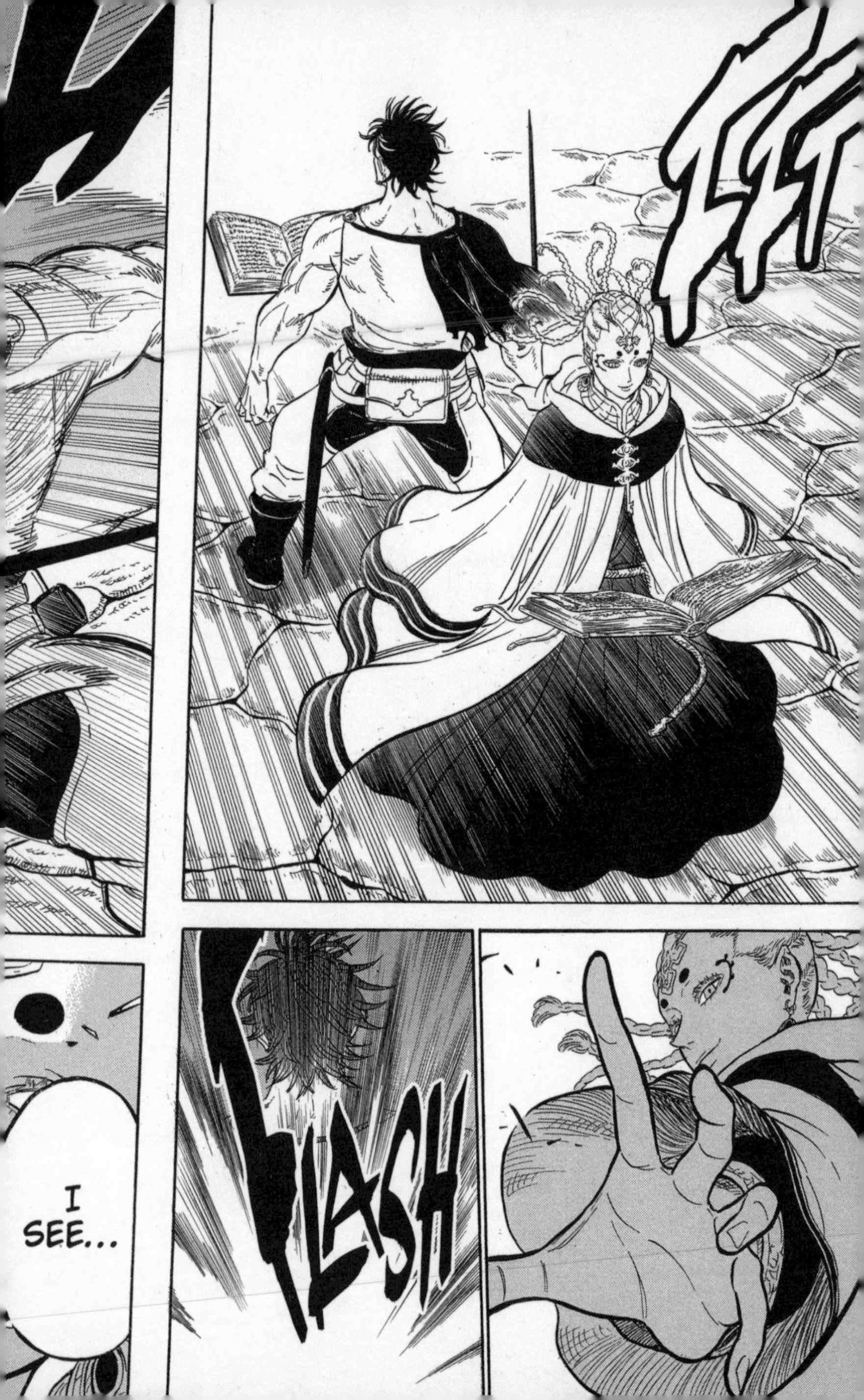
FLASH
I SEE...

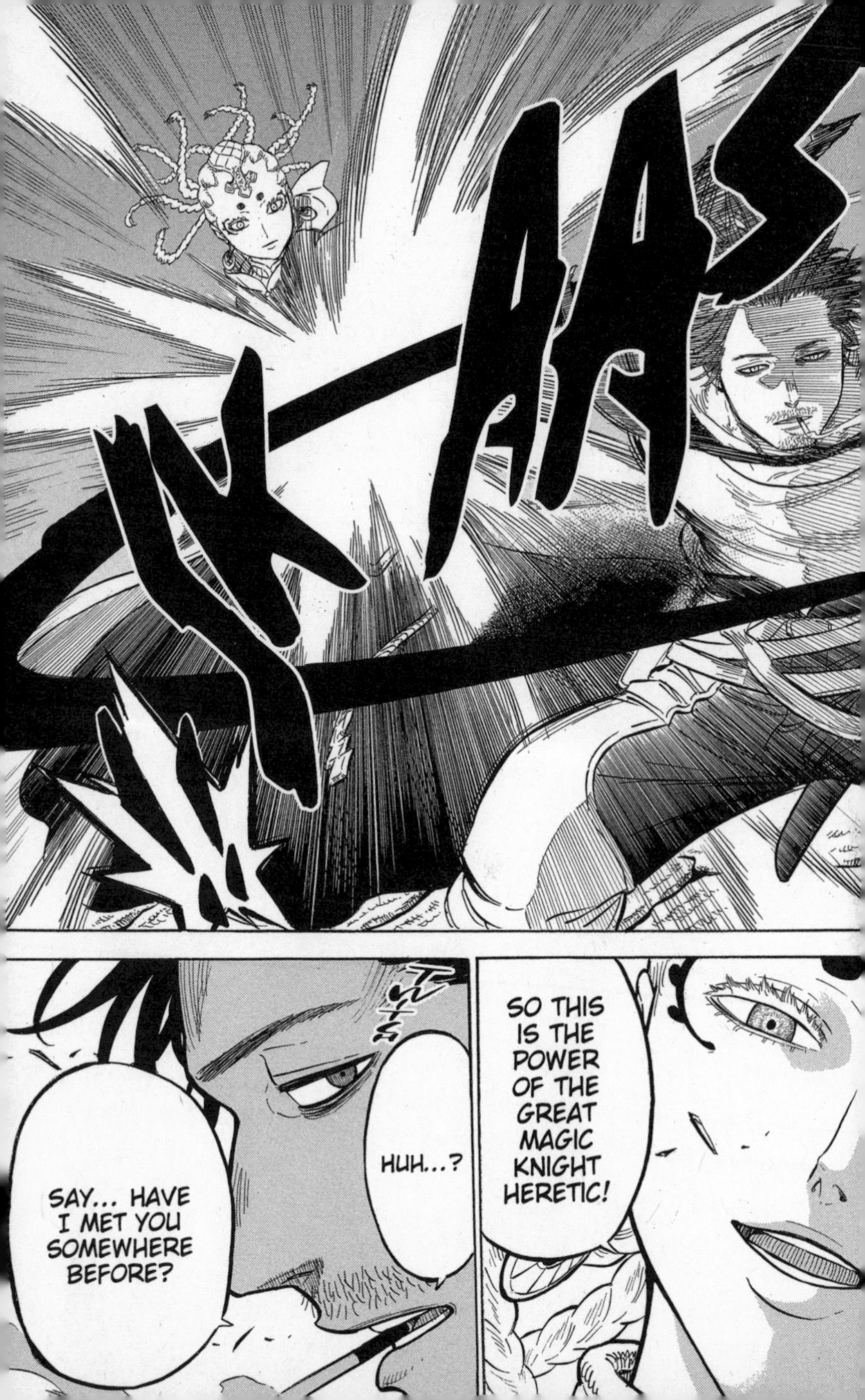
SO THIS IS THE POWER OF THE GREAT MAGIC KNIGHT HERETIC!
HUH...?
SAY... HAVE I MET YOU SOMEWHERE BEFORE?

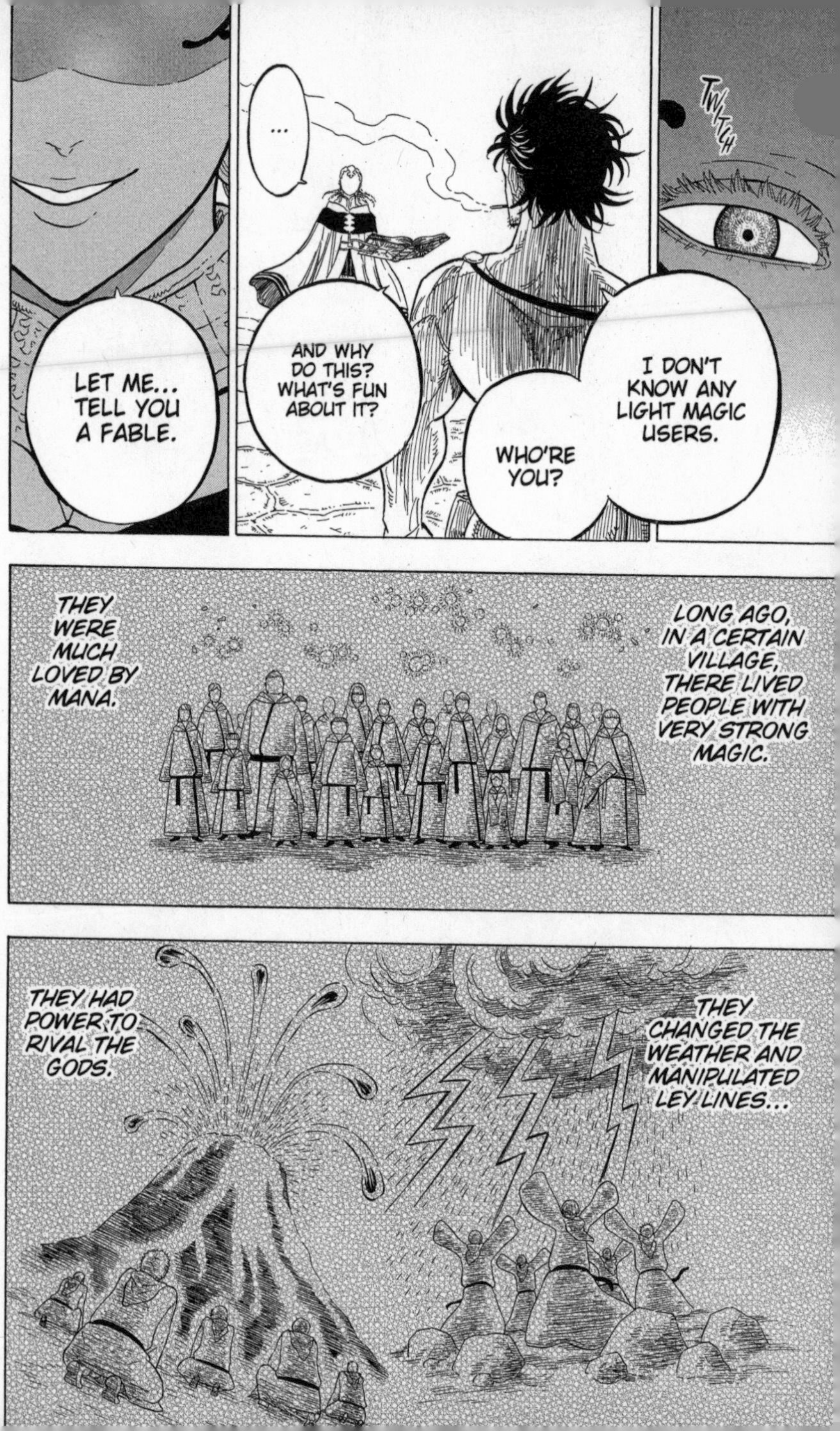
TWITCH
I DON'T KNOW ANY LIGHT MAGIC USERS.
WHO'RE YOU?
...
AND WHY DO THIS? WHAT'S FUN ABOUT IT?
LET ME... TELL YOU A FABLE.
LONG AGO, IN A CERTAIN VILLAGE, THERE LIVED PEOPLE WITH VERY STRONG MAGIC.
THEY WERE MUCH LOVED BY MANA.
THEY CHANGED THE WEATHER AND MANIPULATED LEY LINES...
THEY HAD POWER TO RIVAL THE GODS.

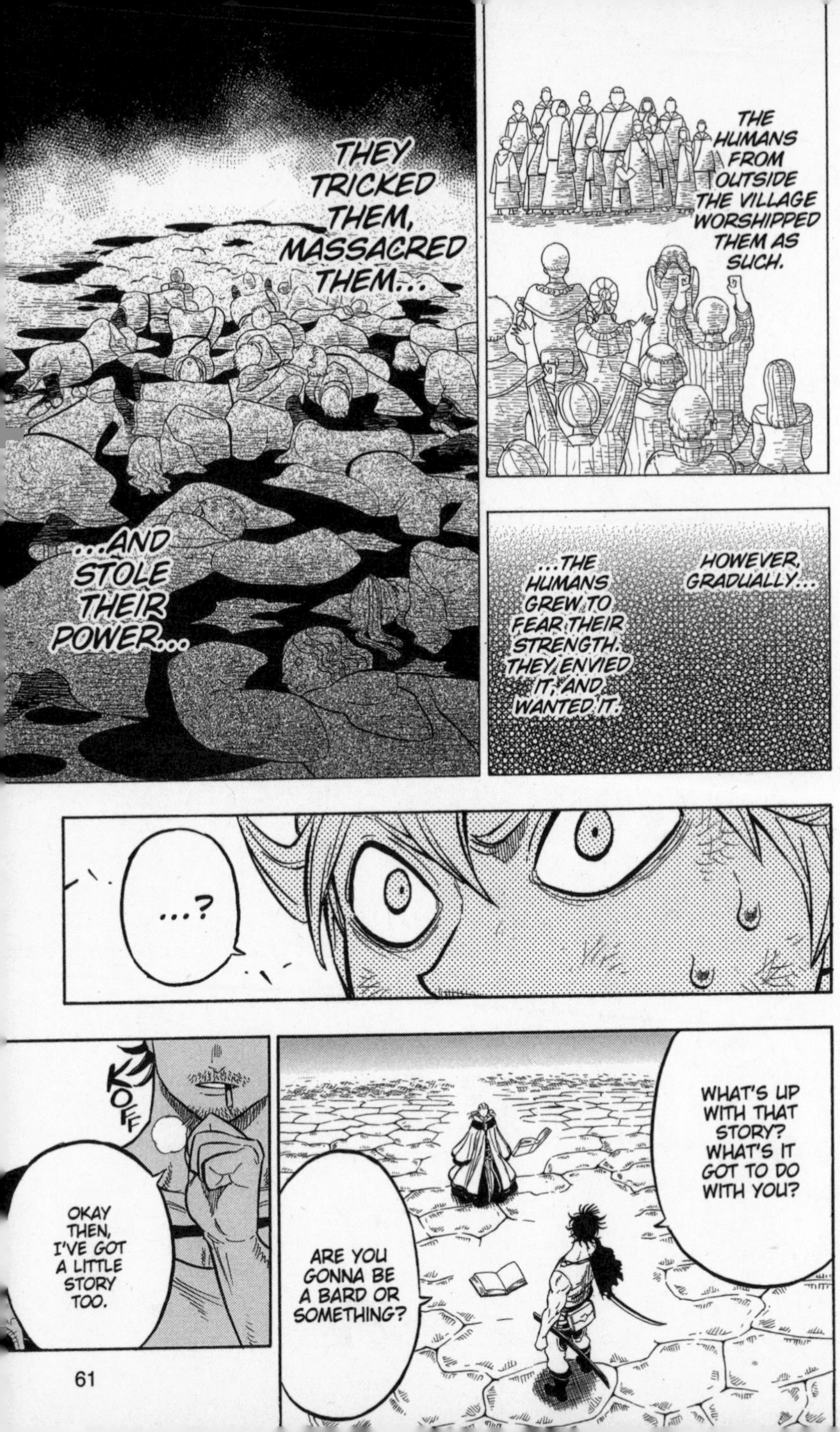
THE HUMANS FROM OUTSIDE THE VILLAGE WORSHIPPED THEM AS SUCH.
HOWEVER, GRADUALLY...
...THE HUMANS GREW TO FEAR THEIR STRENGTH. THEY ENVIED IT, AND WANTED IT.
THEY TRICKED THEM, MASSACRED THEM...
...AND STOLE THEIR POWER...
...?
WHAT'S UP WITH THAT STORY? WHAT'S IT GOT TO DO WITH YOU?
ARE YOU GONNA BE A BARD OR SOMETHING?
KOFF
OKAY THEN, I'VE GOT A LITTLE STORY TOO.

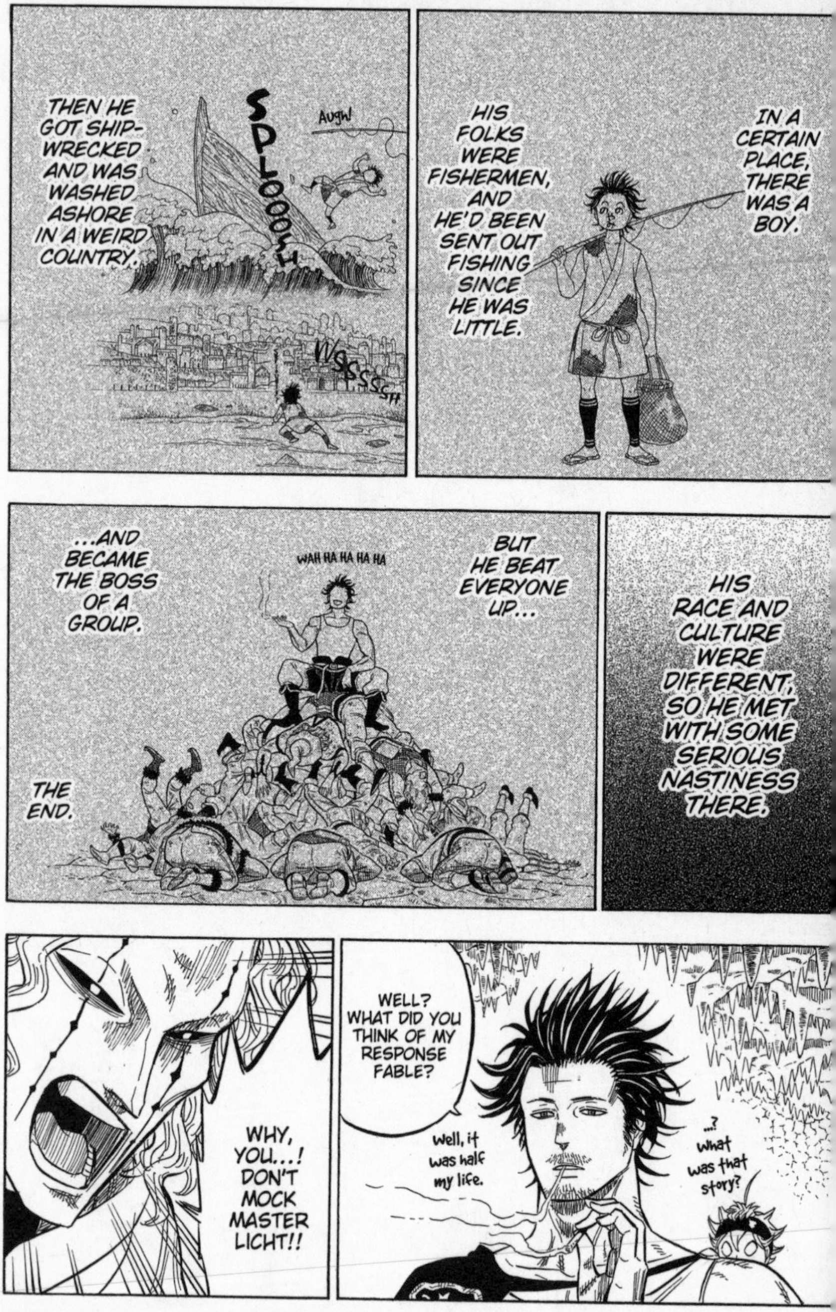
IN A CERTAIN PLACE, THERE WAS A BOY.
HIS FOLKS WERE FISHERMEN, AND HE'D BEEN SENT OUT FISHING SINCE HE WAS LITTLE.
THEN HE GOT SHIP-WRECKED AND WAS WASHED ASHORE IN A WEIRD COUNTRY.
Augh!
SPLOOOOSH
WSSSSSH
HIS RACE AND CULTURE WERE DIFFERENT, SO HE MET WITH SOME SERIOUS NASTINESS THERE.
BUT HE BEAT EVERYONE UP...
...AND BECAME THE BOSS OF A GROUP.
WAH HA HA HA HA
THE END.
WELL? WHAT DID YOU THINK OF MY RESPONSE FABLE?
Well, it was half my life.
...? what was that story?
WHY, YOU...! DON'T MOCK MASTER LICHT!!

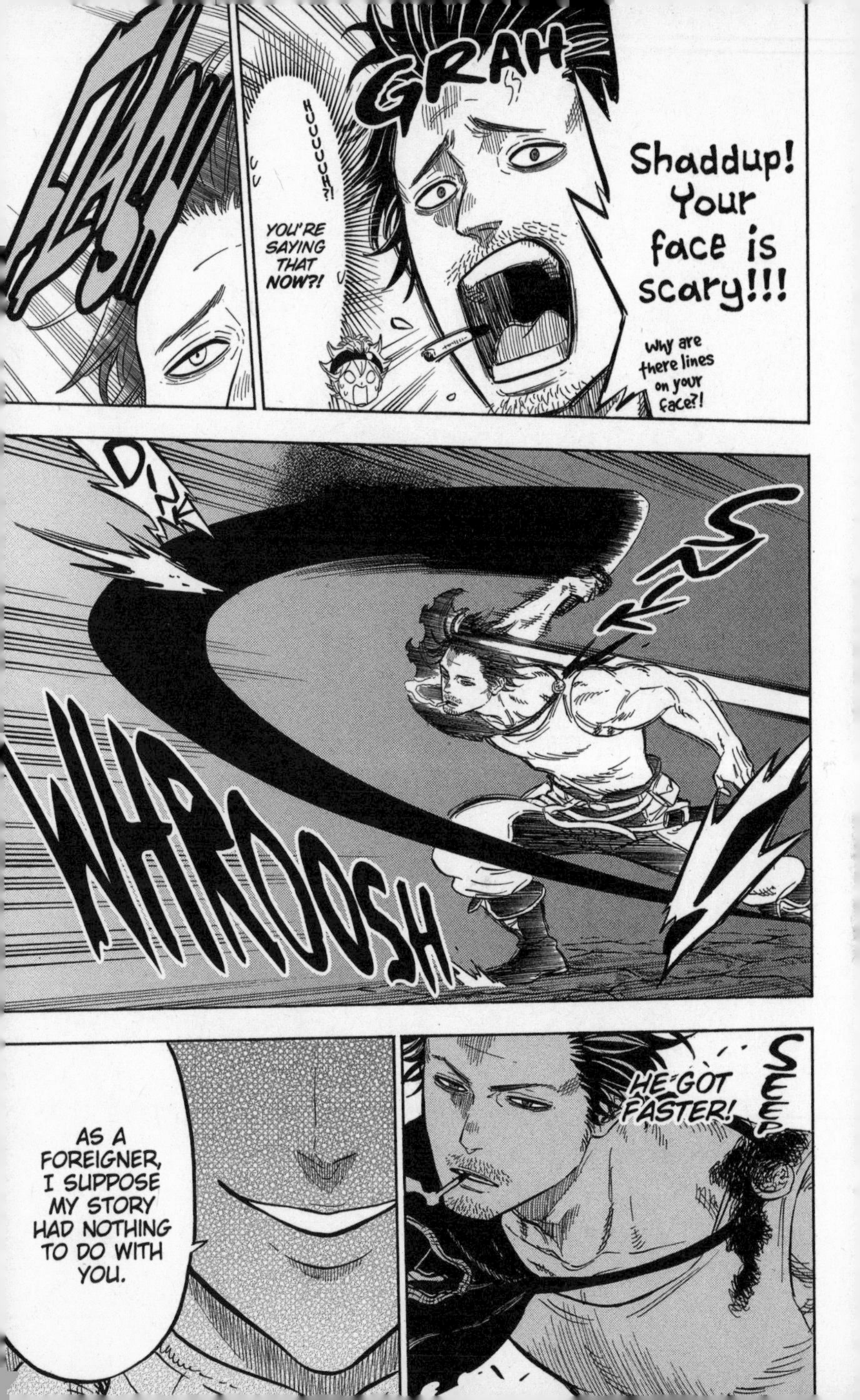
GRAH
Shaddup! Your face is scary!!!
why are there lines on your face?!
HUUUUUH?!
YOU'RE SAYING THAT NOW?!
DINK
WHROOSH
HE GOT FASTER!
AS A FOREIGNER, I SUPPOSE MY STORY HAD NOTHING TO DO WITH YOU.

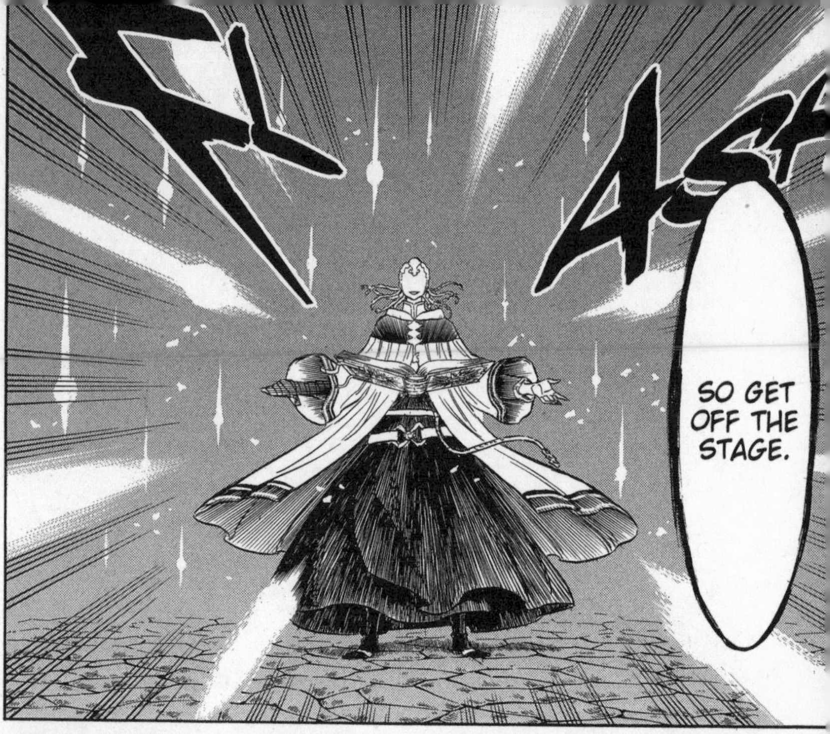
SO GET OFF THE STAGE.
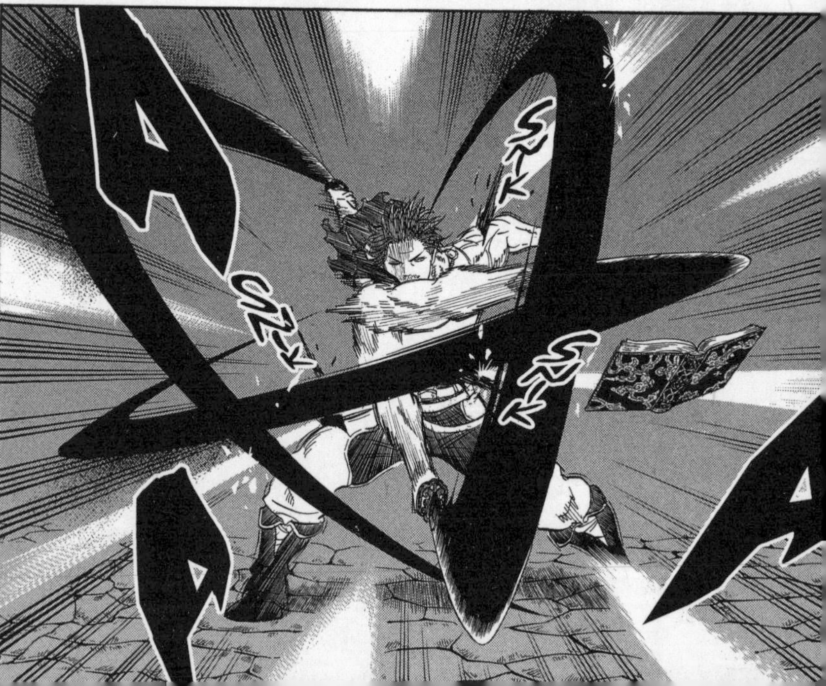
SNIK
SNIK
SNIK

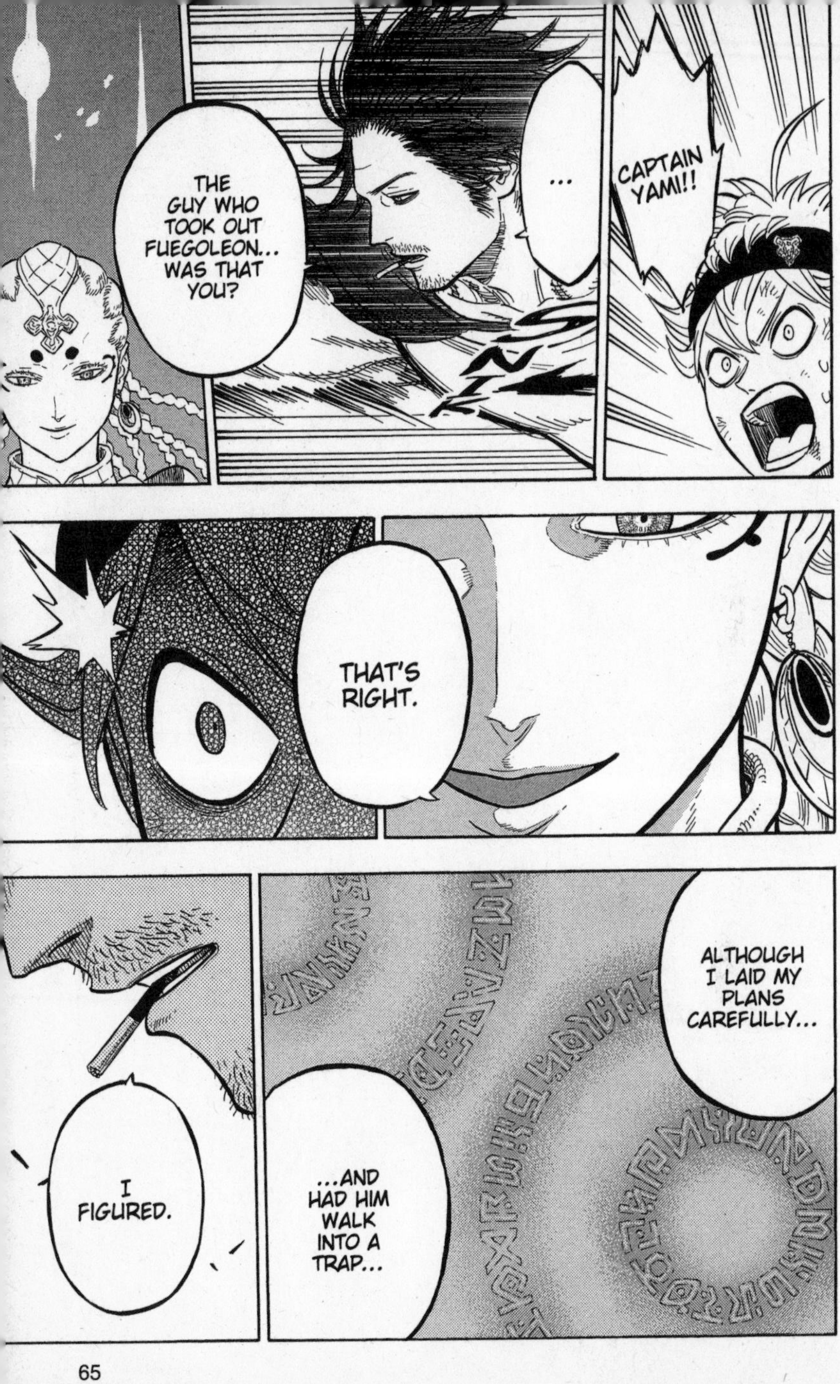

CAPTAIN YAMI!!
...
THE GUY WHO TOOK OUT FUEGOLEON... WAS THAT YOU?
THAT'S RIGHT.
ALTHOUGH I LAID MY PLANS CAREFULLY...
...AND HAD HIM WALK INTO A TRAP...
I FIGURED.

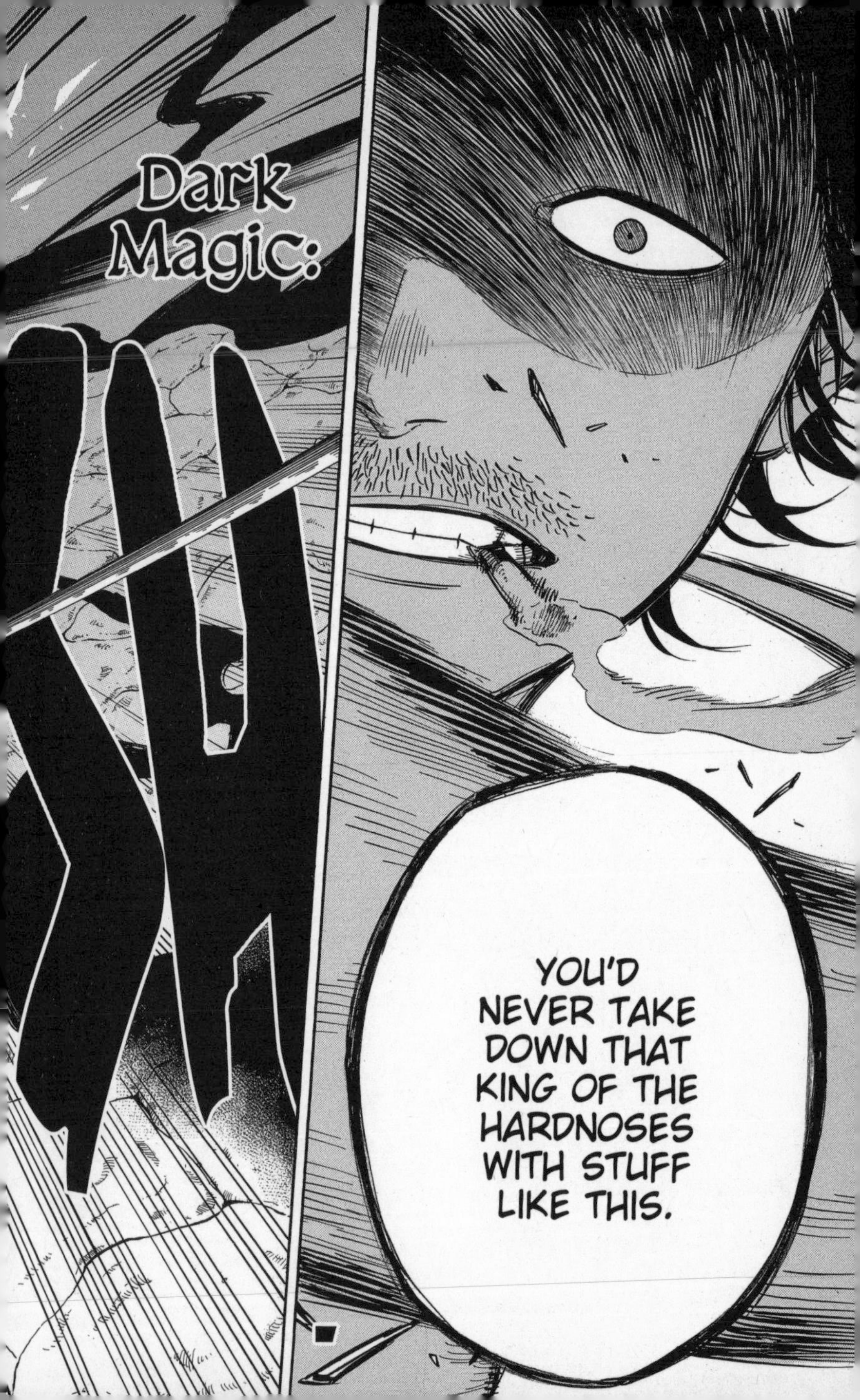
YOU'D NEVER TAKE DOWN THAT KING OF THE HARDNOSES WITH STUFF LIKE THIS.
Dark Magic:

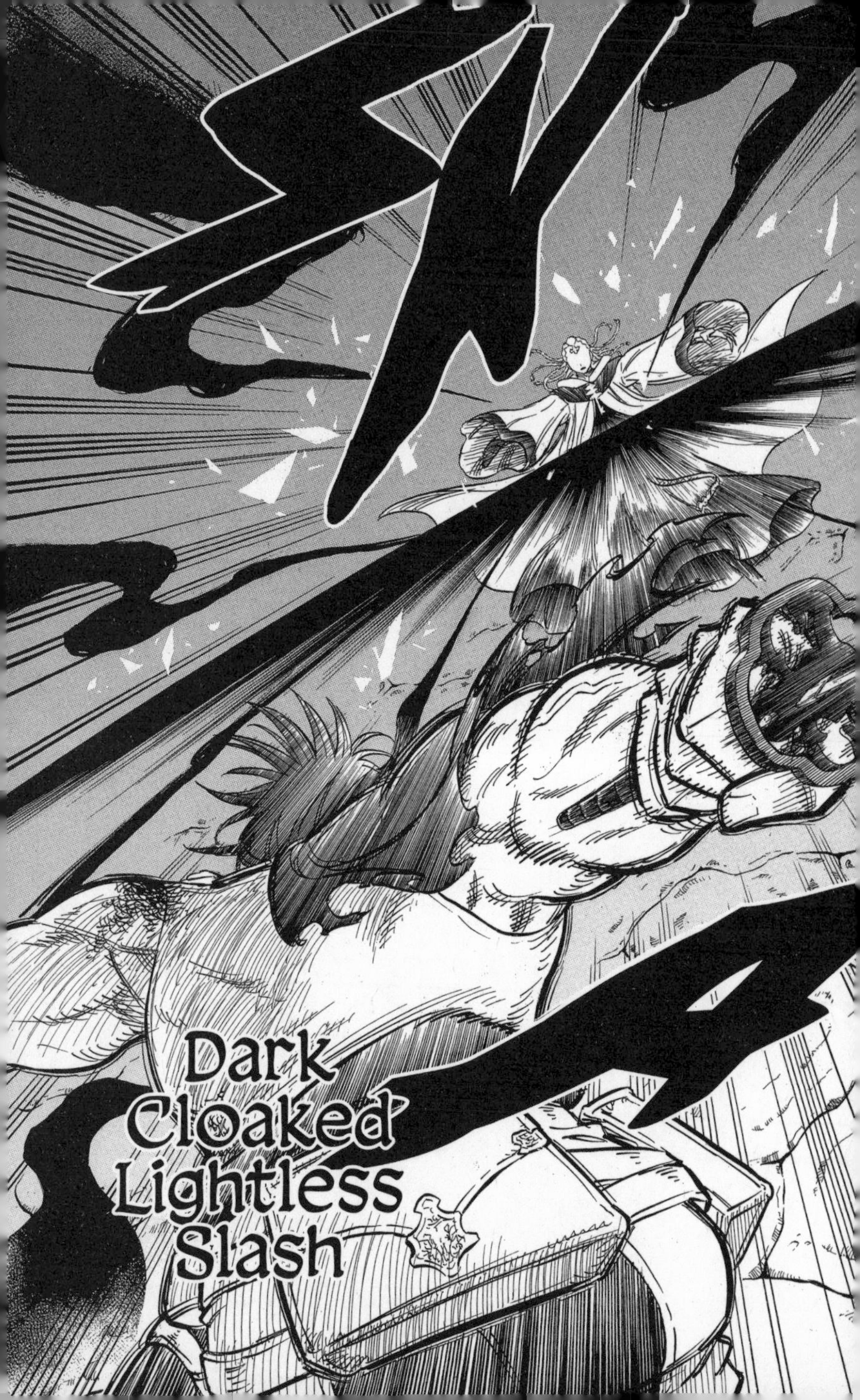
Dark Cloaked Lightless Slash

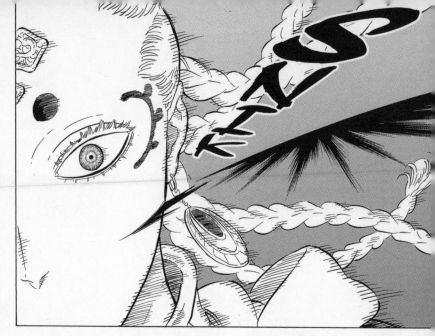

MASTER
LICHT!!

WHY,
YOU
...!!

IF YOU
HADN'T
PLAYED
DIRTY, YOU
COULDN'T
HAVE WON,
COULD YOU?

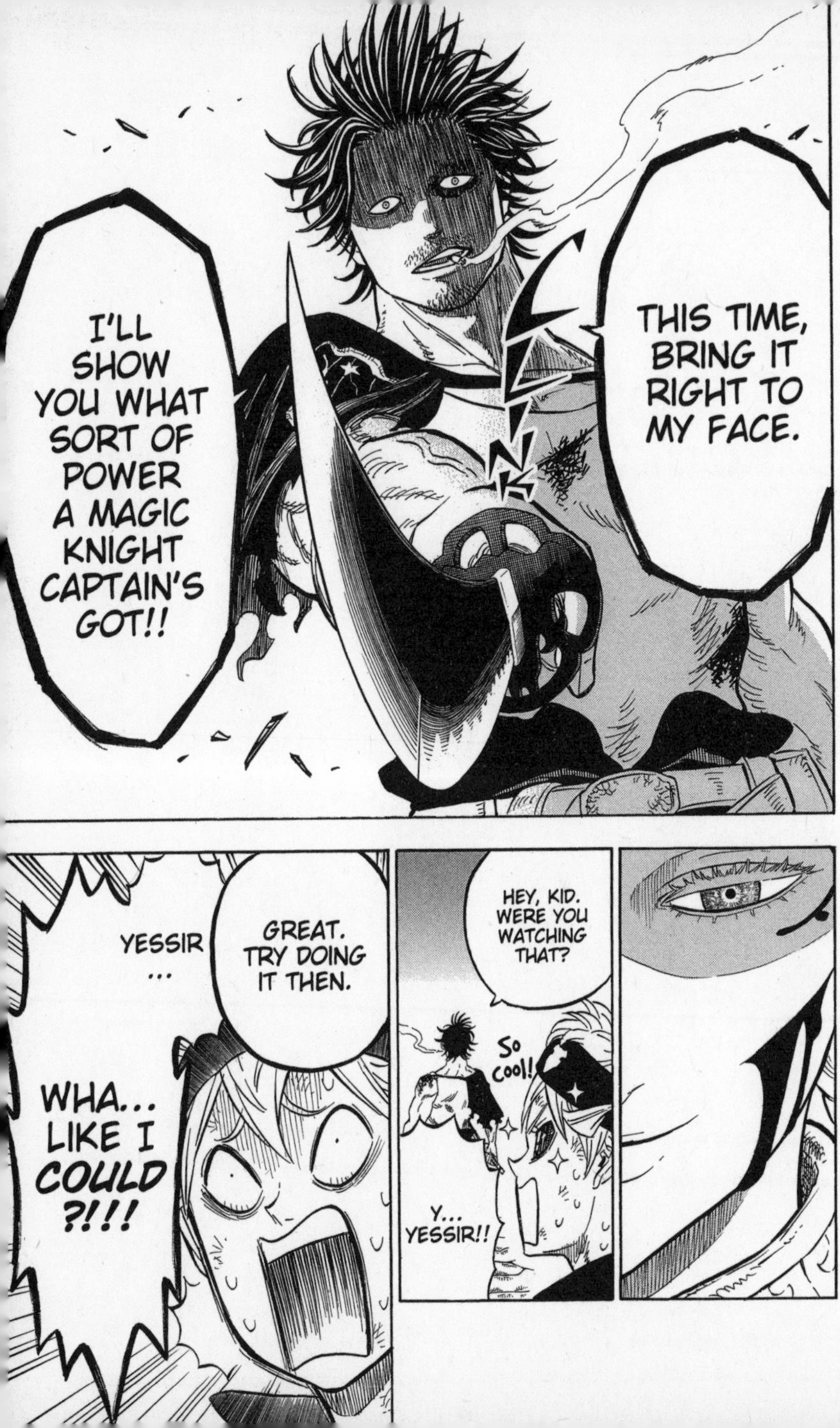
THIS TIME, BRING IT RIGHT TO MY FACE.
I'LL SHOW YOU WHAT SORT OF POWER A MAGIC KNIGHT CAPTAIN'S GOT!!
HEY, KID. WERE YOU WATCHING THAT?
SO COOL!
Y... YESSIR!!
GREAT. TRY DOING IT THEN.
YESSIR ...
WHA... LIKE I COULD ?!!!

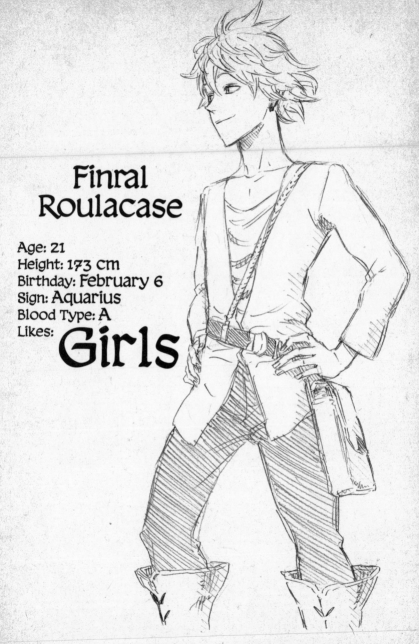

Finral Roulacase

Age: 21
Height: 173 cm
Birthday: February 6
Sign: Aquarius
Blood Type: A
Likes:
Girls

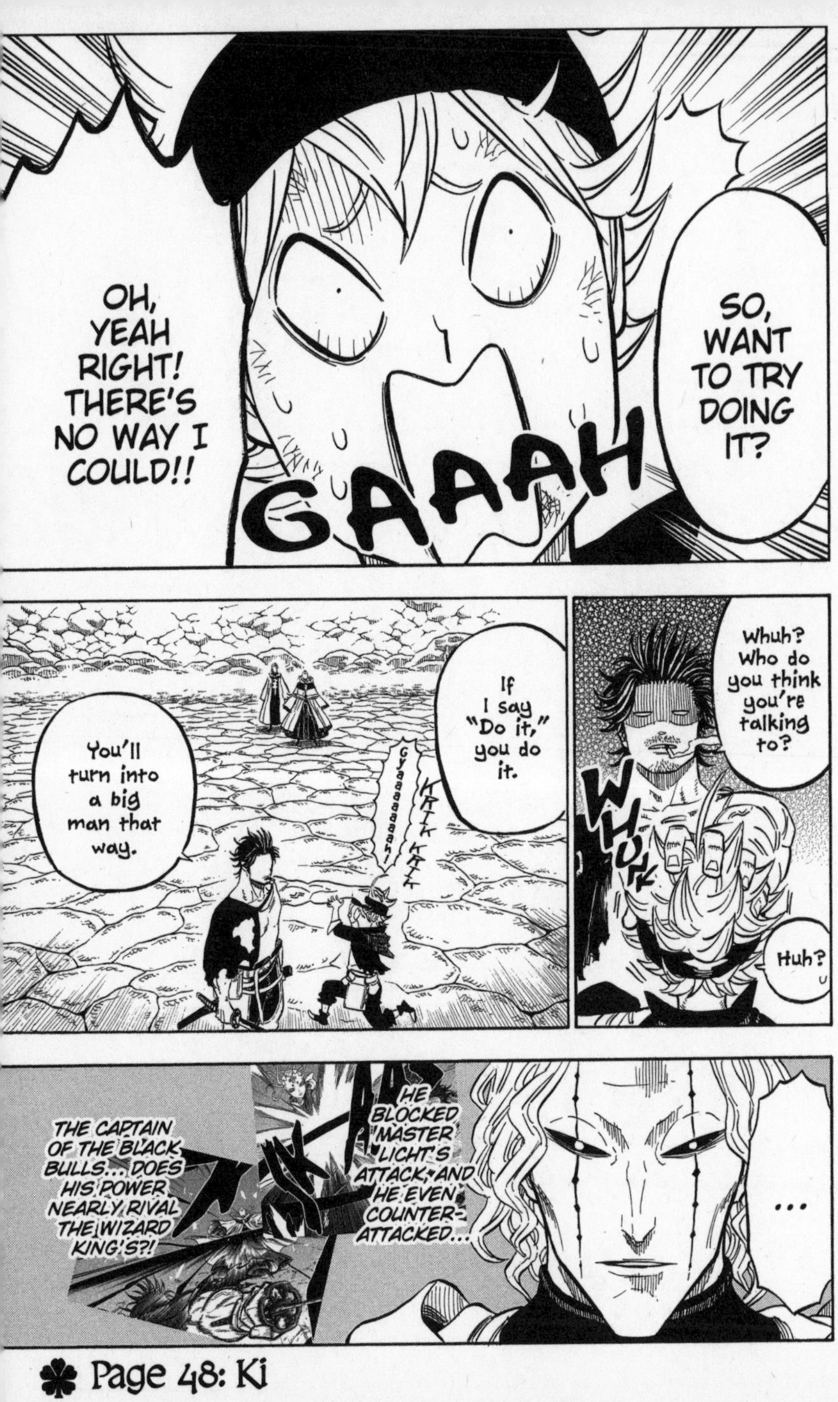
SO, WANT TO TRY DOING IT?
GAAAH
OH, YEAH RIGHT! THERE'S NO WAY I COULD!!
Whuh? Who do you think you're talking to?
WHUNK
Huh?
If I say "Do it," you do it.
KRIK KRIK
Gyaaaaaaaah!
You'll turn into a big man that way.
...
HE BLOCKED MASTER LICHT'S ATTACK, AND HE EVEN COUNTER-ATTACKED...
THE CAPTAIN OF THE BLACK BULLS... DOES HIS POWER NEARLY RIVAL THE WIZARD KING'S?!

Page 48: Ki

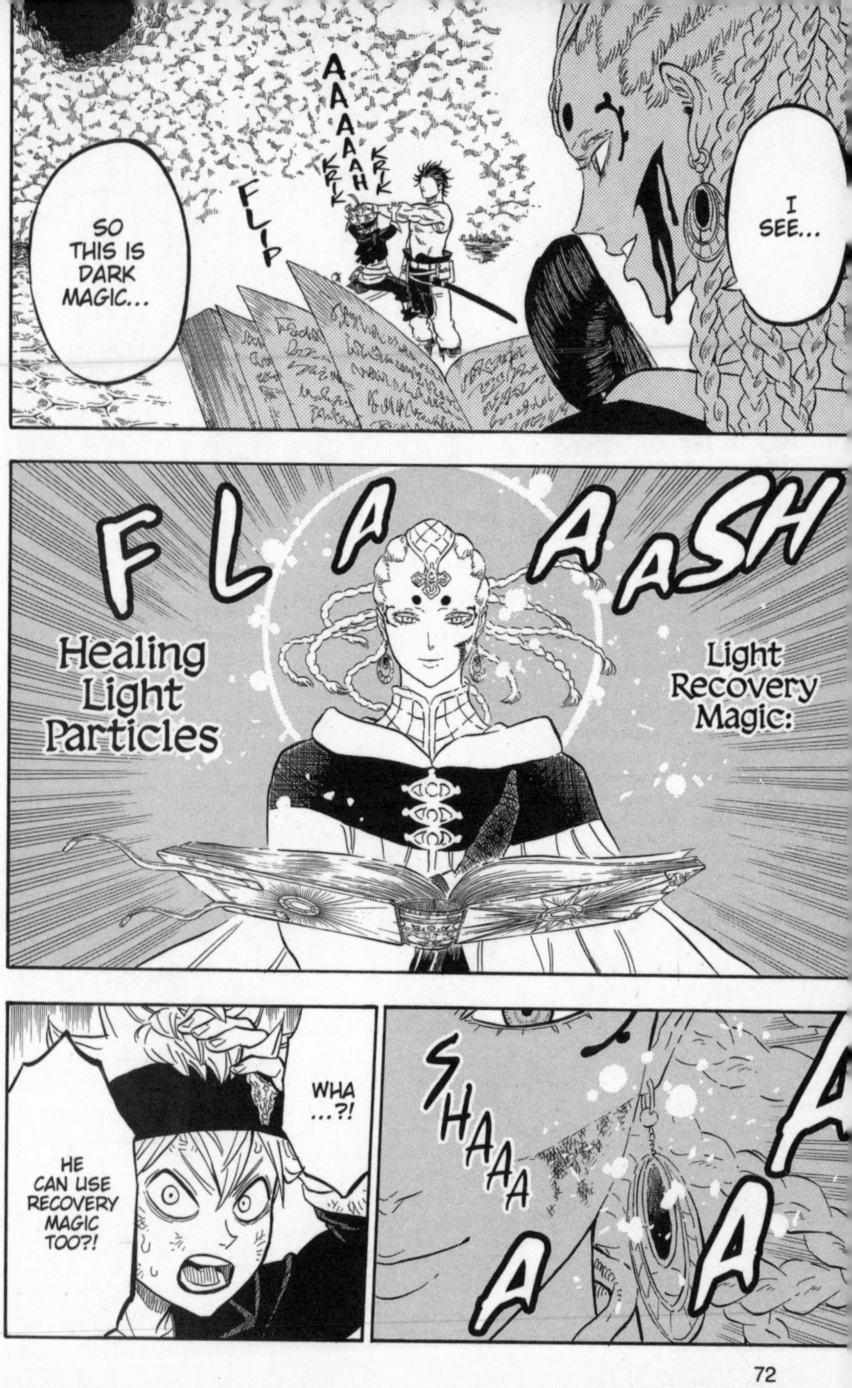
I SEE...
AAAAAAH
KRIK KRIK
FLIP
SO THIS IS DARK MAGIC...
FLAAASH
Light Recovery Magic:
Healing Light Particles
SHAAAAAAA
WHA...?!
HE CAN USE RECOVERY MAGIC TOO?!

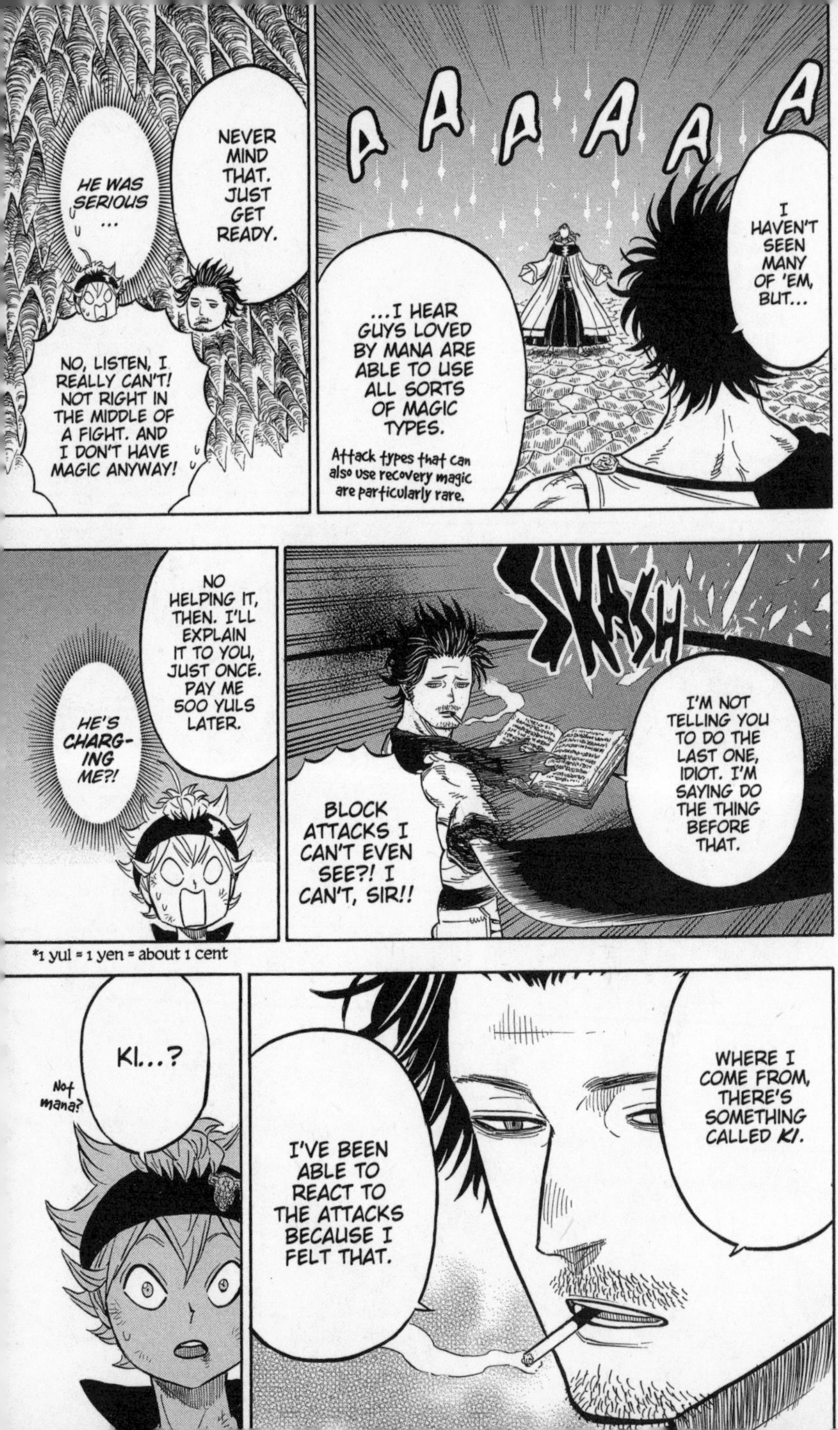
AAAAAA
I HAVEN'T SEEN MANY OF 'EM, BUT...
...I HEAR GUYS LOVED BY MANA ARE ABLE TO USE ALL SORTS OF MAGIC TYPES.
Attack types that can also use recovery magic are particularly rare.
NEVER MIND THAT. JUST GET READY.
HE WAS SERIOUS...
NO, LISTEN, I REALLY CAN'T! NOT RIGHT IN THE MIDDLE OF A FIGHT. AND I DON'T HAVE MAGIC ANYWAY!
SLASH
I'M NOT TELLING YOU TO DO THE LAST ONE, IDIOT. I'M SAYING DO THE THING BEFORE THAT.
BLOCK ATTACKS I CAN'T EVEN SEE?! I CAN'T, SIR!!
NO HELPING IT, THEN. I'LL EXPLAIN IT TO YOU, JUST ONCE. PAY ME 500 YULS LATER.
HE'S CHARGING ME?!
WHERE I COME FROM, THERE'S SOMETHING CALLED *KI*.
I'VE BEEN ABLE TO REACT TO THE ATTACKS BECAUSE I FELT THAT.
KI...?
Not mana?

*1 yul = 1 yen = about 1 cent

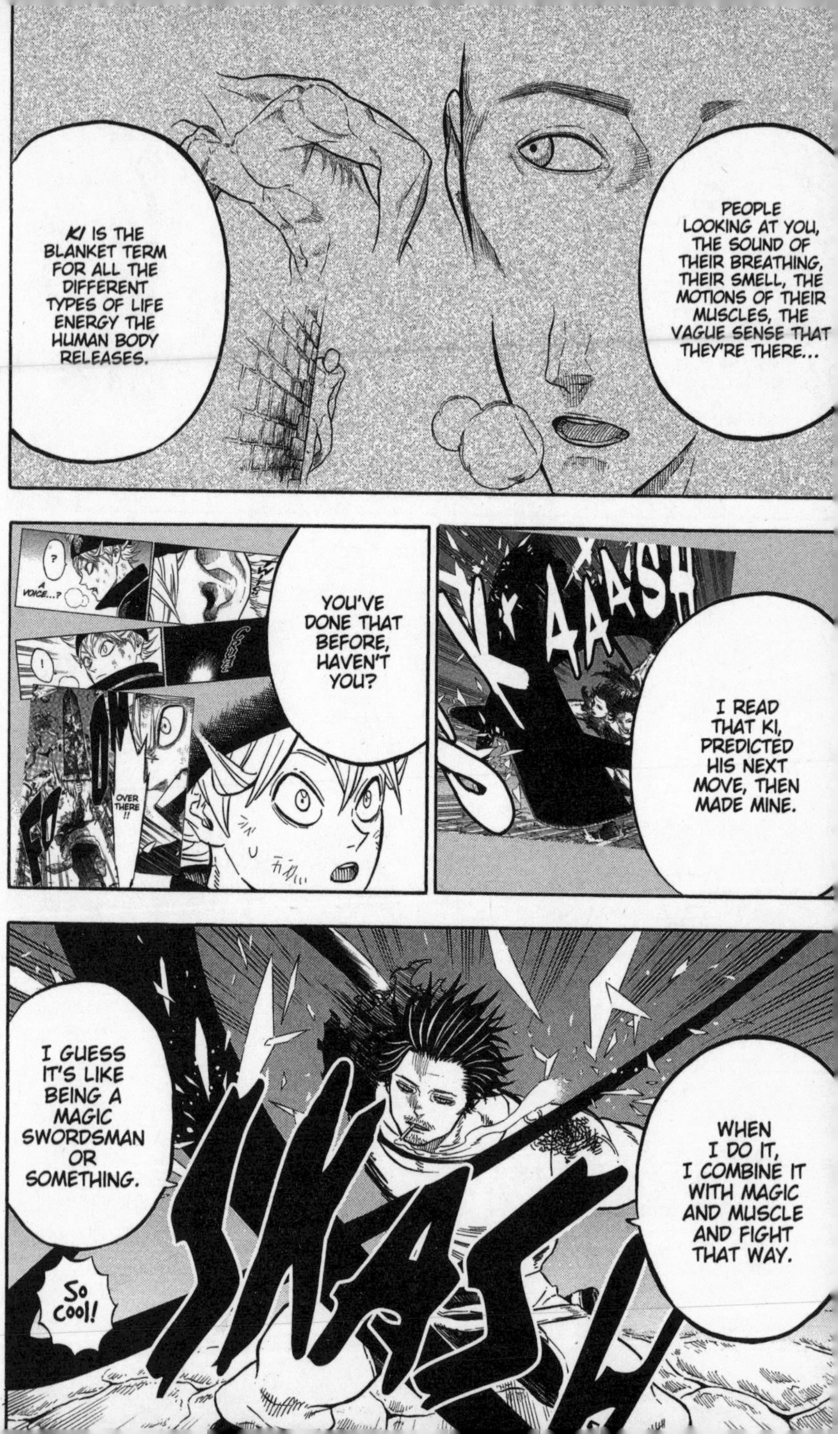
PEOPLE LOOKING AT YOU, THE SOUND OF THEIR BREATHING, THEIR SMELL, THE MOTIONS OF THEIR MUSCLES, THE VAGUE SENSE THAT THEY'RE THERE...
KI IS THE BLANKET TERM FOR ALL THE DIFFERENT TYPES OF LIFE ENERGY THE HUMAN BODY RELEASES.
I READ THAT KI, PREDICTED HIS NEXT MOVE, THEN MADE MINE.
YOU'VE DONE THAT BEFORE, HAVEN'T YOU?
?
A VOICE...?
!
OVER THERE!!
WHEN I DO IT, I COMBINE IT WITH MAGIC AND MUSCLE AND FIGHT THAT WAY.
I GUESS IT'S LIKE BEING A MAGIC SWORDSMAN OR SOMETHING.
So cool!

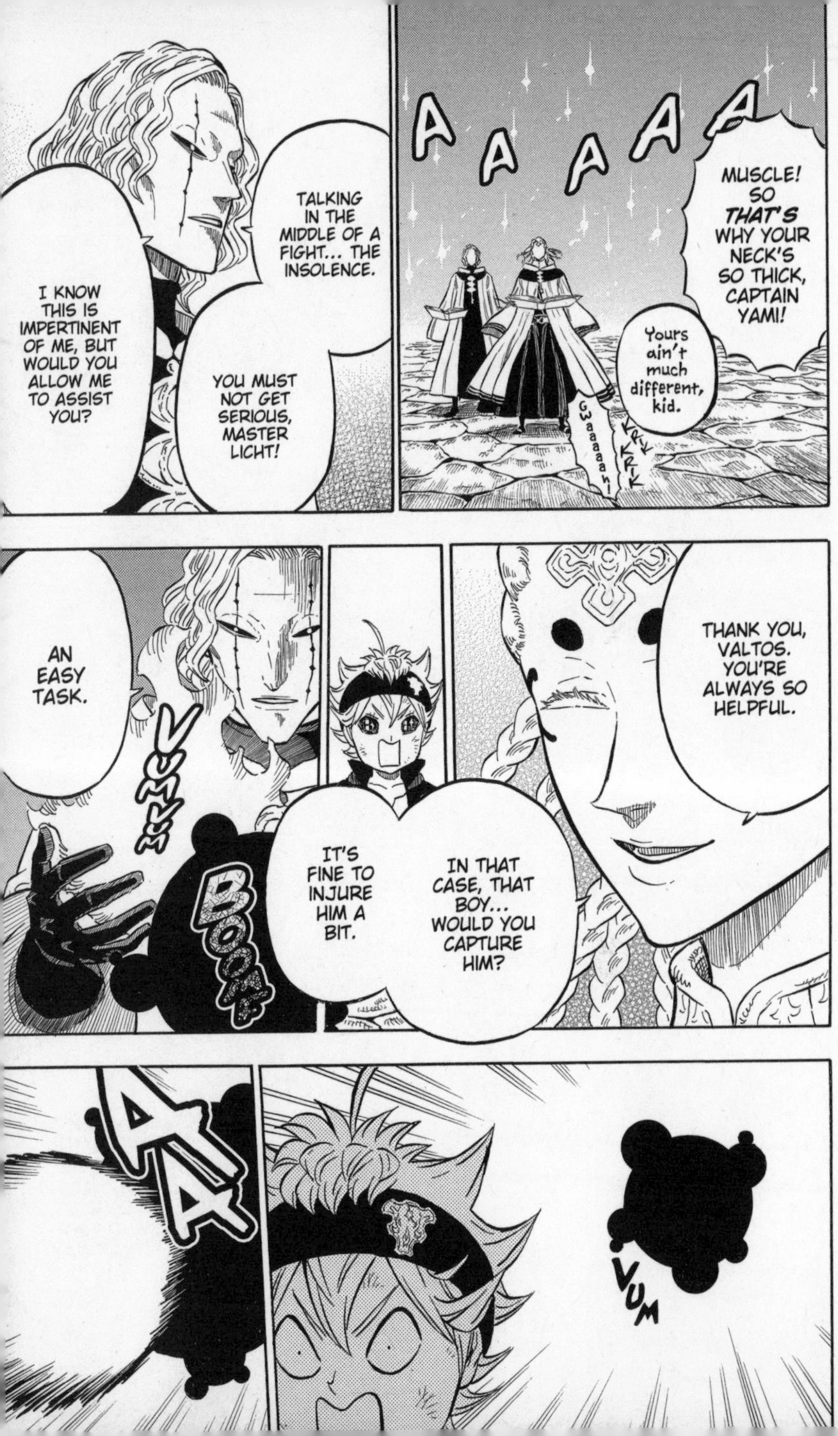
AAAAA
MUSCLE! SO THAT'S WHY YOUR NECK'S SO THICK, CAPTAIN YAMI!
Yours ain't much different, kid.
KRIK KRIK
Gwaaaaah!
TALKING IN THE MIDDLE OF A FIGHT... THE INSOLENCE.
YOU MUST NOT GET SERIOUS, MASTER LICHT!
I KNOW THIS IS IMPERTINENT OF ME, BUT WOULD YOU ALLOW ME TO ASSIST YOU?
THANK YOU, VALTOS. YOU'RE ALWAYS SO HELPFUL.
IN THAT CASE, THAT BOY... WOULD YOU CAPTURE HIM?
IT'S FINE TO INJURE HIM A BIT.
AN EASY TASK.
VUM
AA

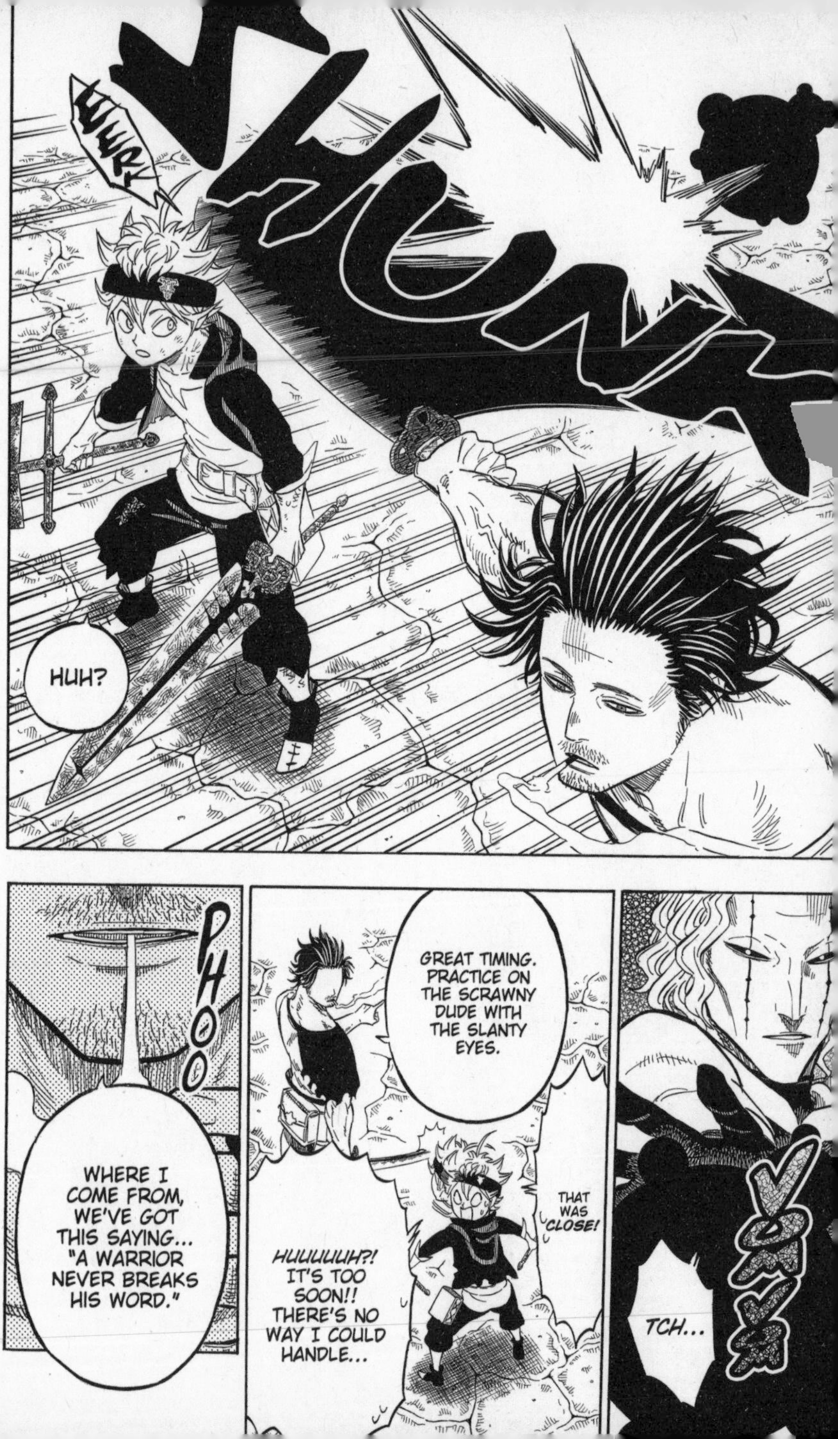
VHUNK
EERK
HUH?
TCH...
GREAT TIMING. PRACTICE ON THE SCRAWNY DUDE WITH THE SLANTY EYES.
THAT WAS CLOSE!
HUUUUUH?! IT'S TOO SOON!! THERE'S NO WAY I COULD HANDLE...
PHOO
WHERE I COME FROM, WE'VE GOT THIS SAYING... "A WARRIOR NEVER BREAKS HIS WORD."

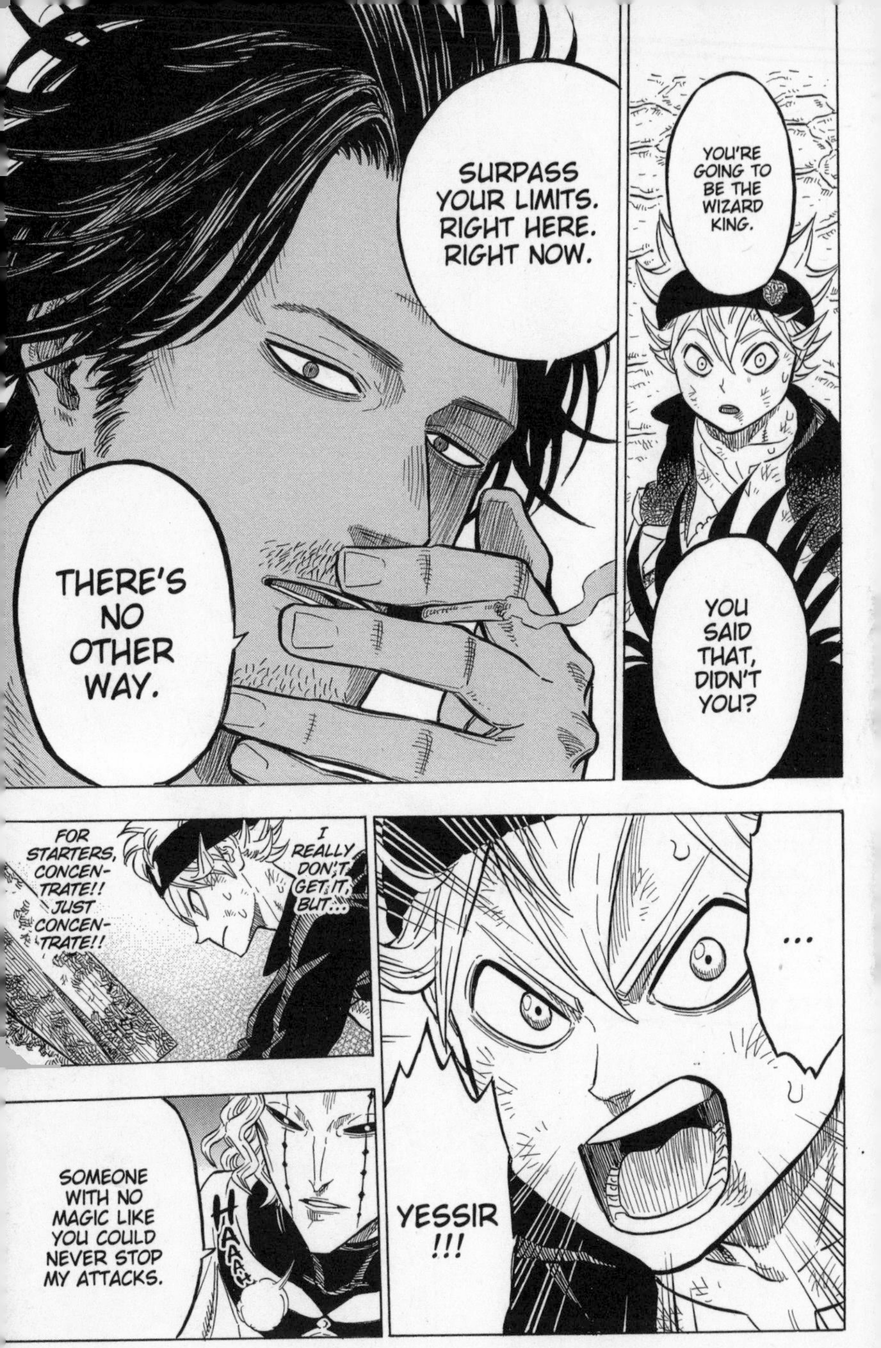
YOU'RE GOING TO BE THE WIZARD KING.
YOU SAID THAT, DIDN'T YOU?
SURPASS YOUR LIMITS. RIGHT HERE. RIGHT NOW.
THERE'S NO OTHER WAY.
...
YESSIR !!!
I REALLY DON'T GET IT, BUT...
FOR STARTERS, CONCENTRATE!! JUST CONCENTRATE!!
HAAA
SOMEONE WITH NO MAGIC LIKE YOU COULD NEVER STOP MY ATTACKS.

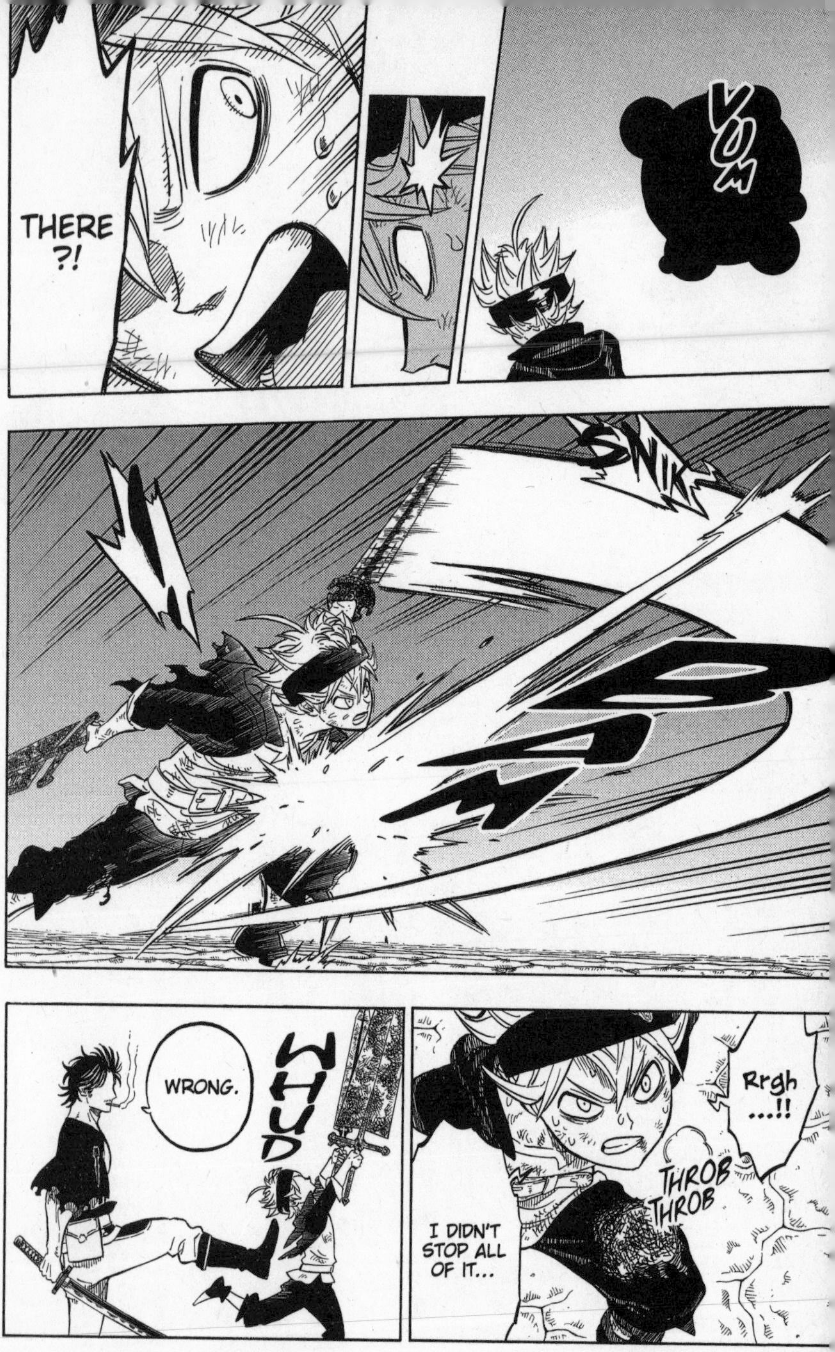
VOM
THERE ?!
SNIK
Rrgh ...!!
THROB THROB
I DIDN'T STOP ALL OF IT...
WHUD
WRONG.

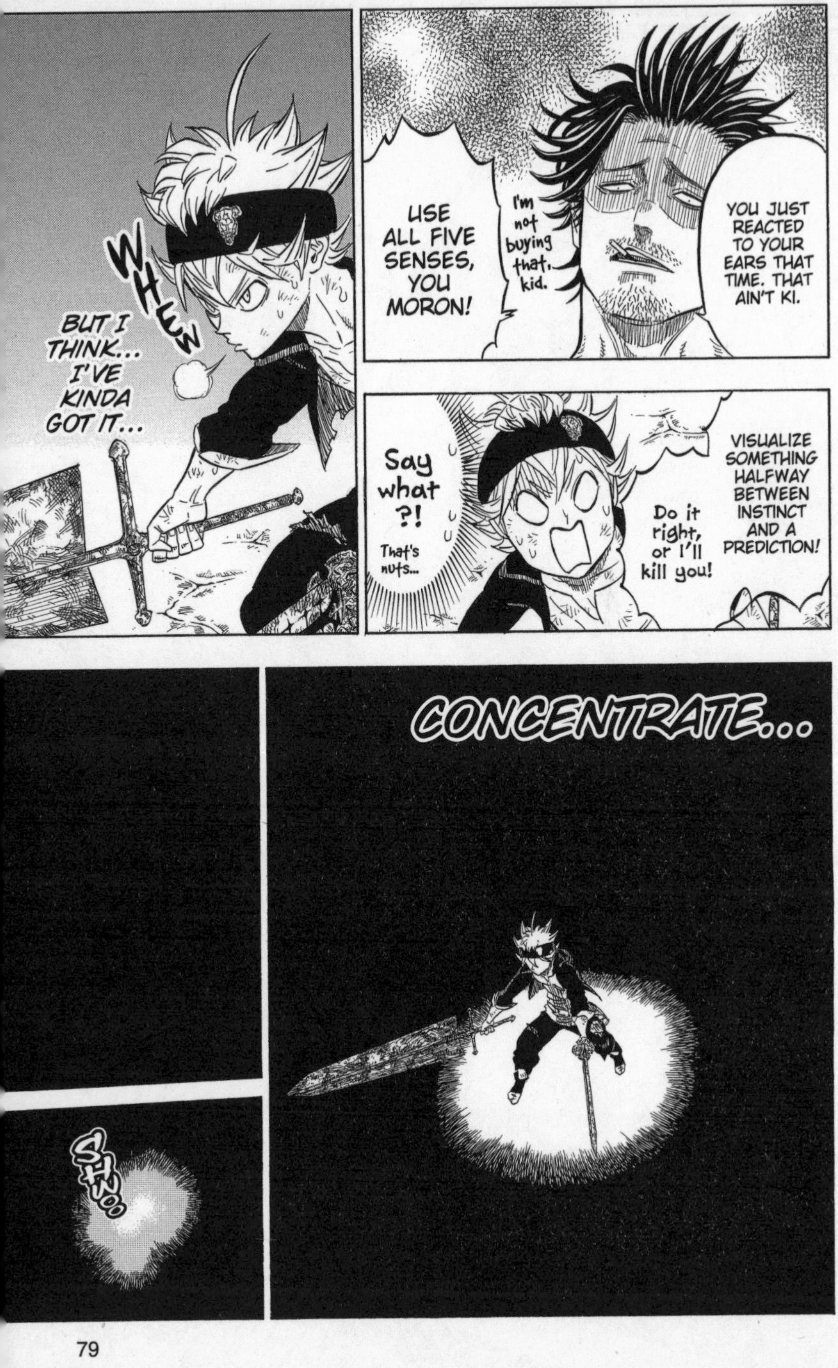
YOU JUST REACTED TO YOUR EARS THAT TIME. THAT AIN'T KI.
I'm not buying that, kid.
USE ALL FIVE SENSES, YOU MORON!
VISUALIZE SOMETHING HALFWAY BETWEEN INSTINCT AND A PREDICTION!
Do it right, or I'll kill you!
Say what?!
That's nuts...
WHEW
BUT I THINK... I'VE KINDA GOT IT...
CONCENTRATE...
SHWOO

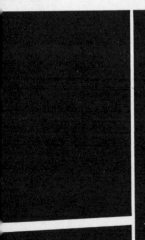

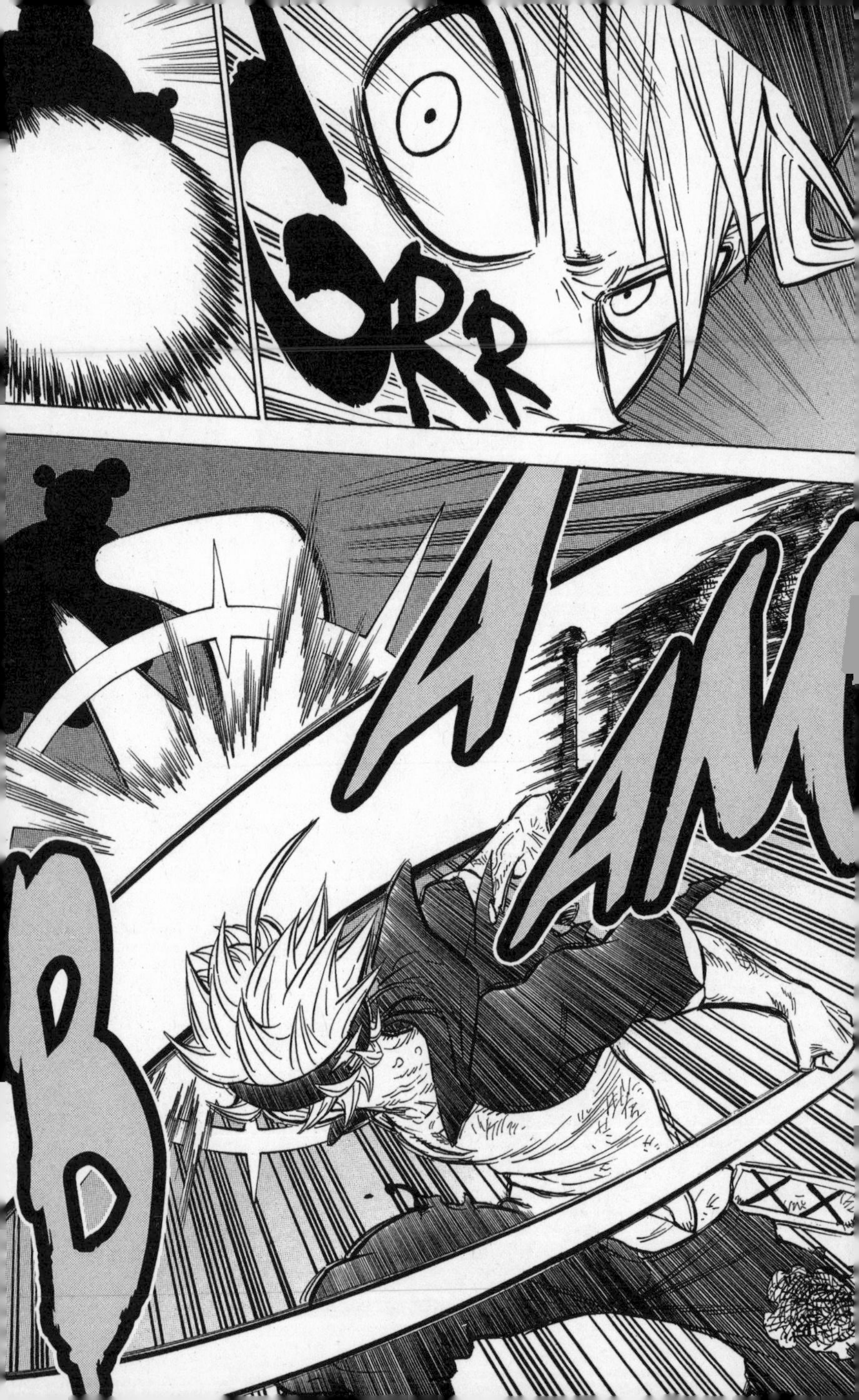
GRR
BAM

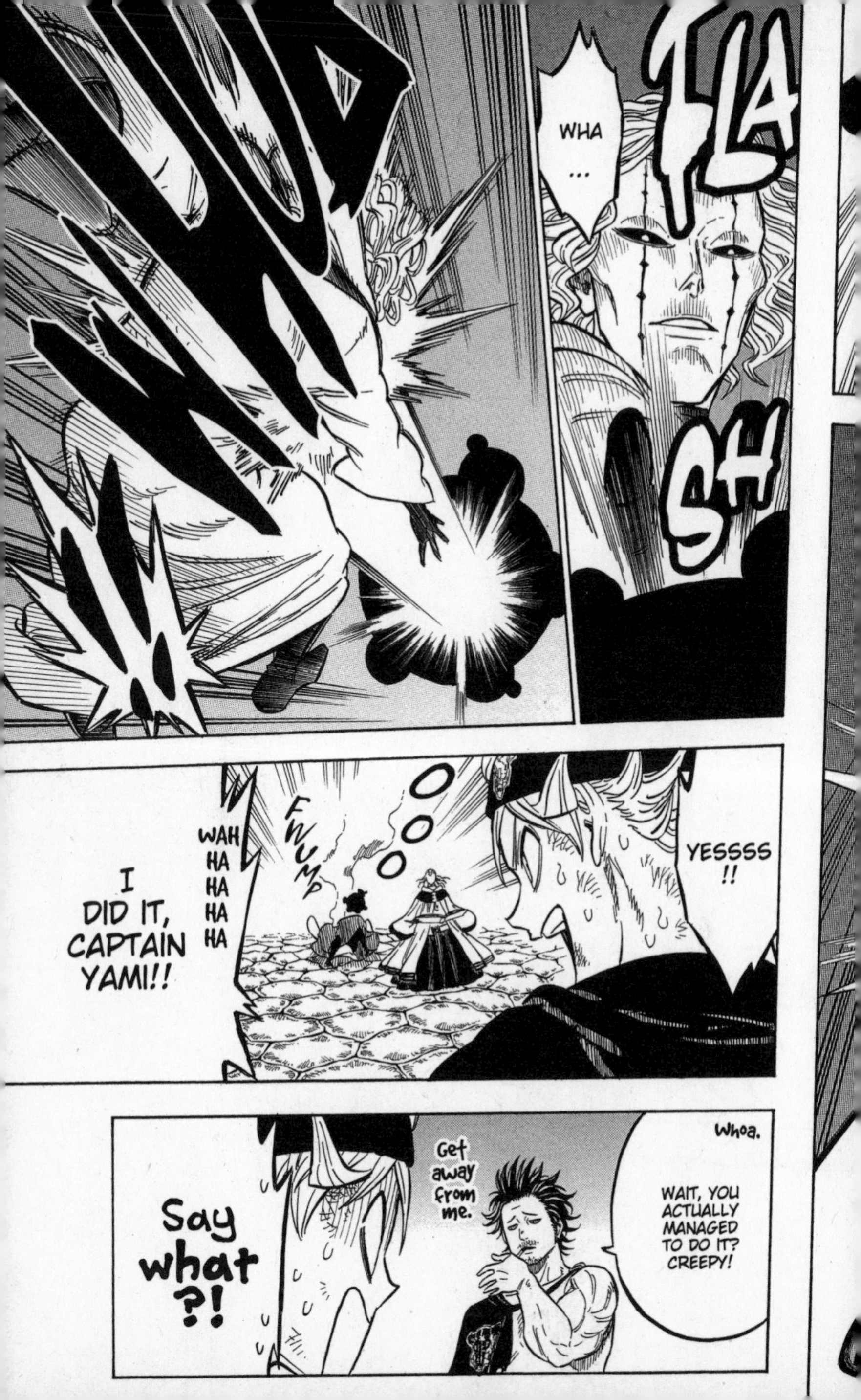
WHA ...
FLA
SH
YESSSS !!
OOOO
FWUMP
WAH HA HA HA HA
I DID IT, CAPTAIN YAMI!!
Whoa.
WAIT, YOU ACTUALLY MANAGED TO DO IT? CREEPY!
Get away from me.
Say what?!

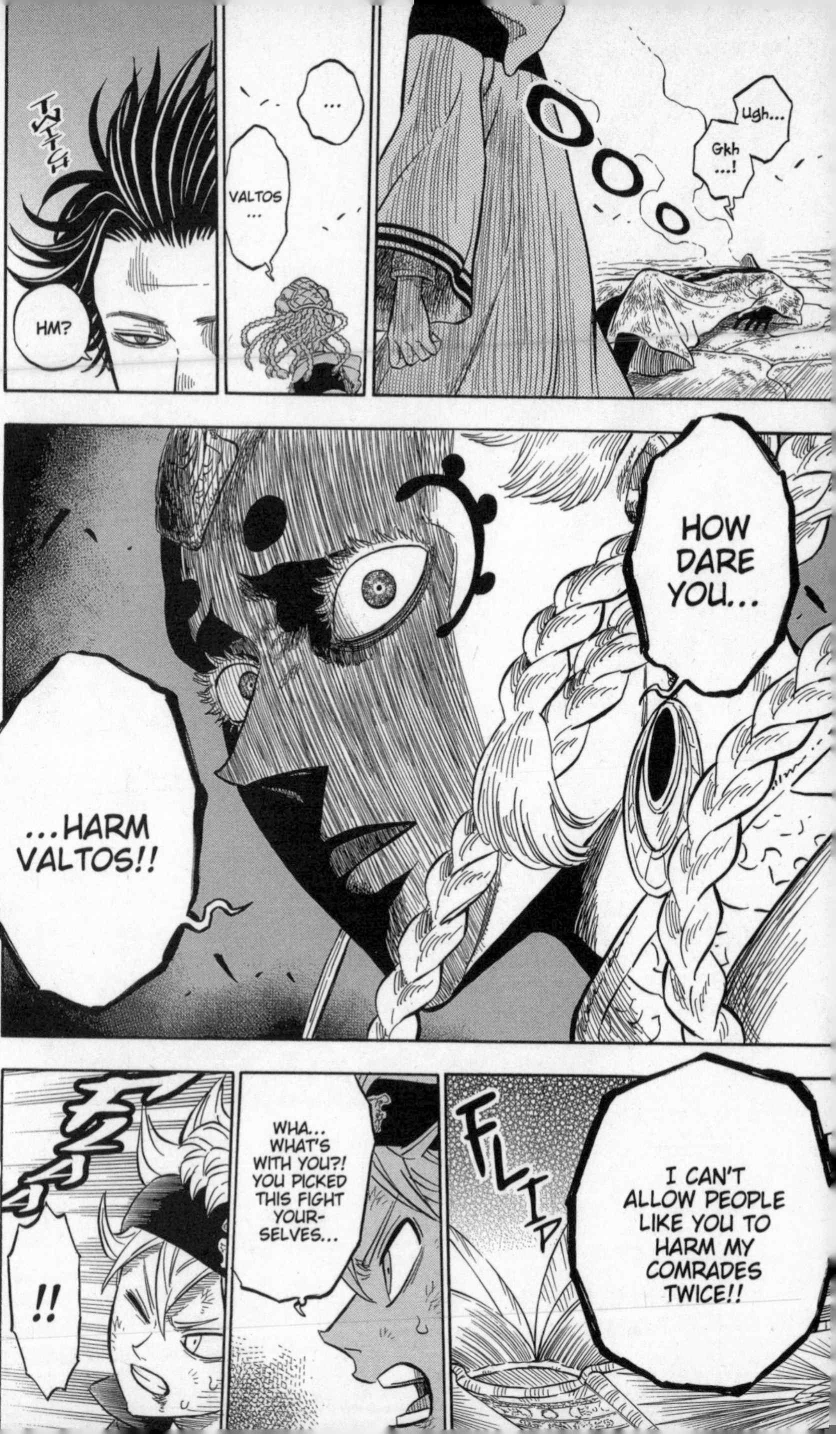
OOOO
Ugh...
Gkh ...!
...
VALTOS ...
TWITCH
HM?
HOW DARE YOU...
...HARM VALTOS!!
FLIP
I CAN'T ALLOW PEOPLE LIKE YOU TO HARM MY COMRADES TWICE!!
WHA... WHAT'S WITH YOU?! YOU PICKED THIS FIGHT YOUR-SELVES...
!!

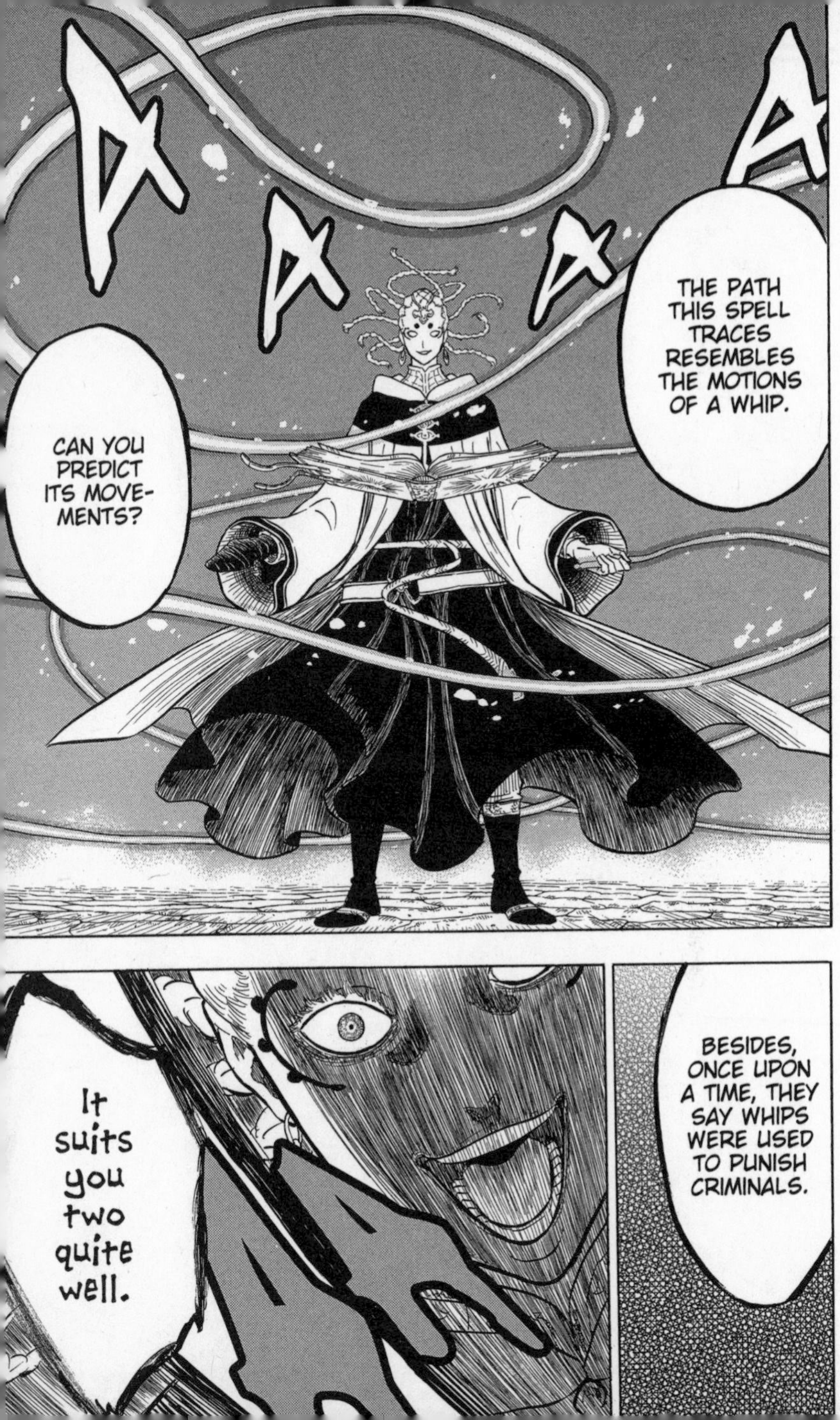
THE PATH THIS SPELL TRACES RESEMBLES THE MOTIONS OF A WHIP.
CAN YOU PREDICT ITS MOVE-MENTS?
BESIDES, ONCE UPON A TIME, THEY SAY WHIPS WERE USED TO PUNISH CRIMINALS.
It suits you two quite well.

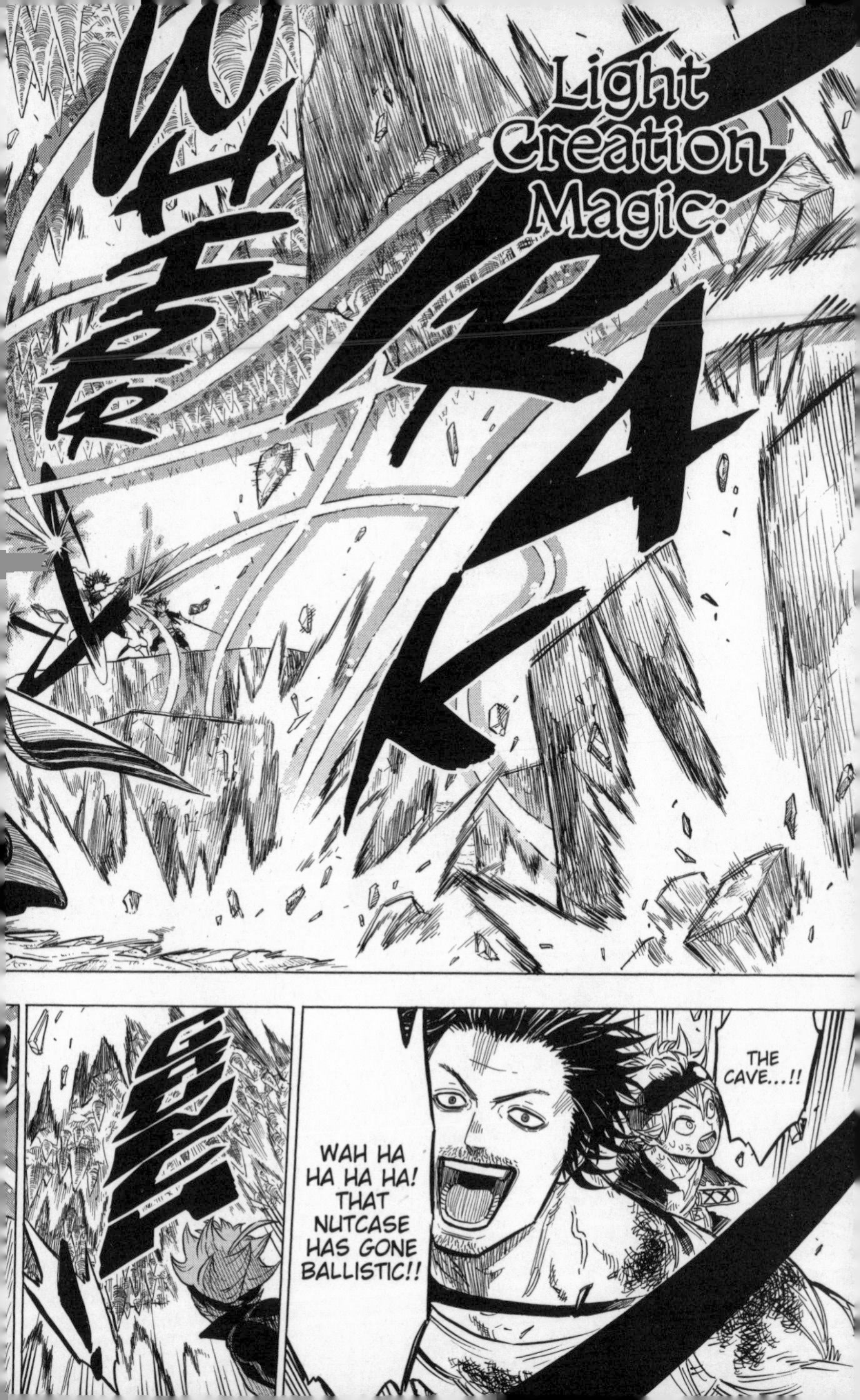
Light Creation Magic:
THE CAVE...!!
WAH HA HA HA HA! THAT NUTCASE HAS GONE BALLISTIC!!

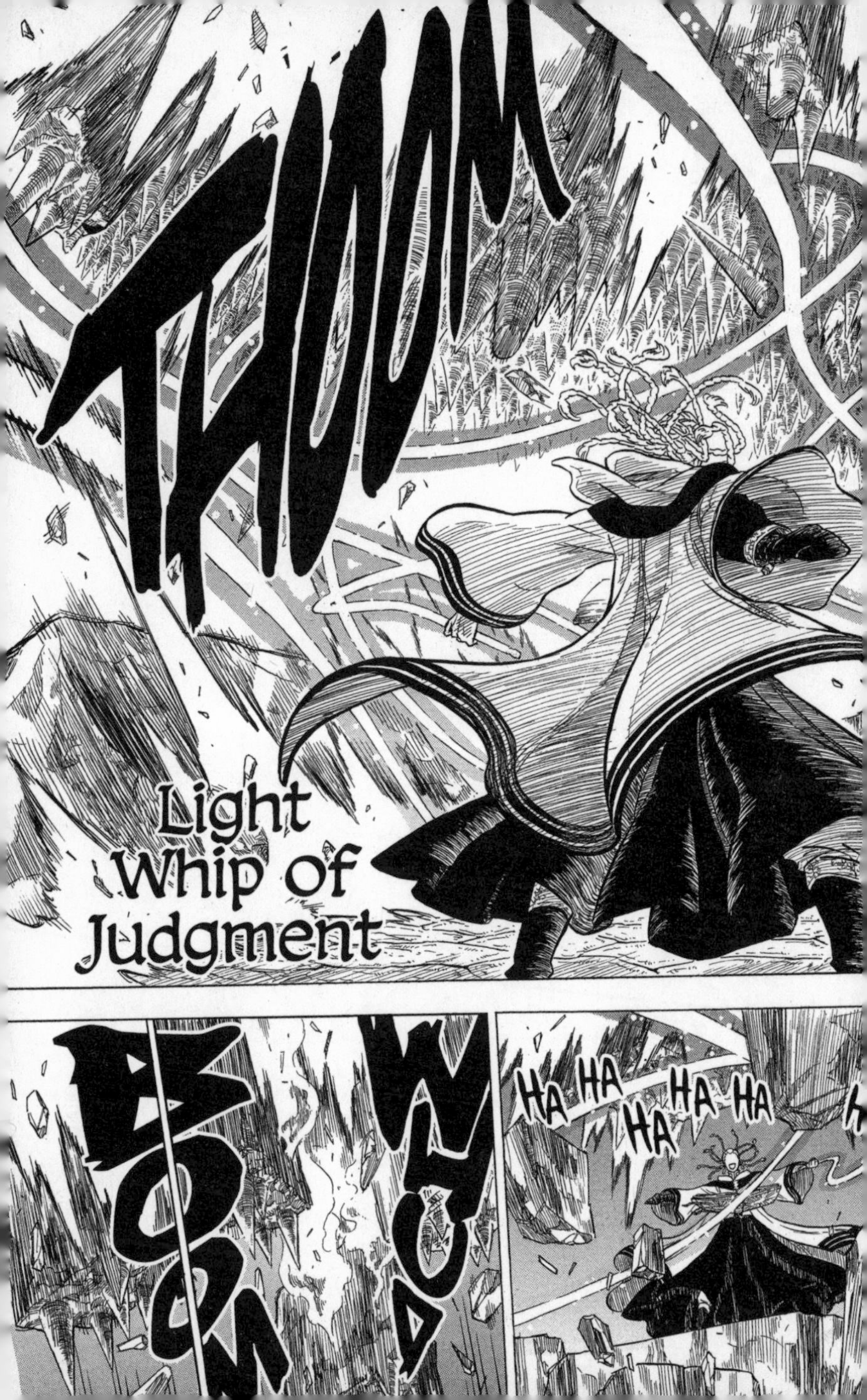
THOOM
Light Whip Of Judgment
HA HA HA HA HA HA

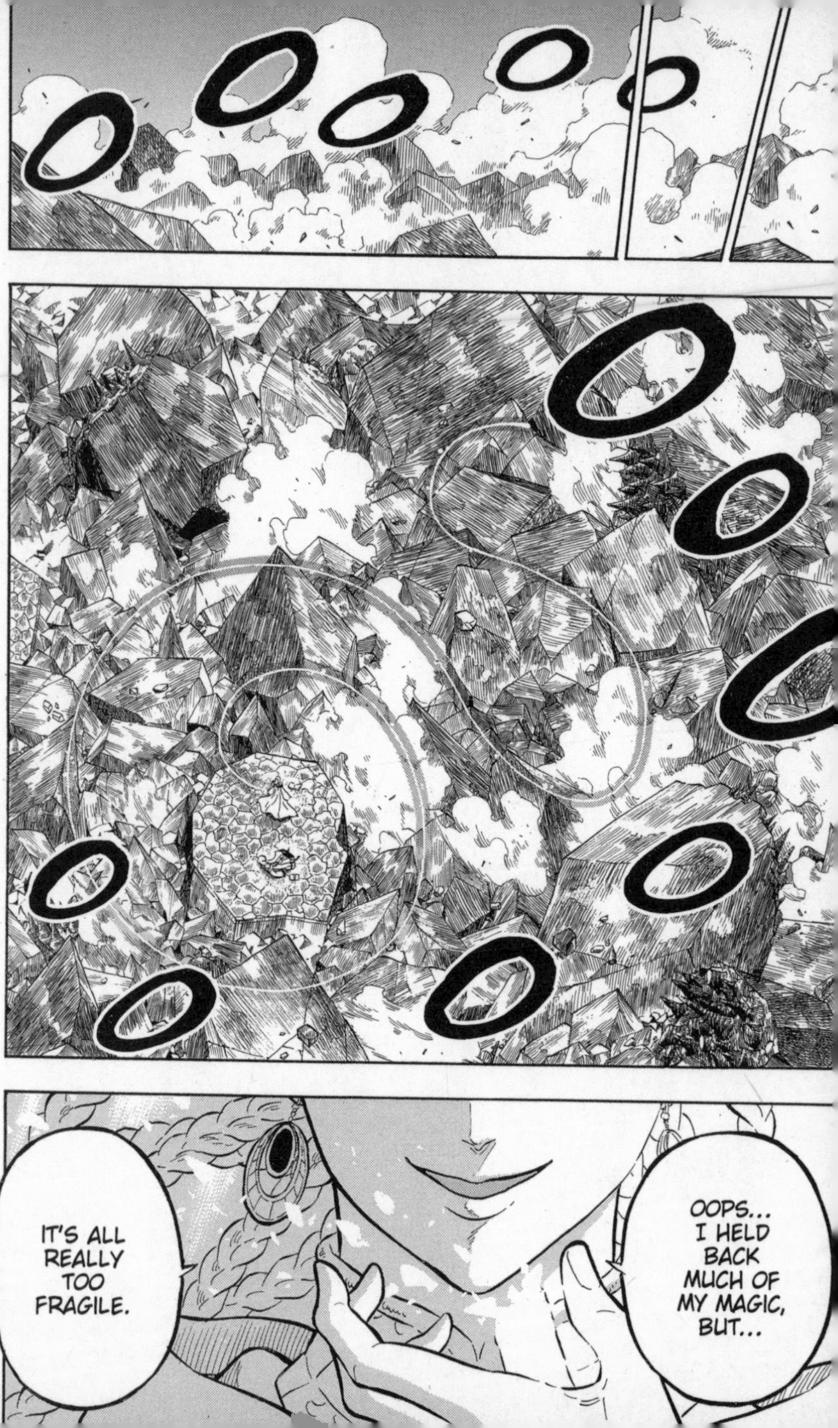
OOPS... I HELD BACK MUCH OF MY MAGIC, BUT...
IT'S ALL REALLY TOO FRAGILE.

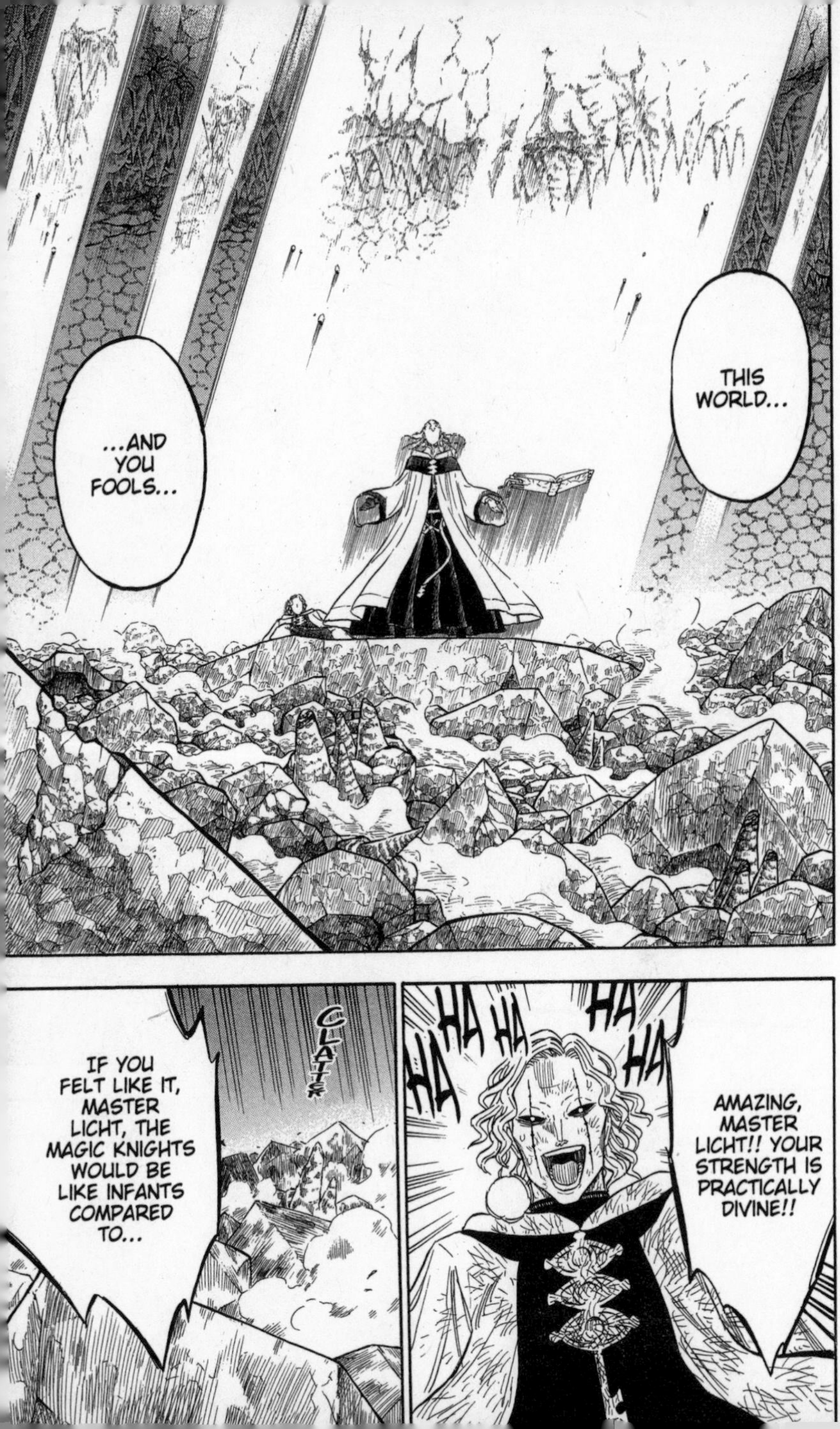
THIS WORLD...
...AND YOU FOOLS...
HA HA HA HA HA HA
AMAZING, MASTER LICHT!! YOUR STRENGTH IS PRACTICALLY DIVINE!!
CLATTER
IF YOU FELT LIKE IT, MASTER LICHT, THE MAGIC KNIGHTS WOULD BE LIKE INFANTS COMPARED TO...

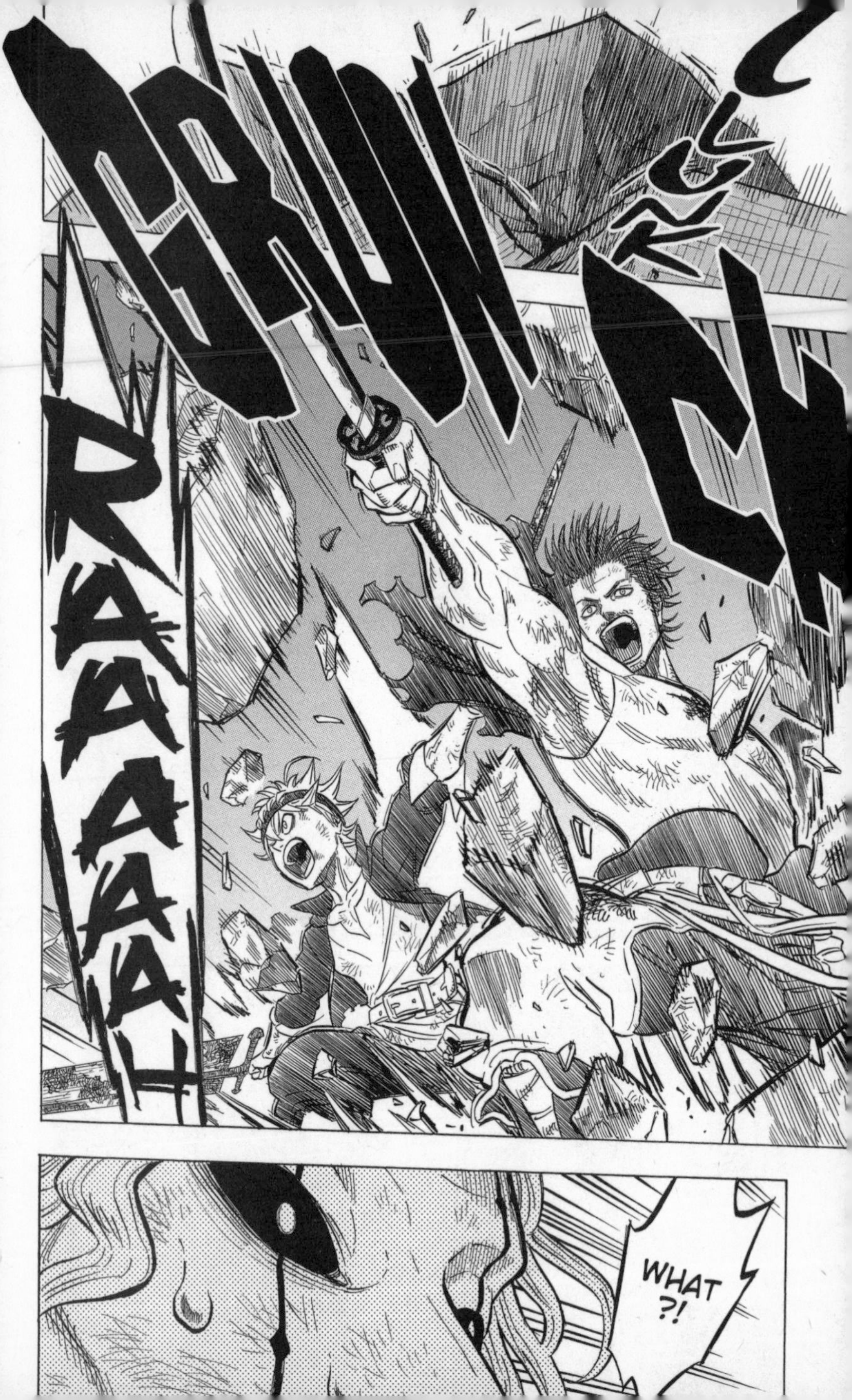
RAAAAAAH
WHAT?!

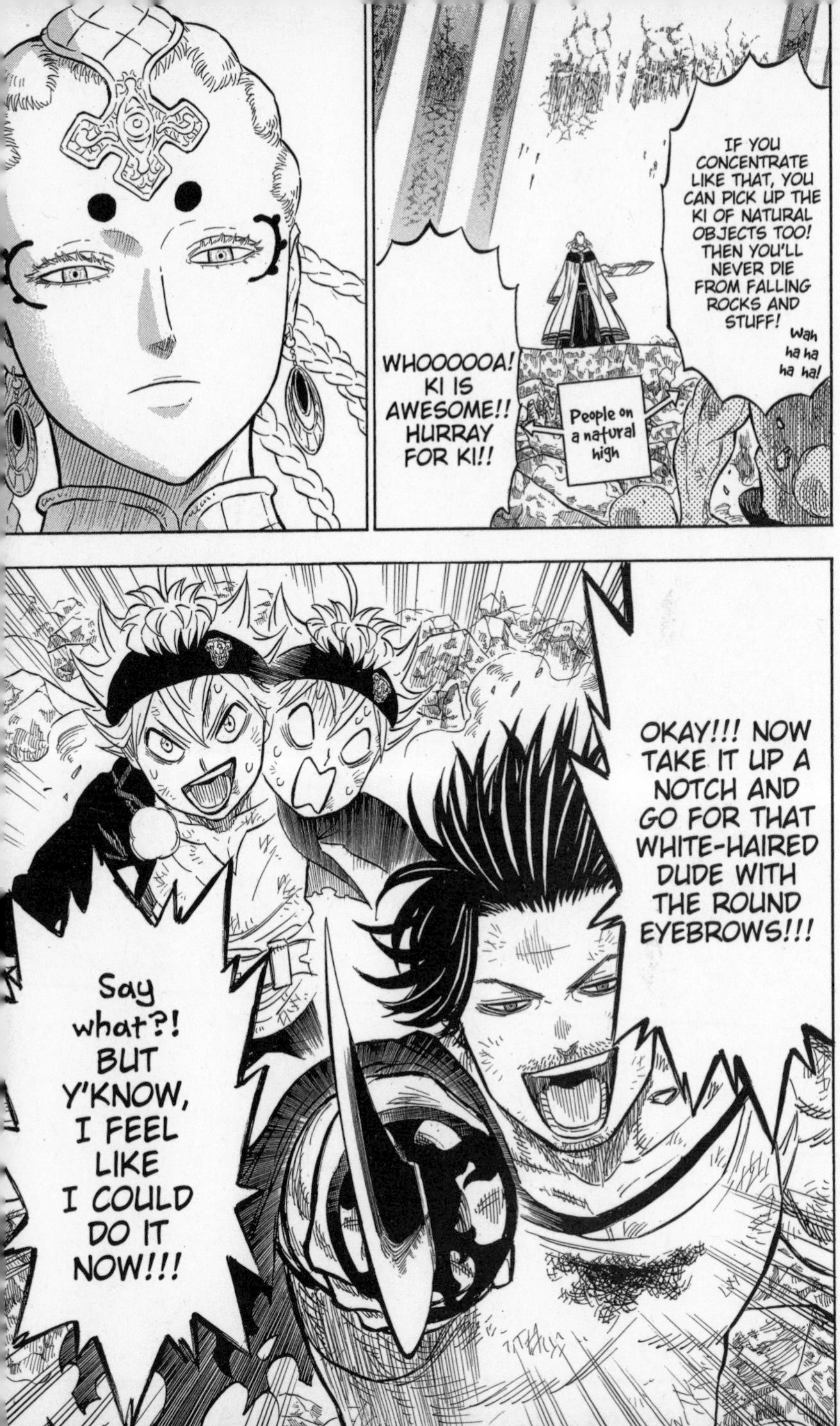
IF YOU CONCENTRATE LIKE THAT, YOU CAN PICK UP THE KI OF NATURAL OBJECTS TOO! THEN YOU'LL NEVER DIE FROM FALLING ROCKS AND STUFF!
Wah ha ha ha ha!
WHOOOOOA! KI IS AWESOME!! HURRAY FOR KI!!
People on a natural high
OKAY!!! NOW TAKE IT UP A NOTCH AND GO FOR THAT WHITE-HAIRED DUDE WITH THE ROUND EYEBROWS!!!
Say what?! BUT Y'KNOW, I FEEL LIKE I COULD DO IT NOW!!!

Valtos

Age: 25
Height: 178 cm
Birthday: December 27
Sign: Capricorn
Blood Type: A
Likes: Quiet places

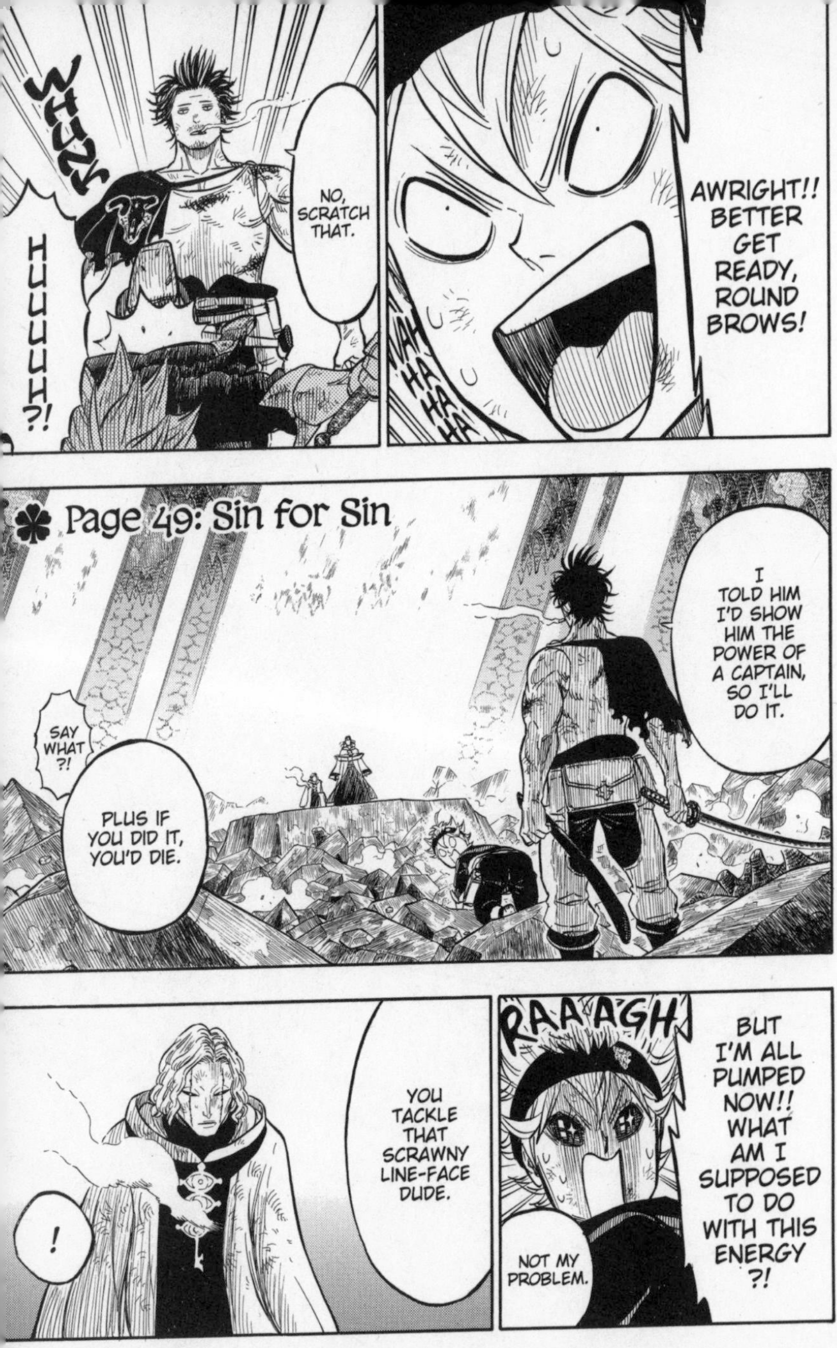
AWRIGHT!! BETTER GET READY, ROUND BROWS!
WAHAHAHAHA
NO, SCRATCH THAT.
WHUN
HUUUUUH?!
Page 49: Sin for Sin
I TOLD HIM I'D SHOW HIM THE POWER OF A CAPTAIN, SO I'LL DO IT.
SAY WHAT?!
PLUS IF YOU DID IT, YOU'D DIE.
RAAAGH
BUT I'M ALL PUMPED NOW!! WHAT AM I SUPPOSED TO DO WITH THIS ENERGY?!
NOT MY PROBLEM.
YOU TACKLE THAT SCRAWNY LINE-FACE DUDE.
!

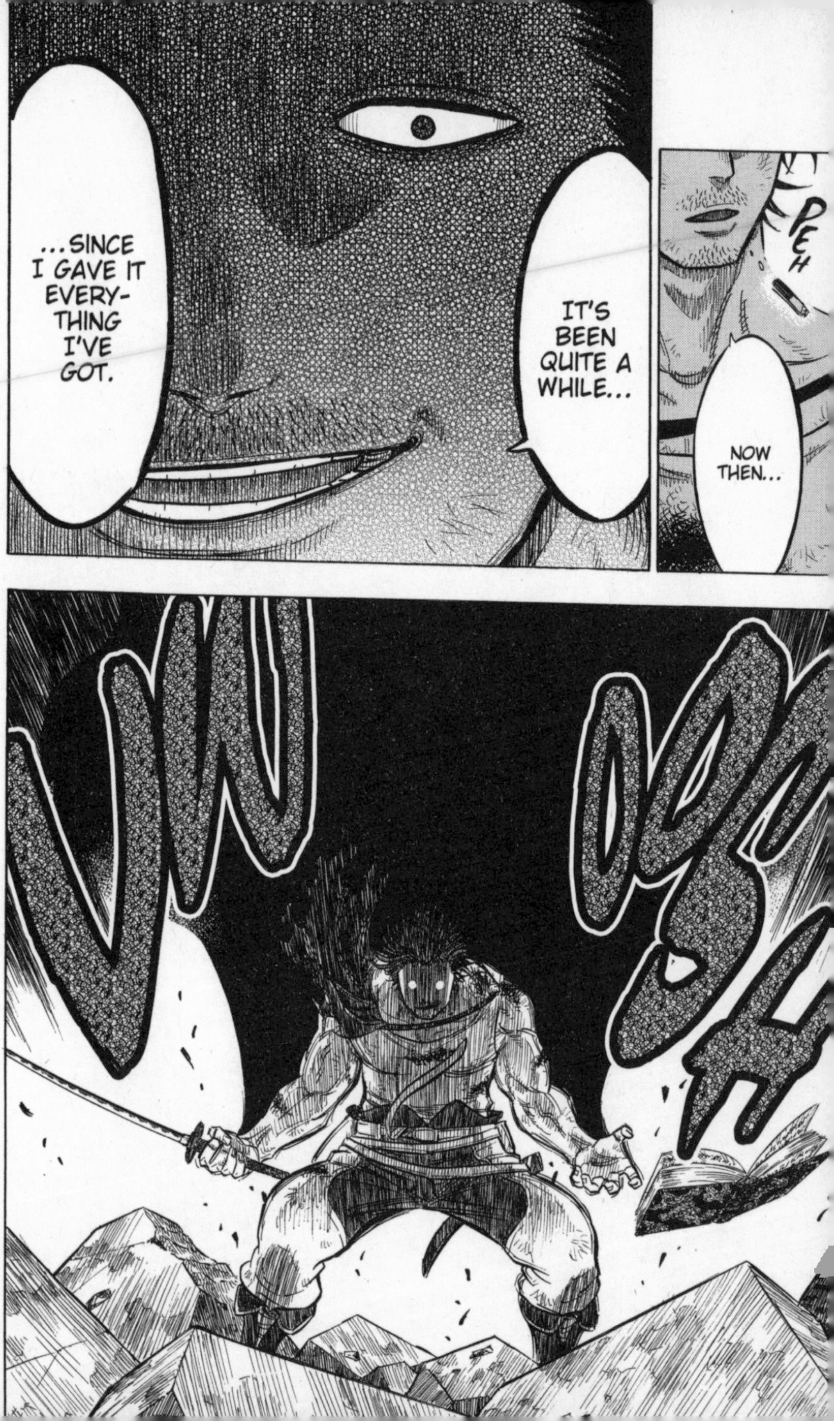
PEH
NOW THEN...
IT'S BEEN QUITE A WHILE...
...SINCE I GAVE IT EVERYTHING I'VE GOT.

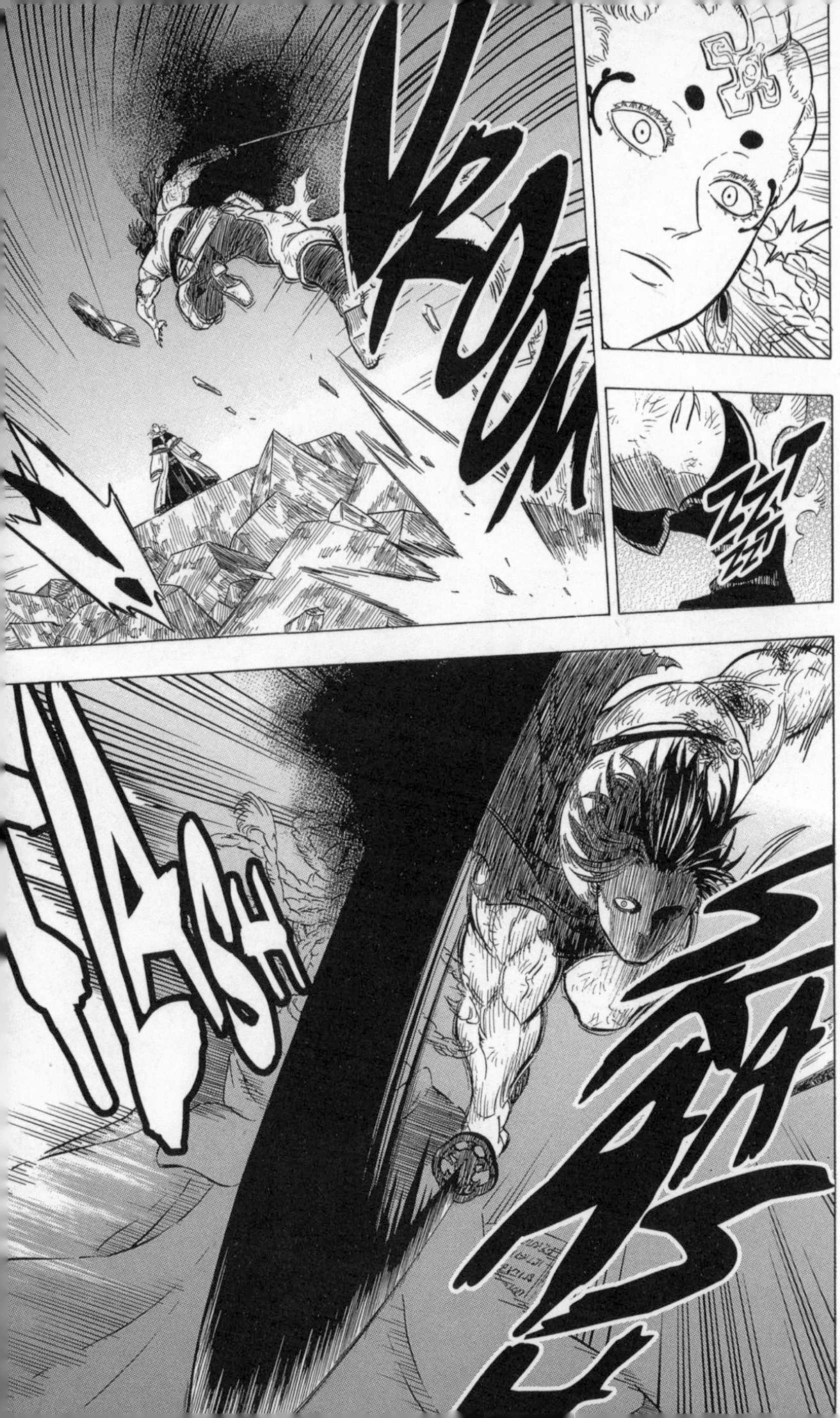
ZZZT
FLASH

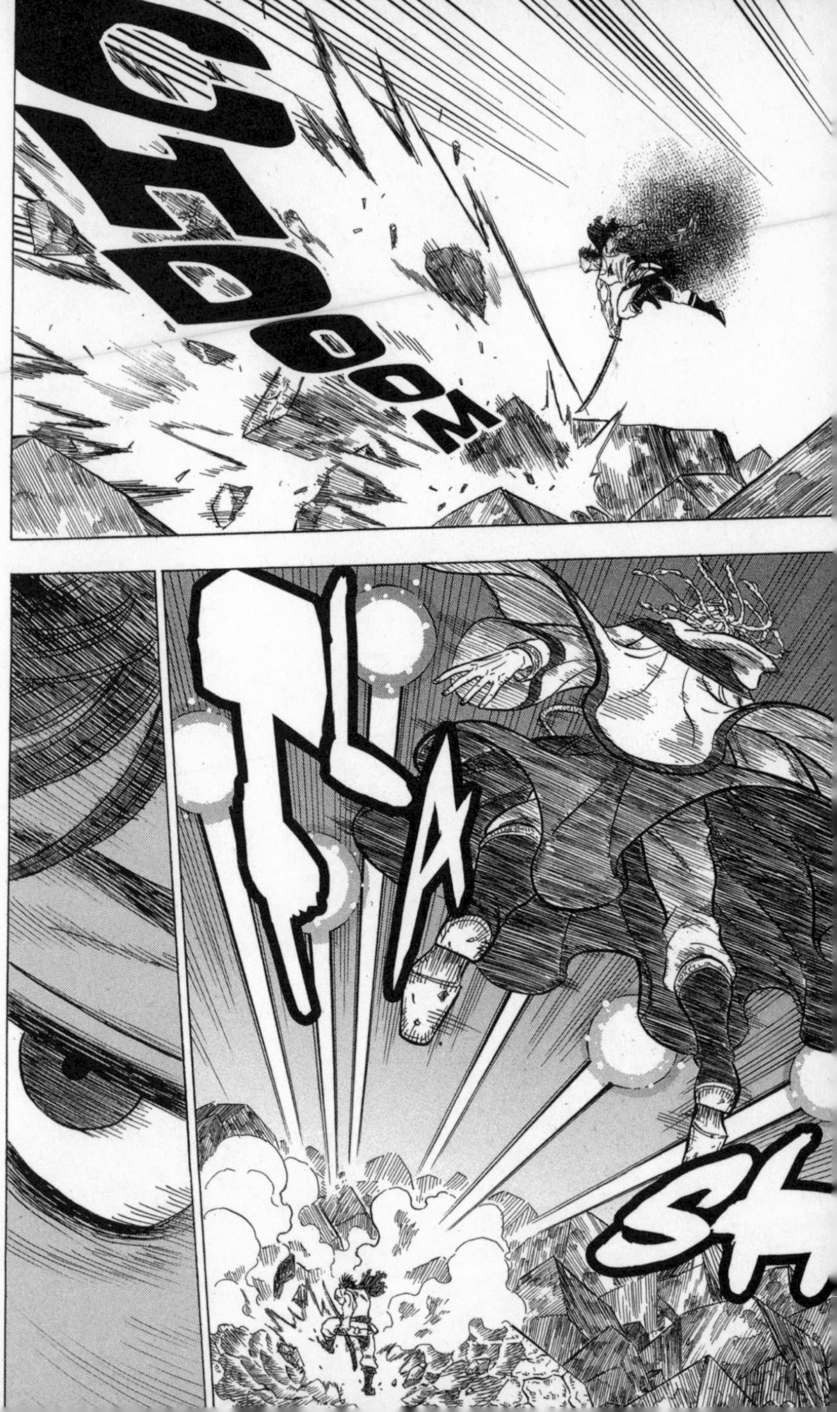

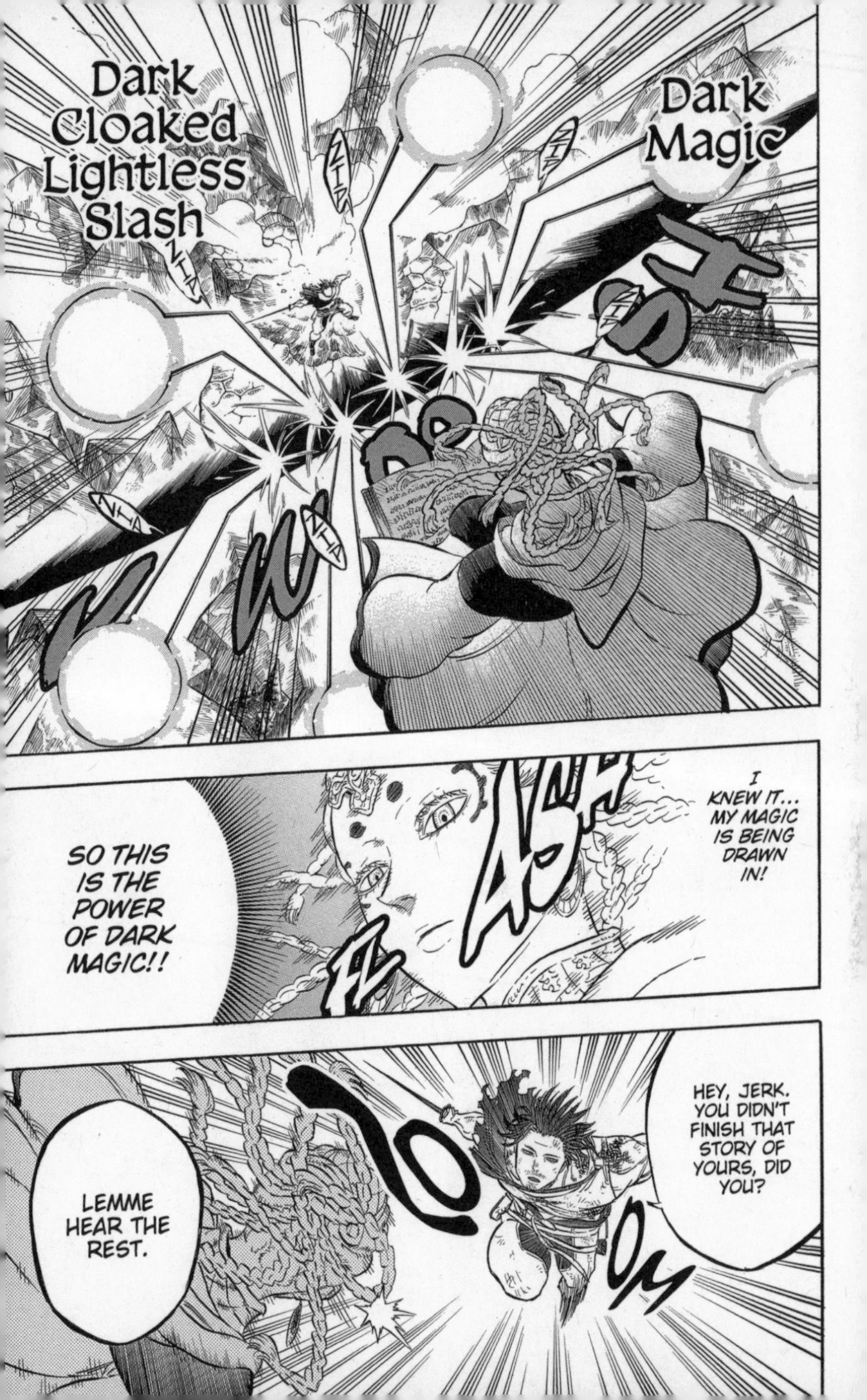
Dark Magic
Dark Cloaked Lightless Slash
ZIP
ZIP
ZIP
ZIP
ZHA
ZHA
I KNEW IT... MY MAGIC IS BEING DRAWN IN!
SO THIS IS THE POWER OF DARK MAGIC!!
HEY, JERK. YOU DIDN'T FINISH THAT STORY OF YOURS, DID YOU?
LEMME HEAR THE REST.

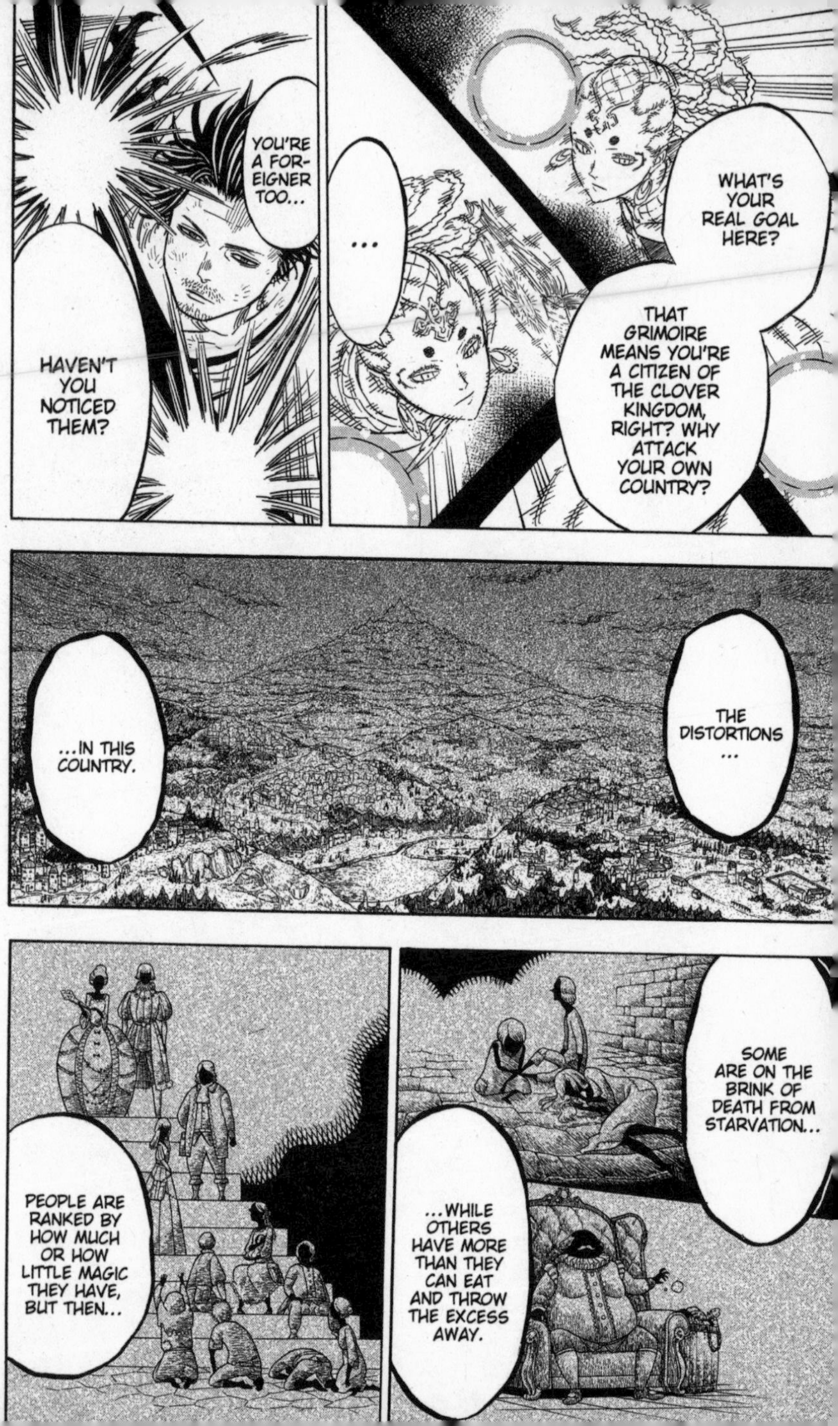
WHAT'S YOUR REAL GOAL HERE?
THAT GRIMOIRE MEANS YOU'RE A CITIZEN OF THE CLOVER KINGDOM, RIGHT? WHY ATTACK YOUR OWN COUNTRY?
...
YOU'RE A FOR-EIGNER TOO...
HAVEN'T YOU NOTICED THEM?
THE DISTORTIONS...
...IN THIS COUNTRY.
SOME ARE ON THE BRINK OF DEATH FROM STARVATION...
...WHILE OTHERS HAVE MORE THAN THEY CAN EAT AND THROW THE EXCESS AWAY.
PEOPLE ARE RANKED BY HOW MUCH OR HOW LITTLE MAGIC THEY HAVE, BUT THEN...

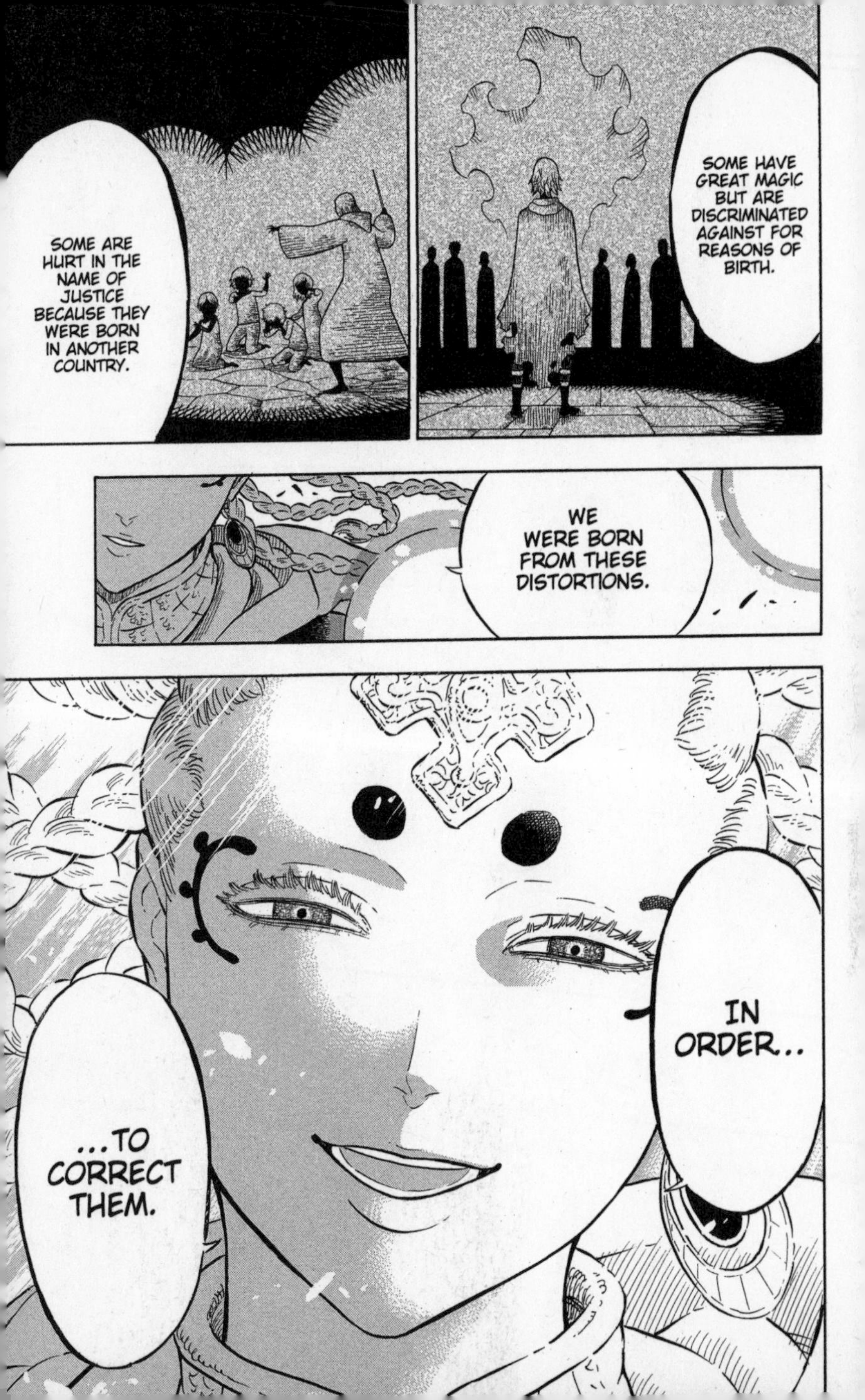
SOME HAVE GREAT MAGIC BUT ARE DISCRIMINATED AGAINST FOR REASONS OF BIRTH.
SOME ARE HURT IN THE NAME OF JUSTICE BECAUSE THEY WERE BORN IN ANOTHER COUNTRY.
WE WERE BORN FROM THESE DISTORTIONS.
IN ORDER...
...TO CORRECT THEM.

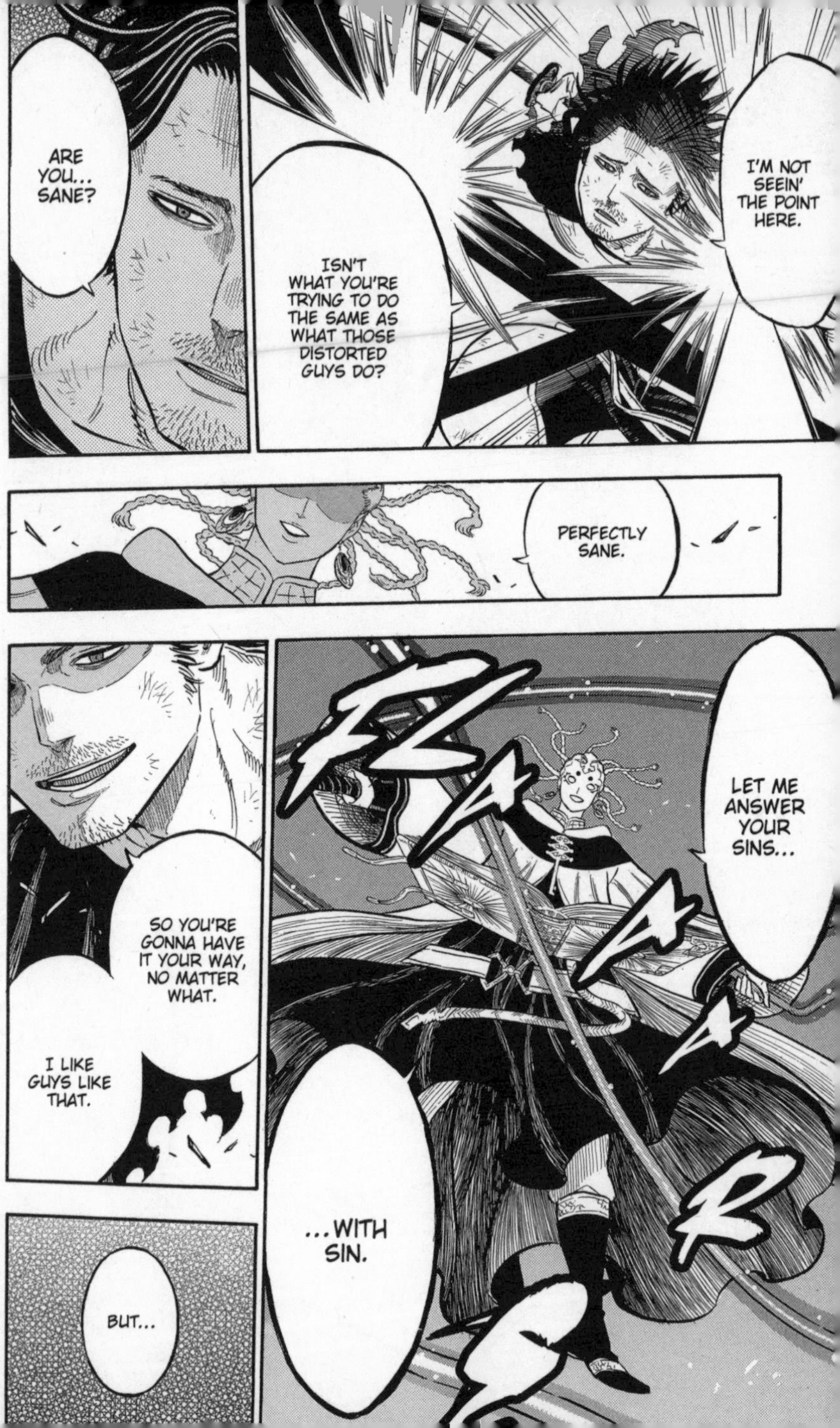
I'M NOT SEEIN' THE POINT HERE.
ISN'T WHAT YOU'RE TRYING TO DO THE SAME AS WHAT THOSE DISTORTED GUYS DO?
ARE YOU... SANE?
PERFECTLY SANE.
LET ME ANSWER YOUR SINS...
...WITH SIN.
SO YOU'RE GONNA HAVE IT YOUR WAY, NO MATTER WHAT.
I LIKE GUYS LIKE THAT.
BUT...

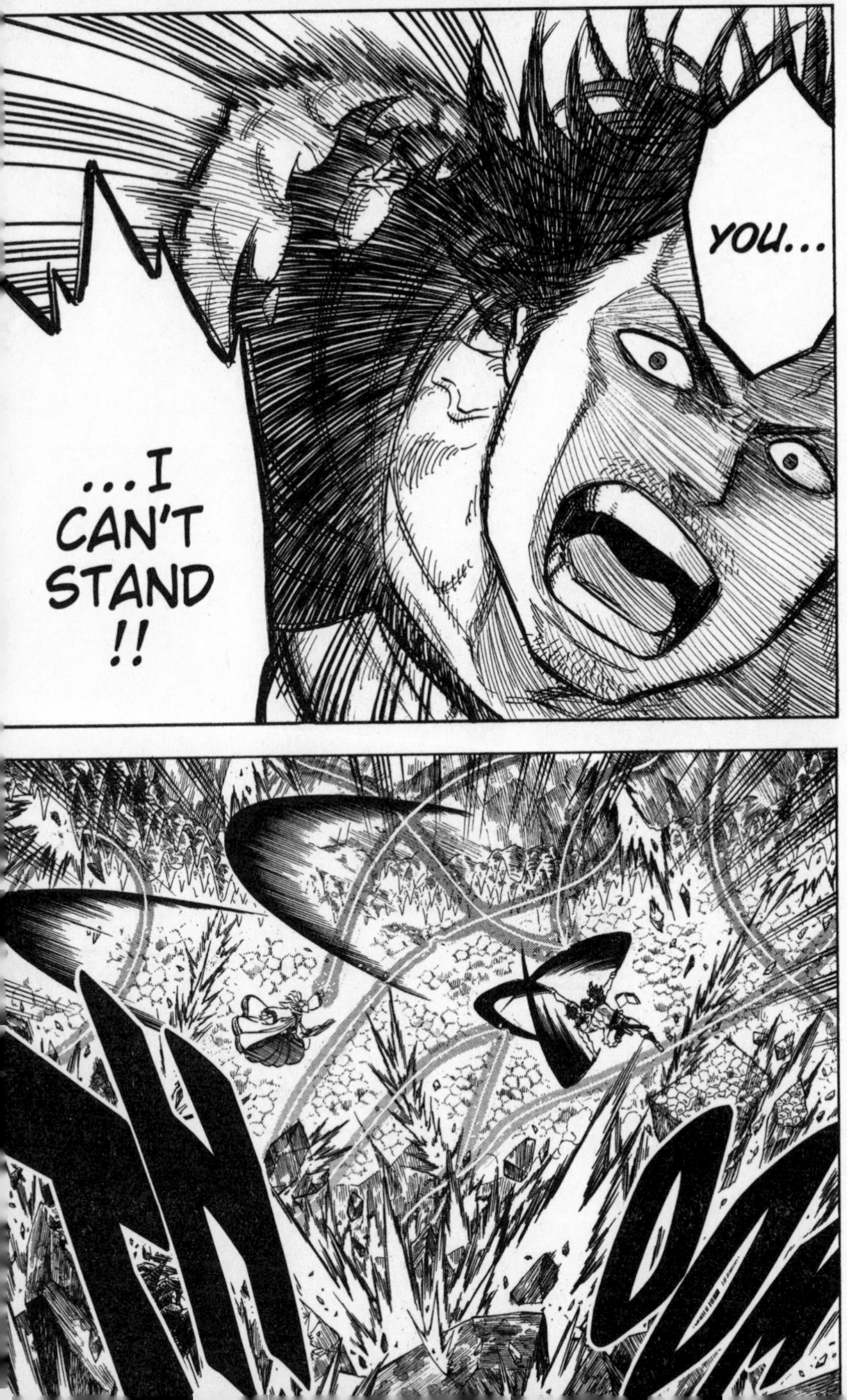
YOU...
...I CAN'T STAND !!

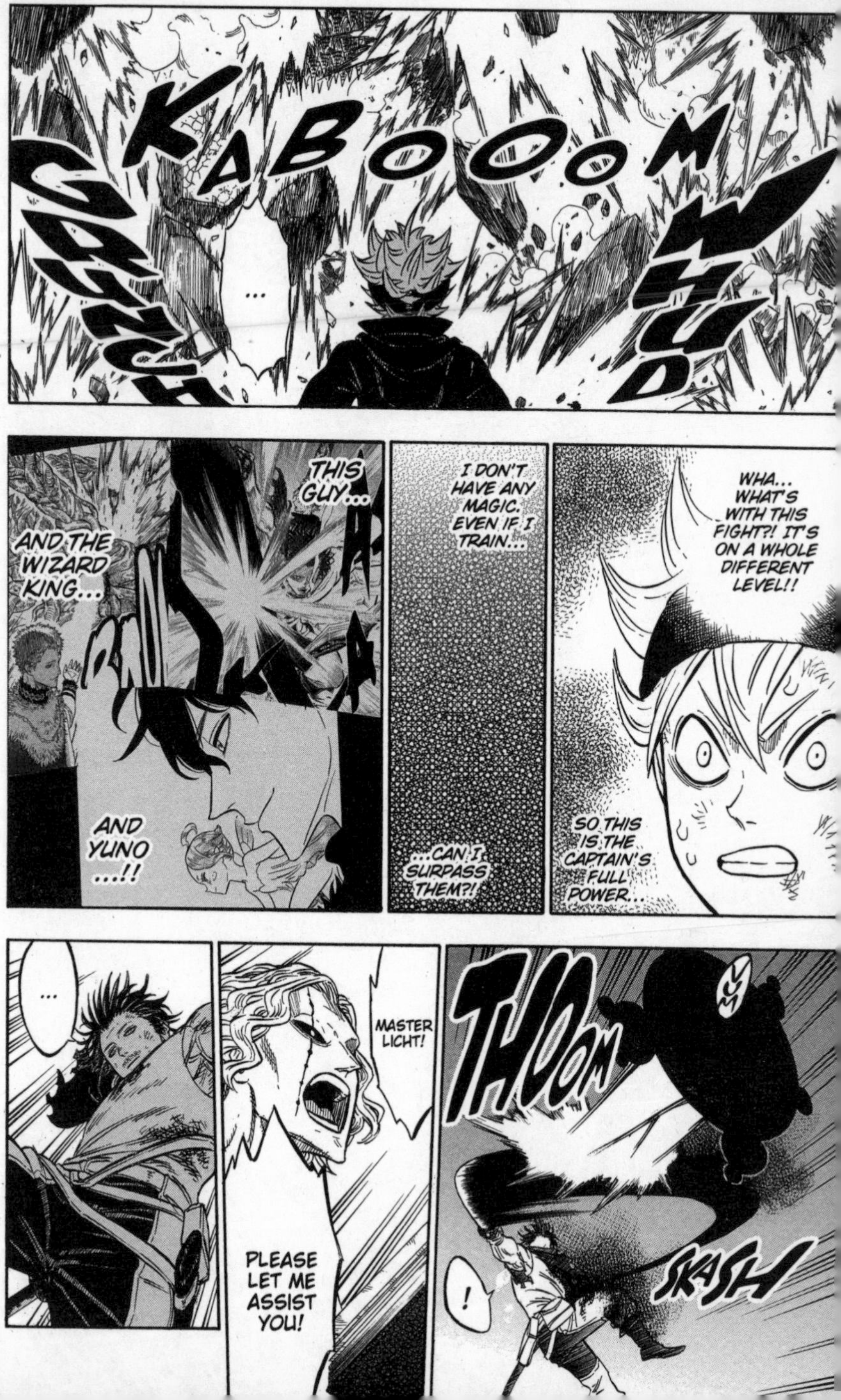
KABOOOOM
...
WHA... WHAT'S WITH THIS FIGHT?! IT'S ON A WHOLE DIFFERENT LEVEL!!
SO THIS IS THE CAPTAIN'S FULL POWER...
I DON'T HAVE ANY MAGIC. EVEN IF I TRAIN...
...CAN I SURPASS THEM?!
THIS GUY...
AND THE WIZARD KING...
AND YUNO ...!!
THOOM
SKASH
!
MASTER LICHT!
PLEASE LET ME ASSIST YOU!
...

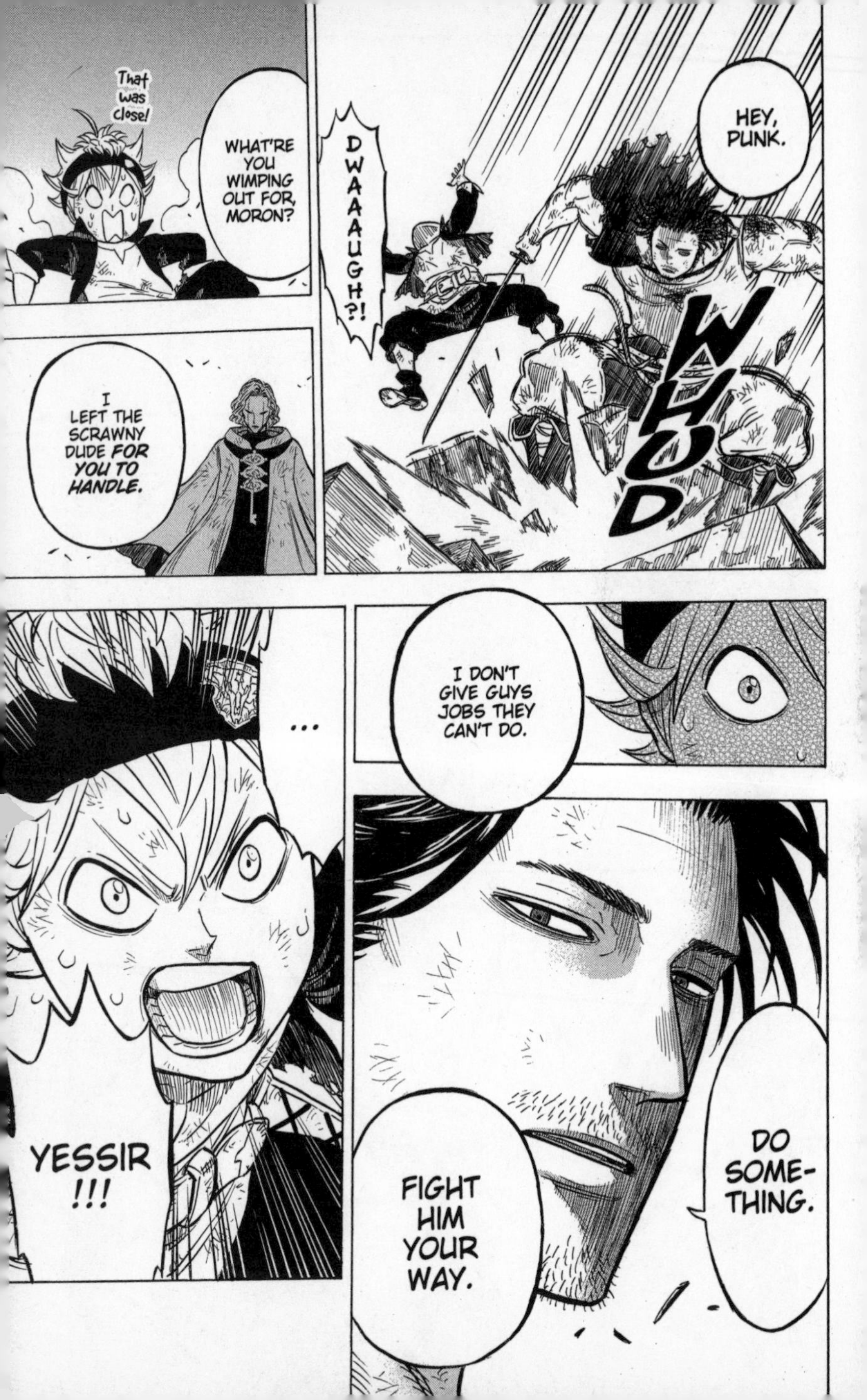
HEY, PUNK.
DWAAAAUGH?!
WHUD
WHAT'RE YOU WIMPING OUT FOR, MORON?
That was close!
I LEFT THE SCRAWNY DUDE *FOR YOU TO HANDLE.*
I DON'T GIVE GUYS JOBS THEY CAN'T DO.
DO SOME-THING.
FIGHT HIM YOUR WAY.
...
YESSIR!!!

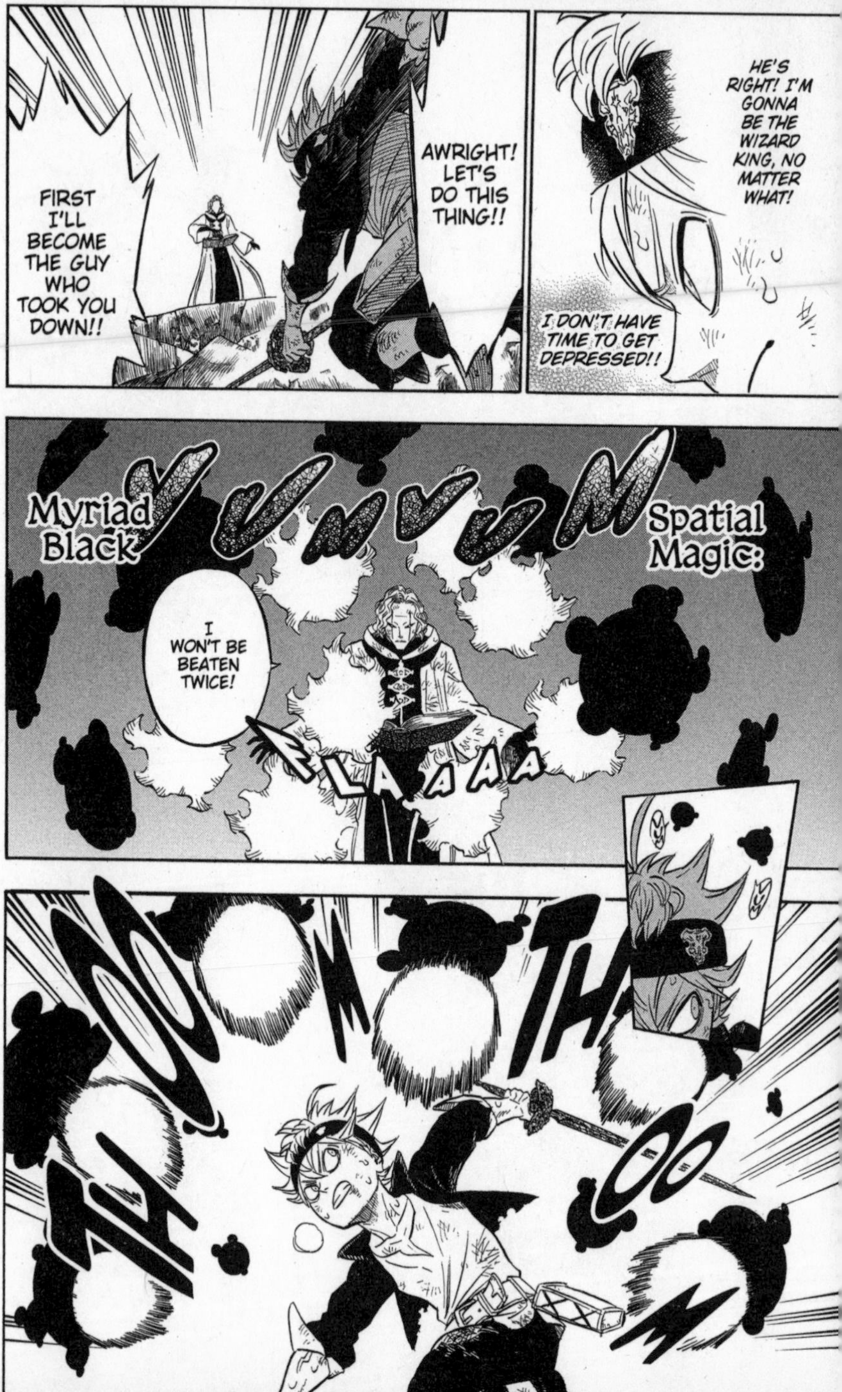
HE'S RIGHT! I'M GONNA BE THE WIZARD KING, NO MATTER WHAT!
I DON'T HAVE TIME TO GET DEPRESSED!!
AWRIGHT! LET'S DO THIS THING!!
FIRST I'LL BECOME THE GUY WHO TOOK YOU DOWN!!
Spatial Magic:
Myriad Black
I WON'T BE BEATEN TWICE!
FLAAAA

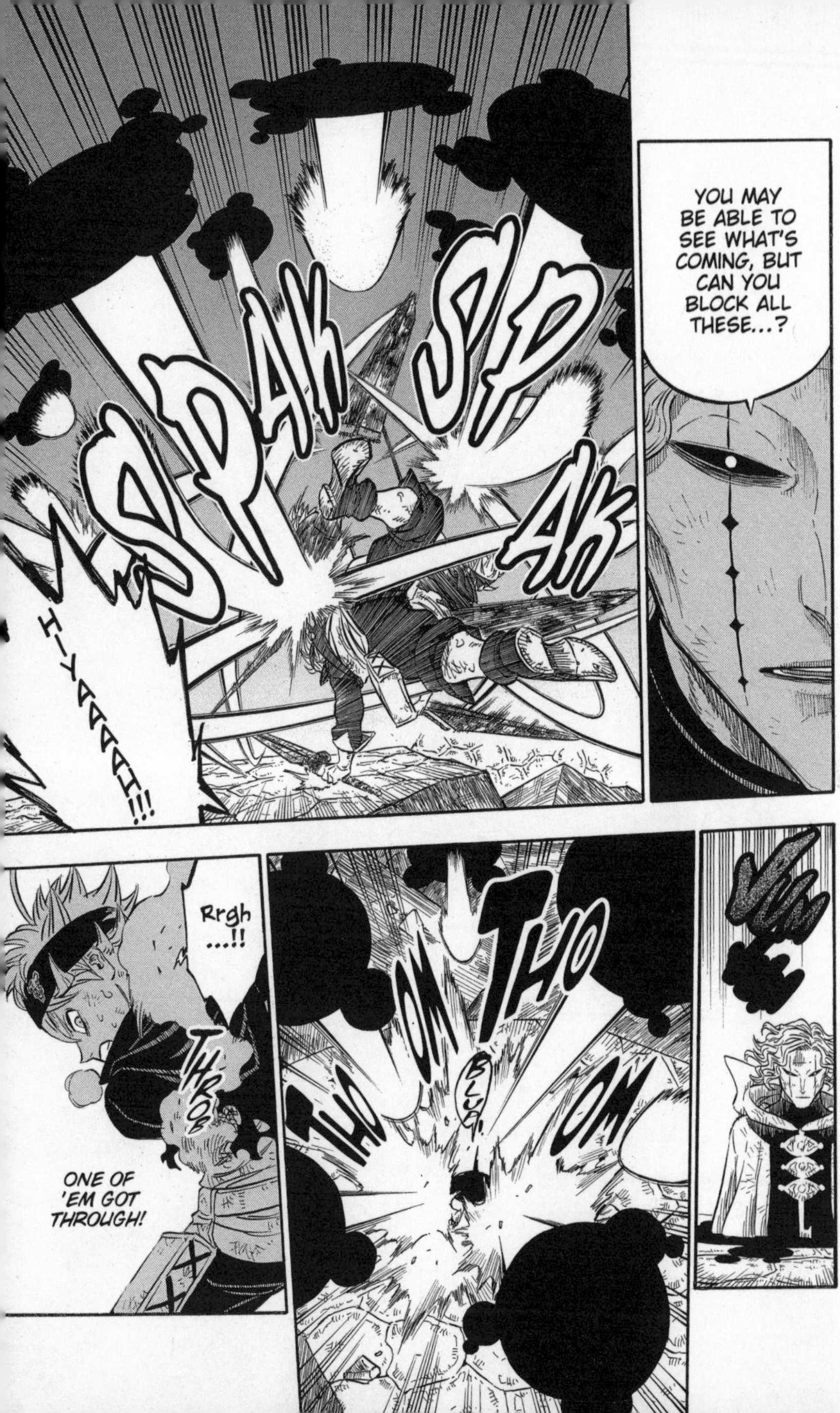
YOU MAY BE ABLE TO SEE WHAT'S COMING, BUT CAN YOU BLOCK ALL THESE...?
SPAK
SPAK
HIYAAAAAH!!!
THOOM
THOOM
BLUP
THOOM
Rrgh ...!!
THROB
ONE OF 'EM GOT THROUGH!

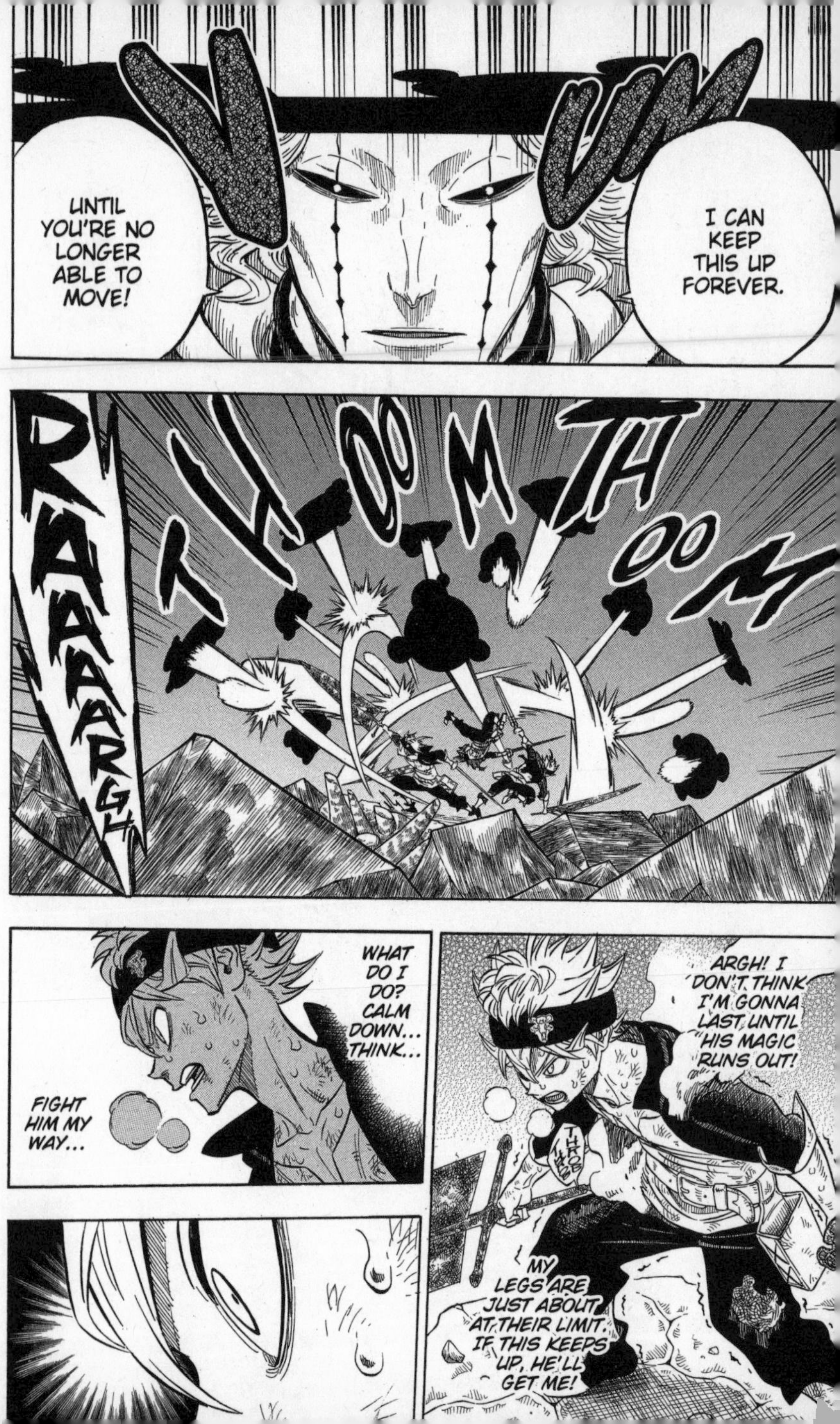

I CAN KEEP THIS UP FOREVER.
UNTIL YOU'RE NO LONGER ABLE TO MOVE!
THOOM THOOM
RAAARGH
ARGH! I DON'T THINK I'M GONNA LAST UNTIL HIS MAGIC RUNS OUT!
THROB THROB
MY LEGS ARE JUST ABOUT AT THEIR LIMIT. IF THIS KEEPS UP, HE'LL GET ME!
WHAT DO I DO? CALM DOWN... THINK...
FIGHT HIM MY WAY...

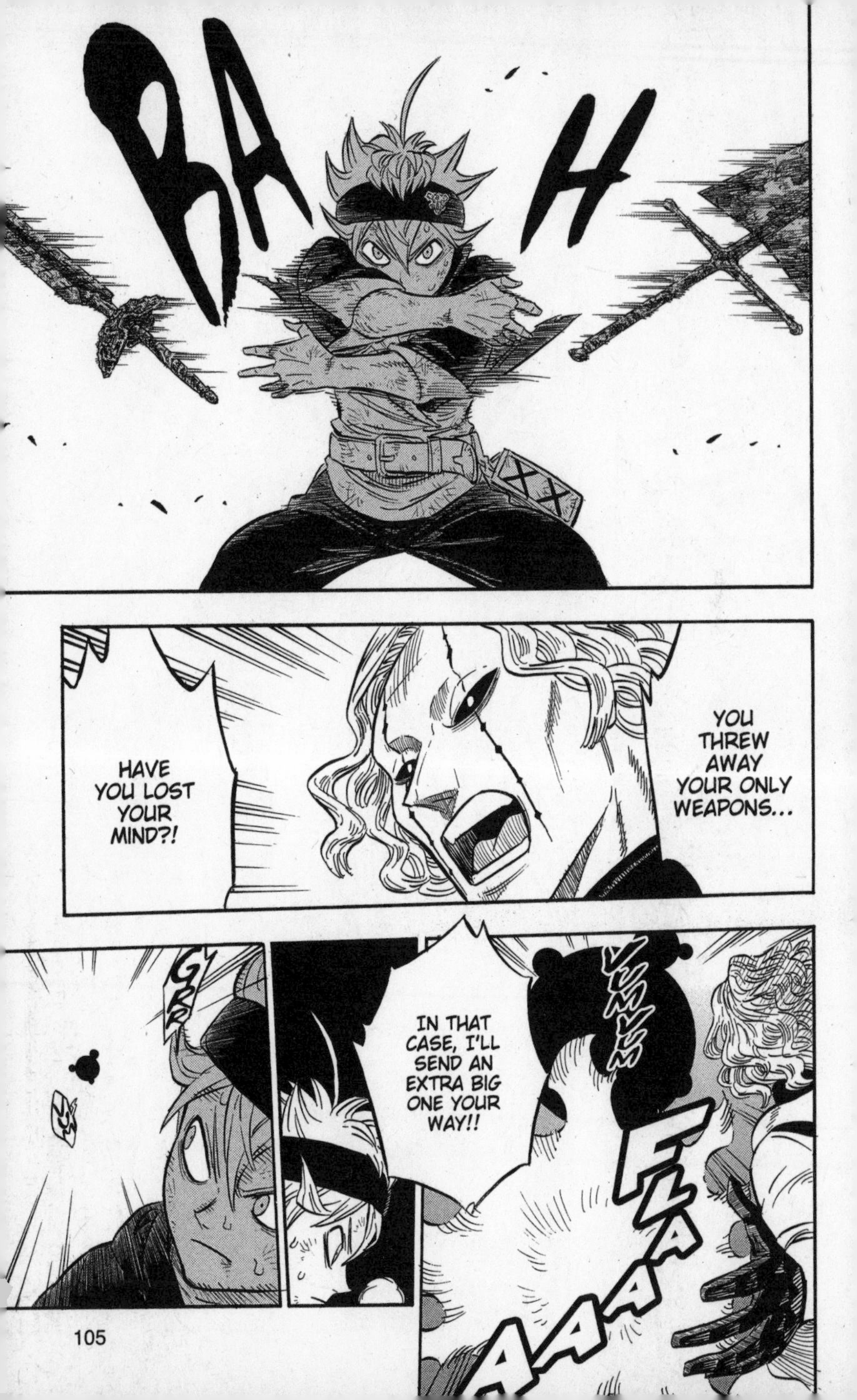
BAH
YOU THREW AWAY YOUR ONLY WEAPONS...
HAVE YOU LOST YOUR MIND?!
MUNYUM
IN THAT CASE, I'LL SEND AN EXTRA BIG ONE YOUR WAY!!
FLAAAAA
GRR

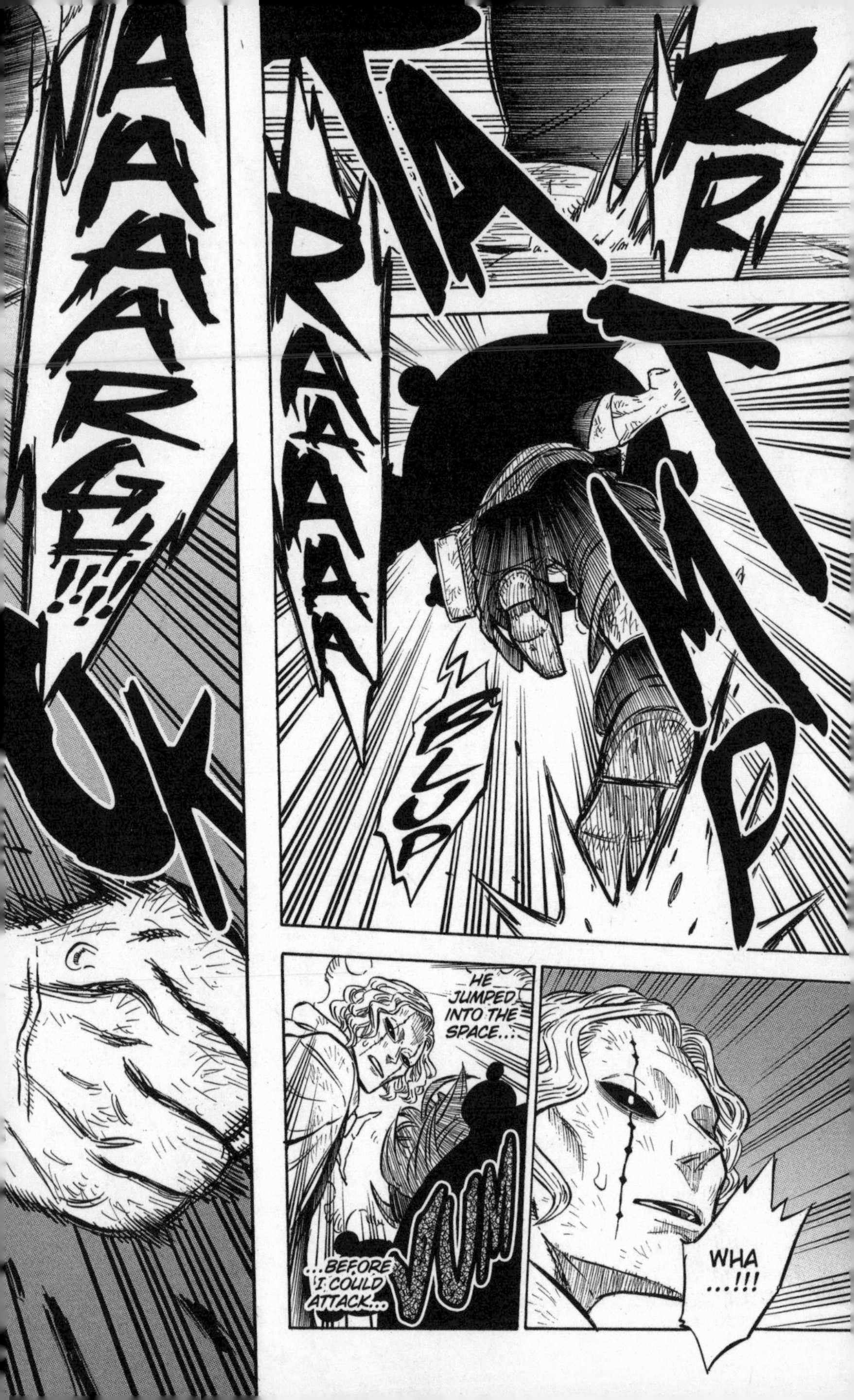
TMP
AAAARGH!!!
HE JUMPED INTO THE SPACE...
...BEFORE I COULD ATTACK...
WHA...!!!

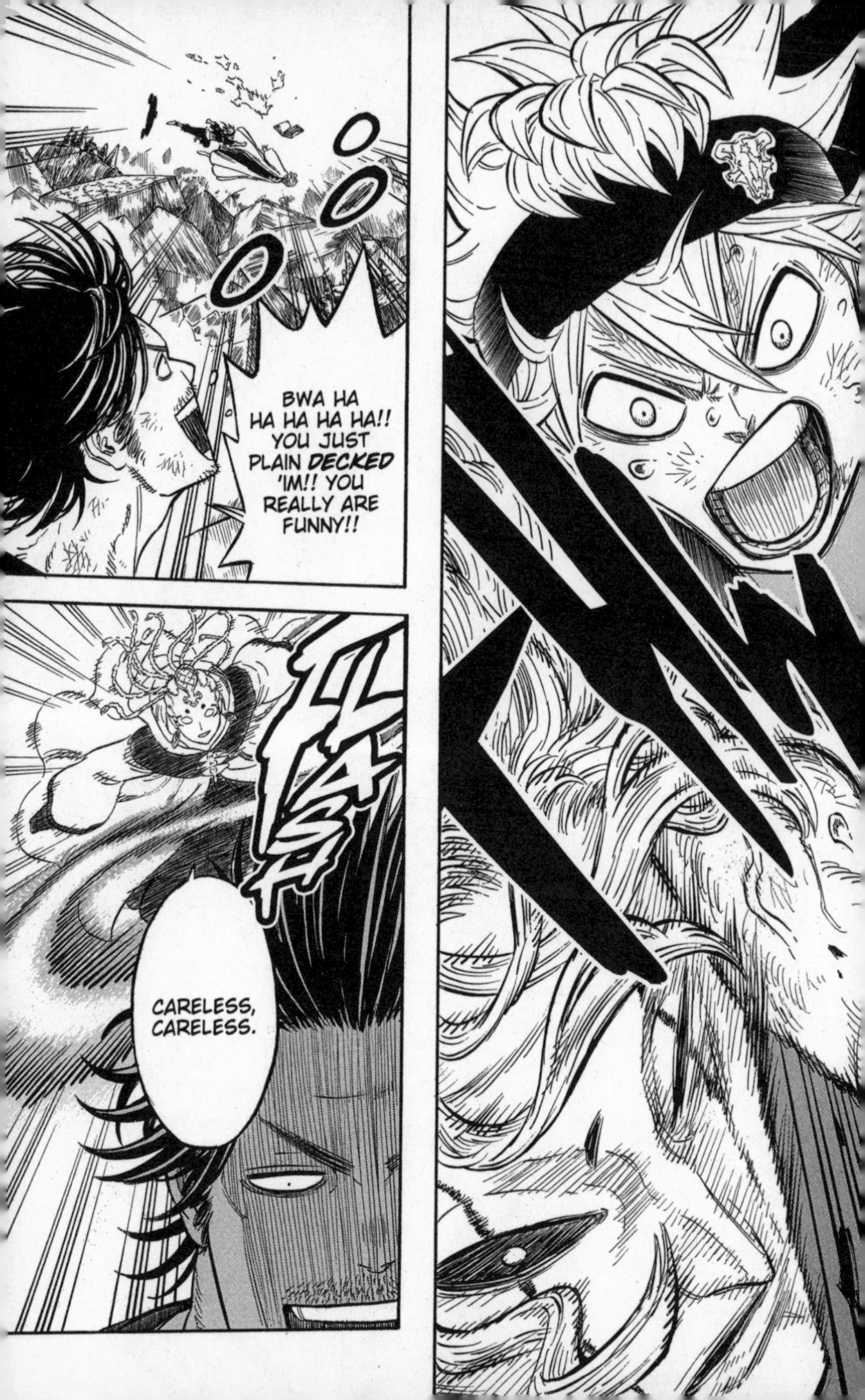
BWA HA HA HA HA HA!! YOU JUST PLAIN *DECKED* 'IM!! YOU REALLY ARE FUNNY!!
CARELESS, CARELESS.

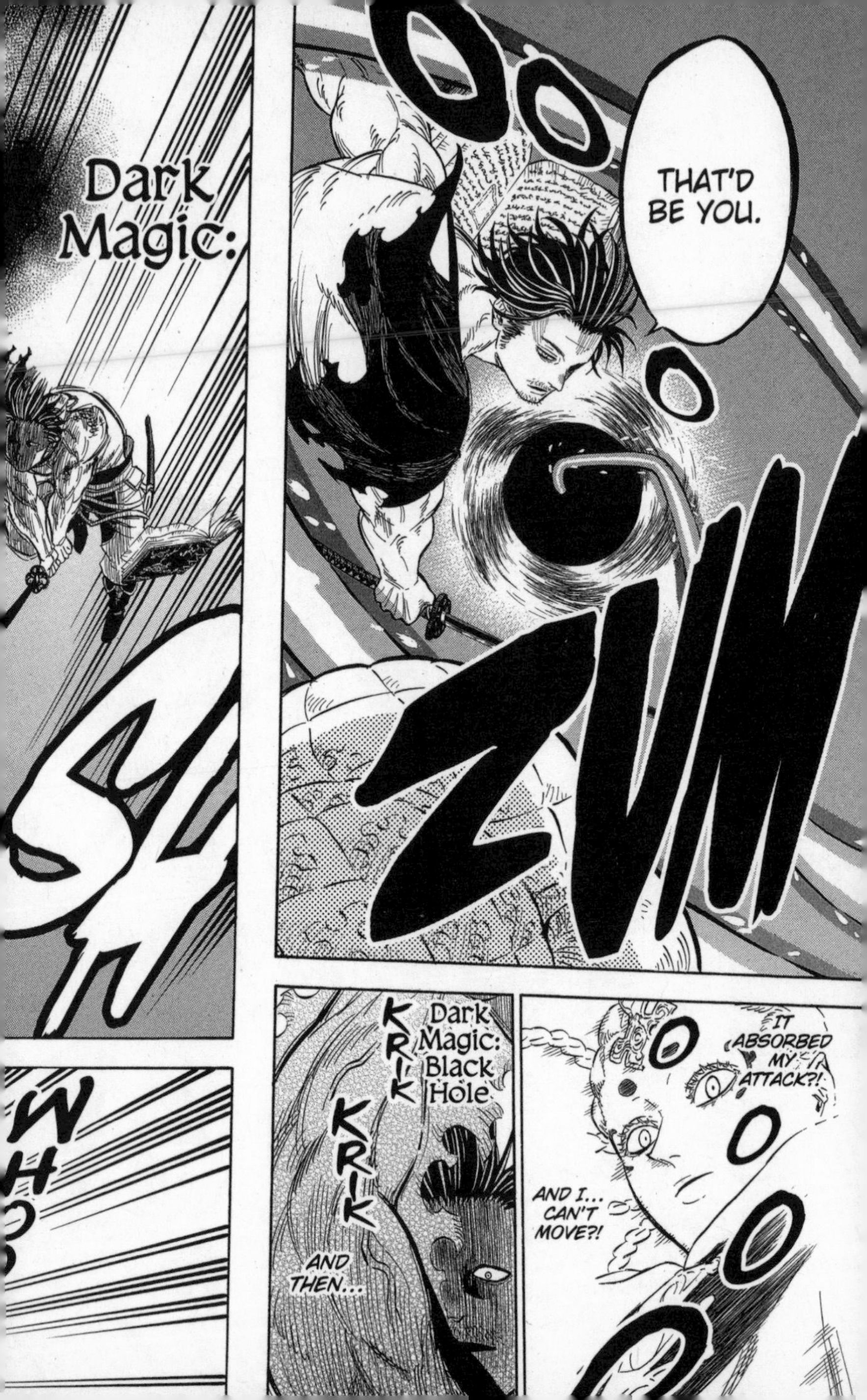
THAT'D BE YOU.
Dark Magic:
IT ABSORBED MY ATTACK?!
AND I... CAN'T MOVE?!
Dark Magic: Black Hole
KRIK
KRIK
AND THEN...

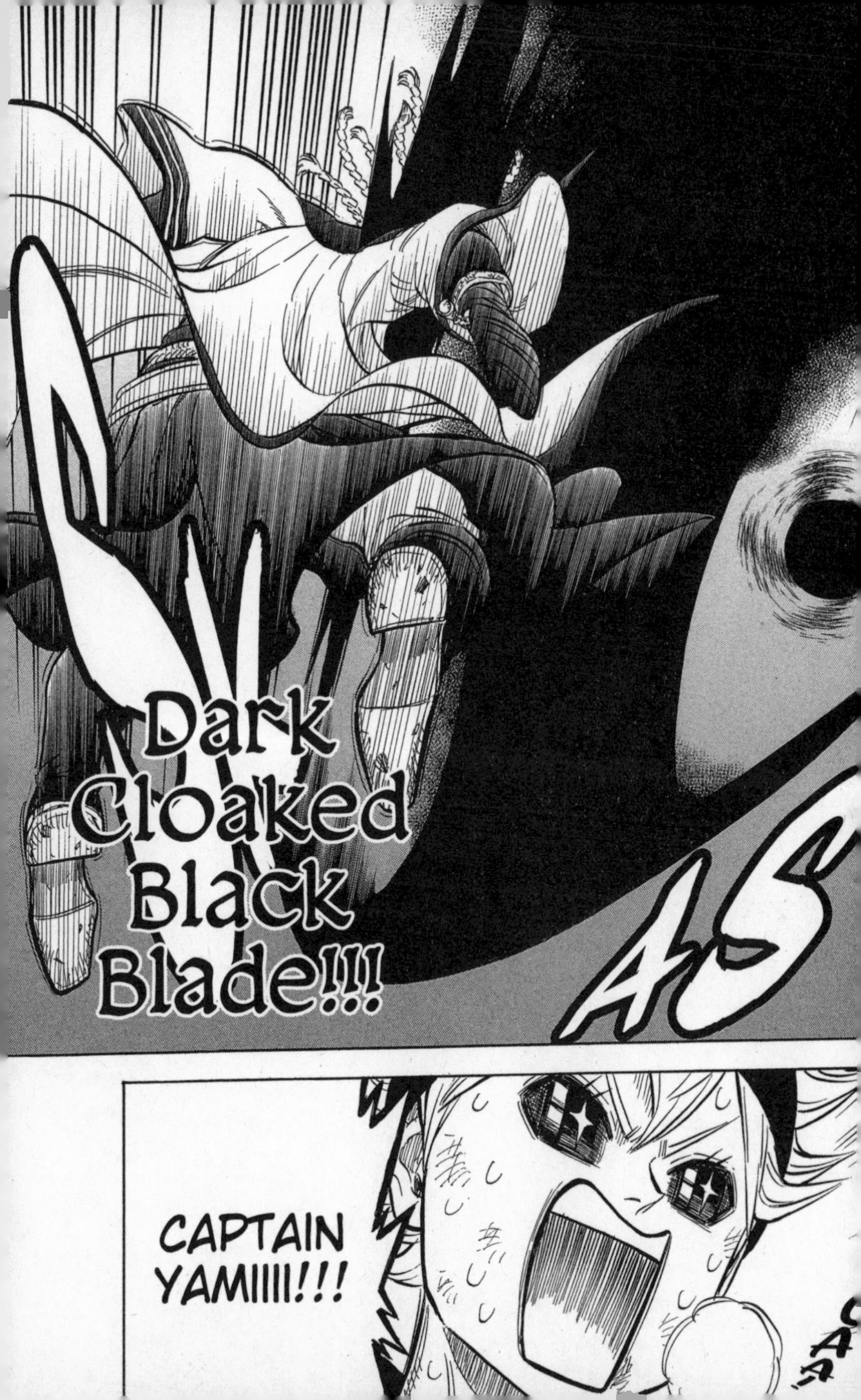
Dark Cloaked Black Blade!!!
CAPTAIN YAMIIIII!!!

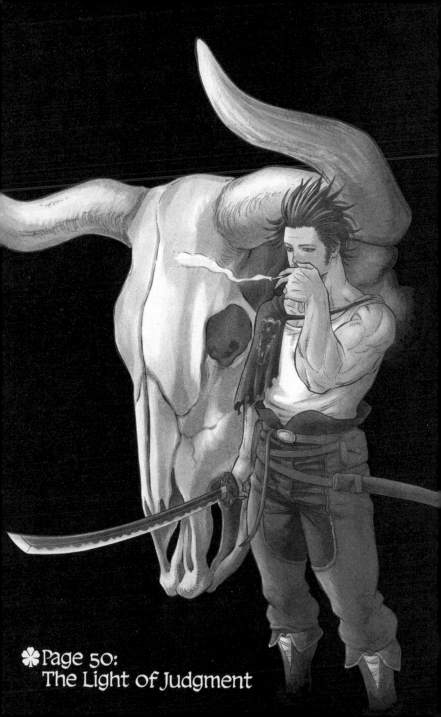

❀Page 50:
The Light of Judgment

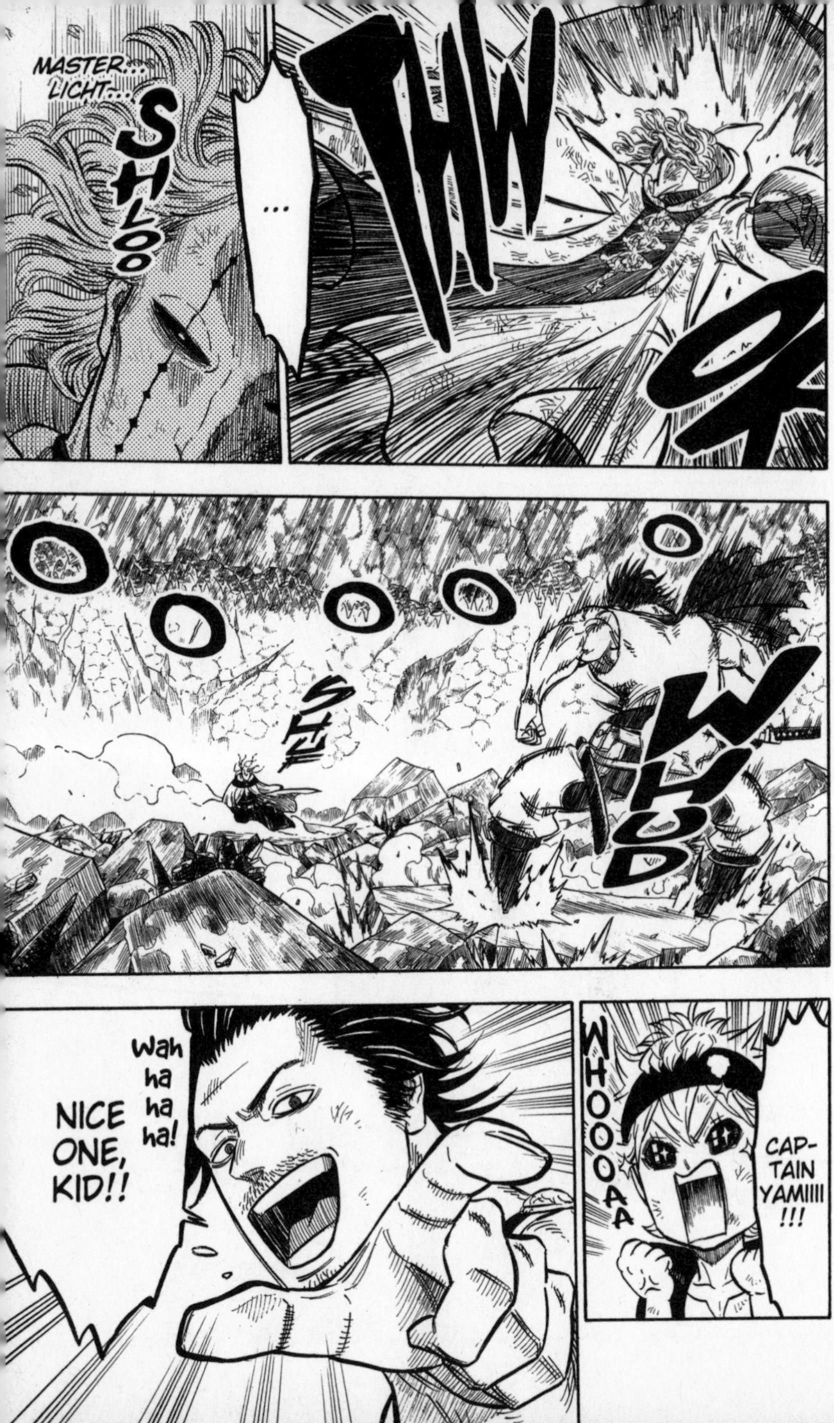
THW
OK
...
MASTER... LICHT...
SHLOO
OOOOOO
WHUD
SHU
WHOOOOAA
CAP-TAIN YAMIIII!!!
Wah ha ha ha!
NICE ONE, KID!!

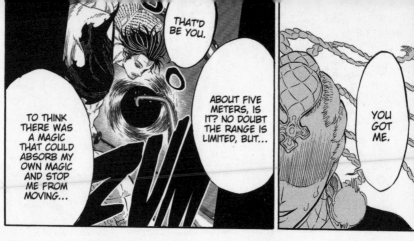

YOU GOT ME.
THAT'D BE YOU.
ABOUT FIVE METERS, IS IT? NO DOUBT THE RANGE IS LIMITED, BUT...
TO THINK THERE WAS A MAGIC THAT COULD ABSORB MY OWN MAGIC AND STOP ME FROM MOVING...
DARK MAGIC... IS AMAZING!
THE ONE ATTRIBUTE THAT'S THE NATURAL ENEMY OF MY LIGHT MAGIC!

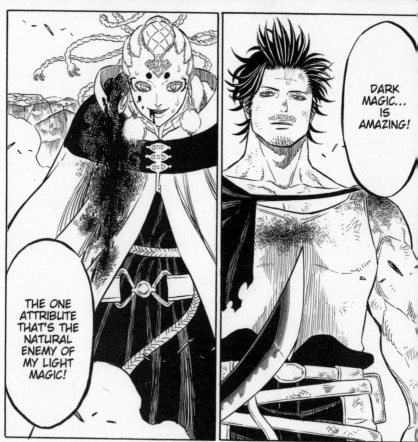

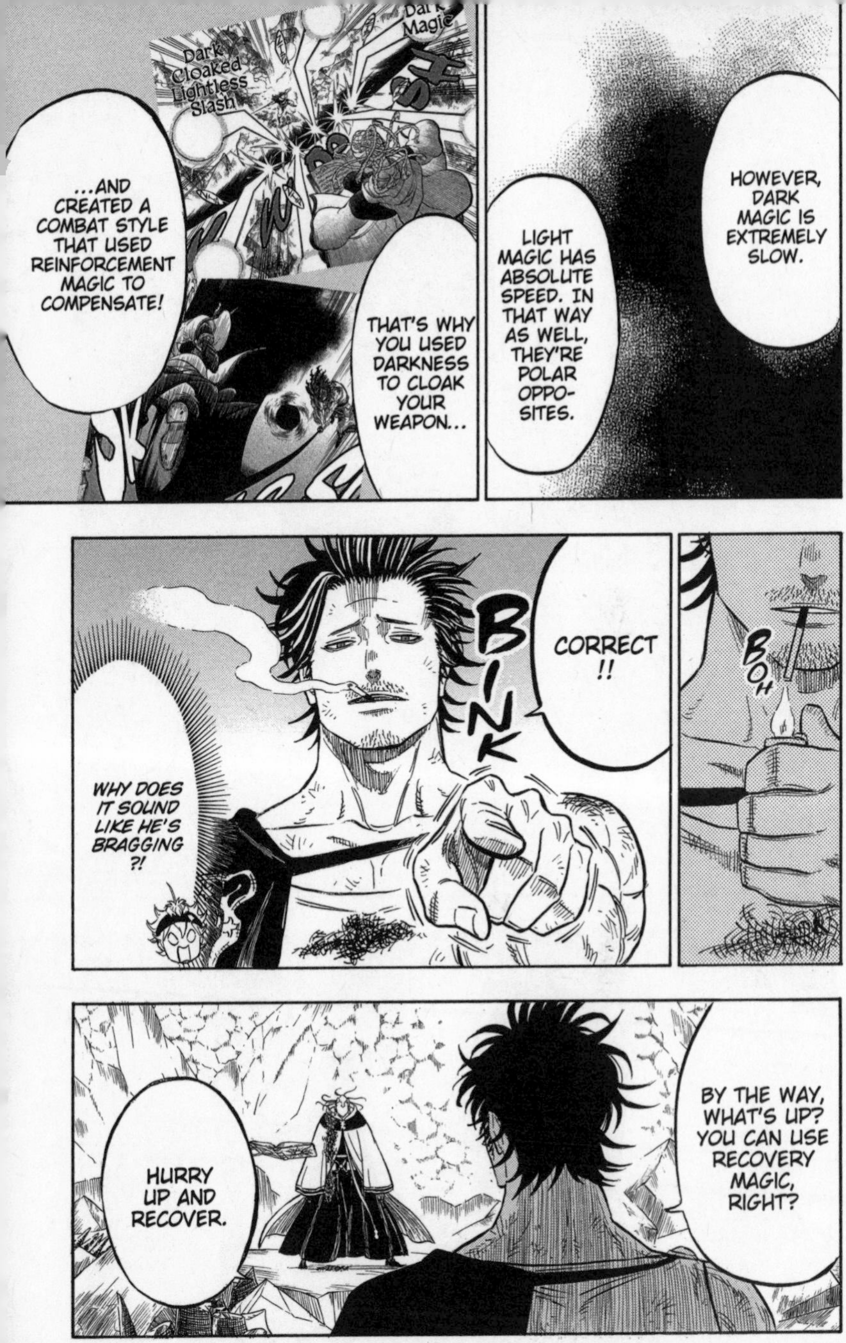
HOWEVER, DARK MAGIC IS EXTREMELY SLOW.
LIGHT MAGIC HAS ABSOLUTE SPEED. IN THAT WAY AS WELL, THEY'RE POLAR OPPO-SITES.
Dark Magic
Dark Cloaked Lightless Slash
THAT'S WHY YOU USED DARKNESS TO CLOAK YOUR WEAPON...
...AND CREATED A COMBAT STYLE THAT USED REINFORCEMENT MAGIC TO COMPENSATE!
BOH
CORRECT!!
BINK
WHY DOES IT SOUND LIKE HE'S BRAGGING?!
BY THE WAY, WHAT'S UP? YOU CAN USE RECOVERY MAGIC, RIGHT?
HURRY UP AND RECOVER.

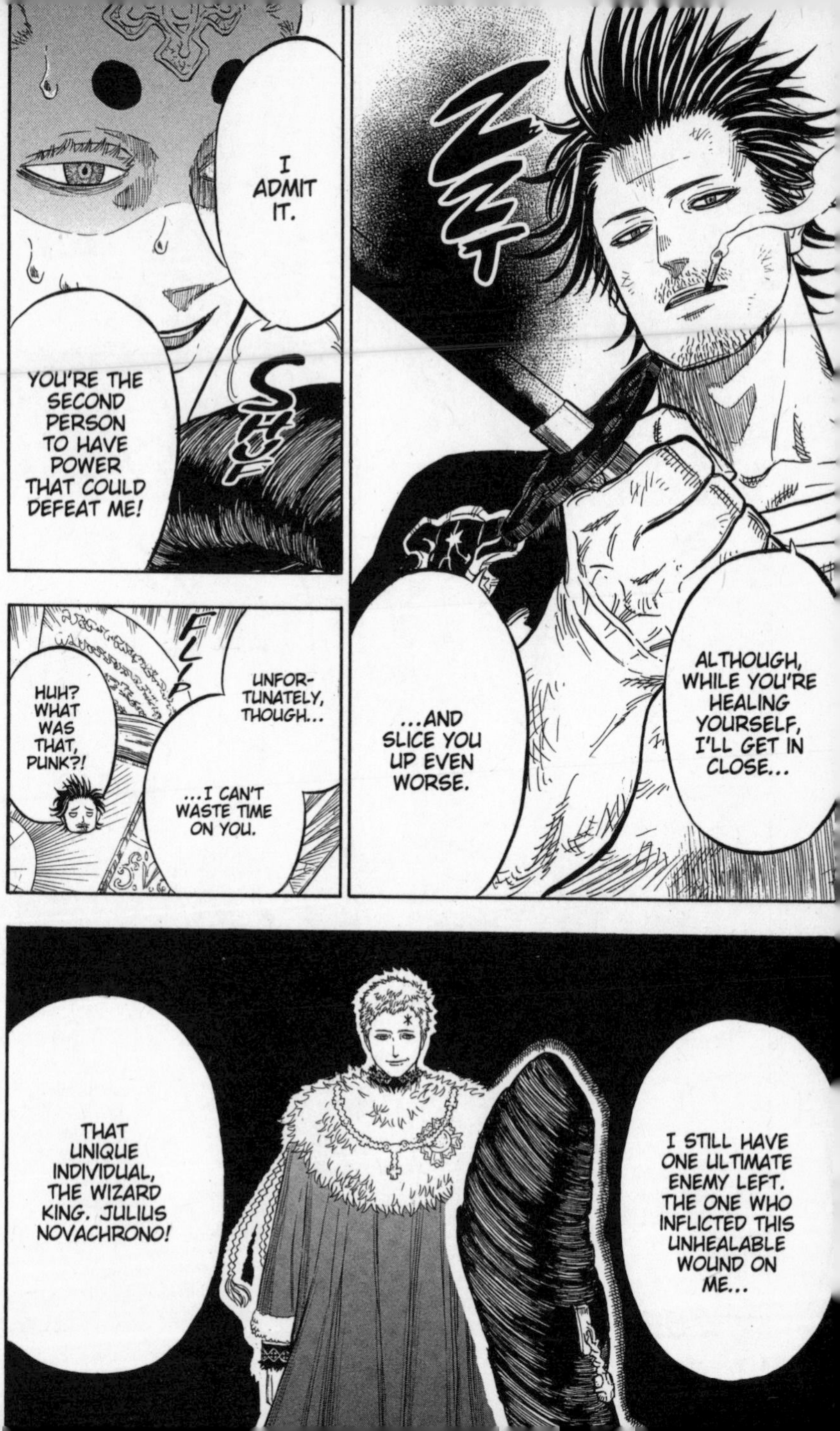
ALTHOUGH, WHILE YOU'RE HEALING YOURSELF, I'LL GET IN CLOSE...
...AND SLICE YOU UP EVEN WORSE.
I ADMIT IT.
YOU'RE THE SECOND PERSON TO HAVE POWER THAT COULD DEFEAT ME!
UNFOR-TUNATELY, THOUGH...
...I CAN'T WASTE TIME ON YOU.
HUH? WHAT WAS THAT, PUNK?!
I STILL HAVE ONE ULTIMATE ENEMY LEFT. THE ONE WHO INFLICTED THIS UNHEALABLE WOUND ON ME...
THAT UNIQUE INDIVIDUAL, THE WIZARD KING. JULIUS NOVACHRONO!

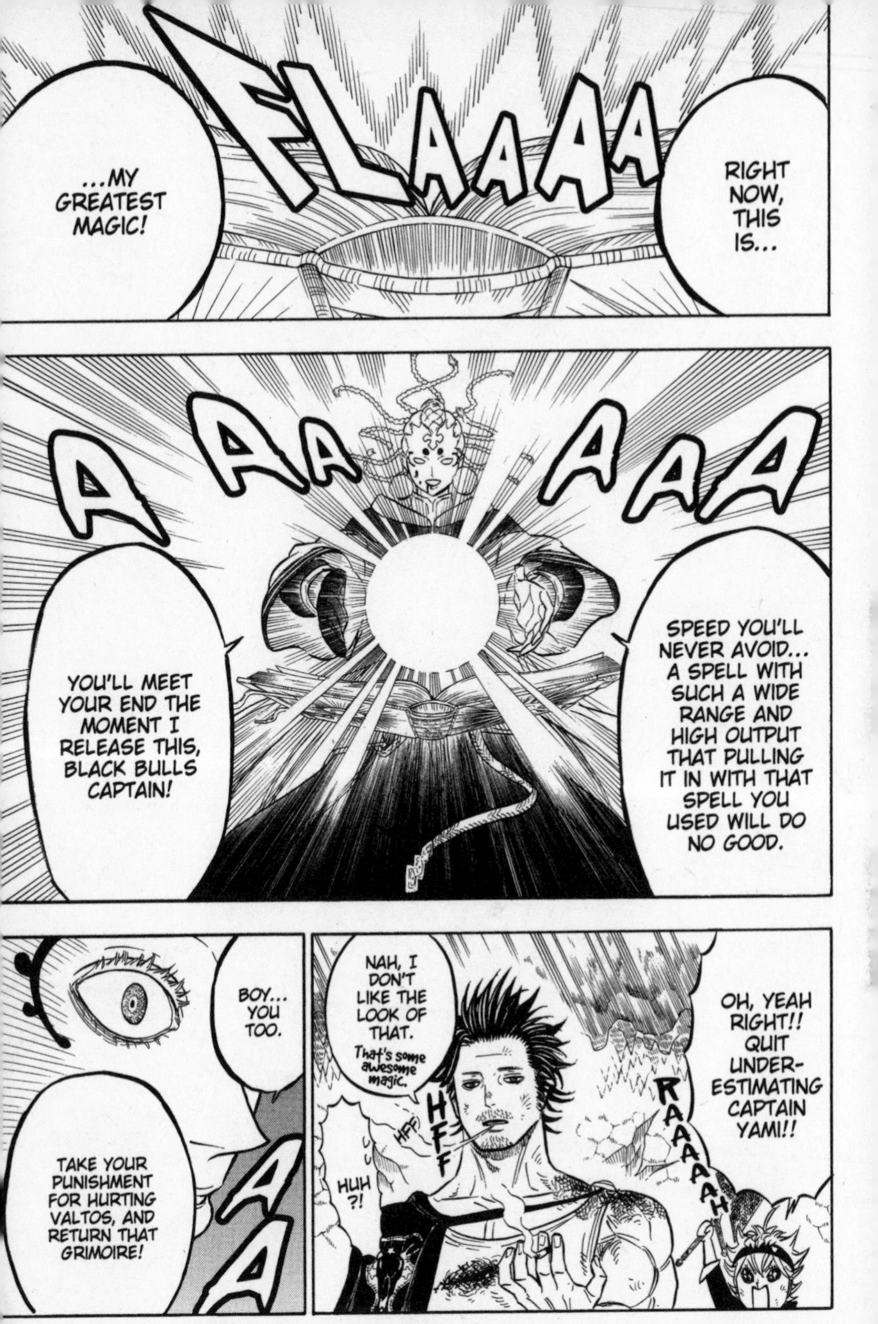
RIGHT NOW, THIS IS...
FLAAAA
...MY GREATEST MAGIC!
AAA AAA
SPEED YOU'LL NEVER AVOID... A SPELL WITH SUCH A WIDE RANGE AND HIGH OUTPUT THAT PULLING IT IN WITH THAT SPELL YOU USED WILL DO NO GOOD.
YOU'LL MEET YOUR END THE MOMENT I RELEASE THIS, BLACK BULLS CAPTAIN!
NAH, I DON'T LIKE THE LOOK OF THAT.
That's some awesome magic.
OH, YEAH RIGHT!! QUIT UNDER-ESTIMATING CAPTAIN YAMI!!
RAAAAAH
HFF HFF
HUH ?!
BOY... YOU TOO.
AA
TAKE YOUR PUNISHMENT FOR HURTING VALTOS, AND RETURN THAT GRIMOIRE!

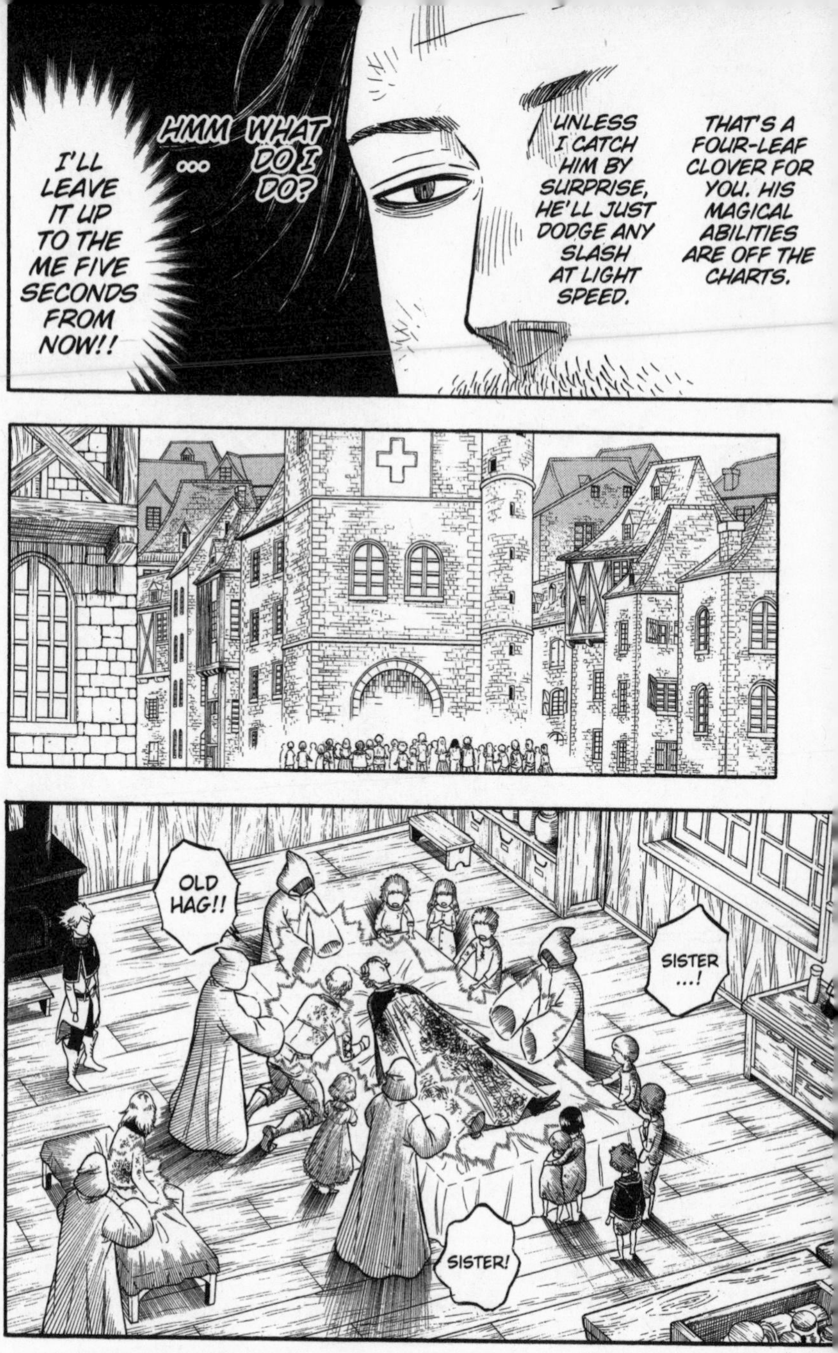
THAT'S A FOUR-LEAF CLOVER FOR YOU. HIS MAGICAL ABILITIES ARE OFF THE CHARTS.
UNLESS I CATCH HIM BY SURPRISE, HE'LL JUST DODGE ANY SLASH AT LIGHT SPEED.
WHAT DO I DO?
HMM...
I'LL LEAVE IT UP TO THE ME FIVE SECONDS FROM NOW!!
SISTER...!
OLD HAG!!
SISTER!

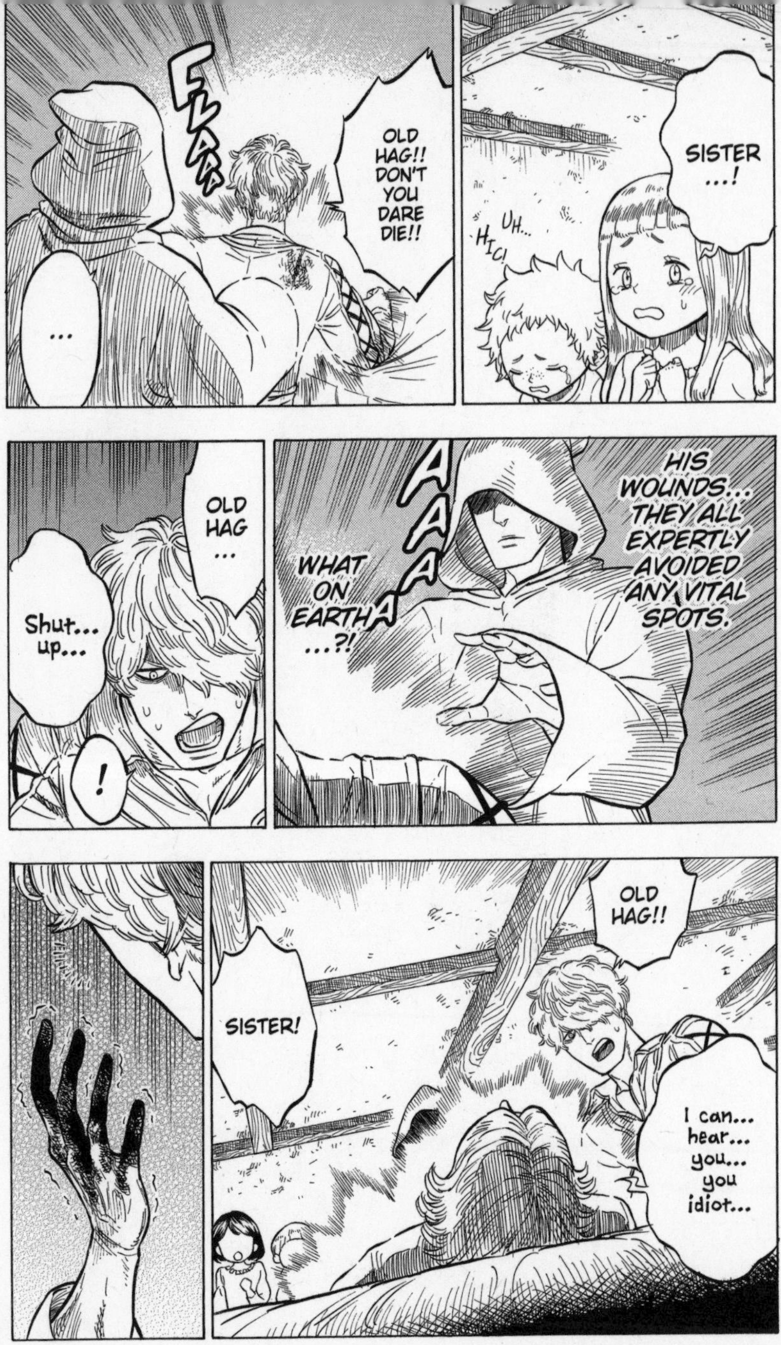
SISTER...!
UH... HIC!
OLD HAG!! DON'T YOU DARE DIE!!
FLAAA
...
HIS WOUNDS... THEY ALL EXPERTLY AVOIDED ANY VITAL SPOTS.
AAAA
WHAT ON EARTH...?!
OLD HAG...
Shut... up...
!
OLD HAG!!
SISTER!
I can... hear... you... you idiot...

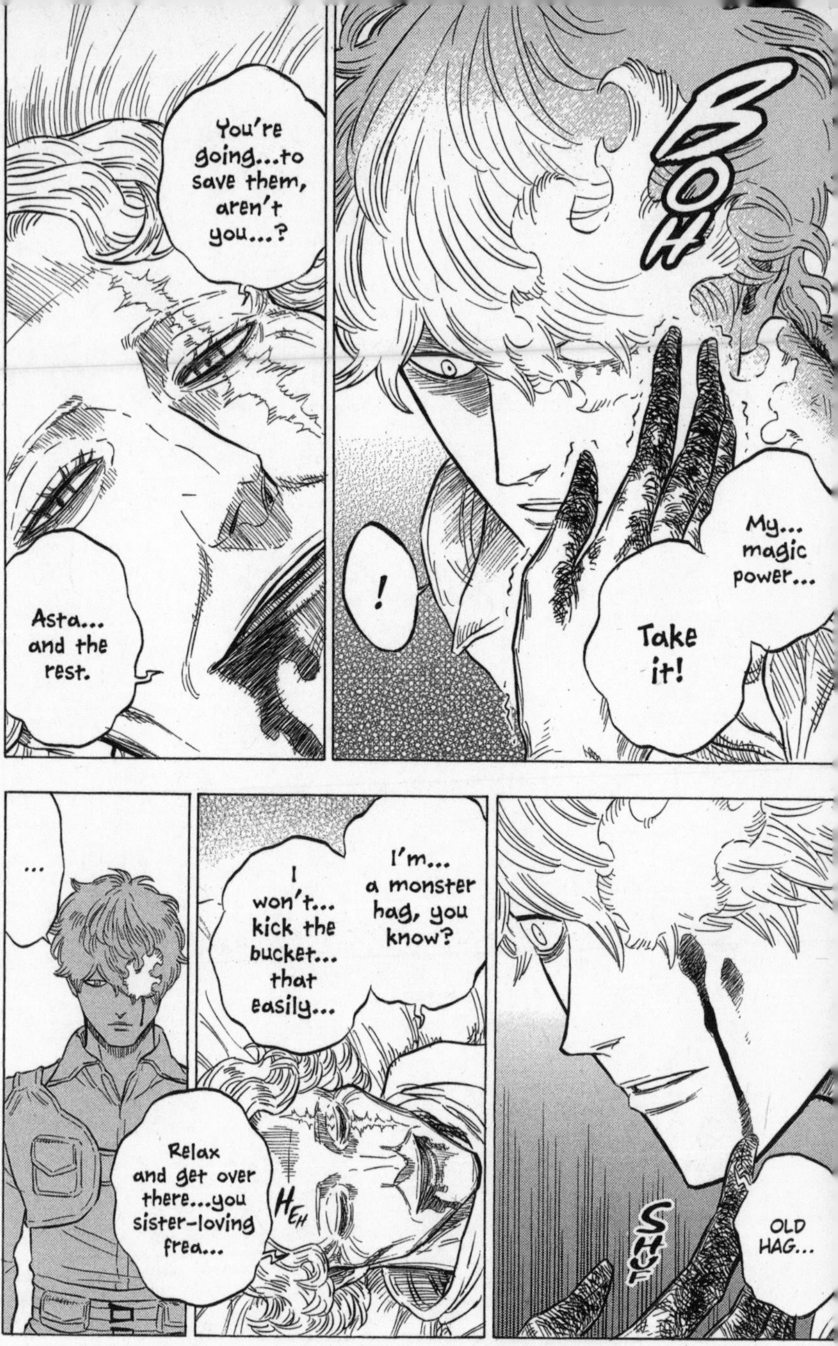
My... magic power...
Take it!
!
You're going...to save them, aren't you...?
Asta... and the rest.
OLD HAG...
I'm... a monster hag, you know?
I won't... kick the bucket... that easily...
HEH
Relax and get over there...you sister-loving frea...
...

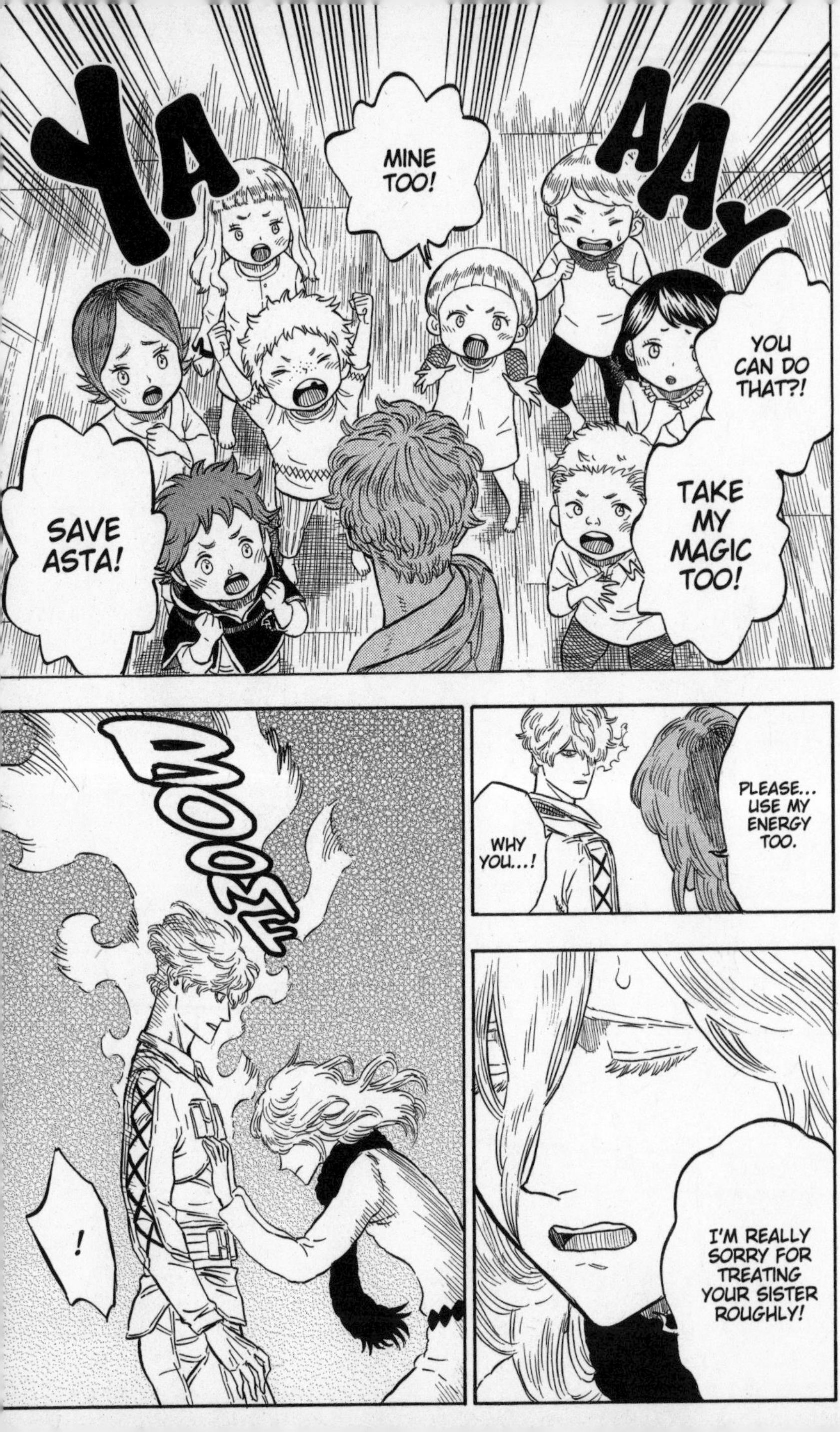
YAAAY
YOU CAN DO THAT?!
MINE TOO!
TAKE MY MAGIC TOO!
SAVE ASTA!
PLEASE... USE MY ENERGY TOO.
WHY YOU...!
I'M REALLY SORRY FOR TREATING YOUR SISTER ROUGHLY!
WOOSH
!

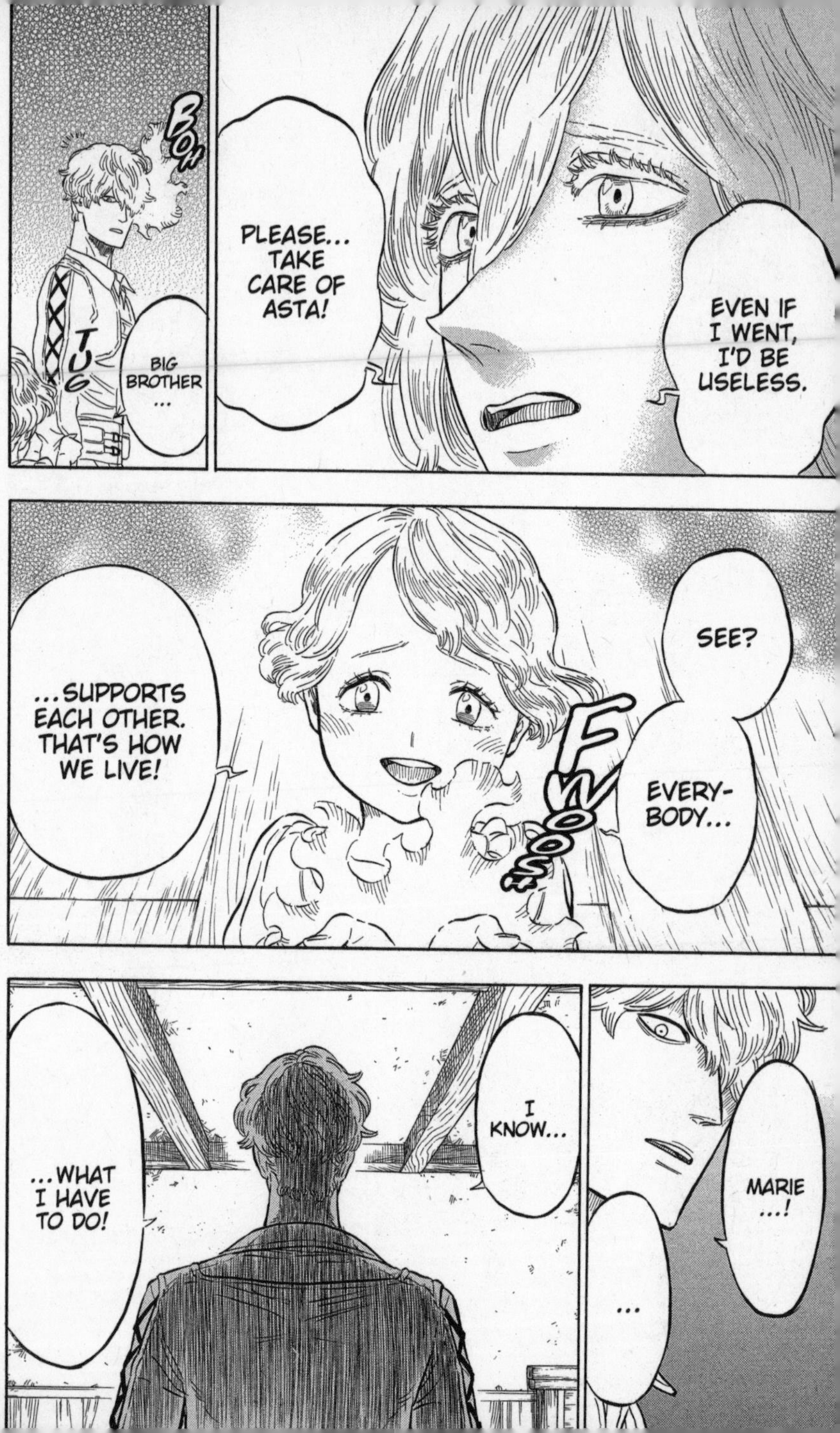
EVEN IF I WENT, I'D BE USELESS.
PLEASE... TAKE CARE OF ASTA!
BOH
TUG
BIG BROTHER...
SEE?
EVERY-BODY...
FWOOSH
...SUPPORTS EACH OTHER. THAT'S HOW WE LIVE!
MARIE...!
...
I KNOW...
...WHAT I HAVE TO DO!

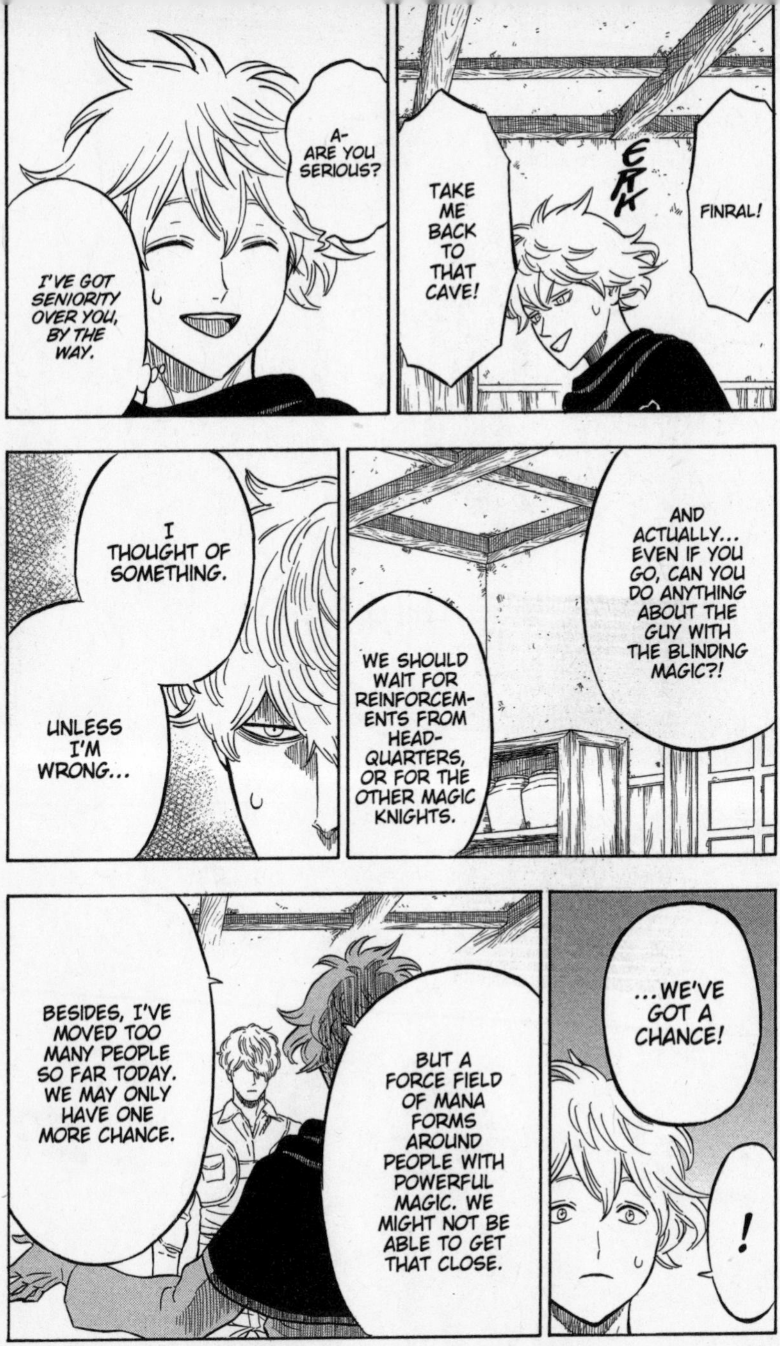
FINRAL!
ERK
TAKE ME BACK TO THAT CAVE!
A- ARE YOU SERIOUS?
I'VE GOT SENIORITY OVER YOU, BY THE WAY.
AND ACTUALLY... EVEN IF YOU GO, CAN YOU DO ANYTHING ABOUT THE GUY WITH THE BLINDING MAGIC?!
WE SHOULD WAIT FOR REINFORCEMENTS FROM HEADQUARTERS, OR FOR THE OTHER MAGIC KNIGHTS.
I THOUGHT OF SOMETHING.
UNLESS I'M WRONG...
...WE'VE GOT A CHANCE!
!
BUT A FORCE FIELD OF MANA FORMS AROUND PEOPLE WITH POWERFUL MAGIC. WE MIGHT NOT BE ABLE TO GET THAT CLOSE.
BESIDES, I'VE MOVED TOO MANY PEOPLE SO FAR TODAY. WE MAY ONLY HAVE ONE MORE CHANCE.

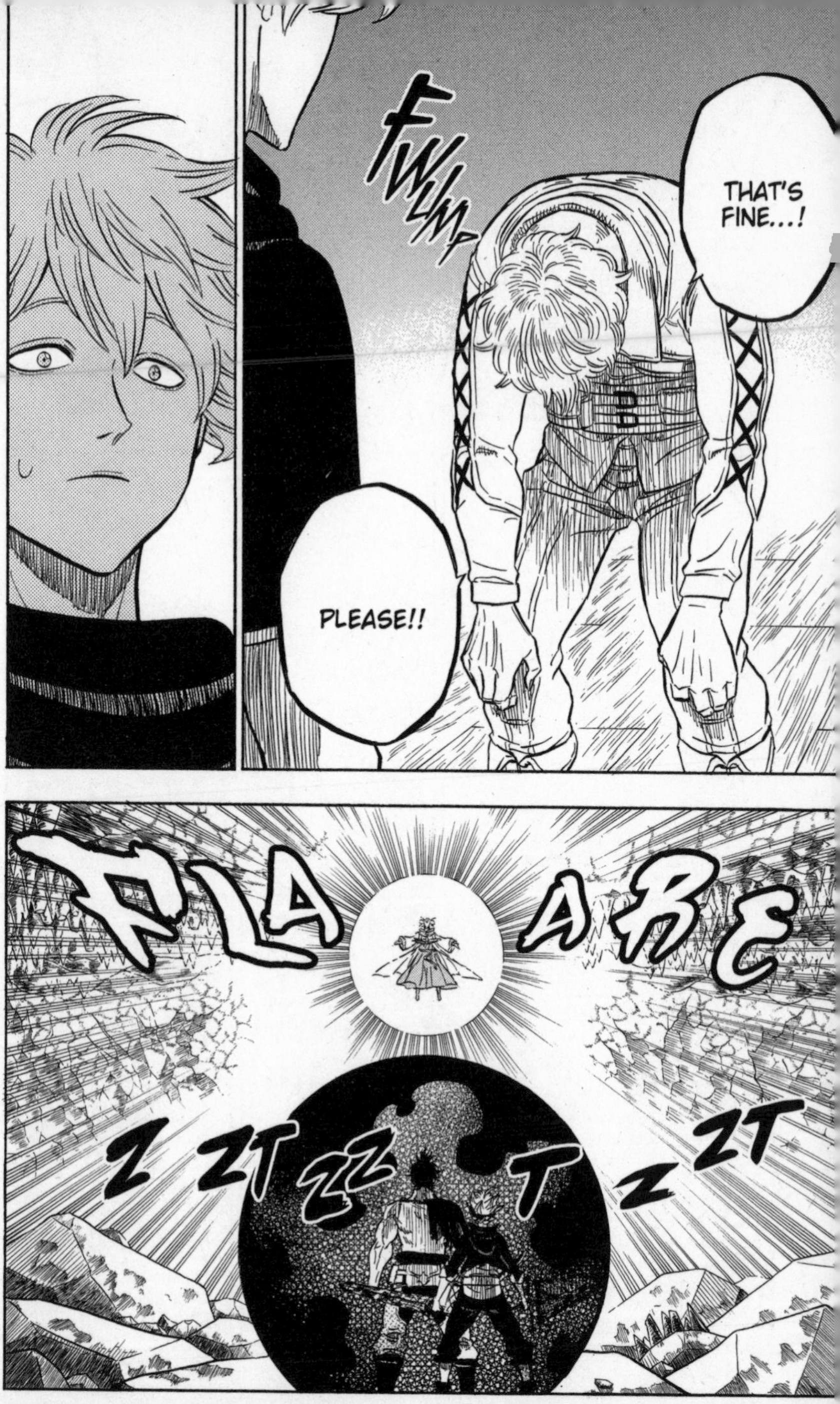
THAT'S FINE...!
FWUMP
PLEASE!!
FLA ARE
Z ZT ZZ T Z ZT

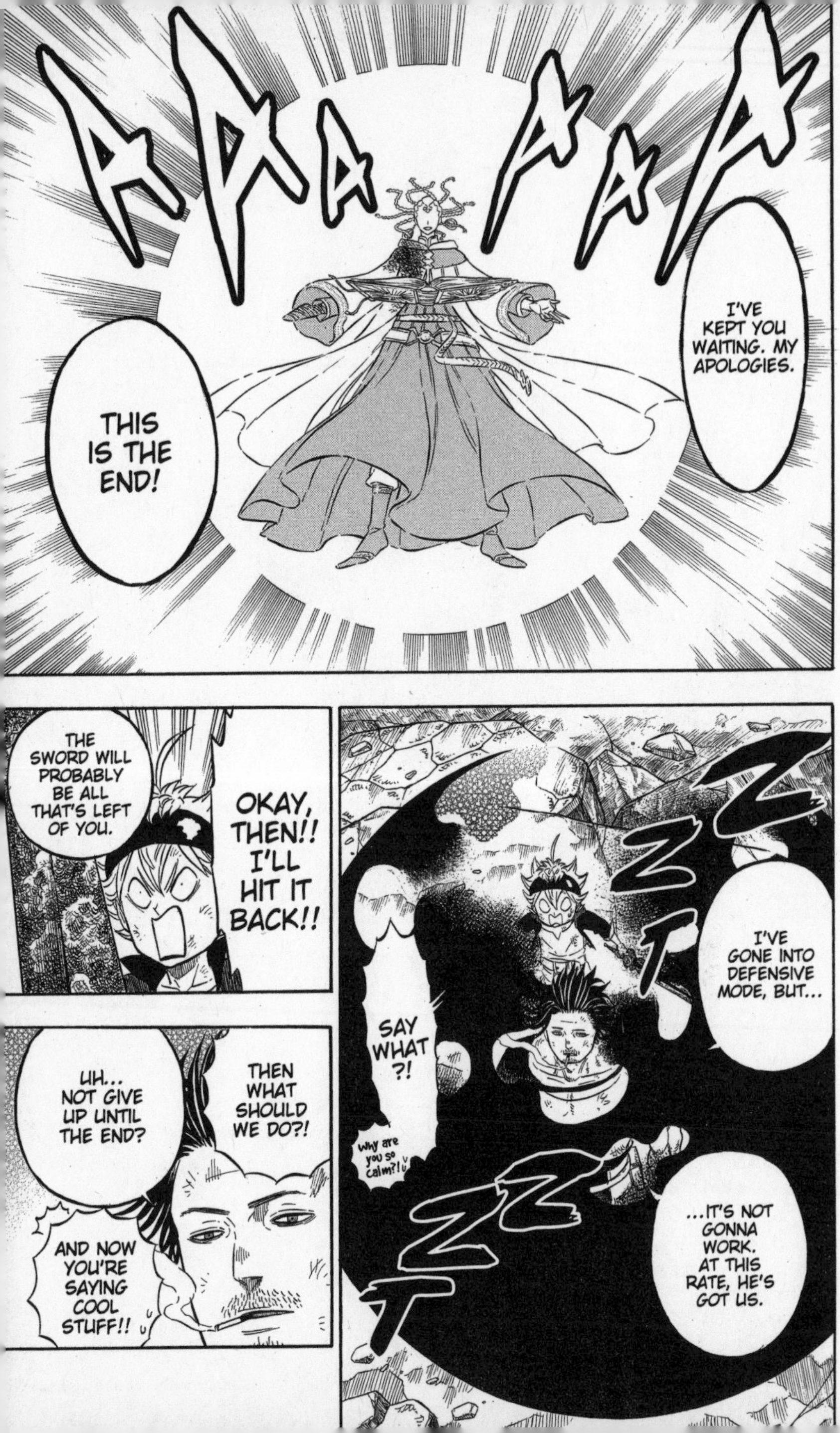
I'VE KEPT YOU WAITING. MY APOLOGIES.
THIS IS THE END!
I'VE GONE INTO DEFENSIVE MODE, BUT...
SAY WHAT?!
Why are you so calm?!
...IT'S NOT GONNA WORK. AT THIS RATE, HE'S GOT US.
OKAY, THEN!! I'LL HIT IT BACK!!
THE SWORD WILL PROBABLY BE ALL THAT'S LEFT OF YOU.
THEN WHAT SHOULD WE DO?!
UH... NOT GIVE UP UNTIL THE END?
AND NOW YOU'RE SAYING COOL STUFF!!

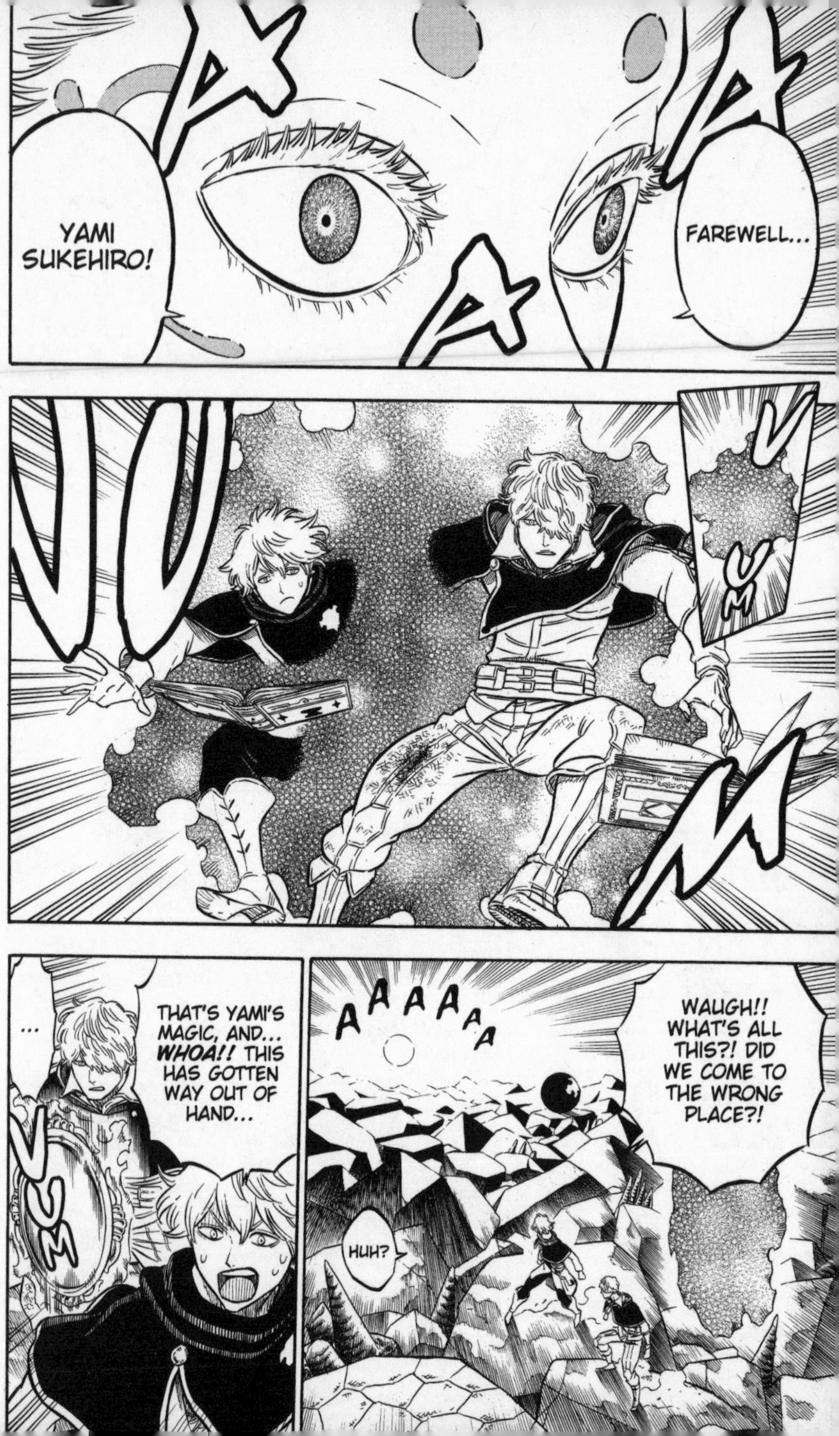
FAREWELL...
YAMI SUKEHIRO!
VVUM
WAUGH!! WHAT'S ALL THIS?! DID WE COME TO THE WRONG PLACE?!
AAAAAAA
HUH?
THAT'S YAMI'S MAGIC, AND... **WHOA!!** THIS HAS GOTTEN WAY OUT OF HAND...
...
VVUM

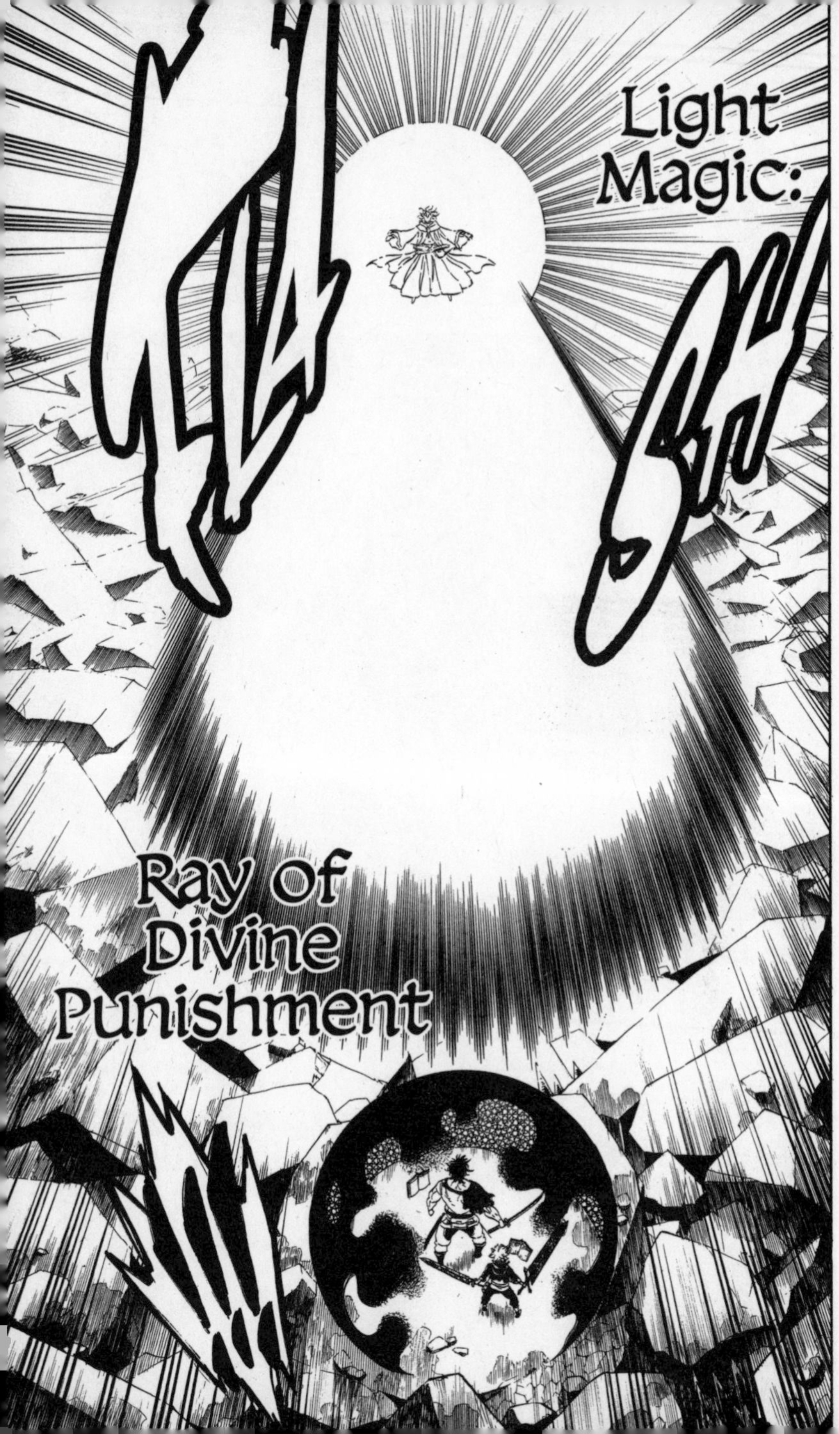
Light Magic:
Ray Of Divine Punishment

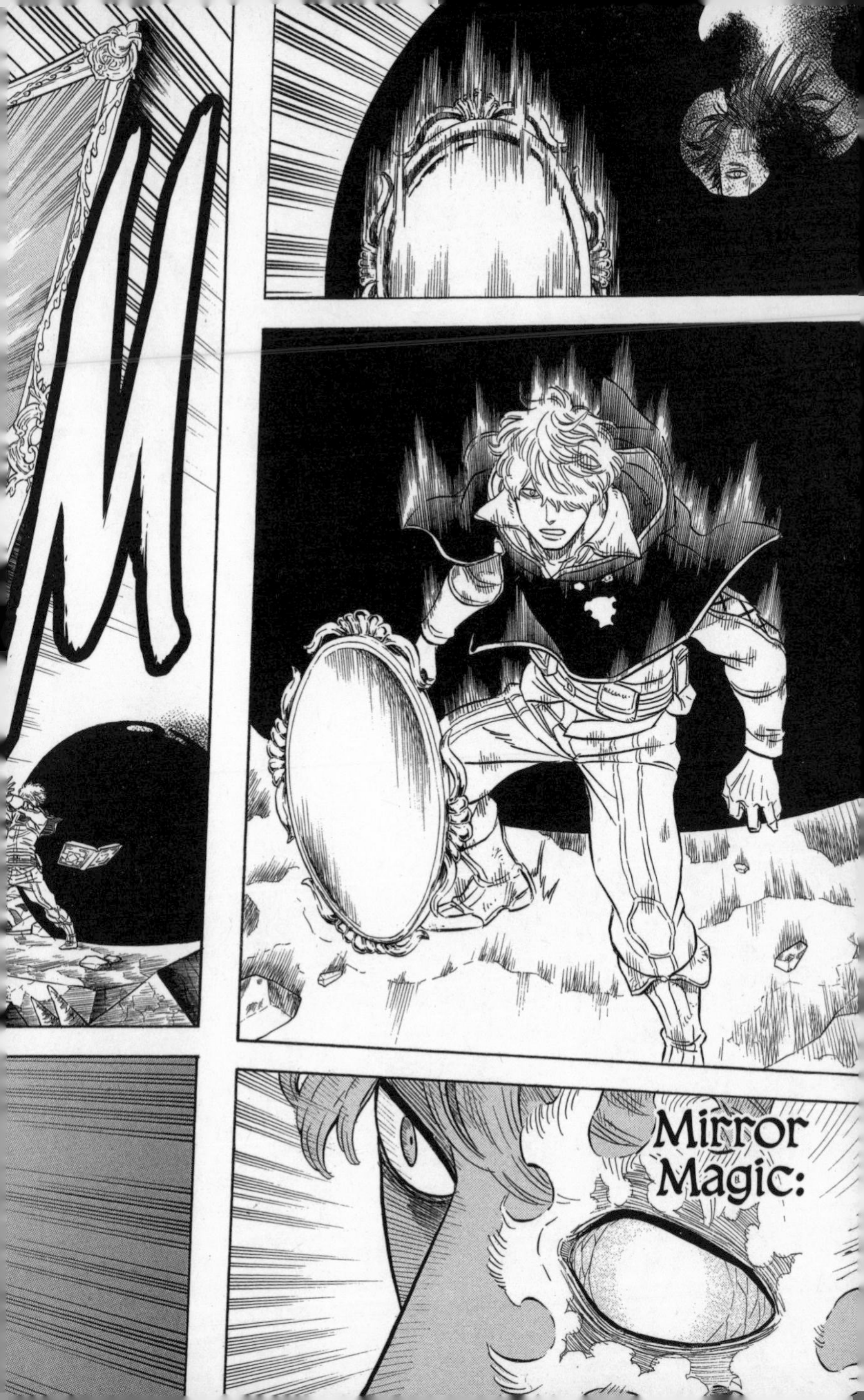
Mirror Magic:

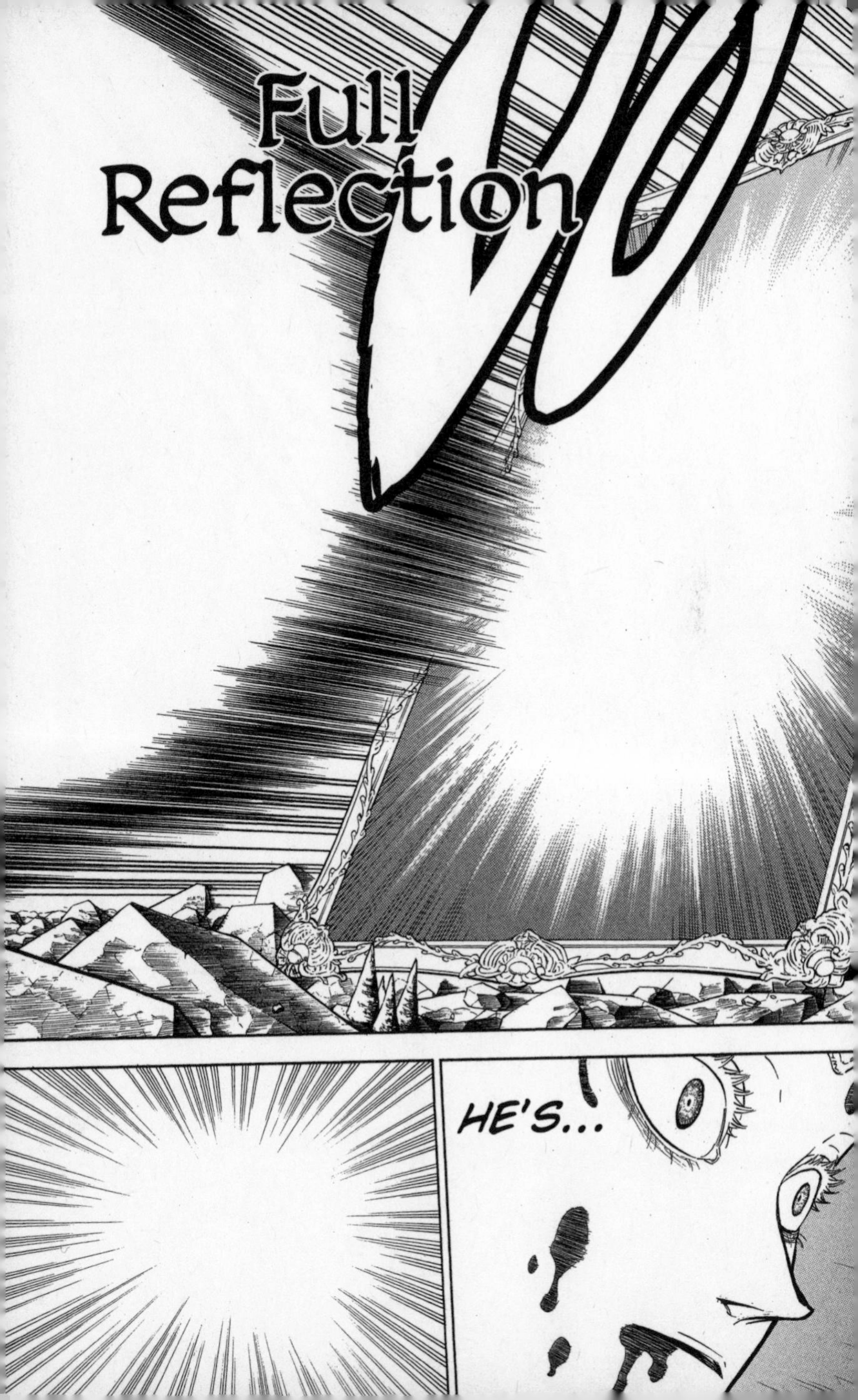
Full Reflection
HE'S...

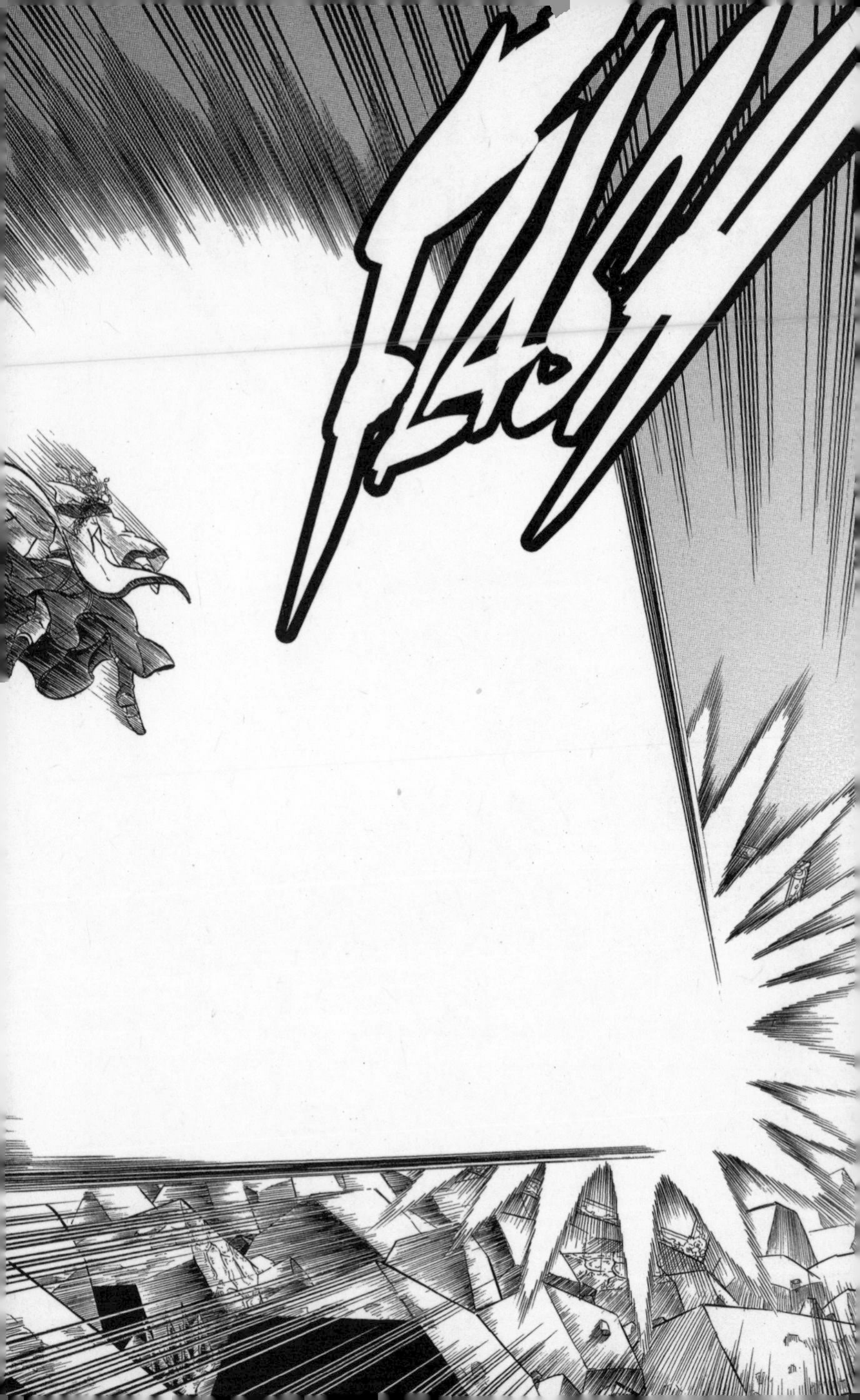

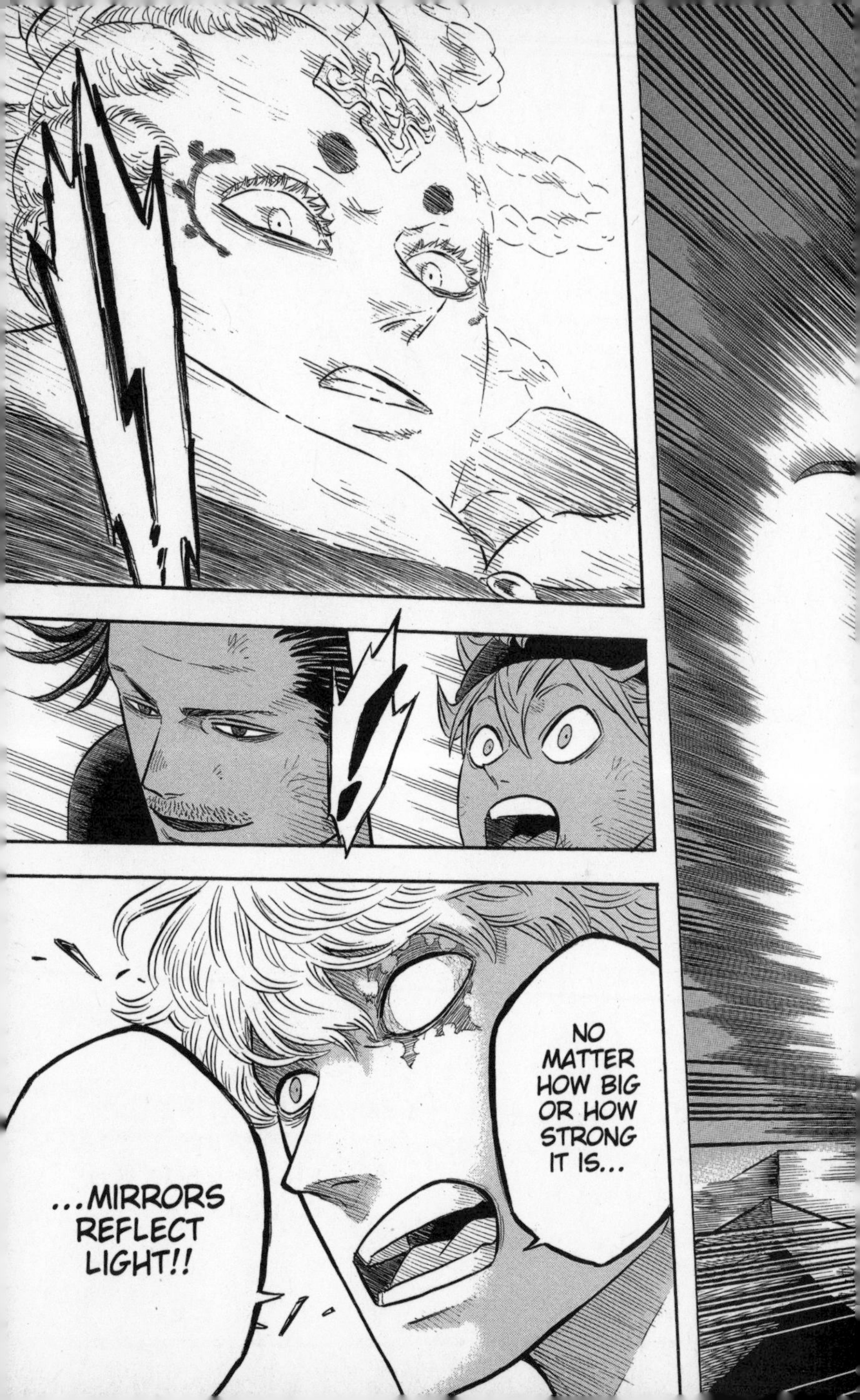
NO MATTER HOW BIG OR HOW STRONG IT IS...
...MIRRORS REFLECT LIGHT!!

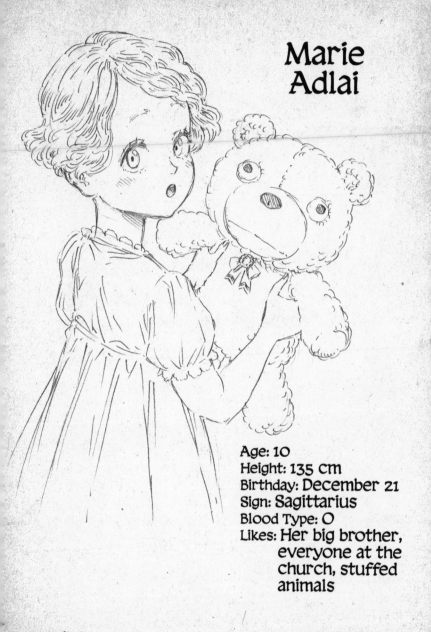

Marie Adlai

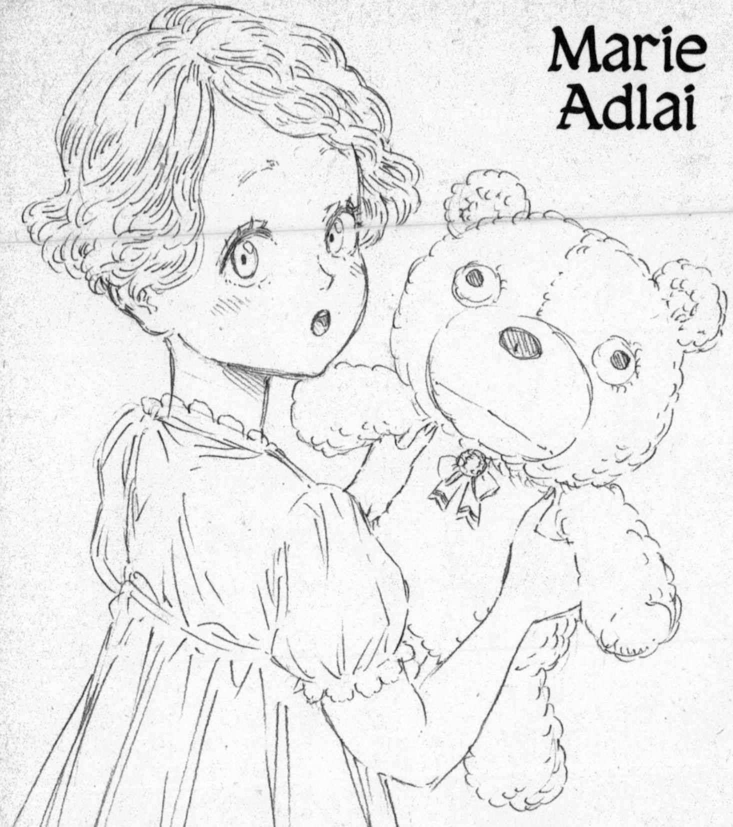

Age: 10
Height: 135 cm
Birthday: December 21
Sign: Sagittarius
Blood Type: O
Likes: Her big brother, everyone at the church, stuffed animals

Character Profile

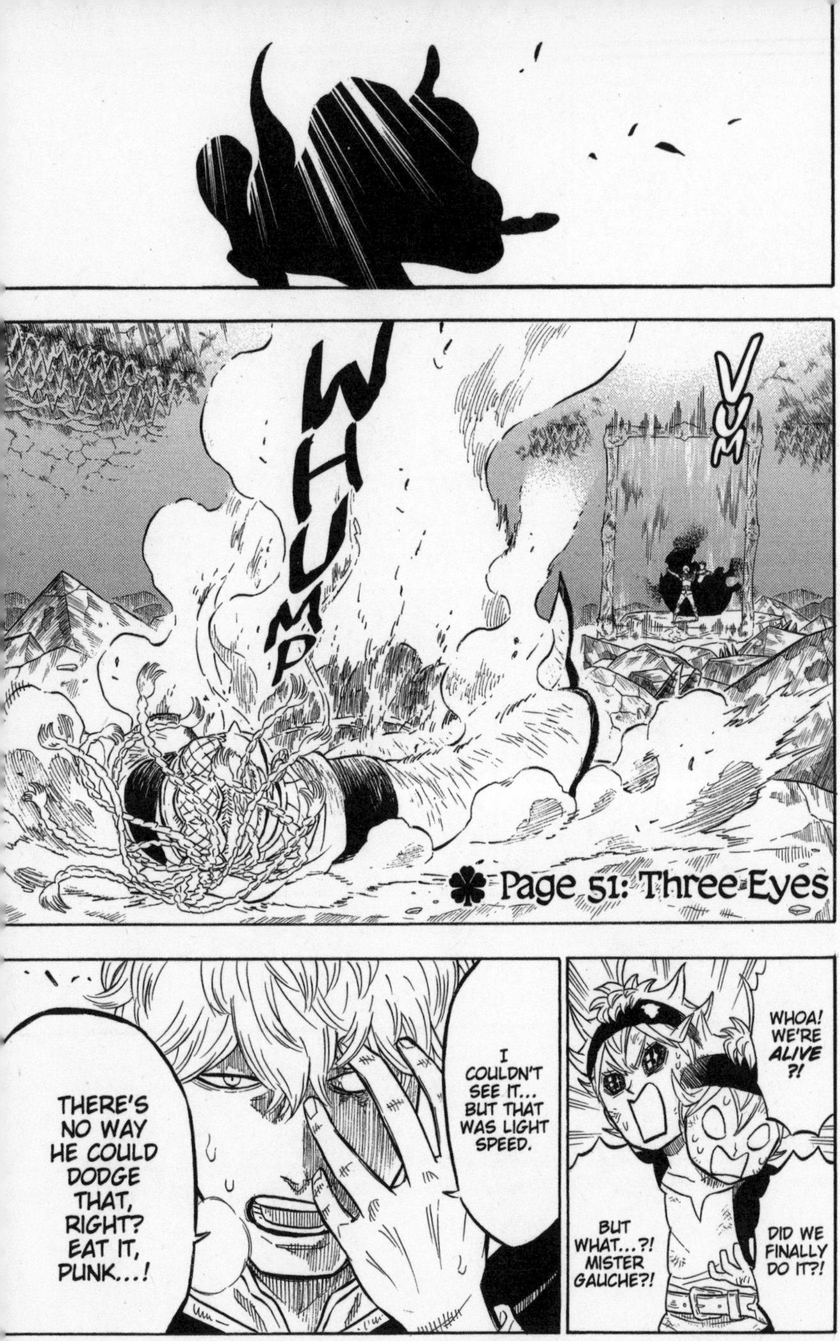

VUM
WHUMP
Page 51: Three Eyes
WHOA! WE'RE ALIVE?!
DID WE FINALLY DO IT?!
BUT WHAT...?! MISTER GAUCHE?!
I COULDN'T SEE IT... BUT THAT WAS LIGHT SPEED.
THERE'S NO WAY HE COULD DODGE THAT, RIGHT? EAT IT, PUNK...!

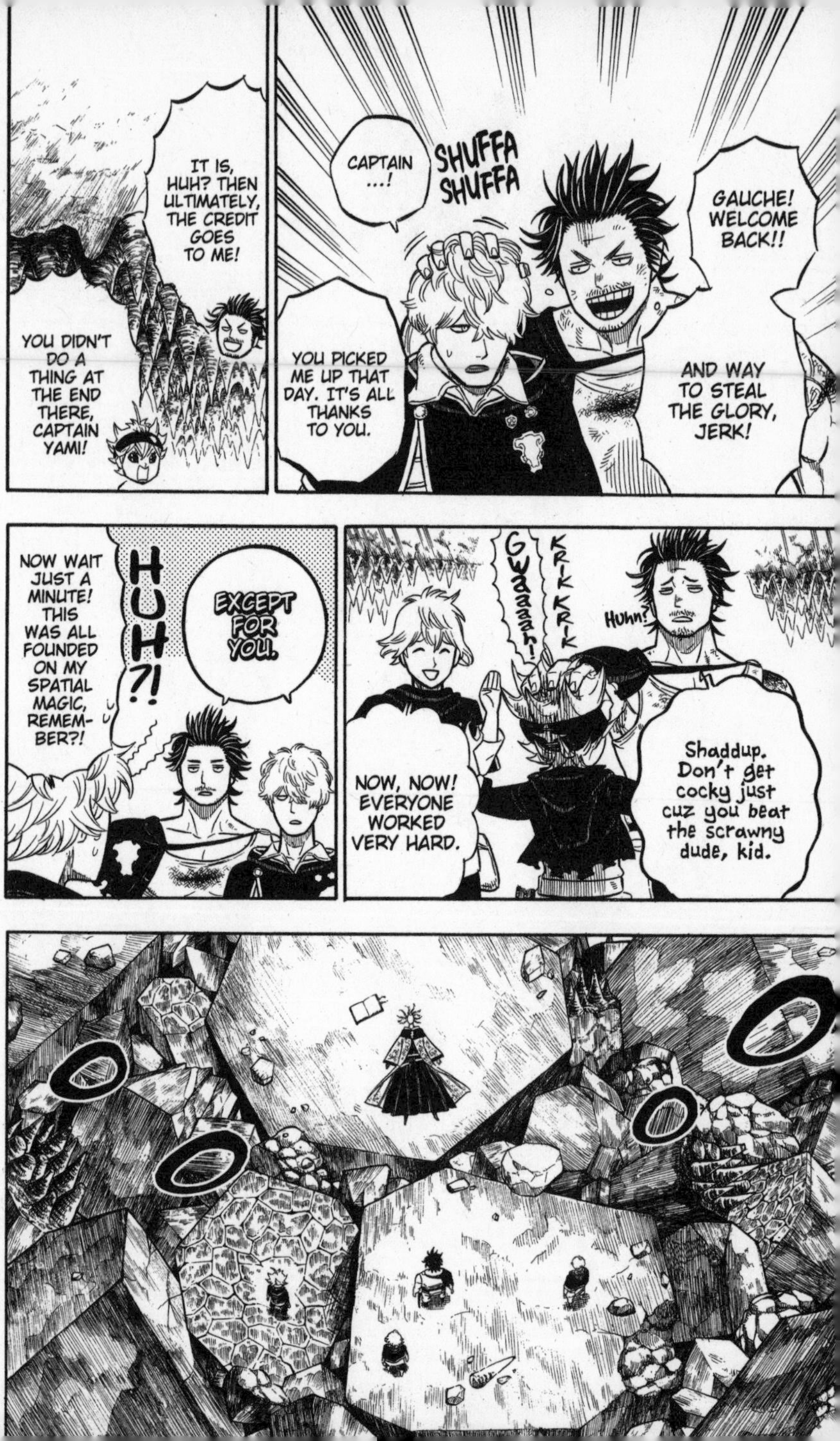
GAUCHE! WELCOME BACK!!
SHUFFA SHUFFA
CAPTAIN ...!
AND WAY TO STEAL THE GLORY, JERK!
YOU PICKED ME UP THAT DAY. IT'S ALL THANKS TO YOU.
IT IS, HUH? THEN ULTIMATELY, THE CREDIT GOES TO ME!
YOU DIDN'T DO A THING AT THE END THERE, CAPTAIN YAMI!
Huhn?
KRIK KRIK
Gwaaaah!
Shaddup. Don't get cocky just cuz you beat the scrawny dude, kid.
NOW, NOW! EVERYONE WORKED VERY HARD.
EXCEPT FOR YOU.
HUH?!
NOW WAIT JUST A MINUTE! THIS WAS ALL FOUNDED ON MY SPATIAL MAGIC, REMEMBER?!

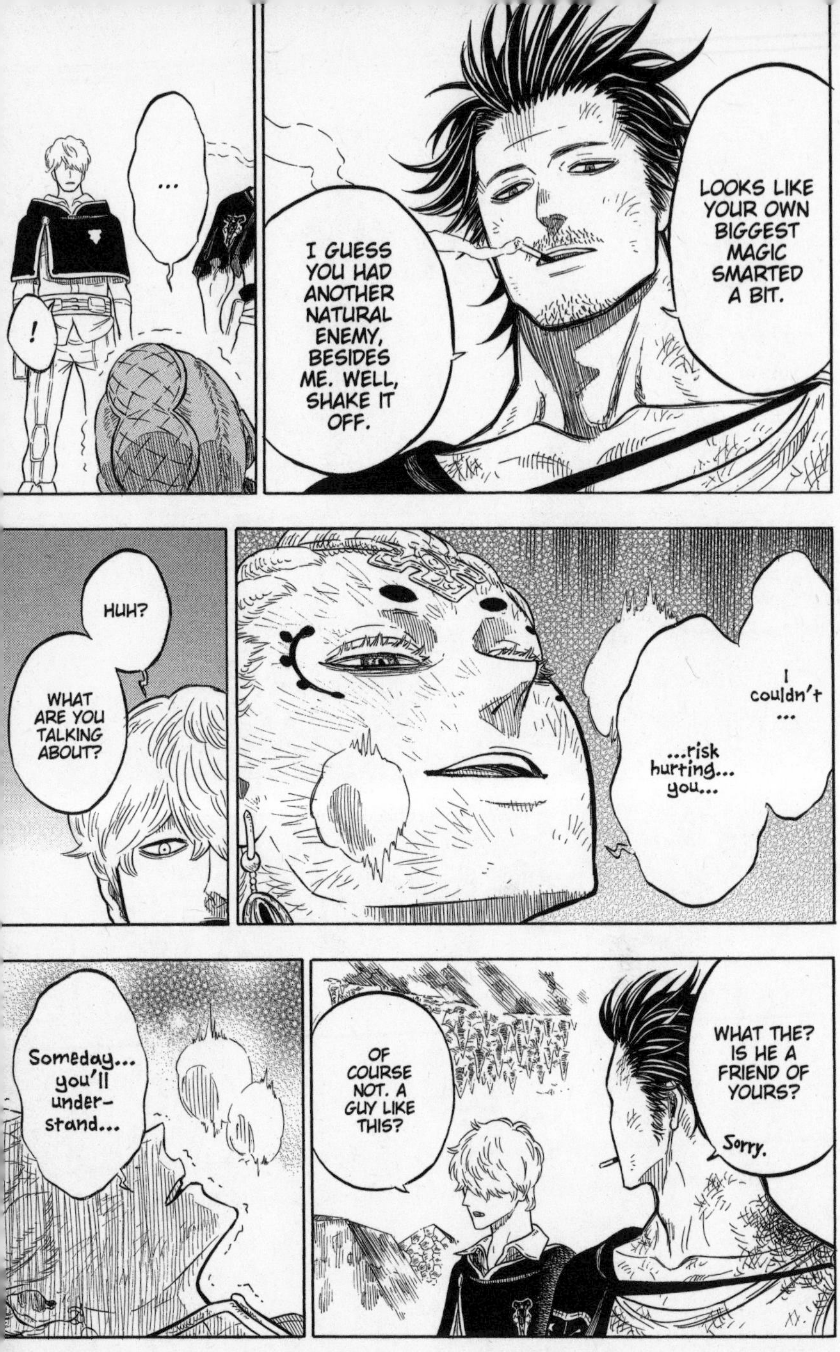
LOOKS LIKE YOUR OWN BIGGEST MAGIC SMARTED A BIT.
I GUESS YOU HAD ANOTHER NATURAL ENEMY, BESIDES ME. WELL, SHAKE IT OFF.
...
!
I couldn't...
...risk hurting... you...
HUH?
WHAT ARE YOU TALKING ABOUT?
WHAT THE? IS HE A FRIEND OF YOURS?
Sorry.
OF COURSE NOT. A GUY LIKE THIS?
Someday... you'll under-stand...

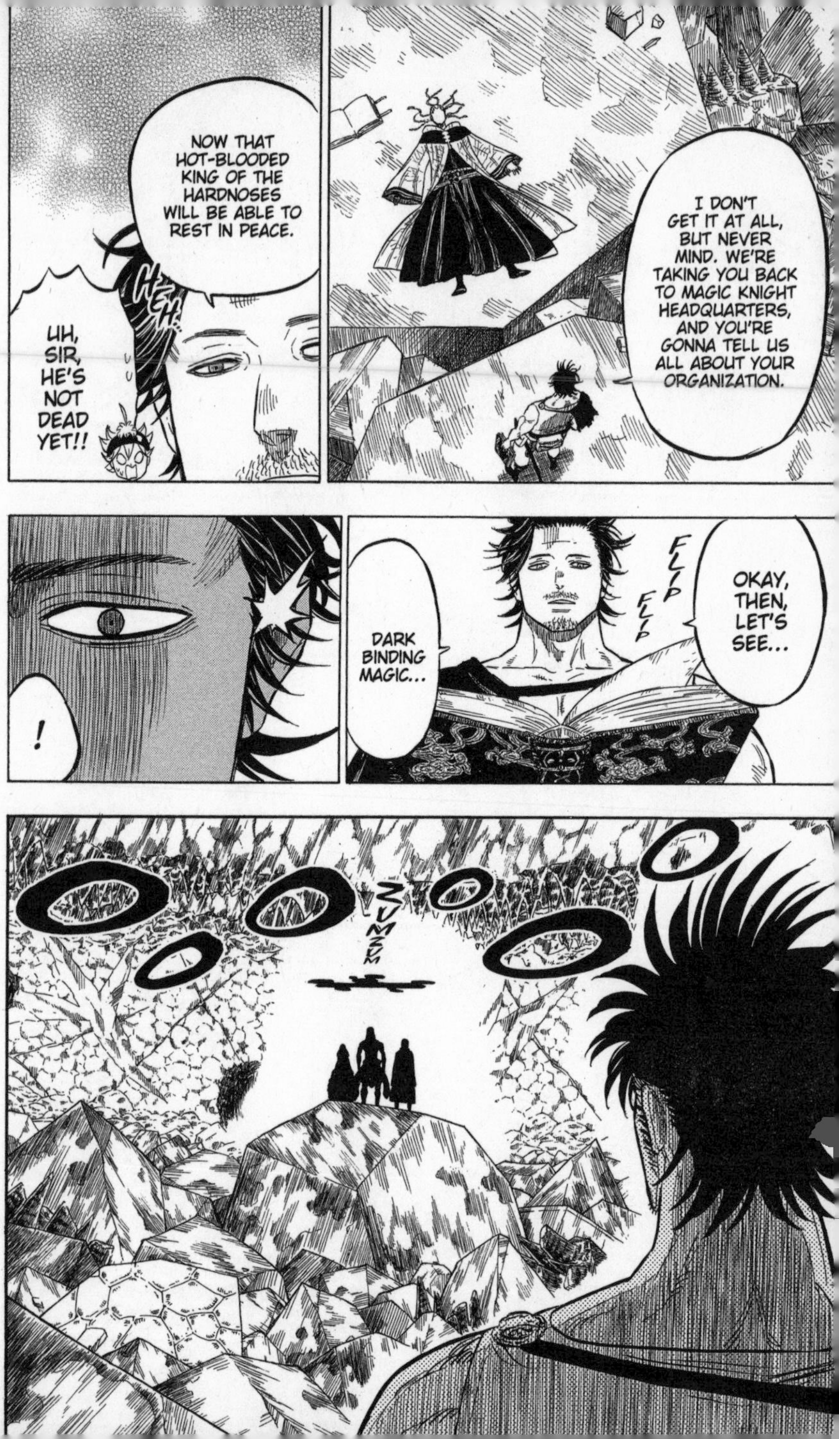
I DON'T GET IT AT ALL, BUT NEVER MIND. WE'RE TAKING YOU BACK TO MAGIC KNIGHT HEADQUARTERS, AND YOU'RE GONNA TELL US ALL ABOUT YOUR ORGANIZATION.
NOW THAT HOT-BLOODED KING OF THE HARDNOSES WILL BE ABLE TO REST IN PEACE.
CHEH
UH, SIR, HE'S NOT DEAD YET!!
OKAY, THEN, LET'S SEE...
FLIP FLIP
DARK BINDING MAGIC...
!
ZUMZUM

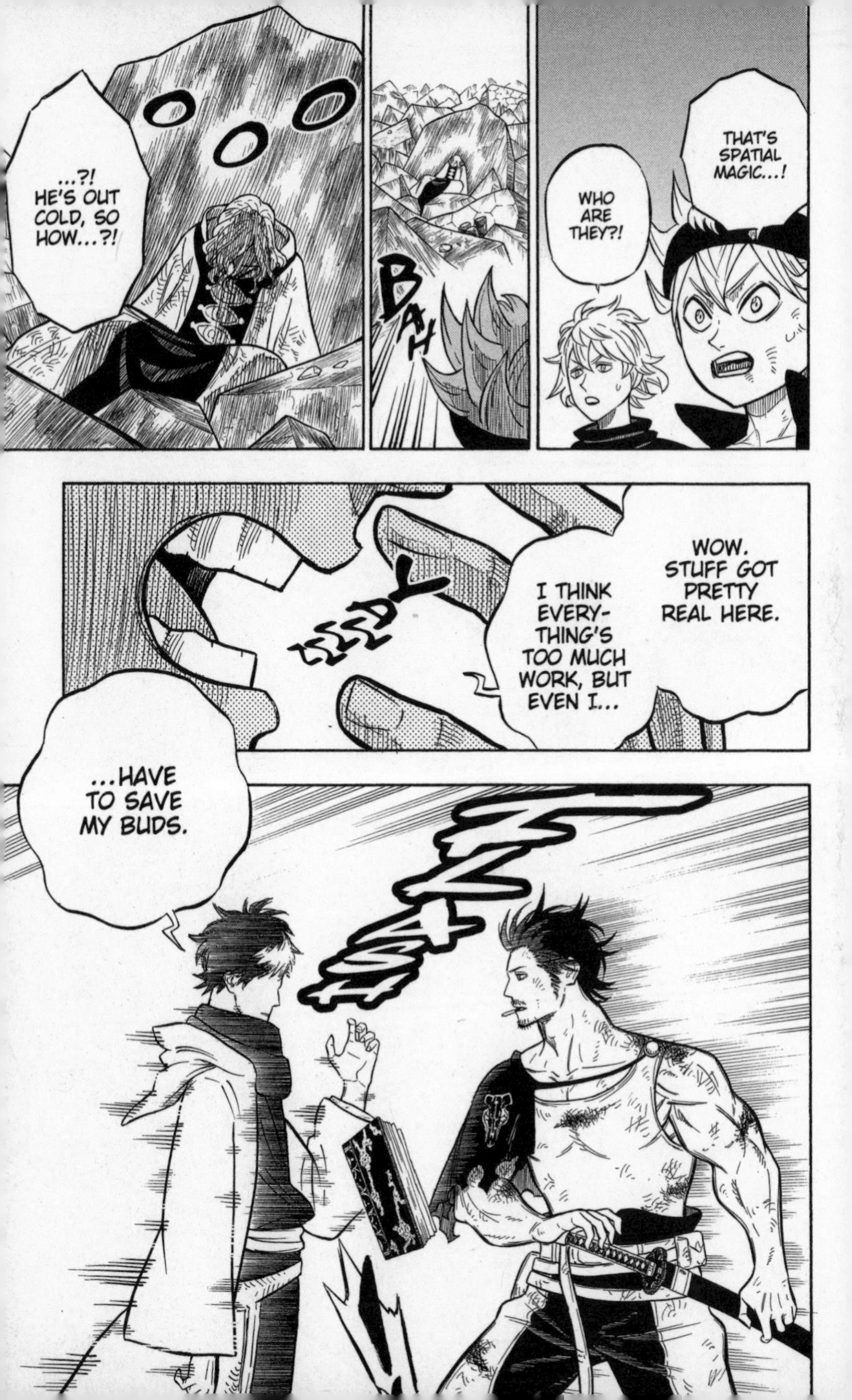

THAT'S SPATIAL MAGIC...!
WHO ARE THEY?!
BAH
...?! HE'S OUT COLD, SO HOW...?!
WOW. STUFF GOT PRETTY REAL HERE.
I THINK EVERY-THING'S TOO MUCH WORK, BUT EVEN I...
...HAVE TO SAVE MY BUDS.

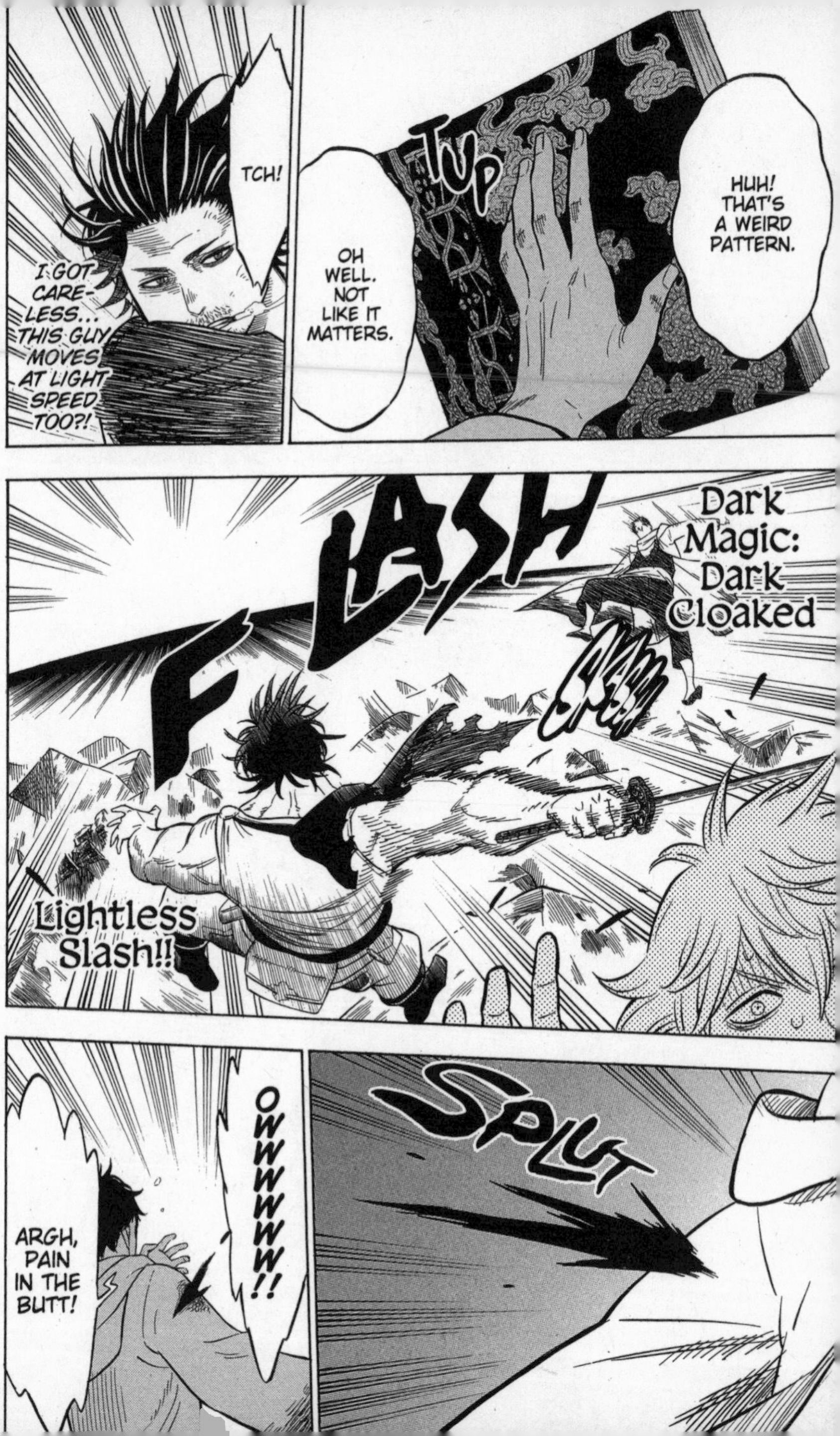
HUH! THAT'S A WEIRD PATTERN.
TUP
OH WELL. NOT LIKE IT MATTERS.
TCH!
I GOT CARELESS... THIS GUY MOVES AT LIGHT SPEED TOO?!
FLASH
Dark Magic: Dark Cloaked
Lightless Slash!!
SPLUT
OWWWWWWW!!
ARGH, PAIN IN THE BUTT!

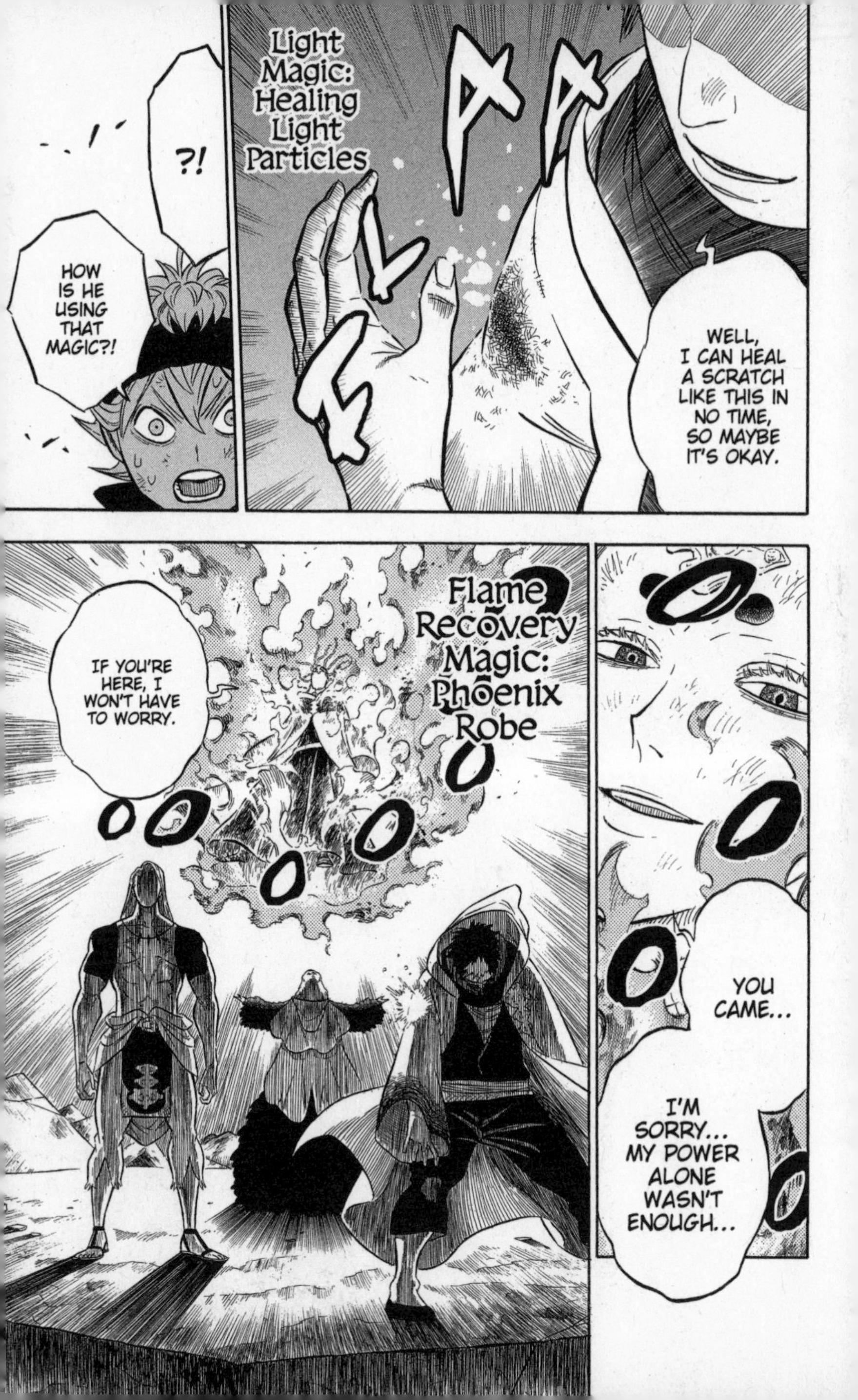
Light Magic: Healing Light Particles
WELL, I CAN HEAL A SCRATCH LIKE THIS IN NO TIME, SO MAYBE IT'S OKAY.
?!
HOW IS HE USING THAT MAGIC?!
YOU CAME...
I'M SORRY... MY POWER ALONE WASN'T ENOUGH...
Flame Recovery Magic: Phoenix Robe
IF YOU'RE HERE, I WON'T HAVE TO WORRY.

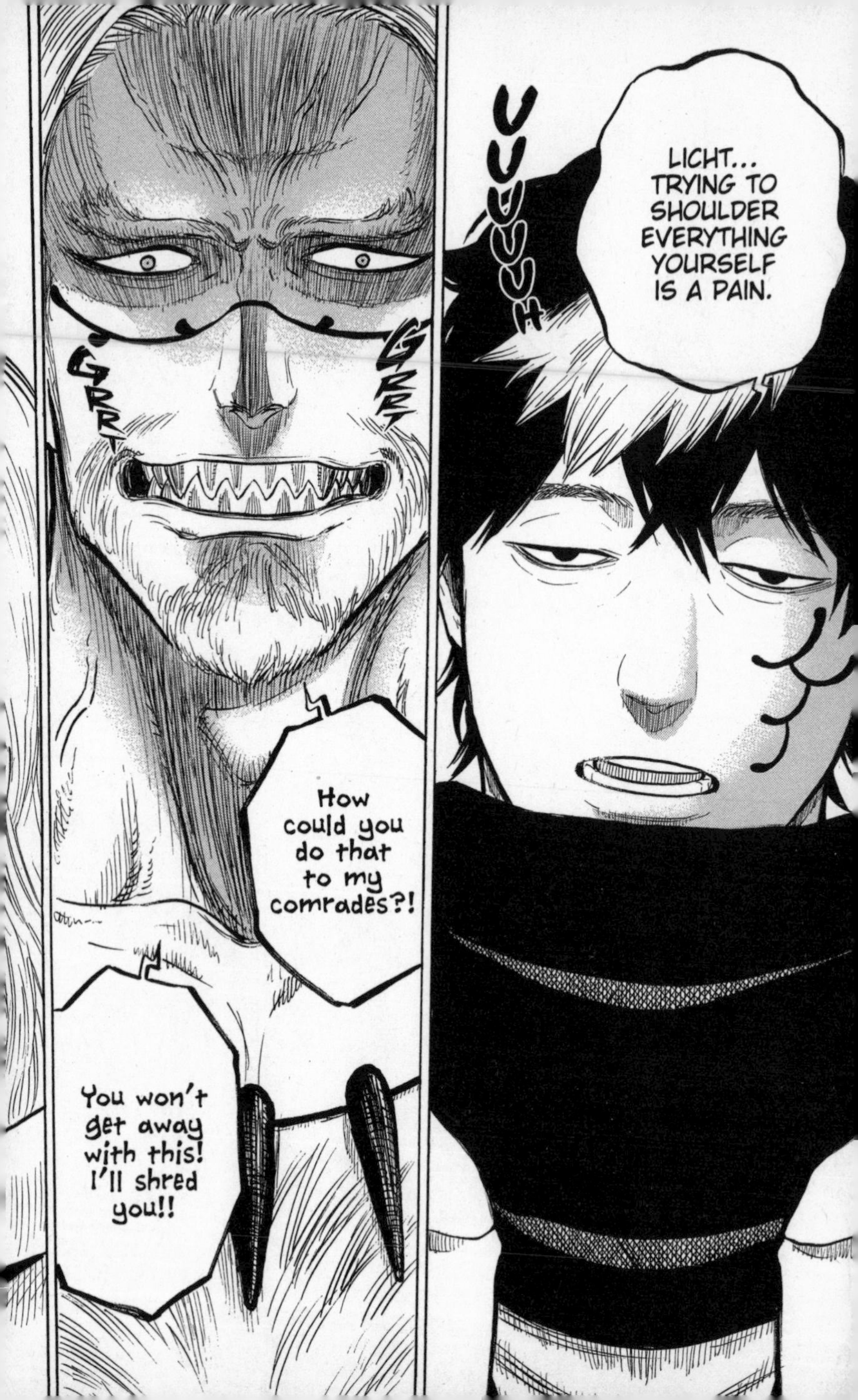
UUUUUH
LICHT... TRYING TO SHOULDER EVERYTHING YOURSELF IS A PAIN.
GRR
GRR
How could you do that to my comrades?!
You won't get away with this! I'll shred you!!

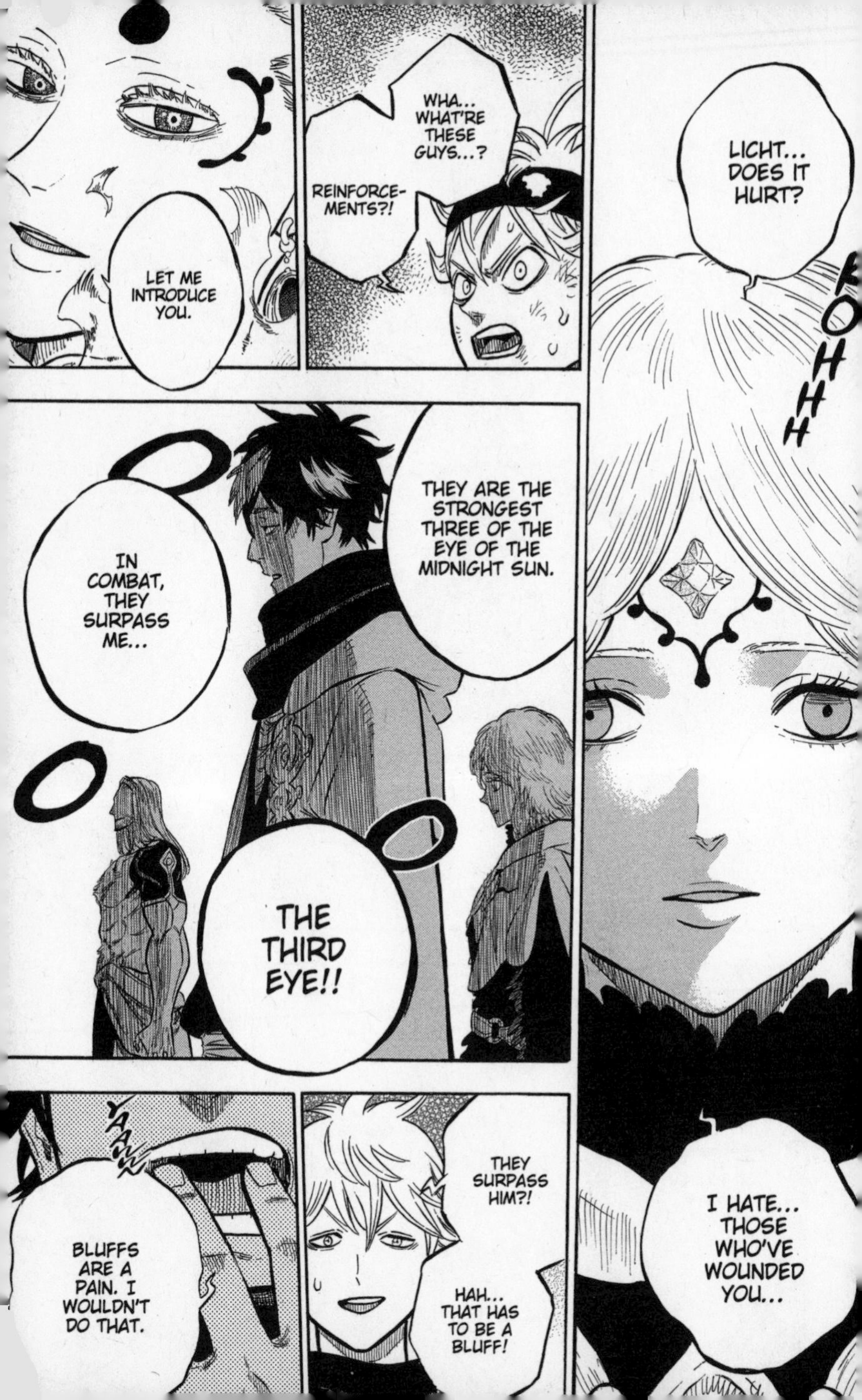
LICHT... DOES IT HURT?
KOHHHH
I HATE... THOSE WHO'VE WOUNDED YOU...
WHA... WHAT'RE THESE GUYS...?
REINFORCE-MENTS?!
LET ME INTRODUCE YOU.
THEY ARE THE STRONGEST THREE OF THE EYE OF THE MIDNIGHT SUN.
IN COMBAT, THEY SURPASS ME...
THE THIRD EYE!!
THEY SURPASS HIM?!
HAH... THAT HAS TO BE A BLUFF!
YAAAWN
BLUFFS ARE A PAIN. I WOULDN'T DO THAT.

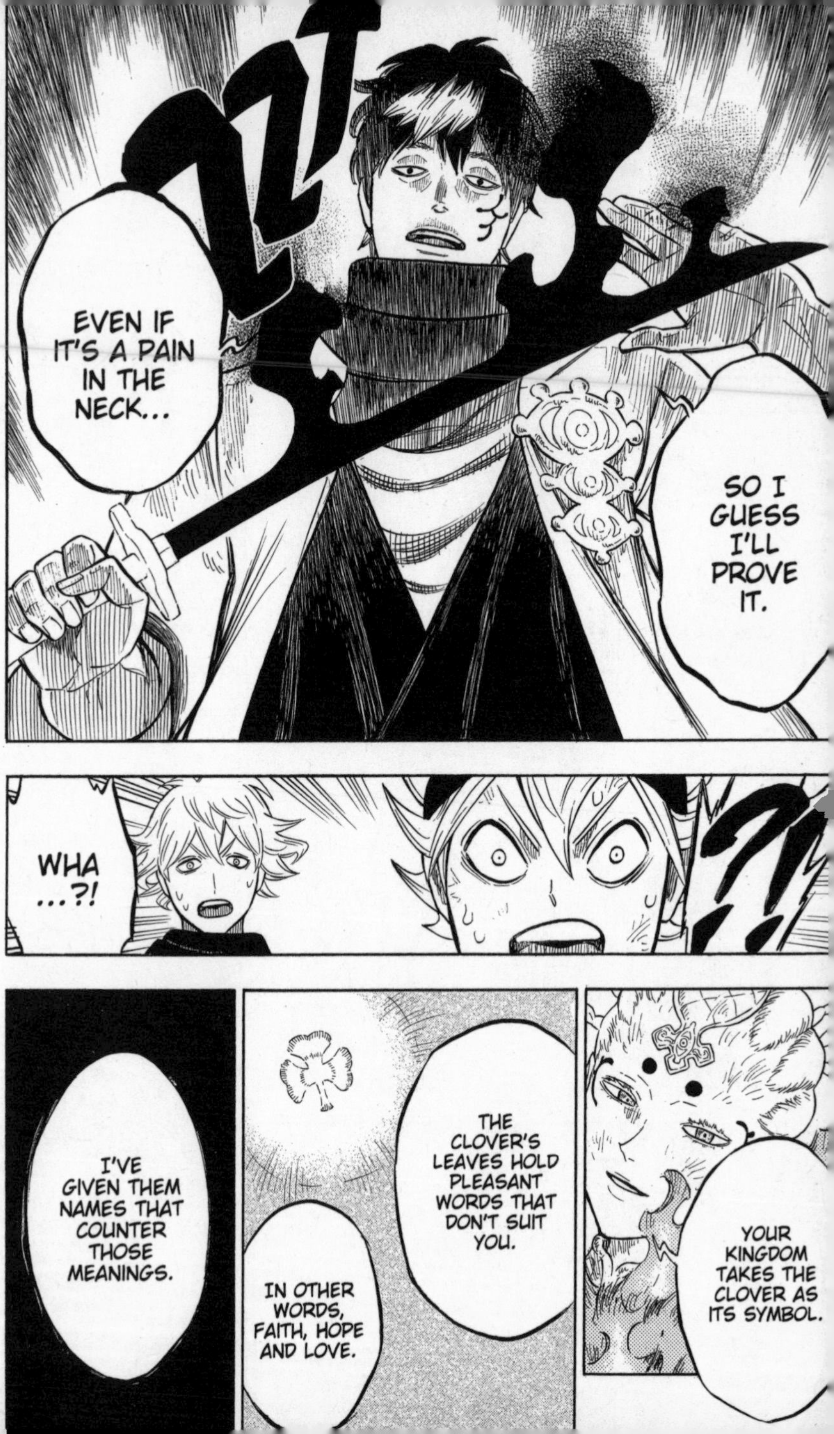
ZZT
EVEN IF IT'S A PAIN IN THE NECK...
SO I GUESS I'LL PROVE IT.
WHA ...?!
YOUR KINGDOM TAKES THE CLOVER AS ITS SYMBOL.
THE CLOVER'S LEAVES HOLD PLEASANT WORDS THAT DON'T SUIT YOU.
IN OTHER WORDS, FAITH, HOPE AND LOVE.
I'VE GIVEN THEM NAMES THAT COUNTER THOSE MEANINGS.

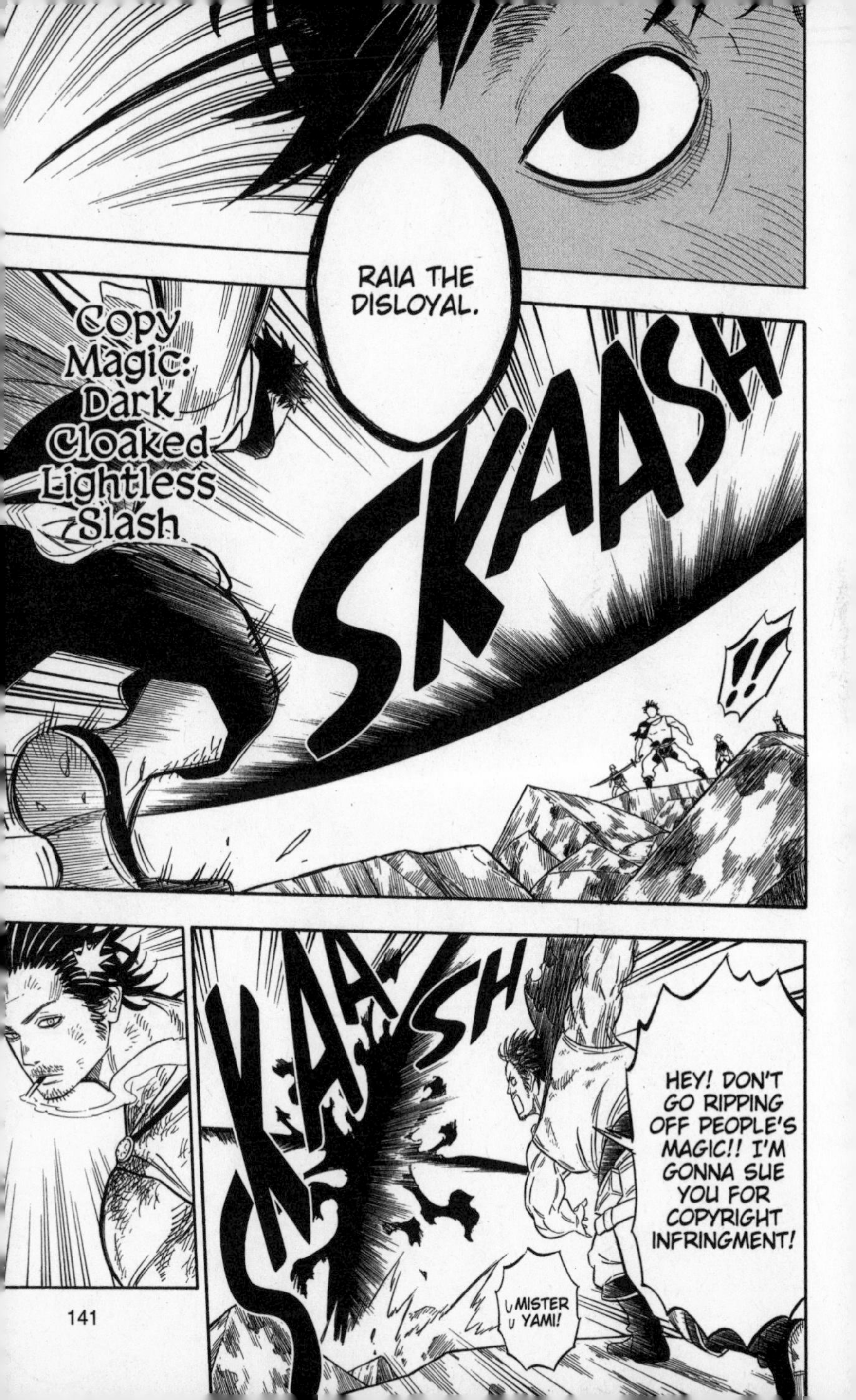
RAIA THE DISLOYAL.
Copy Magic: Dark Cloaked Lightless Slash
SKAASH
!!
SKAASH
HEY! DON'T GO RIPPING OFF PEOPLE'S MAGIC!! I'M GONNA SUE YOU FOR COPYRIGHT INFRINGMENT!
MISTER YAMI!

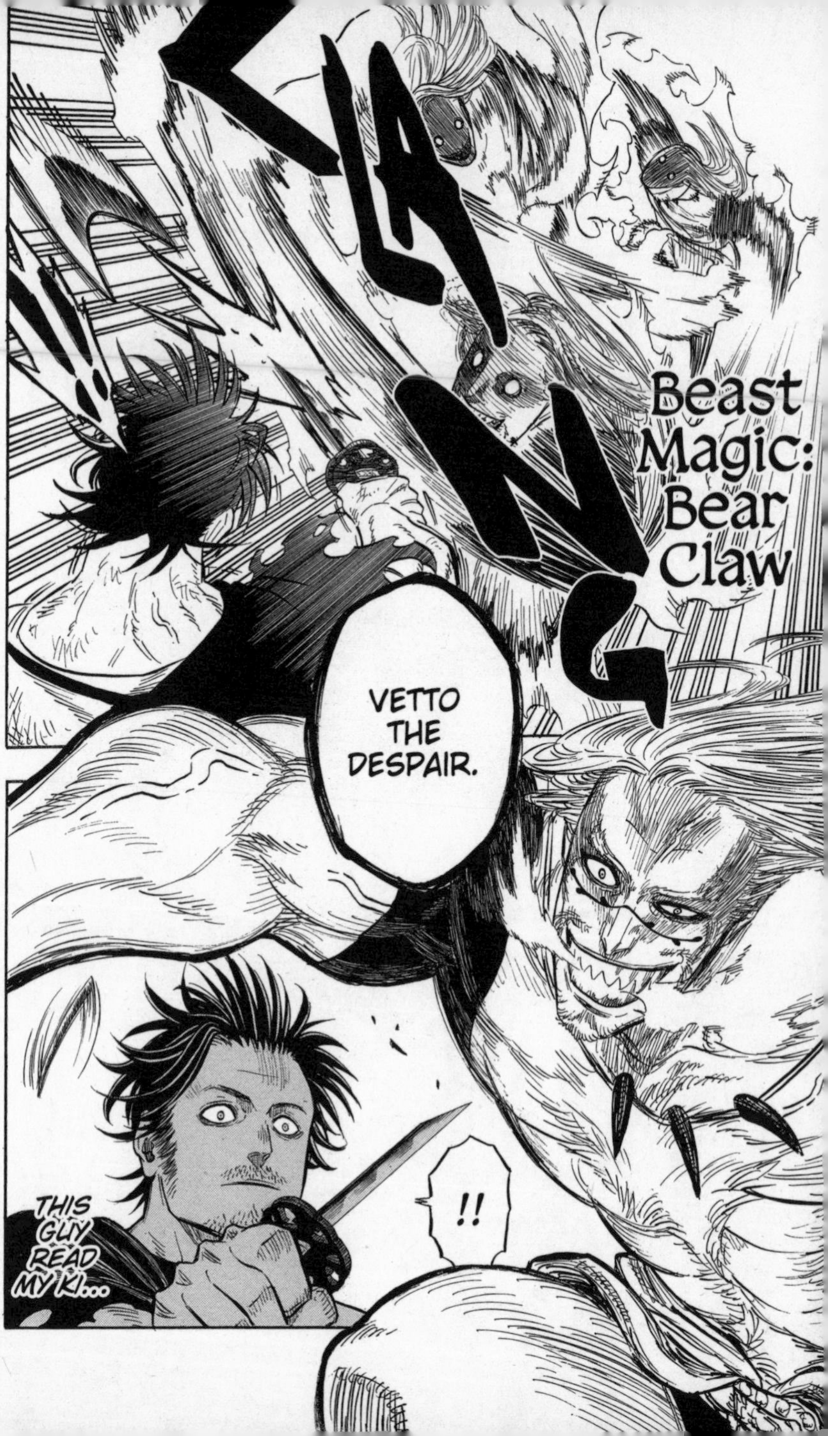
Beast Magic: Bear Claw
!!
VETTO THE DESPAIR.
!!
THIS GUY READ MY KI...

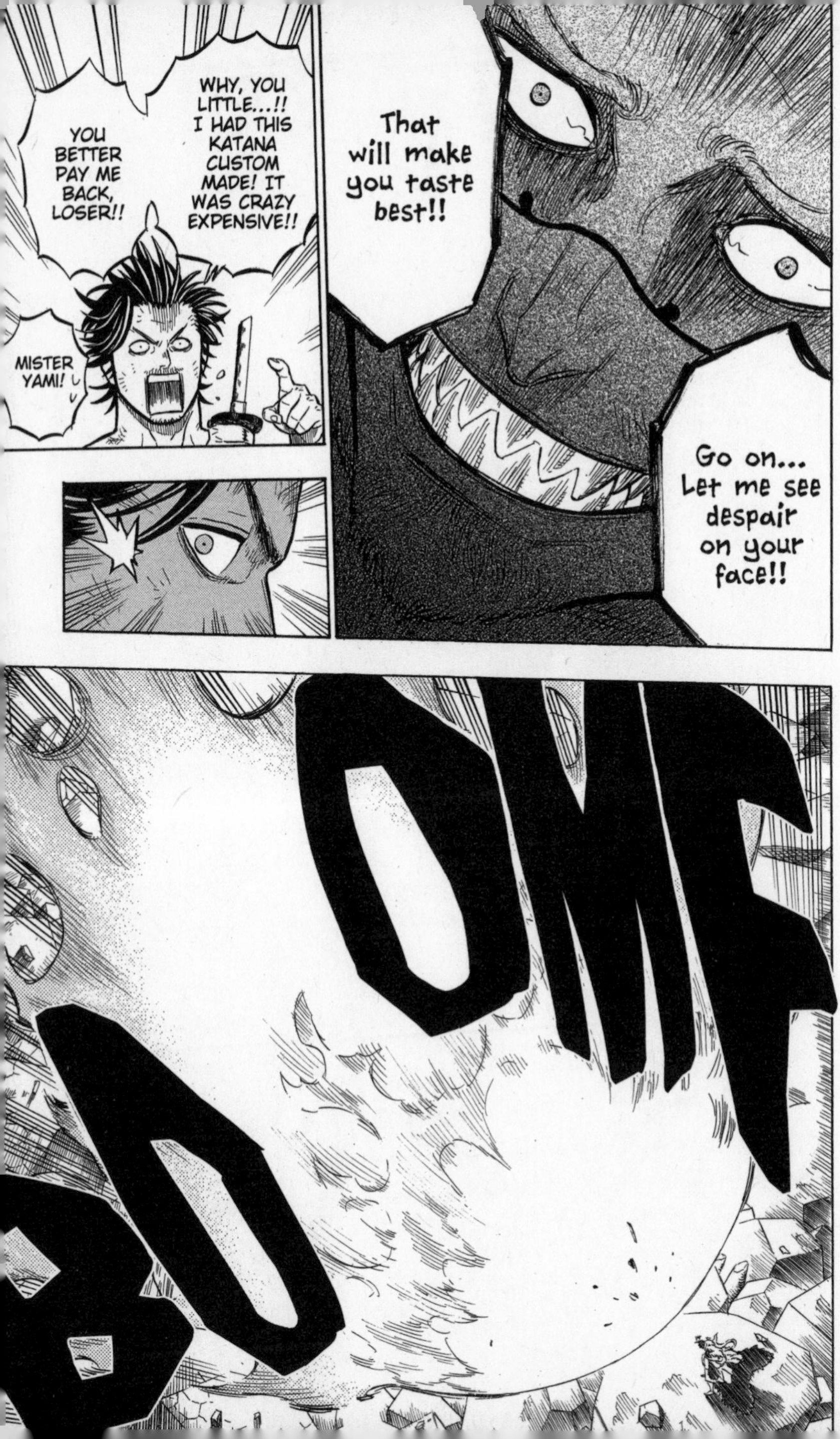

That will make you taste best!!
Go on... Let me see despair on your face!!
WHY, YOU LITTLE...!! I HAD THIS KATANA CUSTOM MADE! IT WAS CRAZY EXPENSIVE!!
YOU BETTER PAY ME BACK, LOSER!!
MISTER YAMI!
BOOMF

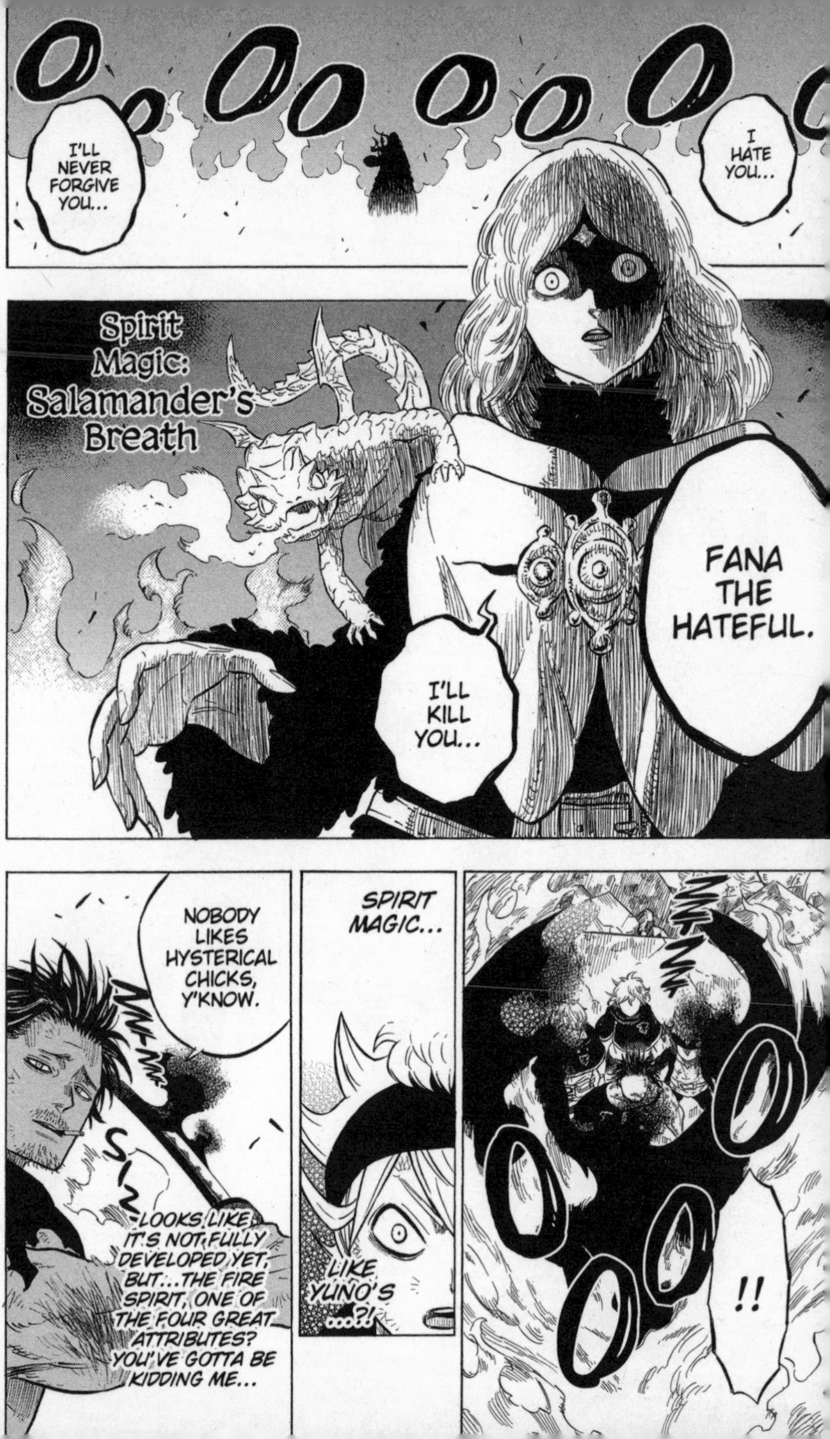
I HATE YOU...
I'LL NEVER FORGIVE YOU...
FANA THE HATEFUL.
I'LL KILL YOU...
Spirit Magic: Salamander's Breath
!!
SPIRIT MAGIC...
LIKE YUNO'S ...?!
NOBODY LIKES HYSTERICAL CHICKS, Y'KNOW.
LOOKS LIKE IT'S NOT FULLY DEVELOPED YET, BUT... THE FIRE SPIRIT, ONE OF THE FOUR GREAT ATTRIBUTES? YOU'VE GOTTA BE KIDDING ME...

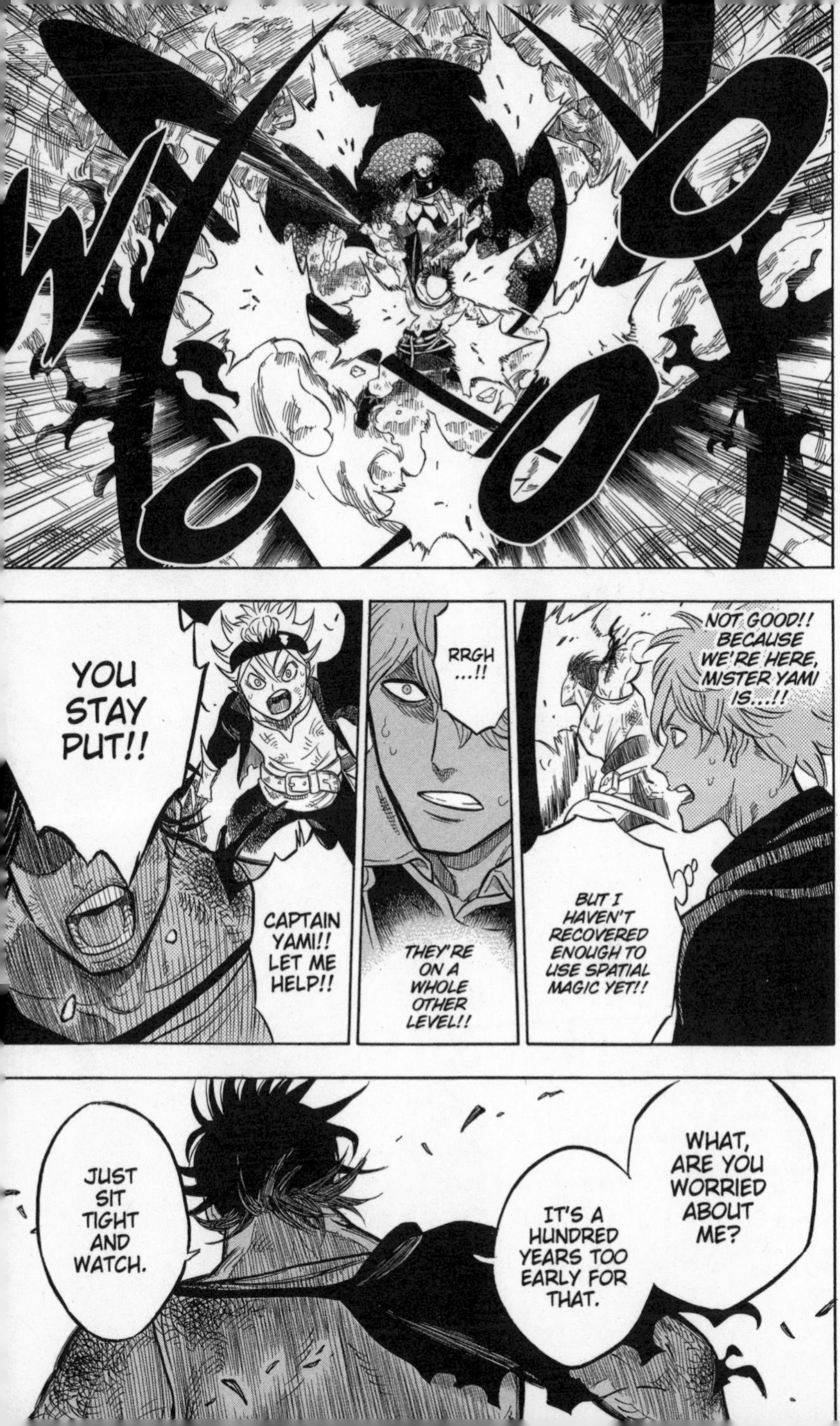
NOT GOOD!! BECAUSE WE'RE HERE, MISTER YAMI IS...!!
BUT I HAVEN'T RECOVERED ENOUGH TO USE SPATIAL MAGIC YET!!
RRGH ...!!
THEY'RE ON A WHOLE OTHER LEVEL!!
CAPTAIN YAMI!! LET ME HELP!!
YOU STAY PUT!!
WHAT, ARE YOU WORRIED ABOUT ME?
IT'S A HUNDRED YEARS TOO EARLY FOR THAT.
JUST SIT TIGHT AND WATCH.

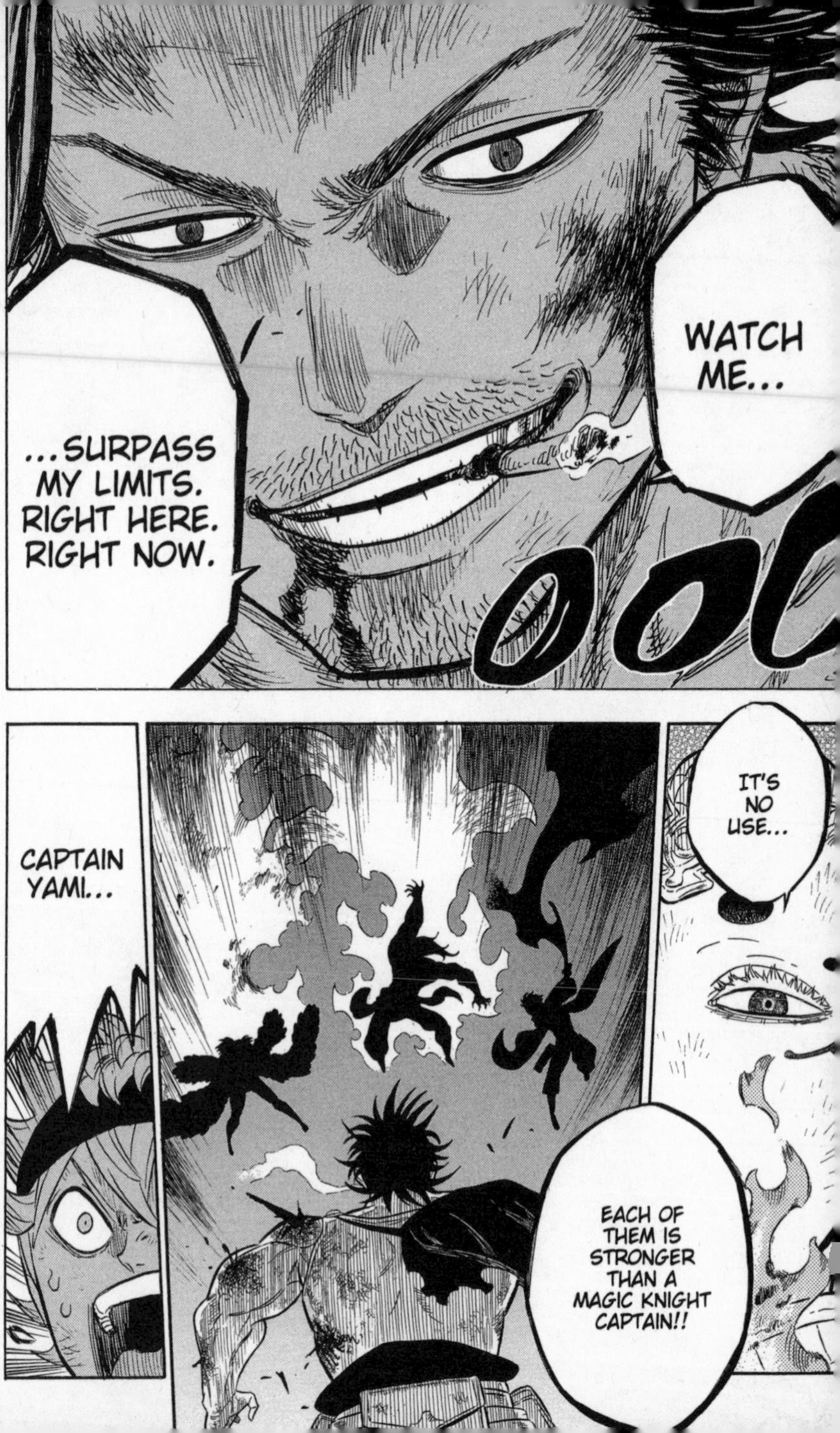
WATCH ME...
...SURPASS MY LIMITS. RIGHT HERE. RIGHT NOW.
OOO
IT'S NO USE...
EACH OF THEM IS STRONGER THAN A MAGIC KNIGHT CAPTAIN!!
CAPTAIN YAMI...

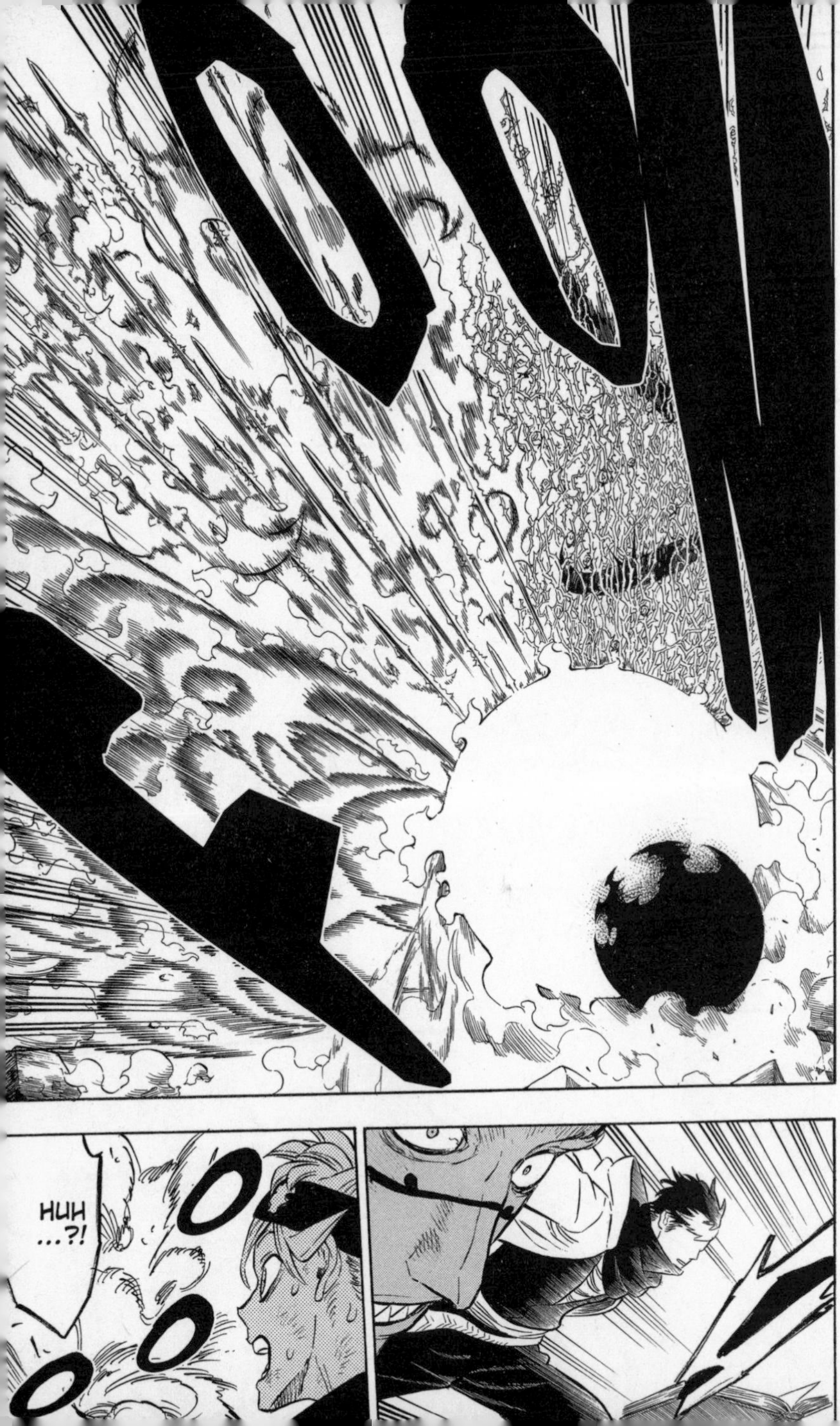
HUH ...?!

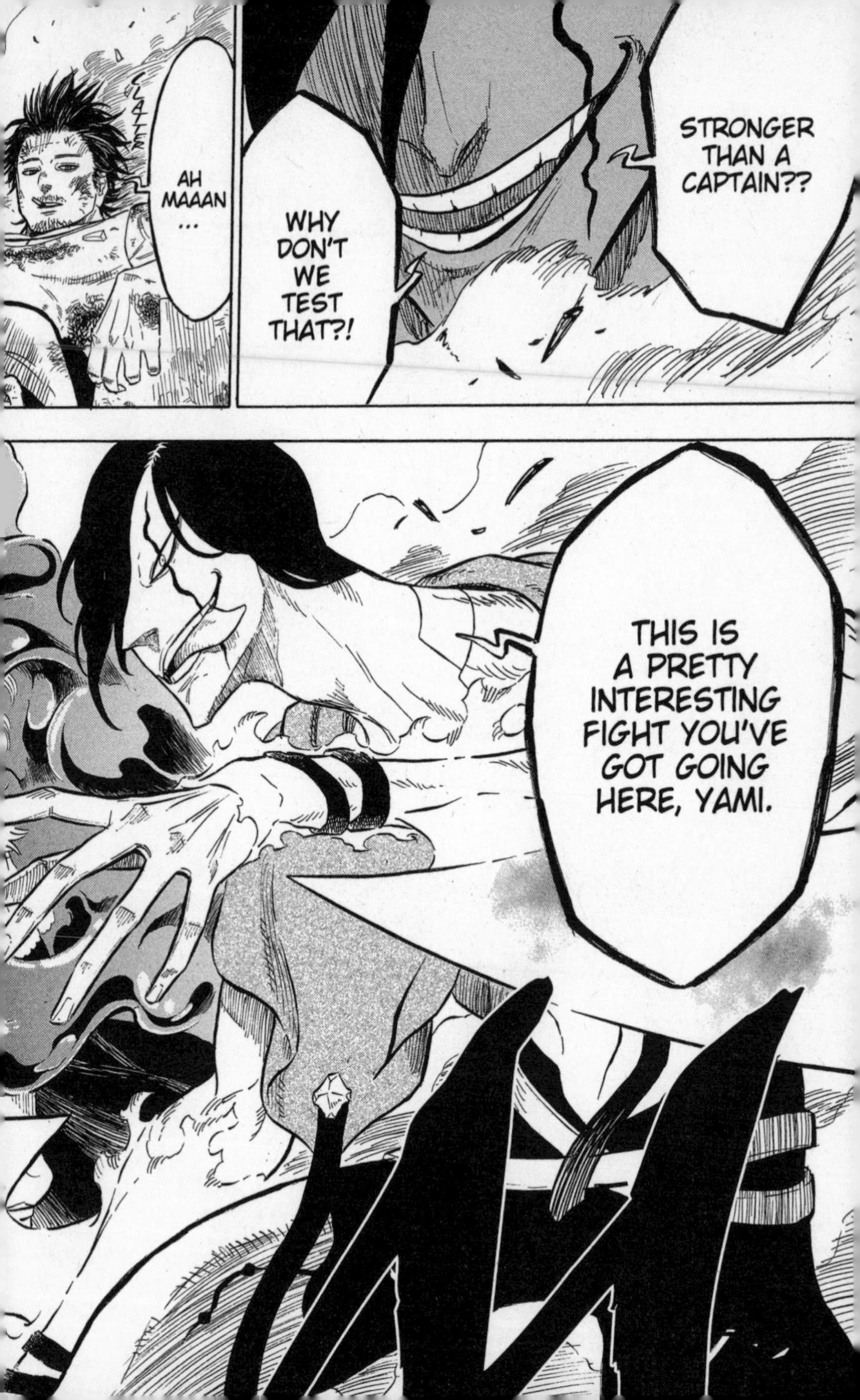
STRONGER THAN A CAPTAIN??
WHY DON'T WE TEST THAT?!
AH MAAAN ...
CLATTER
THIS IS A PRETTY INTERESTING FIGHT YOU'VE GOT GOING HERE, YAMI.

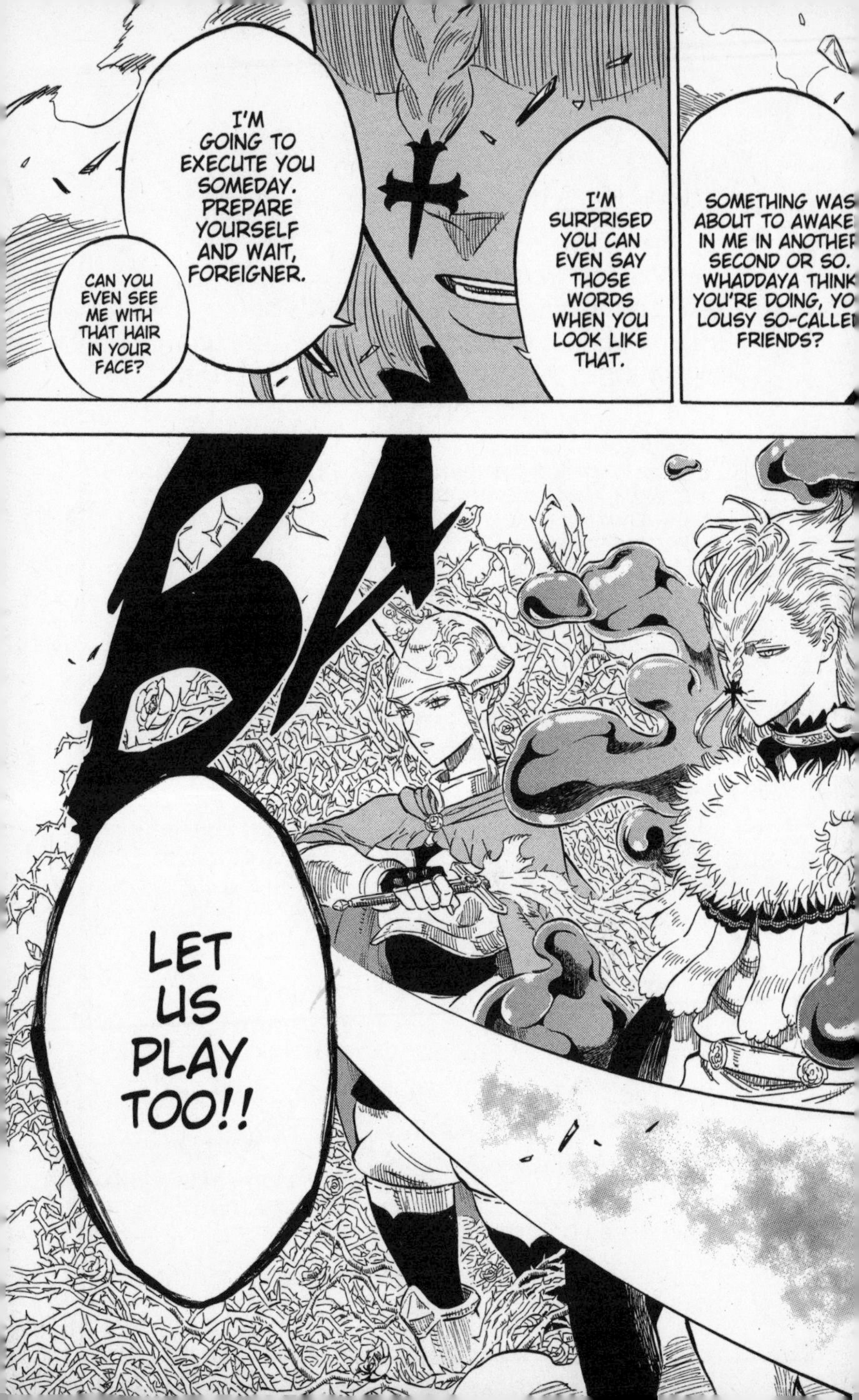
SOMETHING WAS ABOUT TO AWAKE IN ME IN ANOTHE SECOND OR SO. WHADDAYA THINK YOU'RE DOING, YO LOUSY SO-CALLE FRIENDS?
I'M SURPRISED YOU CAN EVEN SAY THOSE WORDS WHEN YOU LOOK LIKE THAT.
I'M GOING TO EXECUTE YOU SOMEDAY. PREPARE YOURSELF AND WAIT, FOREIGNER.
CAN YOU EVEN SEE ME WITH THAT HAIR IN YOUR FACE?
LET US PLAY TOO!!

The Assorted Questions Brigade

Good day! Good evening! Good morning! Here comes the letters corner. My apologies for putting it on hiatus last time!! Starting this volume, I'll be answering questions right and left again.

Q: All the brigades compete over who has more stars, but does a brigade's number of stars go all the way back to when that brigade began, or does it get reset every few years?
(Shunnosuke Tabata, Tokyo)

A: It's reset once a year. The number of stars is reset every March 31, and the count starts on April 1. (Around the time the firefly dandelions flutter.)

That means in the half year between April 1 and the time Asta joined the Black Bulls, the Golden Dawn had earned seventy and the Black Bulls had earned negative thirty! (The Black Bulls are way too hopeless!)

The reset time changes to suit the Wizard King's convenience, but the periods are always at least a year long.

Q: Do wages change depending on rank?
(Yohei Shibayama, Shizuoka)

A: As your rank goes up, so does your pay!

Even the lowest rank makes more than the average annual income of a regular Clover Kingdom citizen.

Stars add achievement rewards to that base pay, so outstanding people have it really good!

Q: As far as Magic Knight brigades are concerned, we've had the Black Bulls and the Crimson Lion Kings. What sort of other Magic Knight brigades are there? I want to know all of them!! (Yushi, Kanagawa)

A: They'll all be shown in volume 7! Hang on a little longer!!

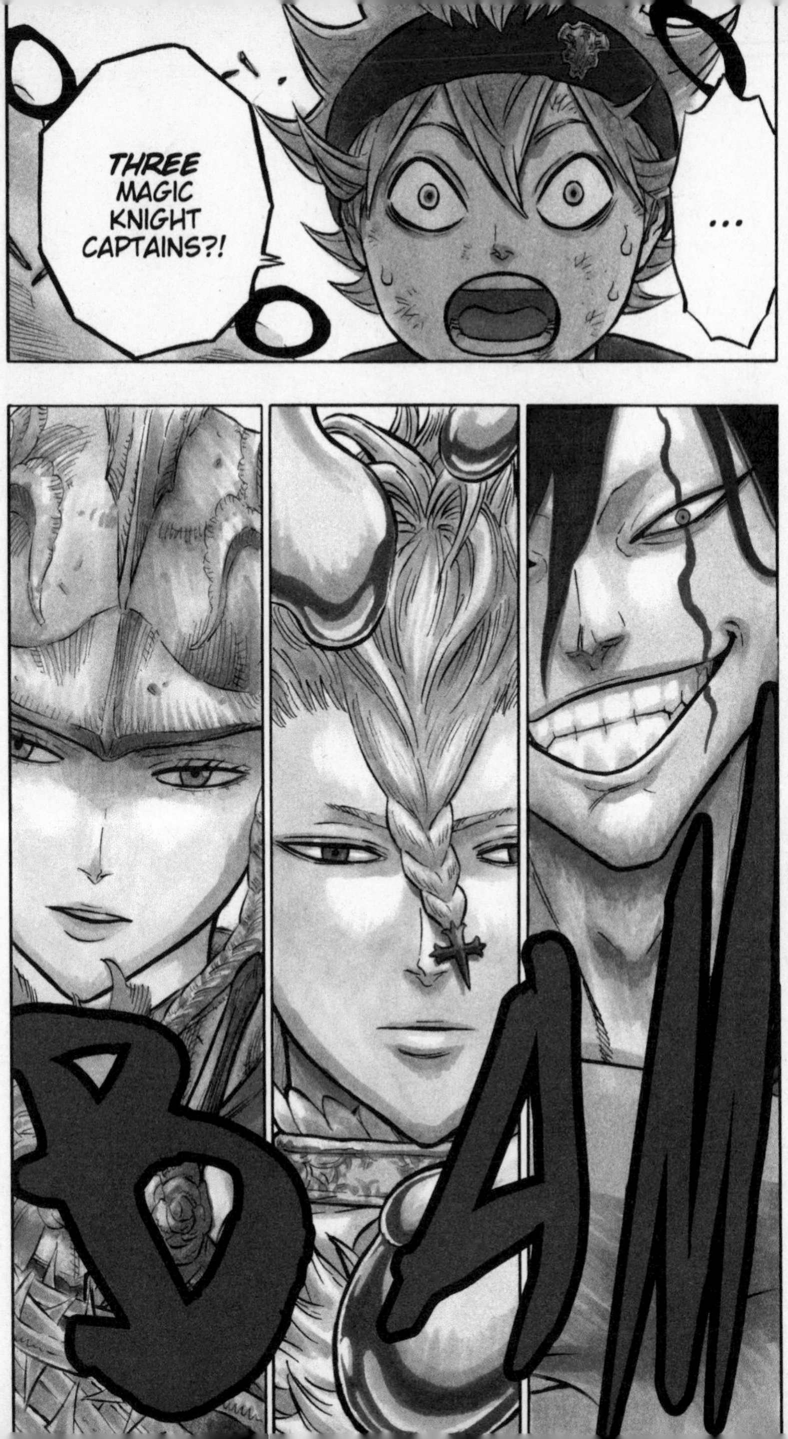
...
THREE MAGIC KNIGHT CAPTAINS?!
BAM

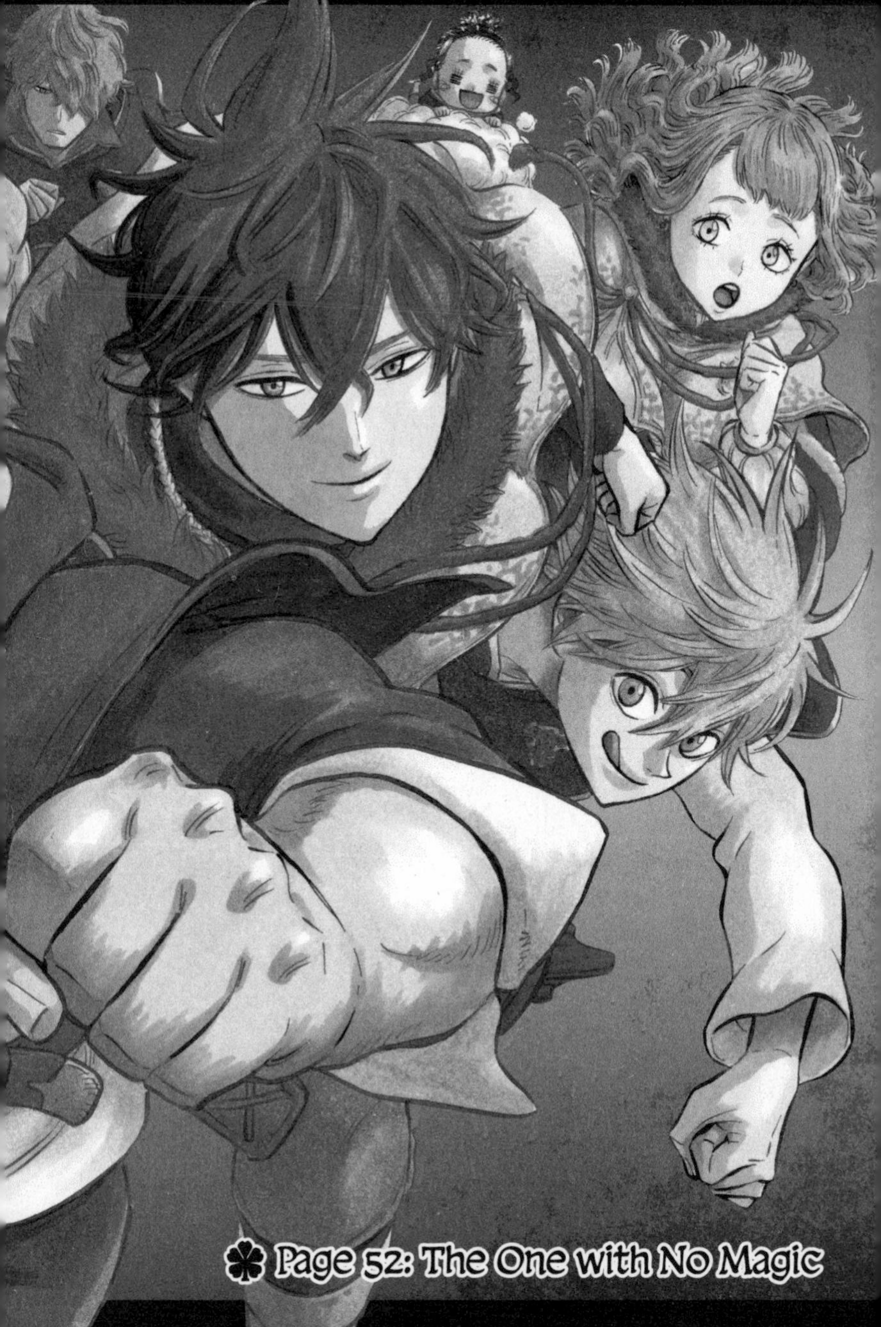

Page 52: The One with No Magic

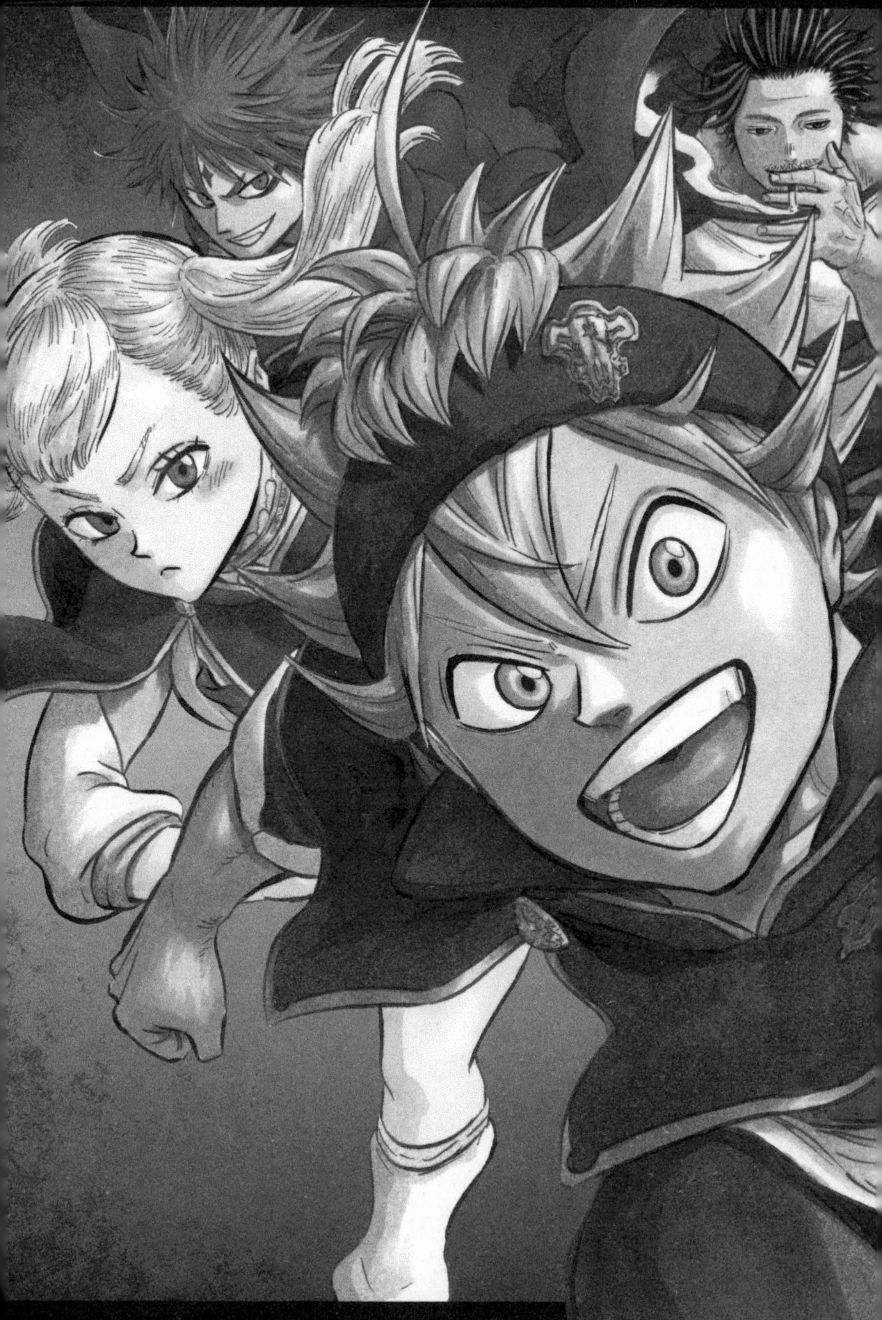

BLACK✻CLOVER

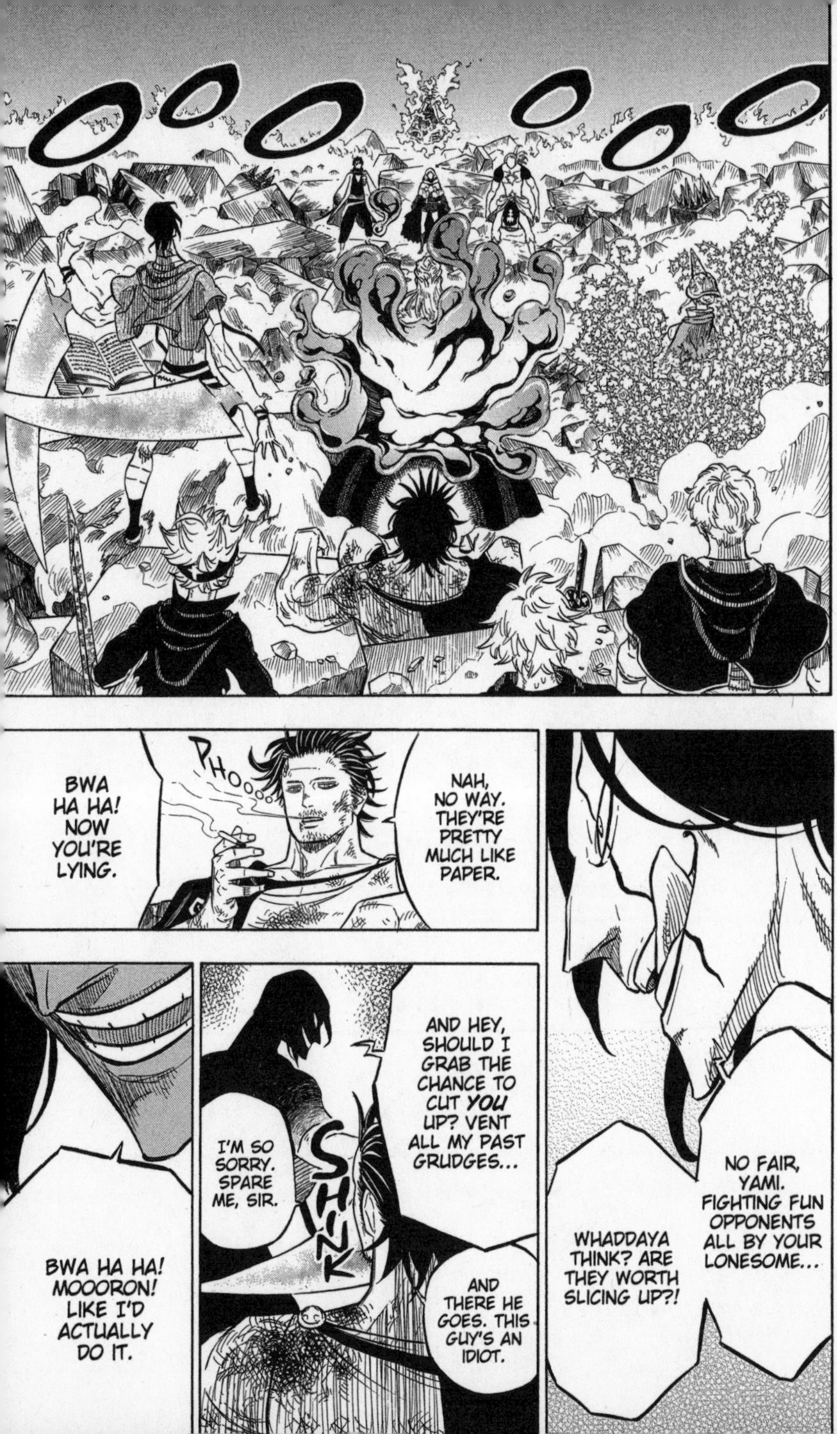
NO FAIR, YAMI. FIGHTING FUN OPPONENTS ALL BY YOUR LONESOME...
WHADDAYA THINK? ARE THEY WORTH SLICING UP?!
NAH, NO WAY. THEY'RE PRETTY MUCH LIKE PAPER.
PHOOO...
BWA HA HA! NOW YOU'RE LYING.
AND HEY, SHOULD I GRAB THE CHANCE TO CUT *YOU* UP? VENT ALL MY PAST GRUDGES...
SHINK
I'M SO SORRY. SPARE ME, SIR.
AND THERE HE GOES. THIS GUY'S AN IDIOT.
BWA HA HA! MOOORON! LIKE I'D ACTUALLY DO IT.

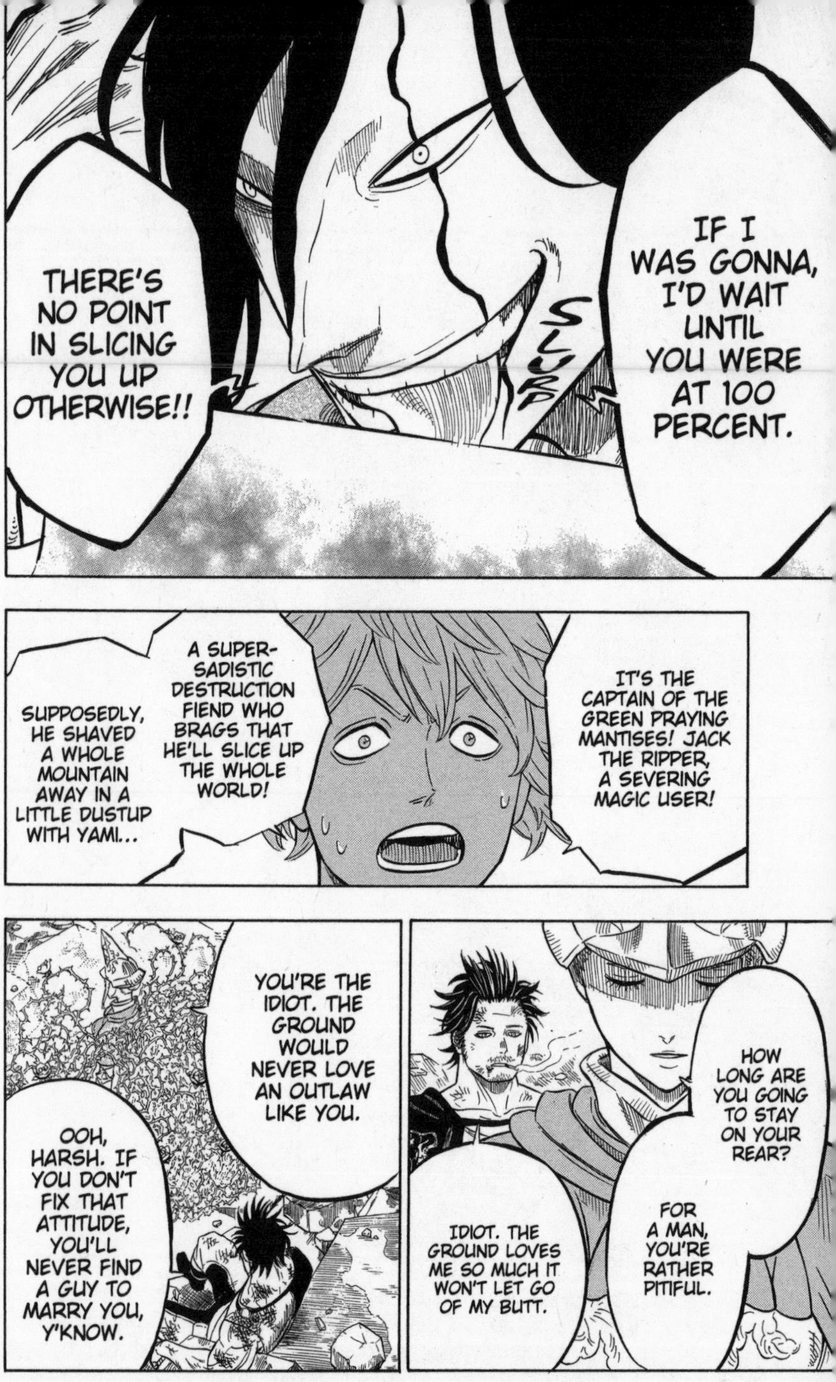
IF I WAS GONNA, I'D WAIT UNTIL YOU WERE AT 100 PERCENT.
SLURP
THERE'S NO POINT IN SLICING YOU UP OTHERWISE!!
IT'S THE CAPTAIN OF THE GREEN PRAYING MANTISES! JACK THE RIPPER, A SEVERING MAGIC USER!
A SUPER-SADISTIC DESTRUCTION FIEND WHO BRAGS THAT HE'LL SLICE UP THE WHOLE WORLD!
SUPPOSEDLY, HE SHAVED A WHOLE MOUNTAIN AWAY IN A LITTLE DUSTUP WITH YAMI...
HOW LONG ARE YOU GOING TO STAY ON YOUR REAR?
FOR A MAN, YOU'RE RATHER PITIFUL.
IDIOT. THE GROUND LOVES ME SO MUCH IT WON'T LET GO OF MY BUTT.
YOU'RE THE IDIOT. THE GROUND WOULD NEVER LOVE AN OUTLAW LIKE YOU.
OOH, HARSH. IF YOU DON'T FIX THAT ATTITUDE, YOU'LL NEVER FIND A GUY TO MARRY YOU, Y'KNOW.

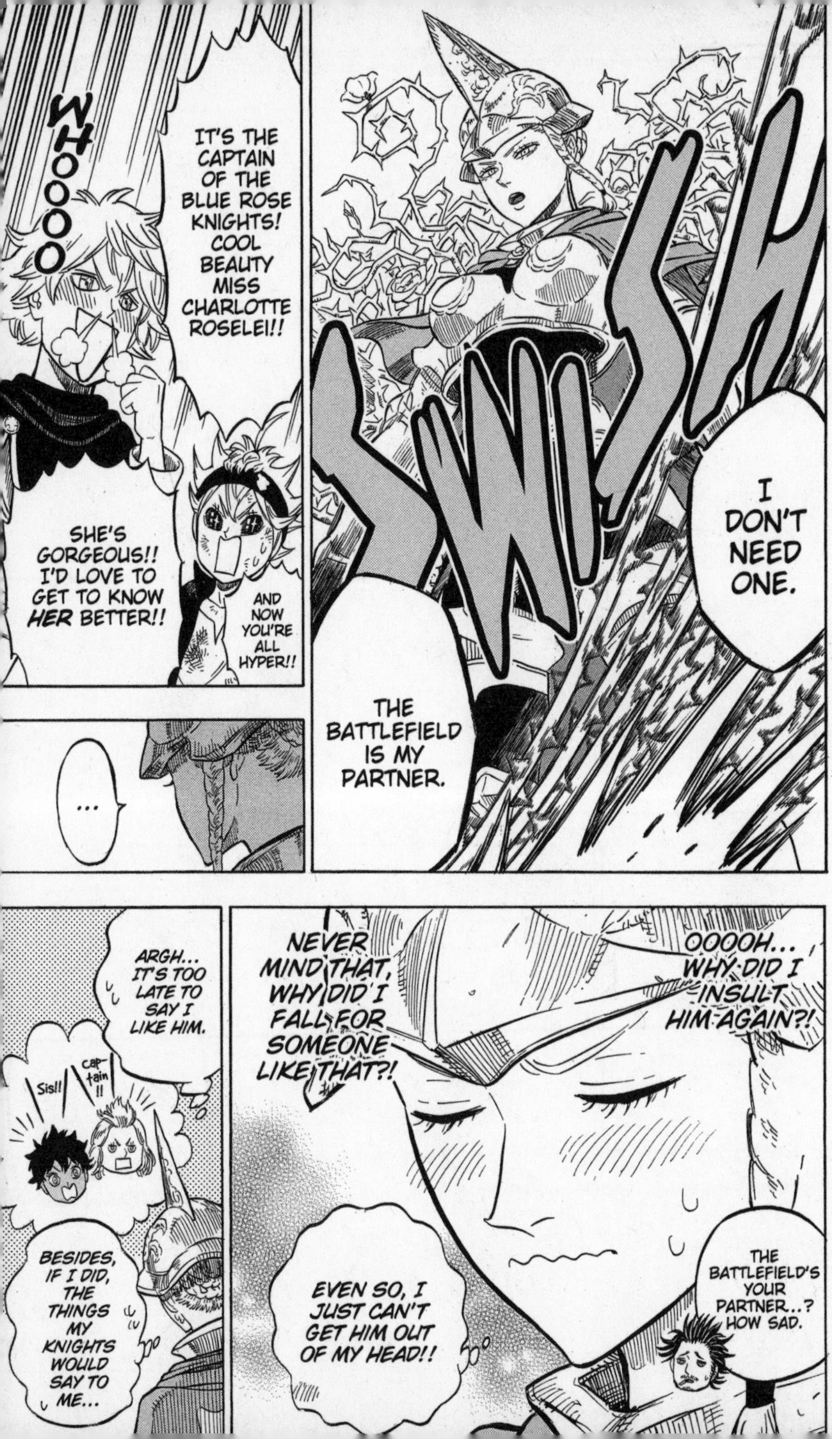
I DON'T NEED ONE.
SWISH
THE BATTLEFIELD IS MY PARTNER.
WHOOOOO
IT'S THE CAPTAIN OF THE BLUE ROSE KNIGHTS! COOL BEAUTY MISS CHARLOTTE ROSELEI!!
SHE'S GORGEOUS!! I'D LOVE TO GET TO KNOW HER BETTER!!
AND NOW YOU'RE ALL HYPER!!
...
OOOOH... WHY DID I INSULT HIM AGAIN?!
NEVER MIND THAT, WHY DID I FALL FOR SOMEONE LIKE THAT?!
THE BATTLEFIELD'S YOUR PARTNER...? HOW SAD.
EVEN SO, I JUST CAN'T GET HIM OUT OF MY HEAD!!
ARGH... IT'S TOO LATE TO SAY I LIKE HIM.
Cap-tain!!
Sis!!
BESIDES, IF I DID, THE THINGS MY KNIGHTS WOULD SAY TO ME...

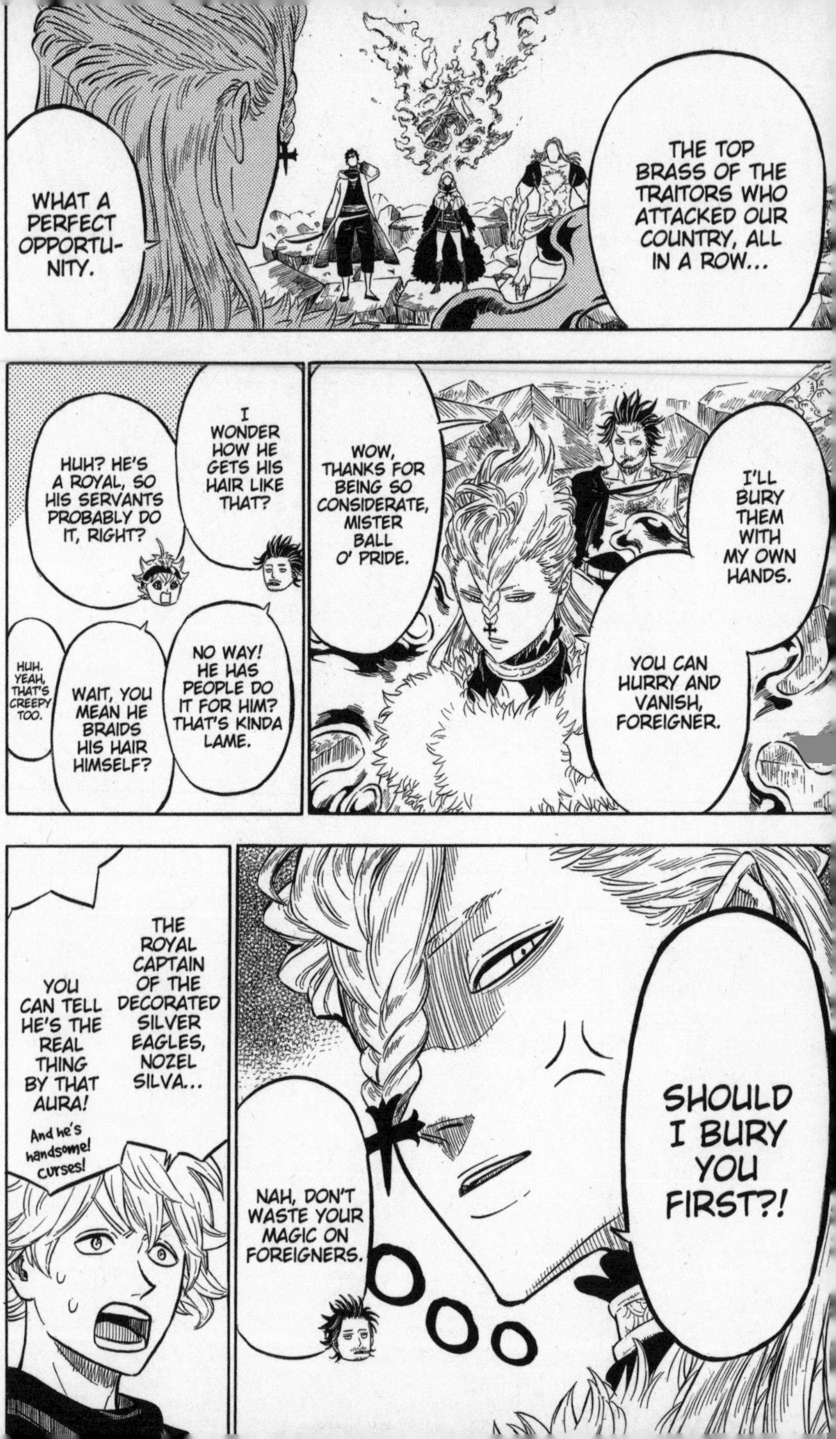
THE TOP BRASS OF THE TRAITORS WHO ATTACKED OUR COUNTRY, ALL IN A ROW...
WHAT A PERFECT OPPORTUNITY.
I'LL BURY THEM WITH MY OWN HANDS.
YOU CAN HURRY AND VANISH, FOREIGNER.
WOW, THANKS FOR BEING SO CONSIDERATE, MISTER BALL O' PRIDE.
I WONDER HOW HE GETS HIS HAIR LIKE THAT?
HUH? HE'S A ROYAL, SO HIS SERVANTS PROBABLY DO IT, RIGHT?
NO WAY! HE HAS PEOPLE DO IT FOR HIM? THAT'S KINDA LAME.
WAIT, YOU MEAN HE BRAIDS HIS HAIR HIMSELF?
HUH. YEAH, THAT'S CREEPY TOO.
SHOULD I BURY YOU FIRST?!
NAH, DON'T WASTE YOUR MAGIC ON FOREIGNERS.
THE ROYAL CAPTAIN OF THE DECORATED SILVER EAGLES, NOZEL SILVA...
YOU CAN TELL HE'S THE REAL THING BY THAT AURA!
And he's handsome! Curses!

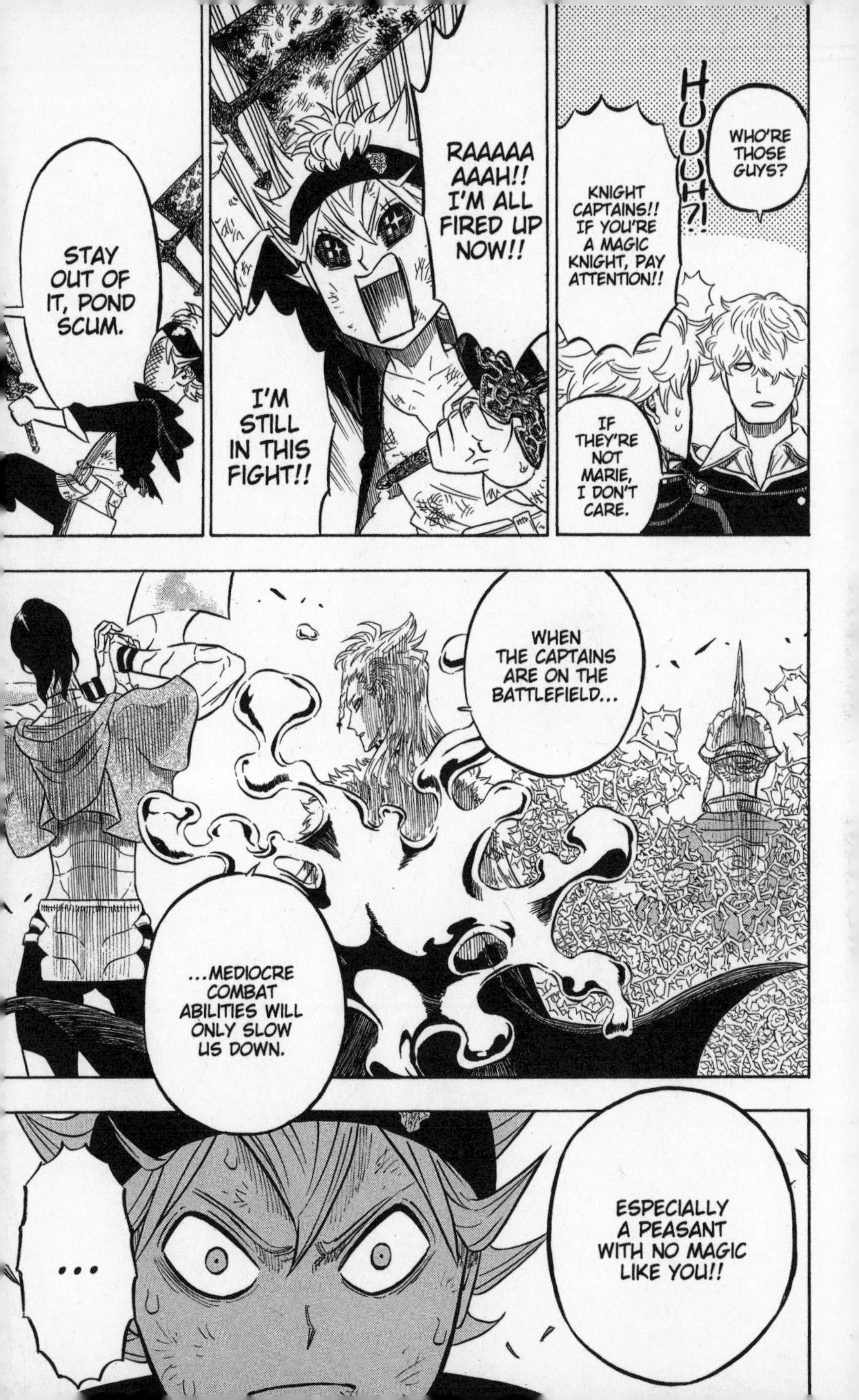
WHO'RE THOSE GUYS?
HUUUH?!
KNIGHT CAPTAINS!! IF YOU'RE A MAGIC KNIGHT, PAY ATTENTION!!
IF THEY'RE NOT MARIE, I DON'T CARE.
RAAAAAAAAH!! I'M ALL FIRED UP NOW!!
I'M STILL IN THIS FIGHT!!
STAY OUT OF IT, POND SCUM.
WHEN THE CAPTAINS ARE ON THE BATTLEFIELD...
...MEDIOCRE COMBAT ABILITIES WILL ONLY SLOW US DOWN.
ESPECIALLY A PEASANT WITH NO MAGIC LIKE YOU!!
...

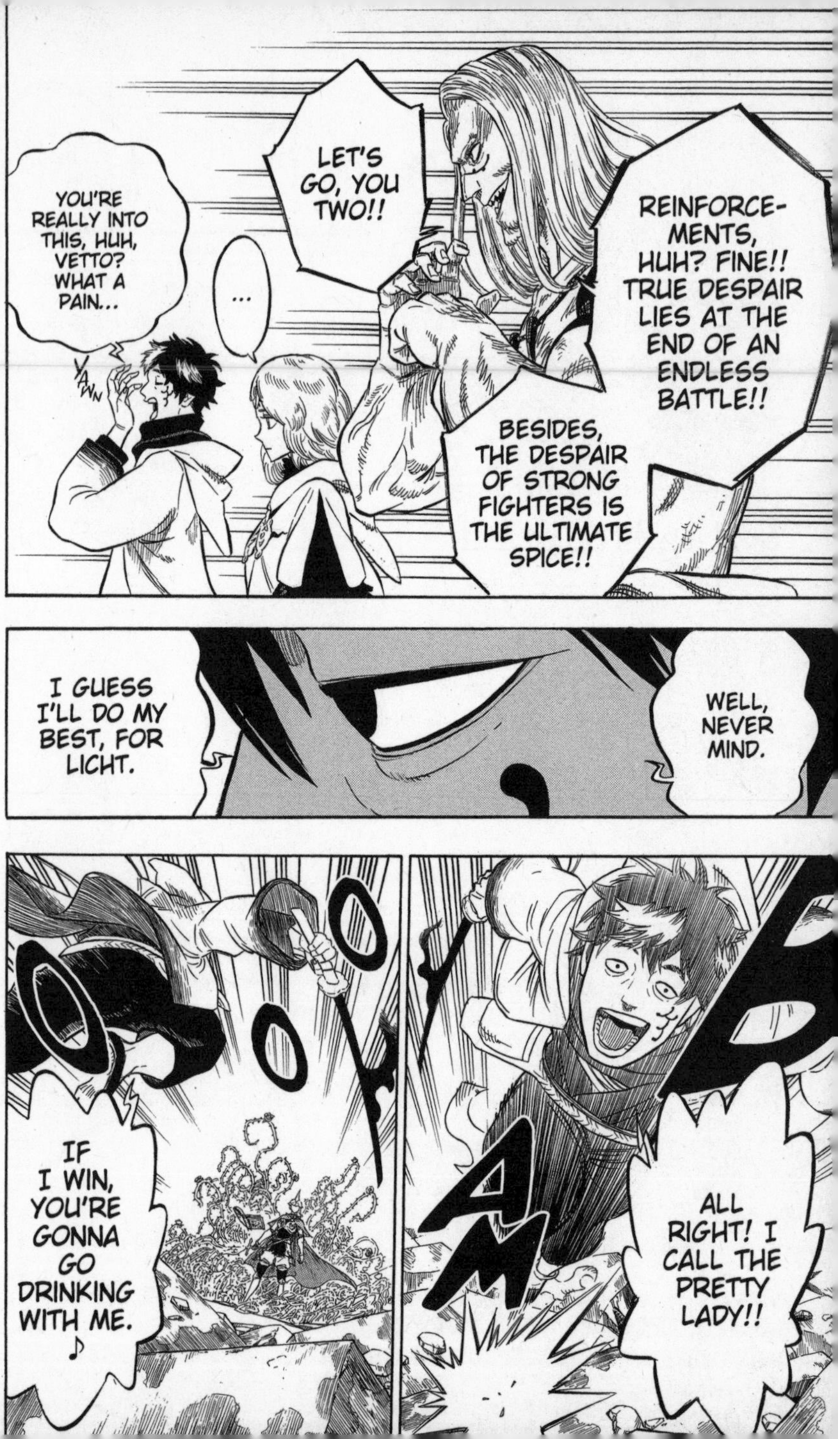
REINFORCEMENTS, HUH? FINE!! TRUE DESPAIR LIES AT THE END OF AN ENDLESS BATTLE!!
BESIDES, THE DESPAIR OF STRONG FIGHTERS IS THE ULTIMATE SPICE!!
LET'S GO, YOU TWO!!
...
YOU'RE REALLY INTO THIS, HUH, VETTO? WHAT A PAIN...
YAWN
WELL, NEVER MIND.
I GUESS I'LL DO MY BEST, FOR LICHT.
ALL RIGHT! I CALL THE PRETTY LADY!!
IF I WIN, YOU'RE GONNA GO DRINKING WITH ME. ♪

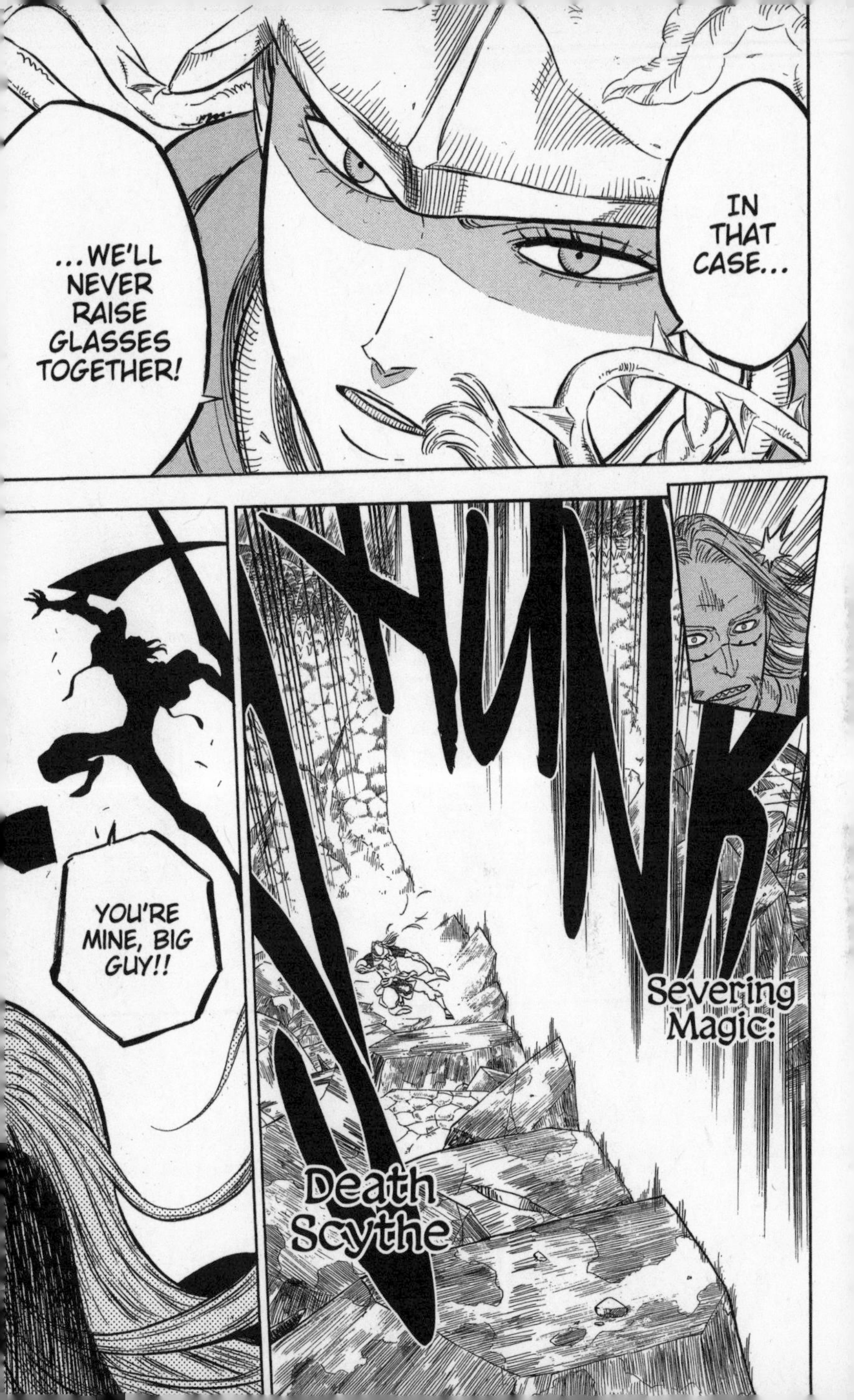
IN THAT CASE...
...WE'LL NEVER RAISE GLASSES TOGETHER!
Severing Magic:
Death Scythe
YOU'RE MINE, BIG GUY!!

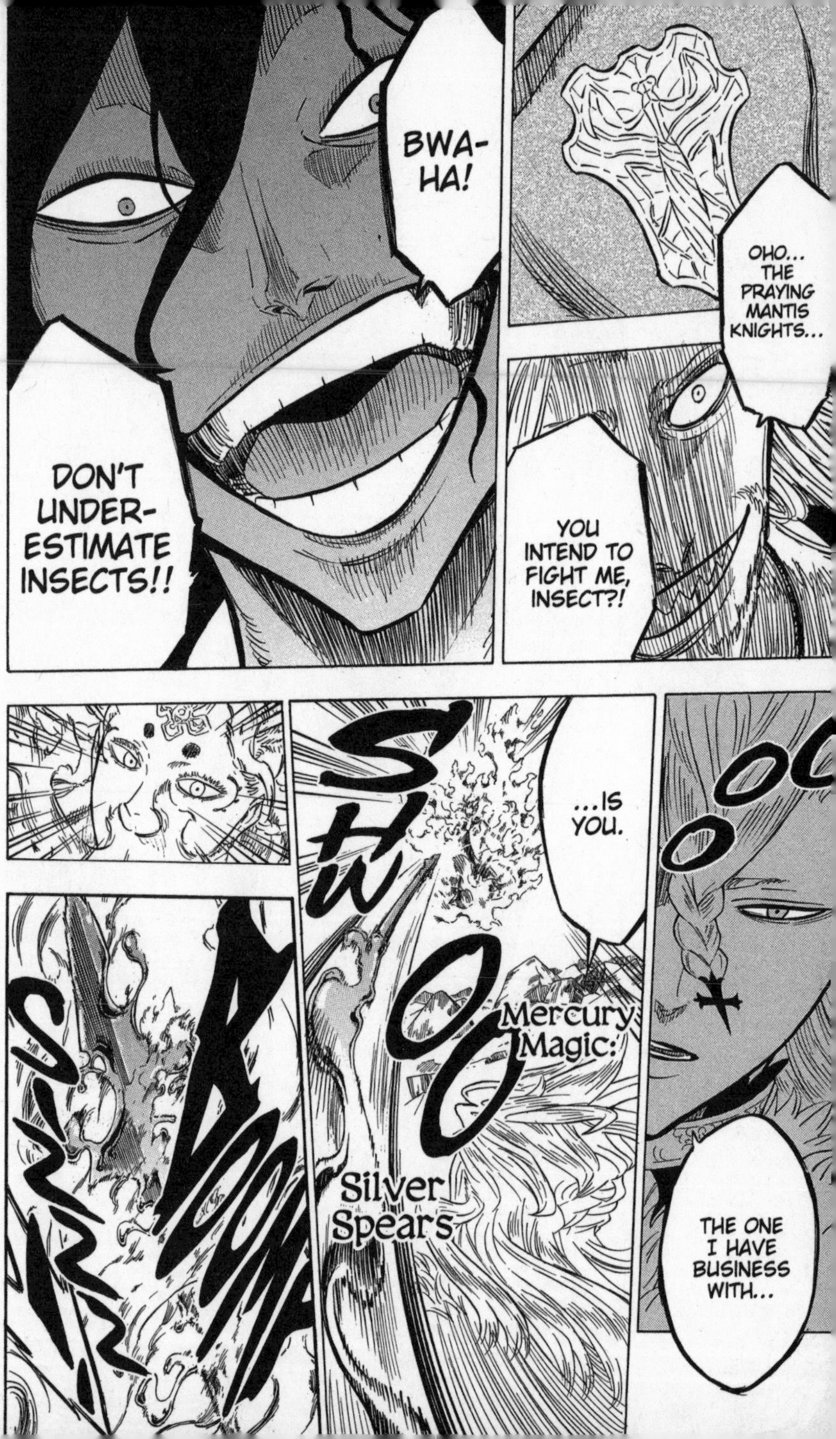

OHO... THE PRAYING MANTIS KNIGHTS...
YOU INTEND TO FIGHT ME, INSECT?!
BWA-HA!
DON'T UNDER-ESTIMATE INSECTS!!
THE ONE I HAVE BUSINESS WITH...
...IS YOU.
SHWOOO
Mercury Magic:
Silver Spears

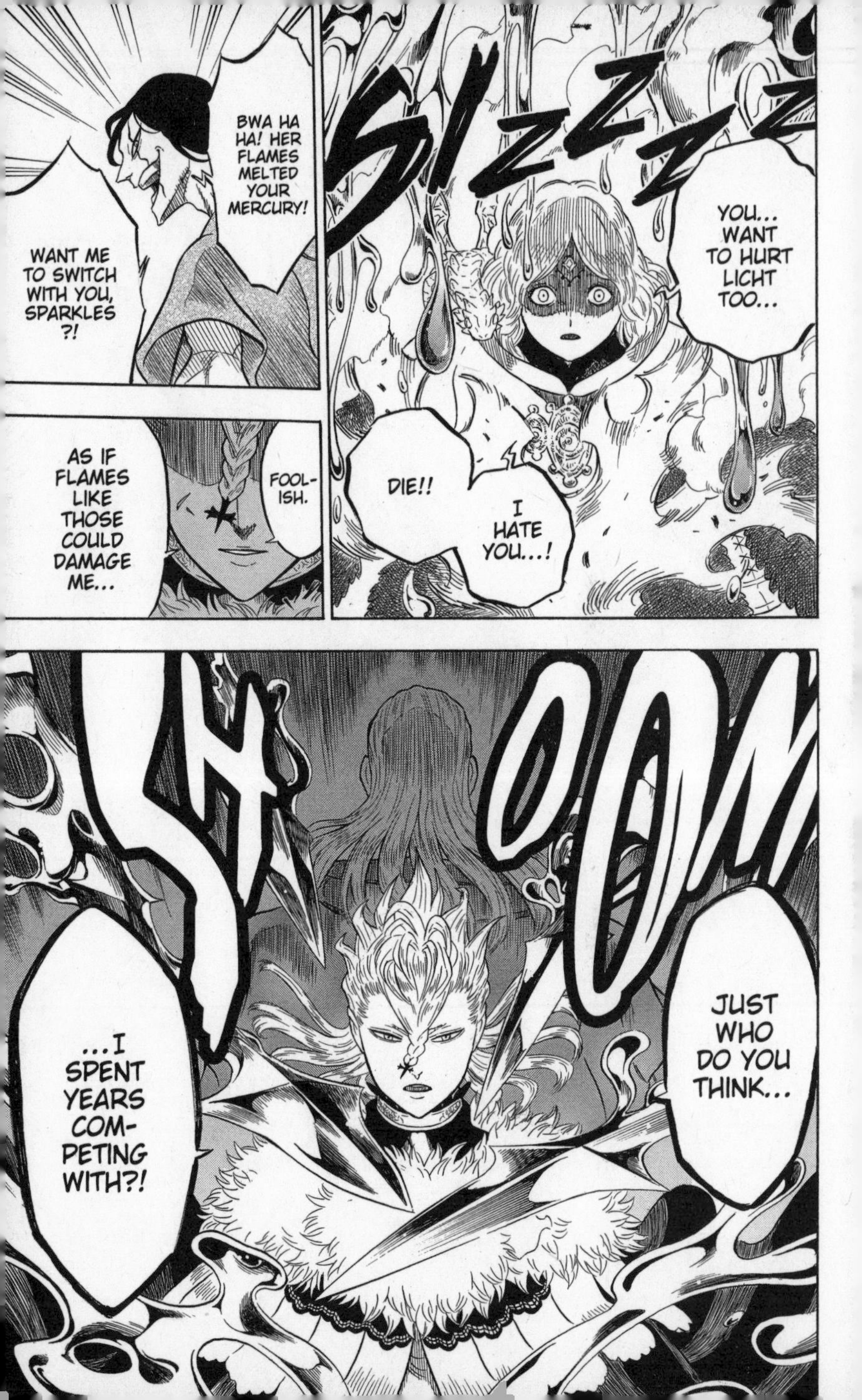
SIZZZZ
YOU... WANT TO HURT LICHT TOO...
I HATE YOU...!
DIE!!
BWA HA HA! HER FLAMES MELTED YOUR MERCURY!
WANT ME TO SWITCH WITH YOU, SPARKLES?!
FOOLISH.
AS IF FLAMES LIKE THOSE COULD DAMAGE ME...
JUST WHO DO YOU THINK...
...I SPENT YEARS COMPETING WITH?!

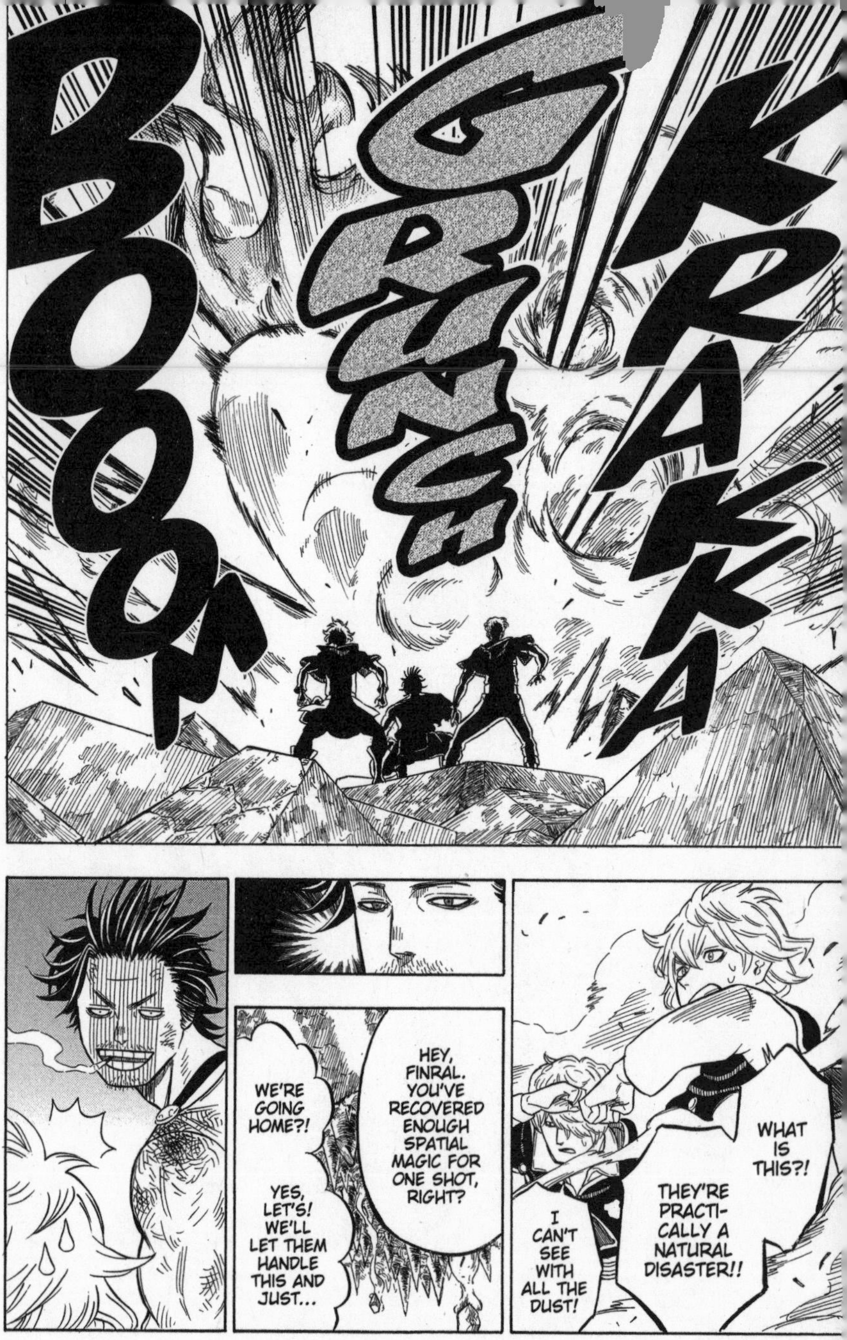
KRAKA
CRUSH
BOOOOM
WHAT IS THIS?!
THEY'RE PRACTICALLY A NATURAL DISASTER!!
I CAN'T SEE WITH ALL THE DUST!
HEY, FINRAL. YOU'VE RECOVERED ENOUGH SPATIAL MAGIC FOR ONE SHOT, RIGHT?
WE'RE GOING HOME?!
YES, LET'S! WE'LL LET THEM HANDLE THIS AND JUST...

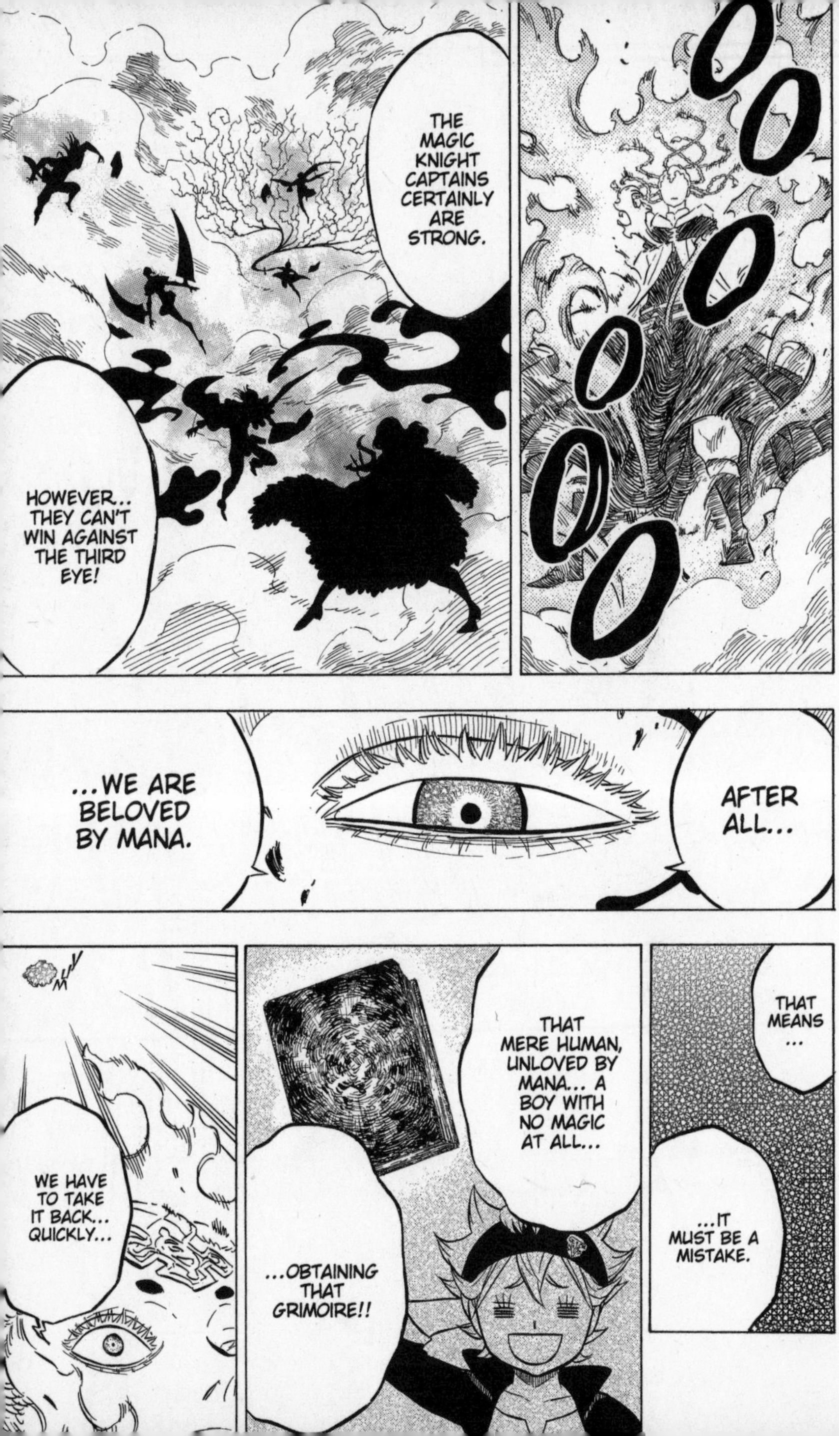
THE MAGIC KNIGHT CAPTAINS CERTAINLY ARE STRONG.
HOWEVER.. THEY CAN'T WIN AGAINST THE THIRD EYE!
AFTER ALL...
...WE ARE BELOVED BY MANA.
THAT MEANS ...
...IT MUST BE A MISTAKE.
THAT MERE HUMAN, UNLOVED BY MANA... A BOY WITH NO MAGIC AT ALL...
...OBTAINING THAT GRIMOIRE!!
WE HAVE TO TAKE IT BACK... QUICKLY...

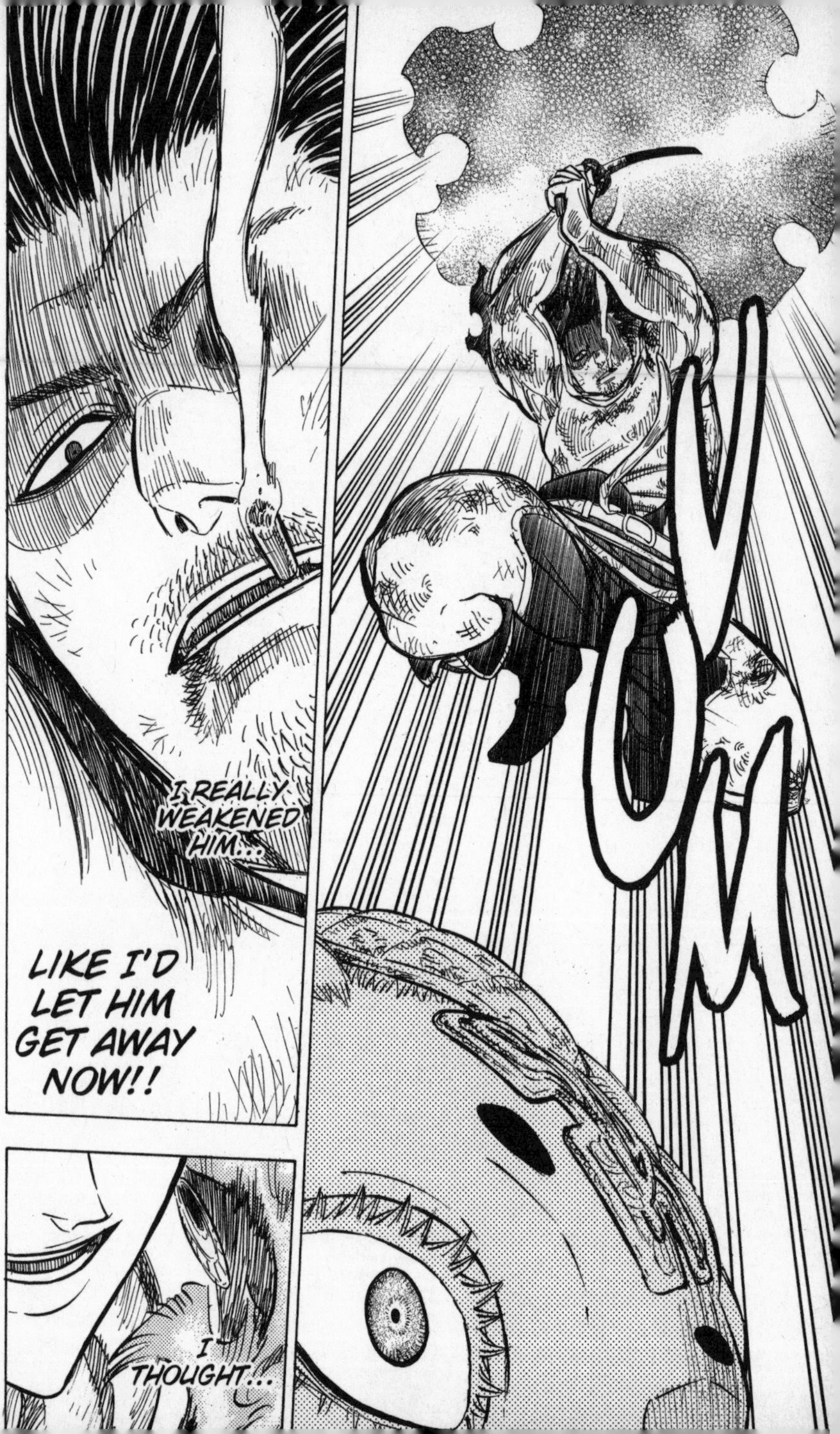
I REALLY WEAKENED HIM...
LIKE I'D LET HIM GET AWAY NOW!!
I THOUGHT...

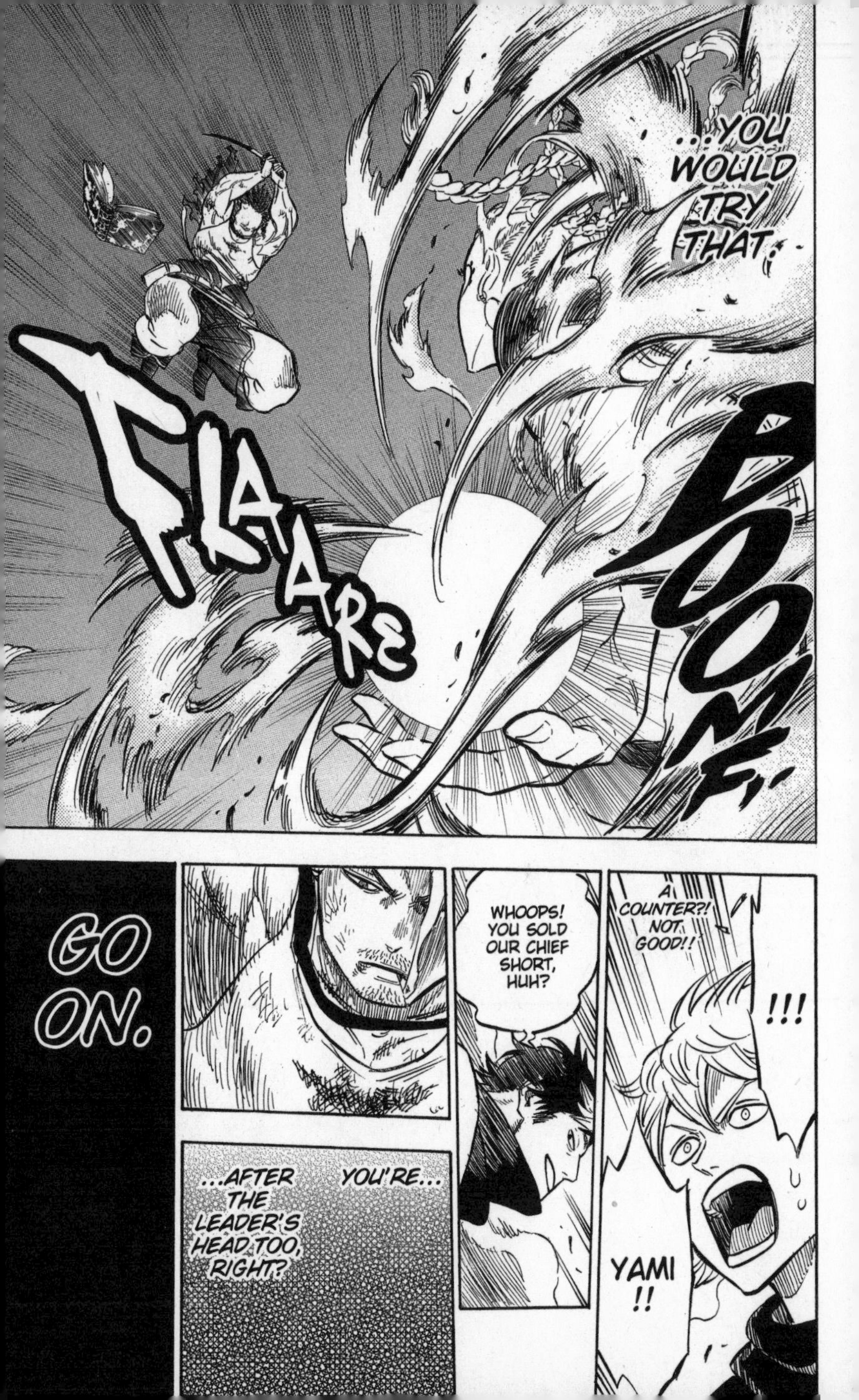

...YOU WOULD TRY THAT...
BOOM!!
FLAARE
A COUNTER?! NOT GOOD!!
!!!
YAMI!!
WHOOPS! YOU SOLD OUR CHIEF SHORT, HUH?
YOU'RE...
...AFTER THE LEADER'S HEAD TOO, RIGHT?
GO ON.

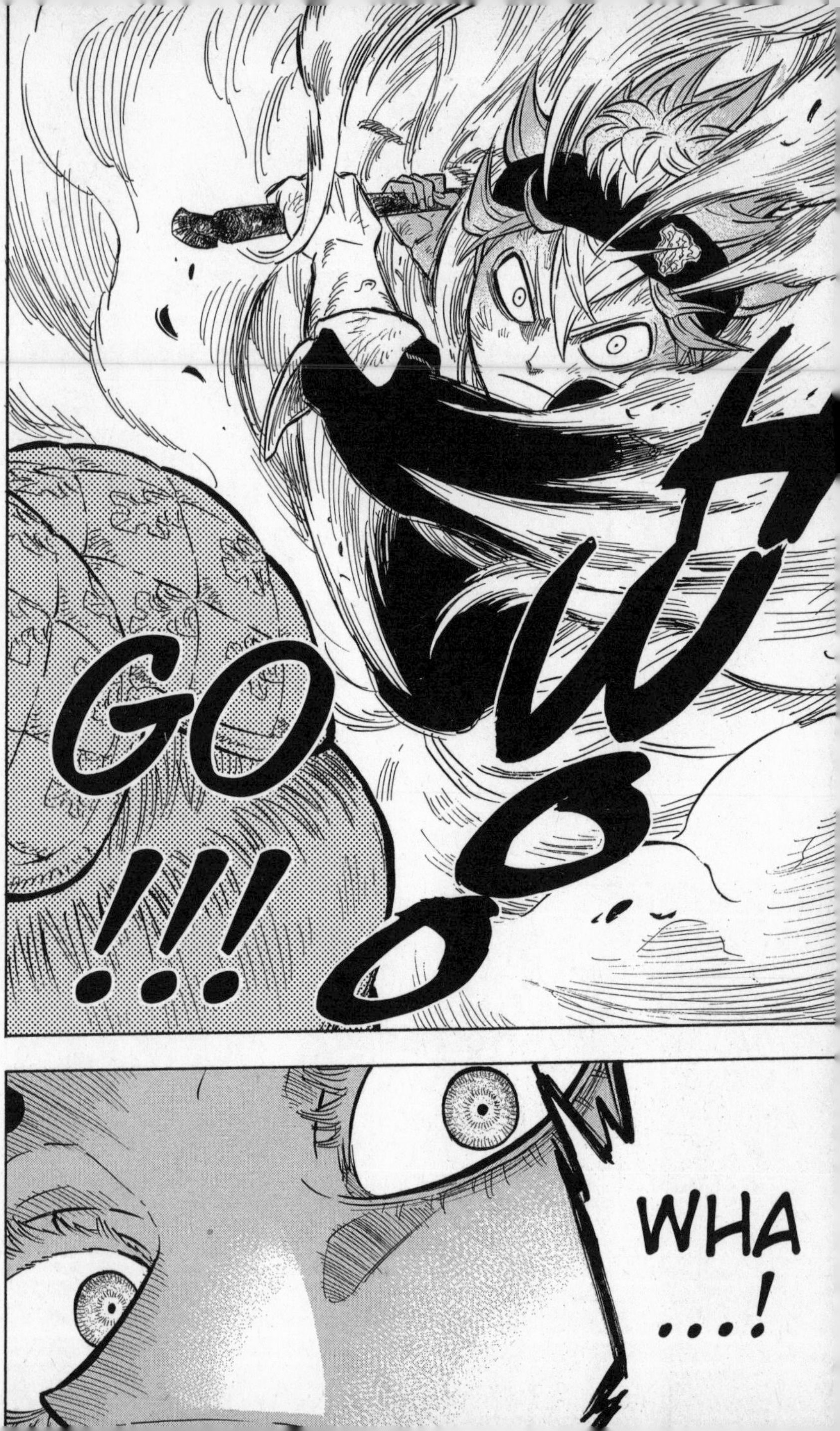
WHA ...!

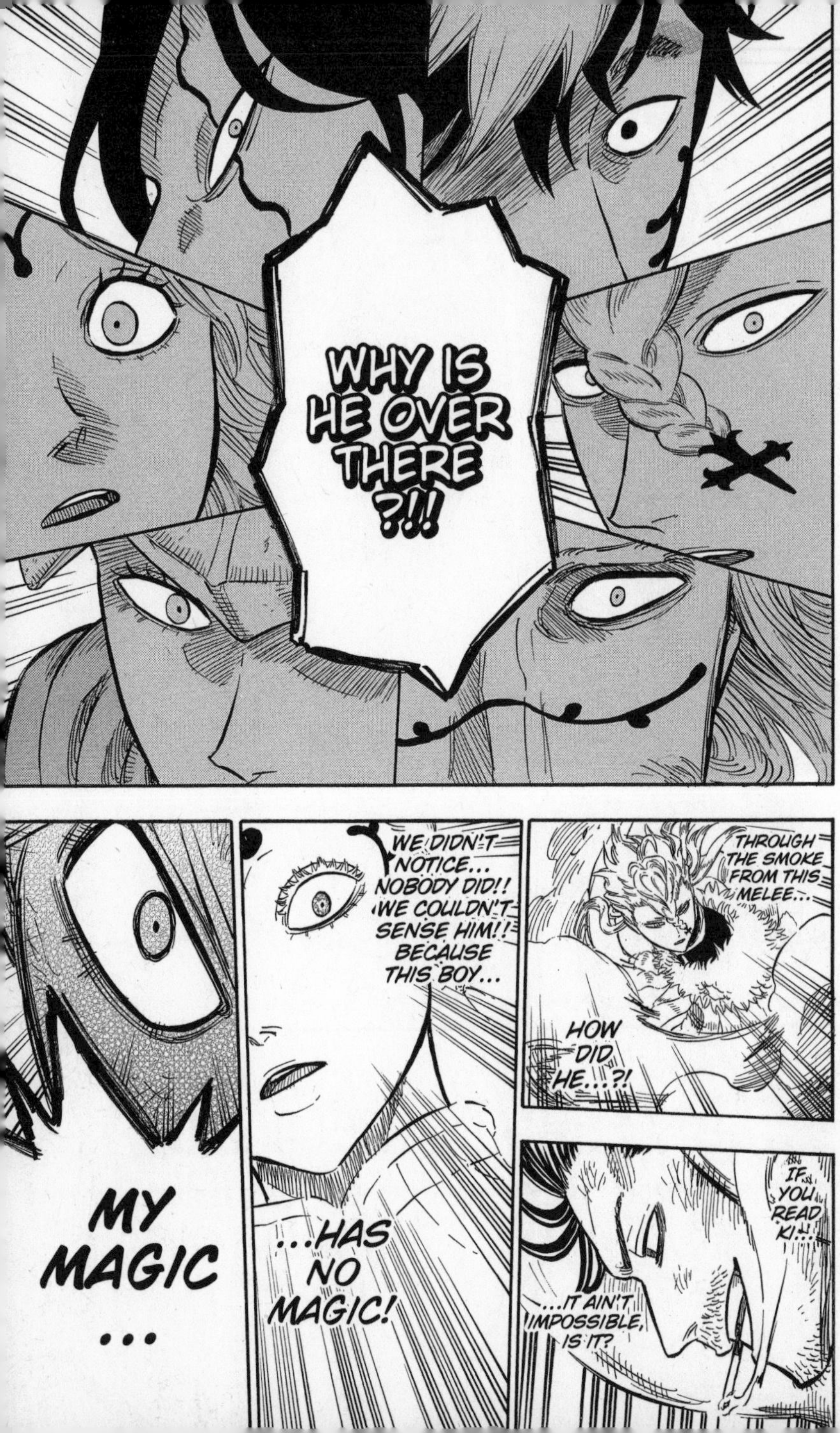
WHY IS HE OVER THERE ?!!
THROUGH THE SMOKE FROM THIS MELEE...
HOW DID HE...?!
IF YOU READ KI...
...IT AIN'T IMPOSSIBLE, IS IT?
WE DIDN'T NOTICE... NOBODY DID!! WE COULDN'T SENSE HIM!! BECAUSE THIS BOY...
...HAS NO MAGIC!
MY MAGIC ...

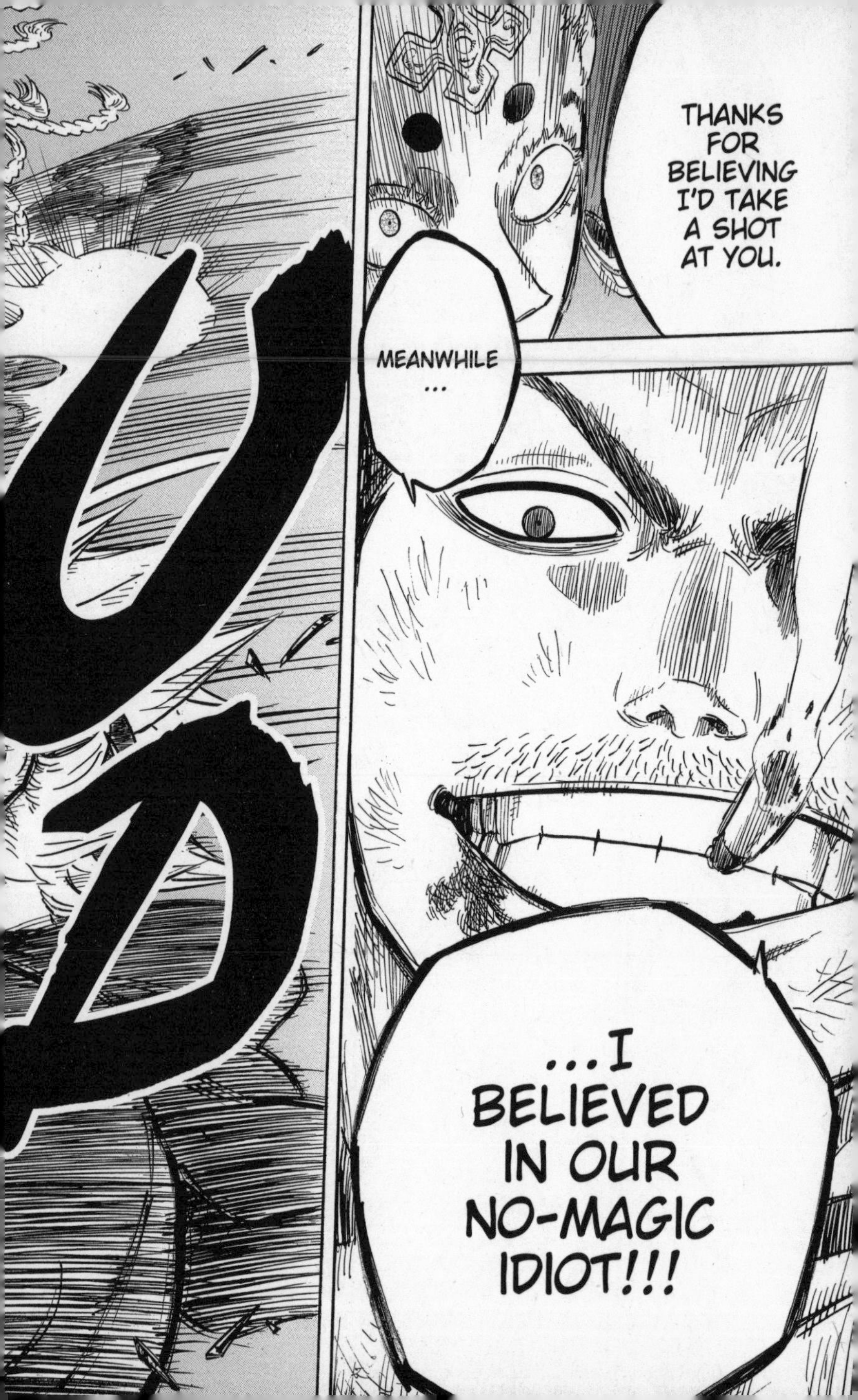
THANKS FOR BELIEVING I'D TAKE A SHOT AT YOU.
MEANWHILE...
...I BELIEVED IN OUR NO-MAGIC IDIOT!!!

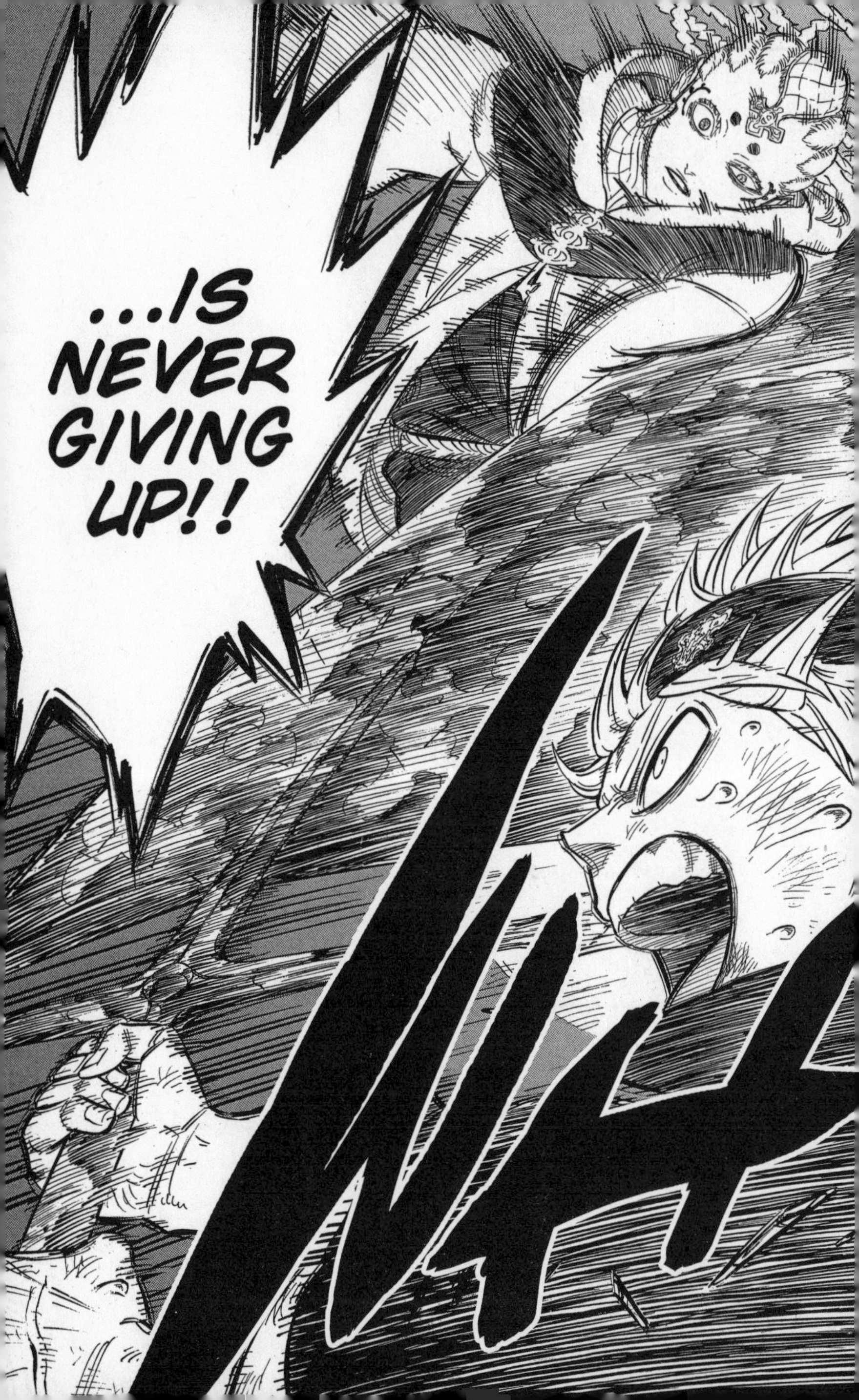
...IS NEVER GIVING UP!!

✤Page 53: They're Not Yours

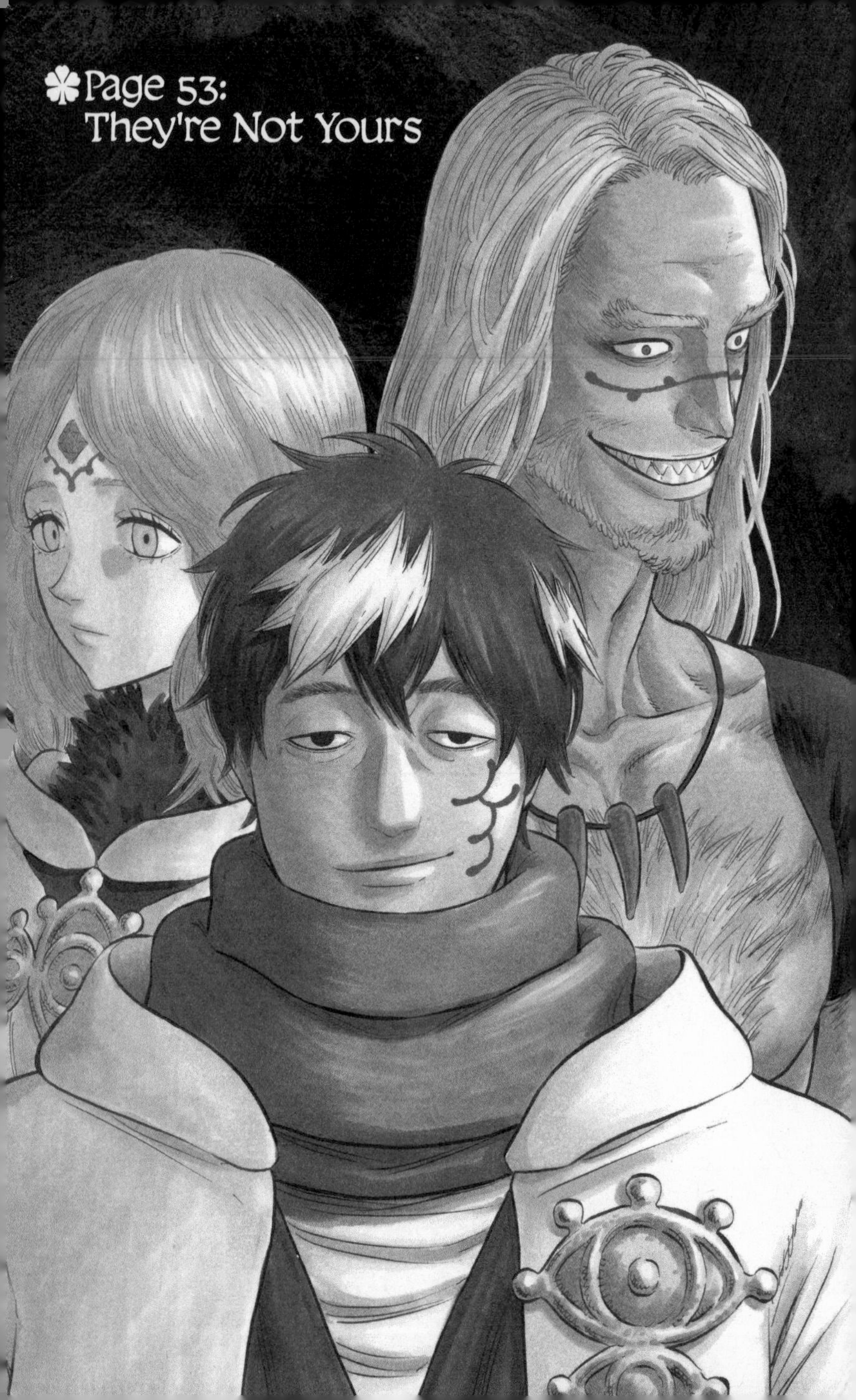

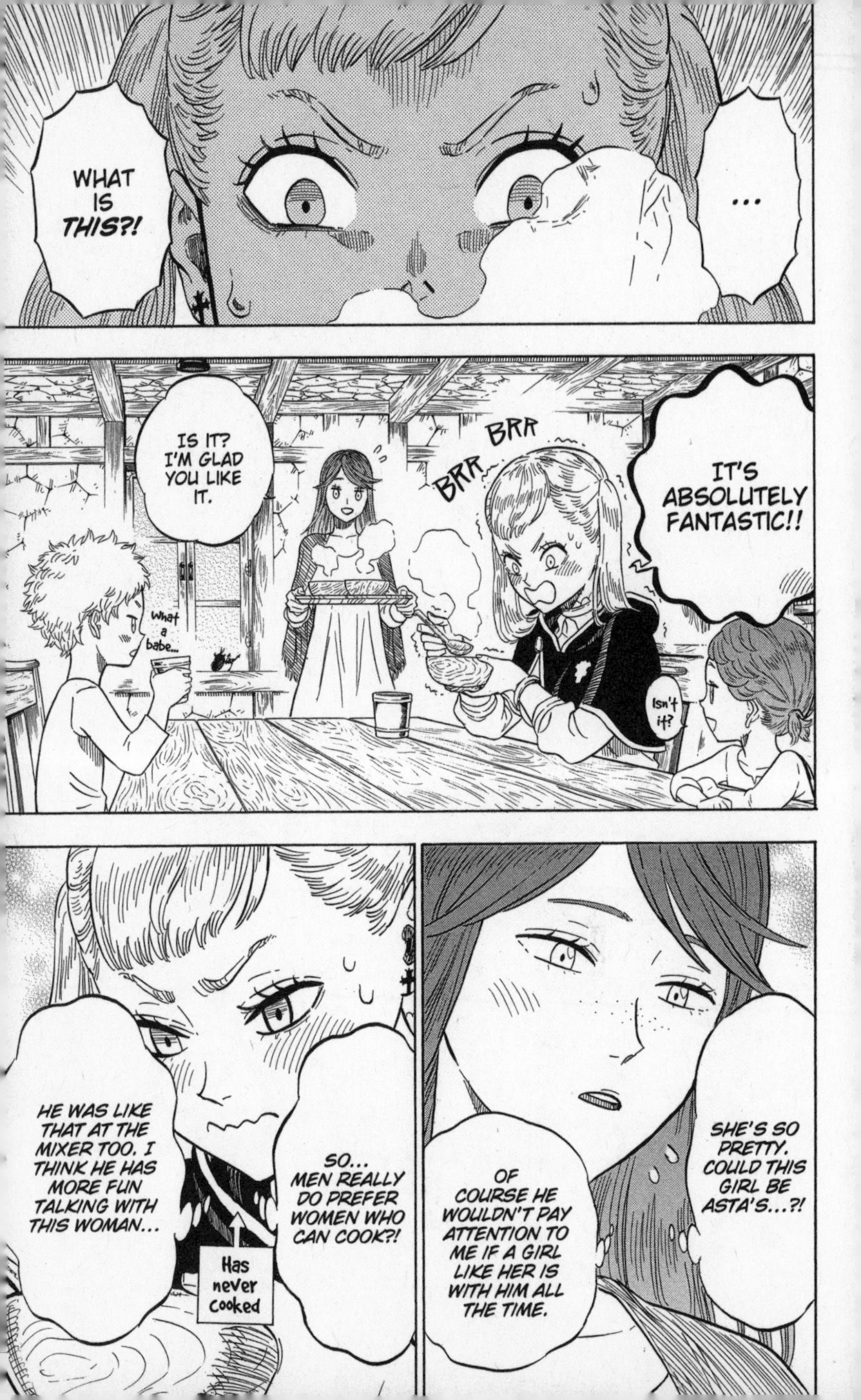
...
WHAT IS THIS?!
IT'S ABSOLUTELY FANTASTIC!!
BRR BRR
IS IT? I'M GLAD YOU LIKE IT.
Isn't it?
what a babe...
SHE'S SO PRETTY. COULD THIS GIRL BE ASTA'S...?!
OF COURSE HE WOULDN'T PAY ATTENTION TO ME IF A GIRL LIKE HER IS WITH HIM ALL THE TIME.
SO... MEN REALLY DO PREFER WOMEN WHO CAN COOK?!
HE WAS LIKE THAT AT THE MIXER TOO. I THINK HE HAS MORE FUN TALKING WITH THIS WOMAN...
Has never cooked

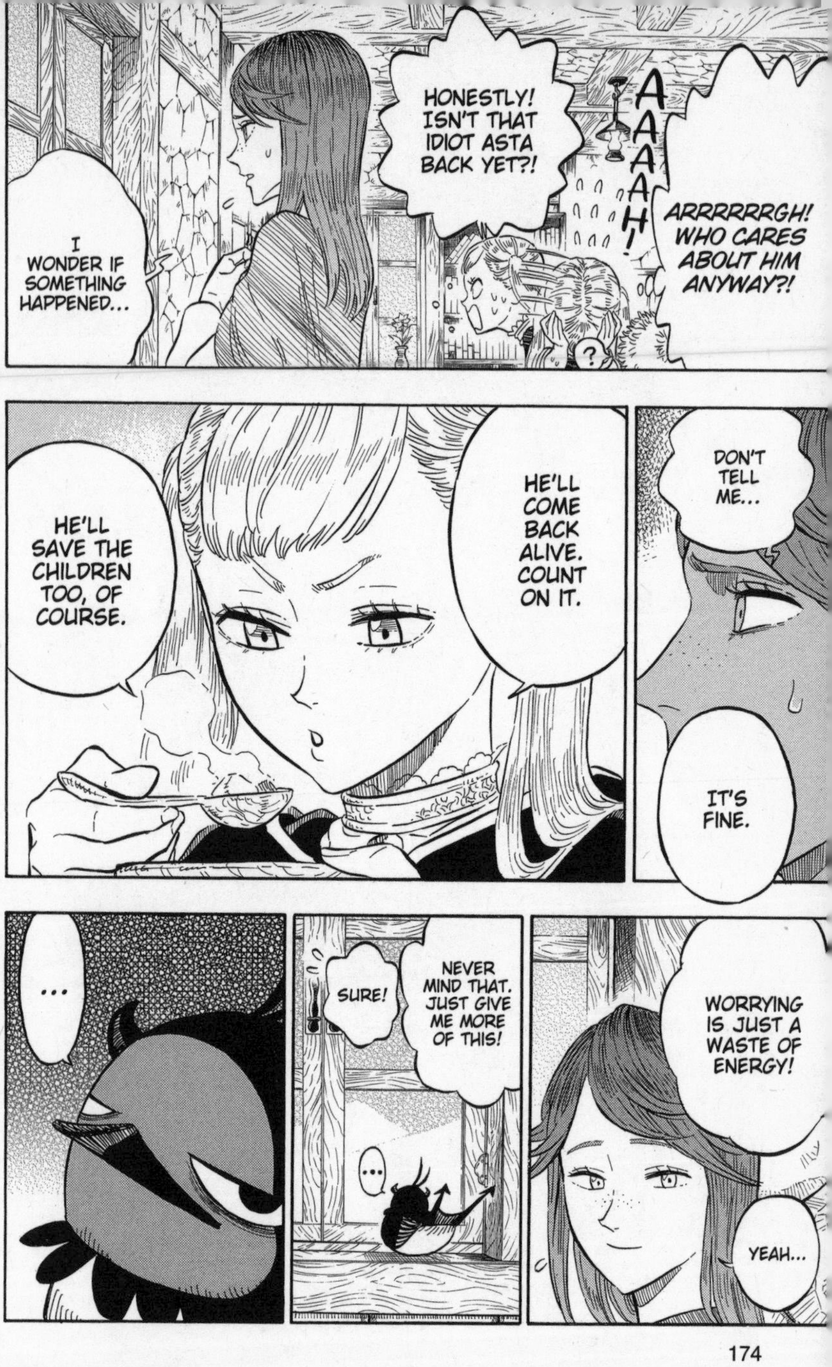
ARRRRRRGH! WHO CARES ABOUT HIM ANYWAY?!
AAAAH!
HONESTLY! ISN'T THAT IDIOT ASTA BACK YET?!
I WONDER IF SOMETHING HAPPENED...
?
DON'T TELL ME...
IT'S FINE.
HE'LL COME BACK ALIVE. COUNT ON IT.
HE'LL SAVE THE CHILDREN TOO, OF COURSE.
WORRYING IS JUST A WASTE OF ENERGY!
YEAH...
NEVER MIND THAT. JUST GIVE ME MORE OF THIS!
SURE!
...
...

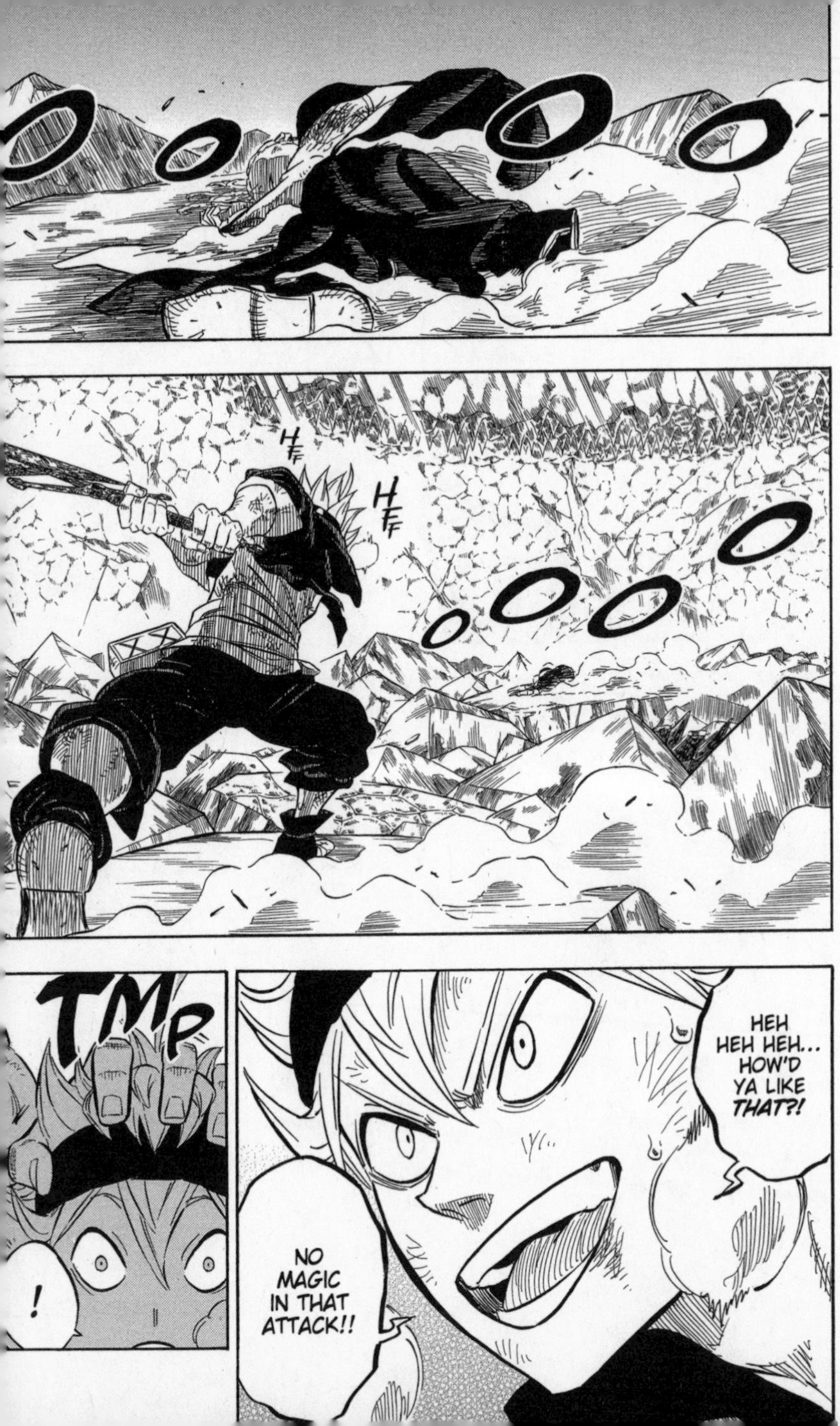
HFF
HFF
HEH HEH HEH... HOW'D YA LIKE THAT?!
NO MAGIC IN THAT ATTACK!!
TMP
!

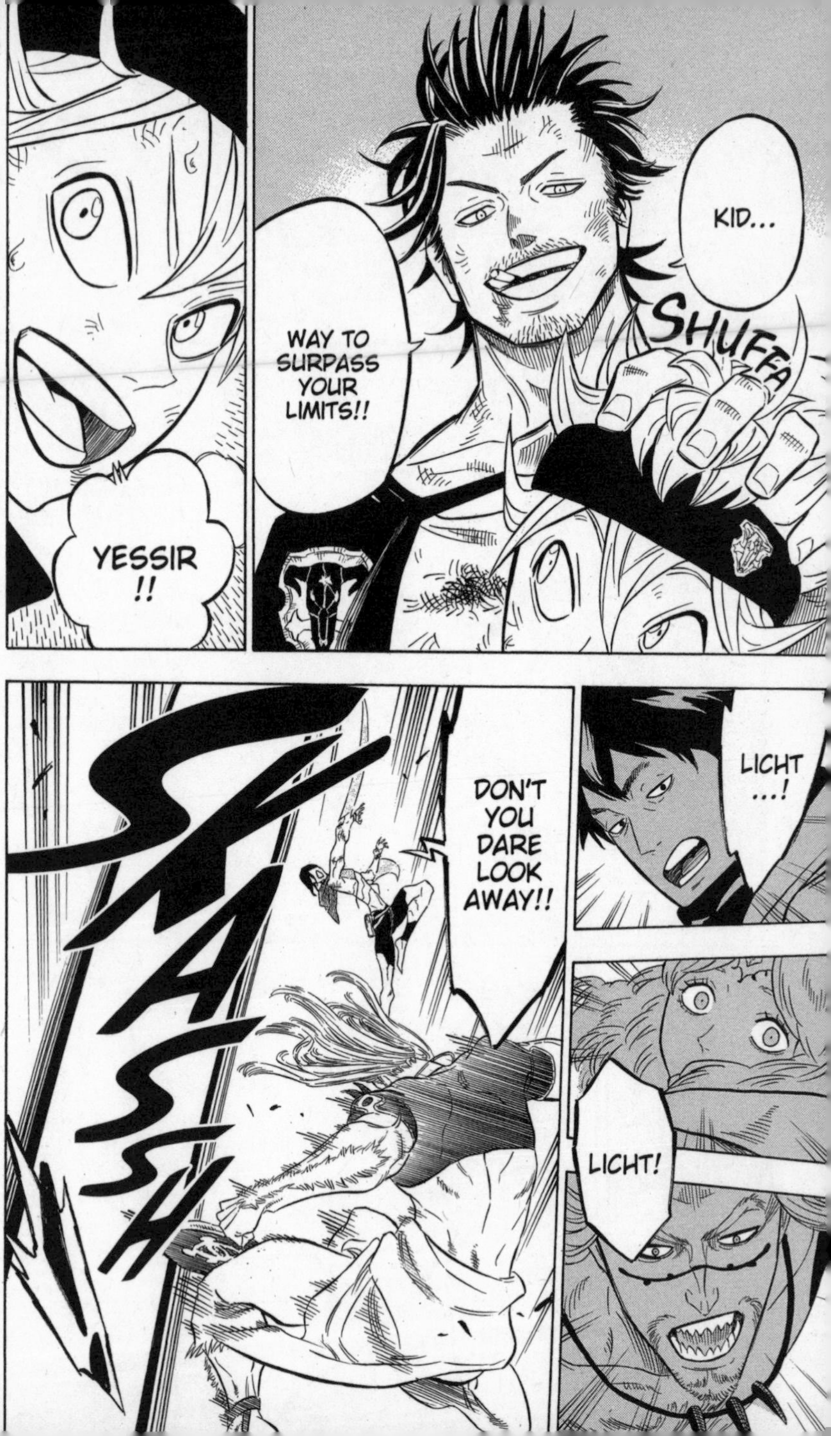
KID...
SHUFFA
WAY TO SURPASS YOUR LIMITS!!
YESSIR!!
LICHT...!
LICHT!
DON'T YOU DARE LOOK AWAY!!
SHASSH

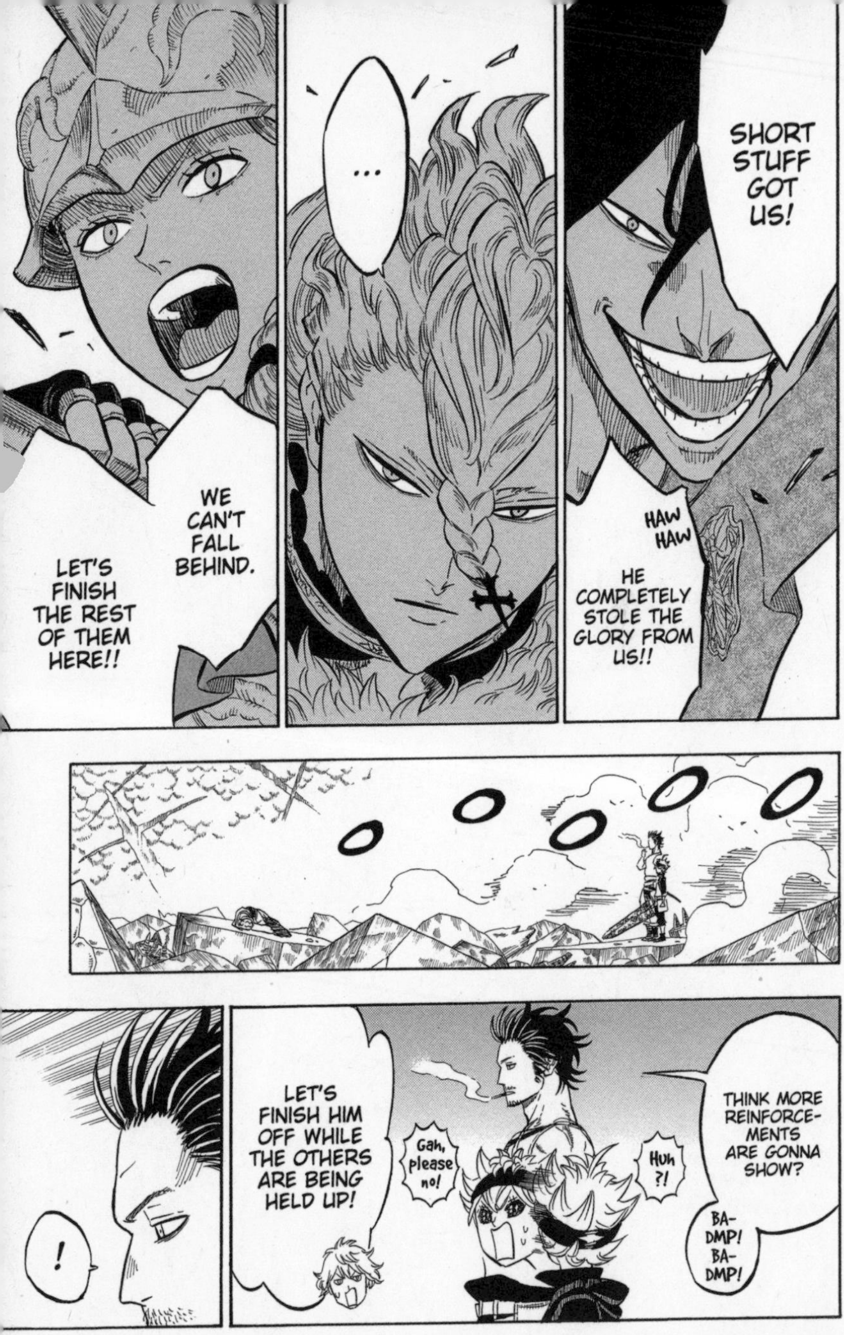
SHORT STUFF GOT US!
HAW HAW
HE COMPLETELY STOLE THE GLORY FROM US!!
...
WE CAN'T FALL BEHIND.
LET'S FINISH THE REST OF THEM HERE!!
THINK MORE REINFORCE-MENTS ARE GONNA SHOW?
BA-DMP! BA-DMP!
Huh?!
Gah, please no!
LET'S FINISH HIM OFF WHILE THE OTHERS ARE BEING HELD UP!
!

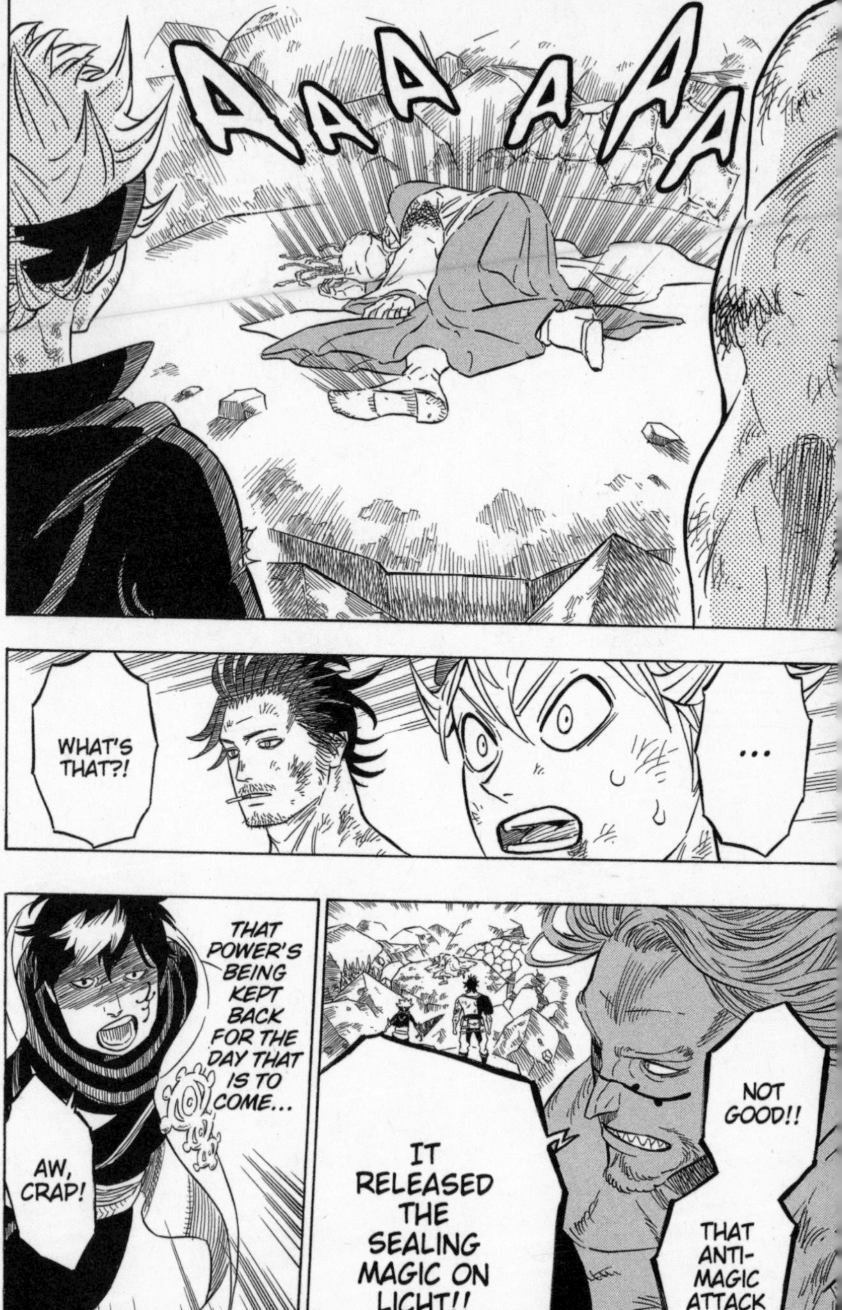
AAAAAA
...
WHAT'S THAT?!
NOT GOOD!!
THAT ANTI-MAGIC ATTACK...
IT RELEASED THE SEALING MAGIC ON LICHT!!
THAT POWER'S BEING KEPT BACK FOR THE DAY THAT IS TO COME...
AW, CRAP!

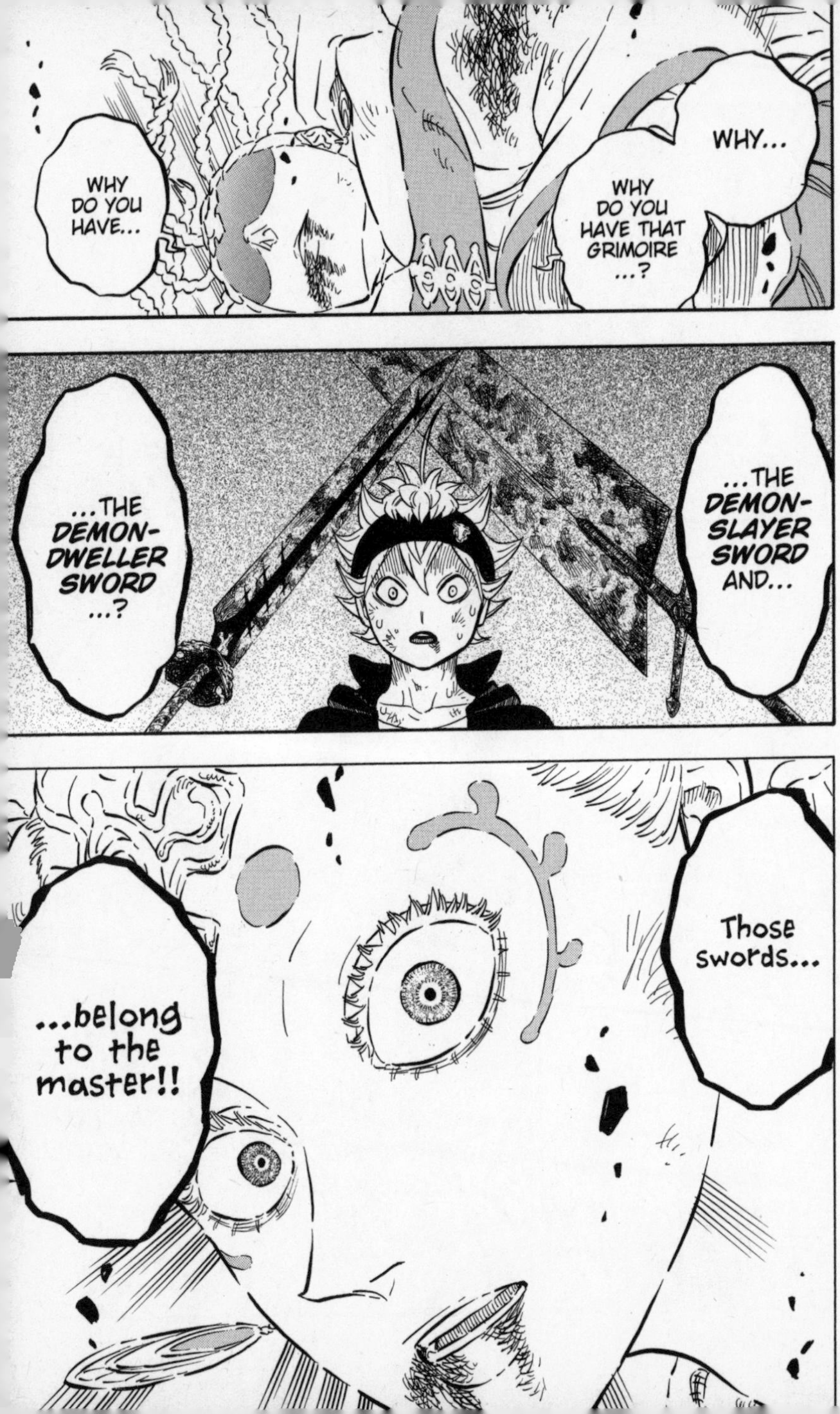
WHY...
WHY DO YOU HAVE THAT GRIMOIRE ...?
WHY DO YOU HAVE...
...THE DEMON-SLAYER SWORD AND...
...THE DEMON-DWELLER SWORD ...?
Those swords...
...belong to the master!!

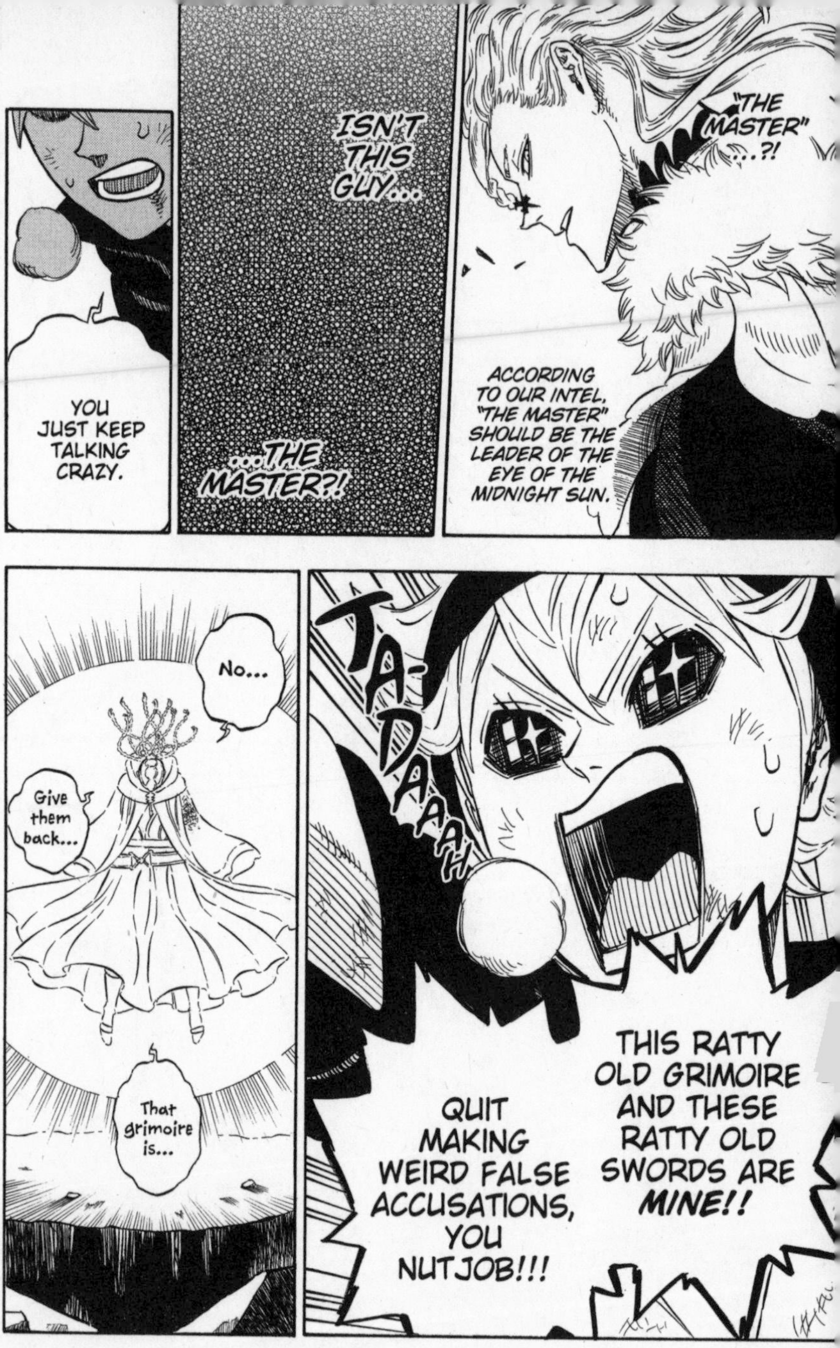
"THE MASTER"...?!
ACCORDING TO OUR INTEL, "THE MASTER" SHOULD BE THE LEADER OF THE EYE OF THE MIDNIGHT SUN.
ISN'T THIS GUY...
...THE MASTER?!
YOU JUST KEEP TALKING CRAZY.
TA-DAAAAH
THIS RATTY OLD GRIMOIRE AND THESE RATTY OLD SWORDS ARE MINE!!
QUIT MAKING WEIRD FALSE ACCUSATIONS, YOU NUTJOB!!!
No...
Give them back...
That grimoire is...

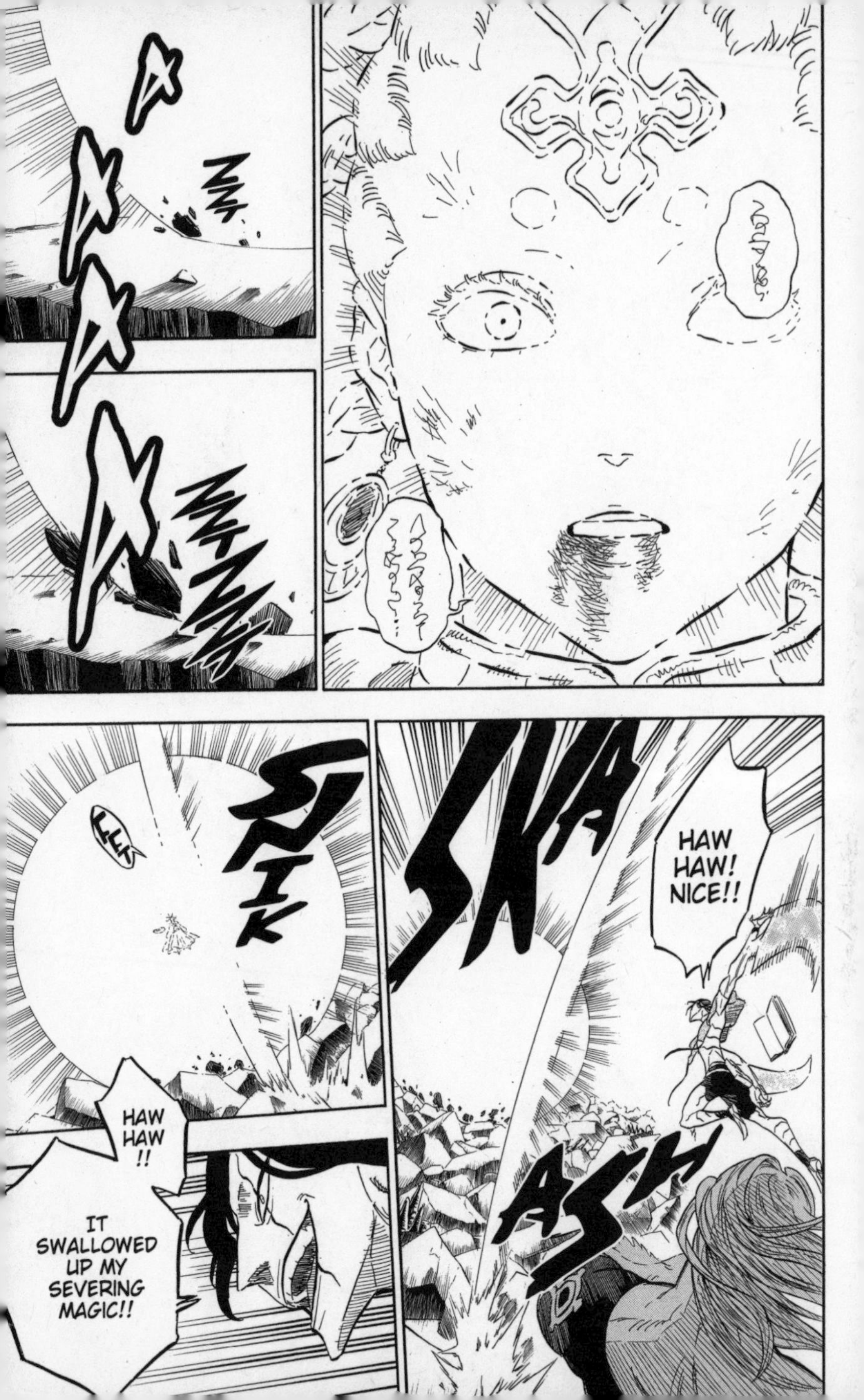
HAW HAW! NICE!!
HAW HAW!!
IT SWALLOWED UP MY SEVERING MAGIC!!

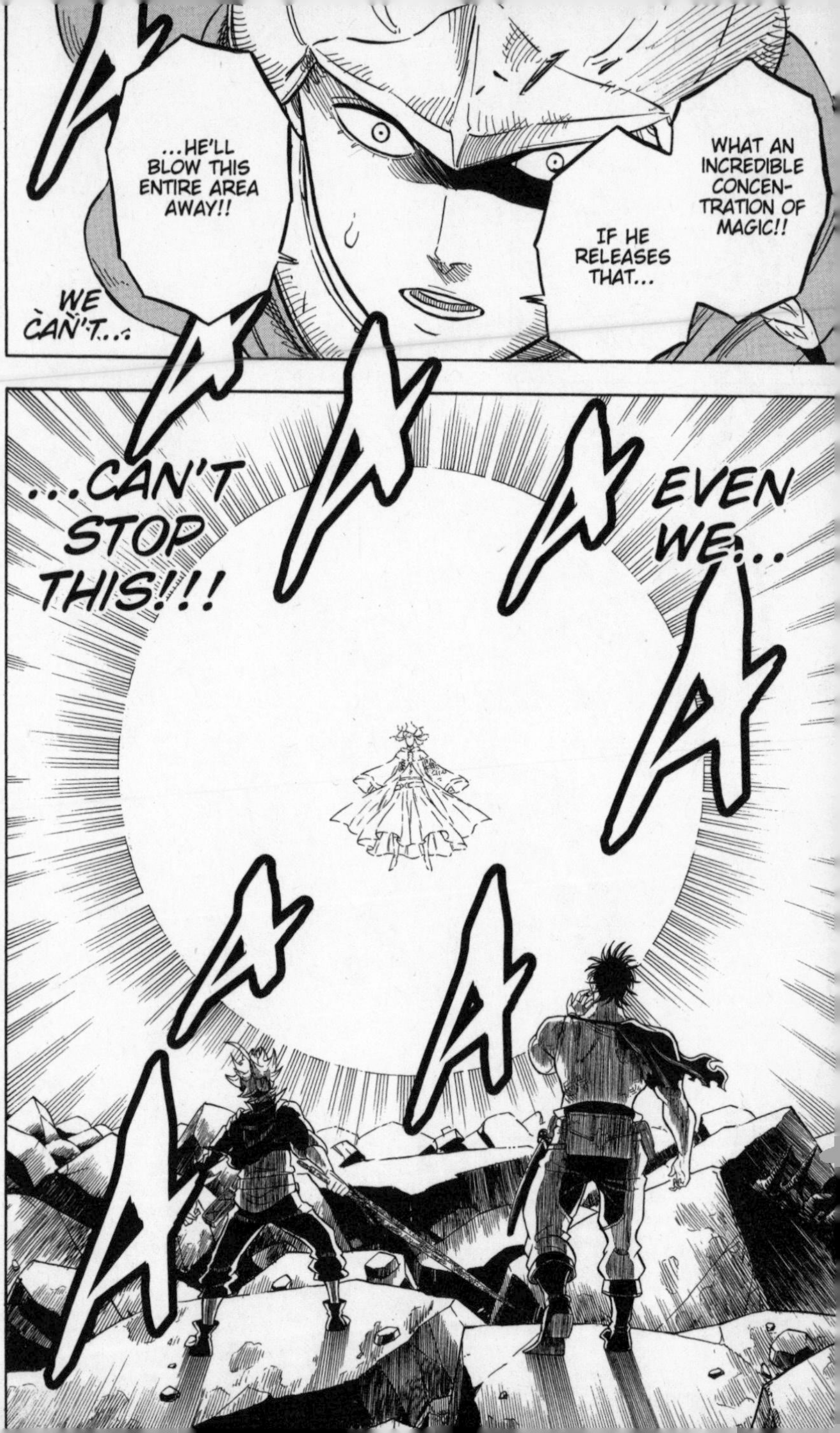
WHAT AN INCREDIBLE CONCEN-TRATION OF MAGIC!!
IF HE RELEASES THAT...
...HE'LL BLOW THIS ENTIRE AREA AWAY!!
WE CAN'T...
EVEN WE...
...CAN'T STOP THIS!!!

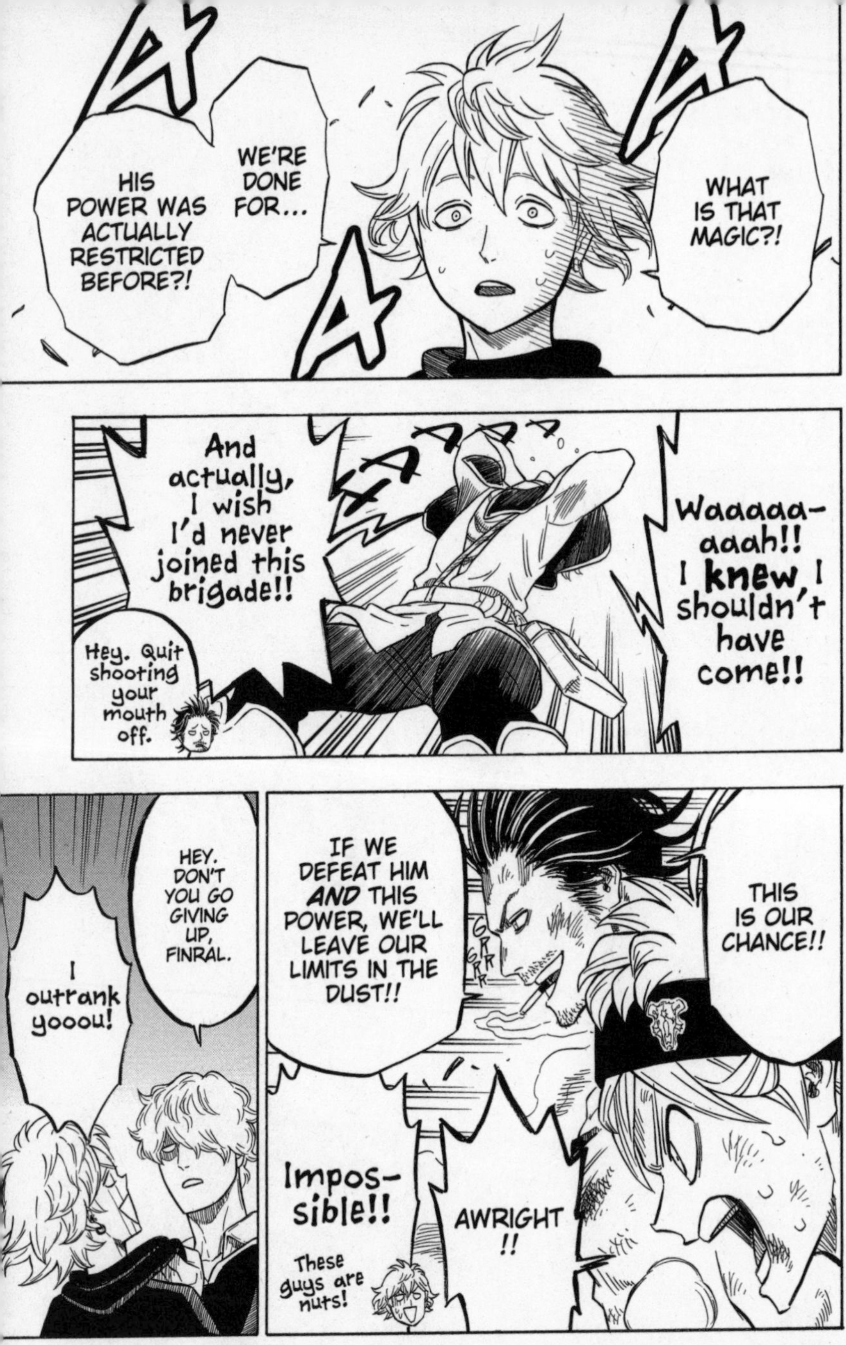
WHAT IS THAT MAGIC?!
WE'RE DONE FOR...
HIS POWER WAS ACTUALLY RESTRICTED BEFORE?!
Waaaaa-aaah!! I **knew** I shouldn't have come!!
And actually, I wish I'd never joined this brigade!!
Hey. Quit shooting your mouth off.
THIS IS OUR CHANCE!!
IF WE DEFEAT HIM *AND* THIS POWER, WE'LL LEAVE OUR LIMITS IN THE DUST!!
AWRIGHT !!
Impos-sible!!
These guys are nuts!
HEY. DON'T YOU GO GIVING UP, FINRAL.
I outrank yooou!

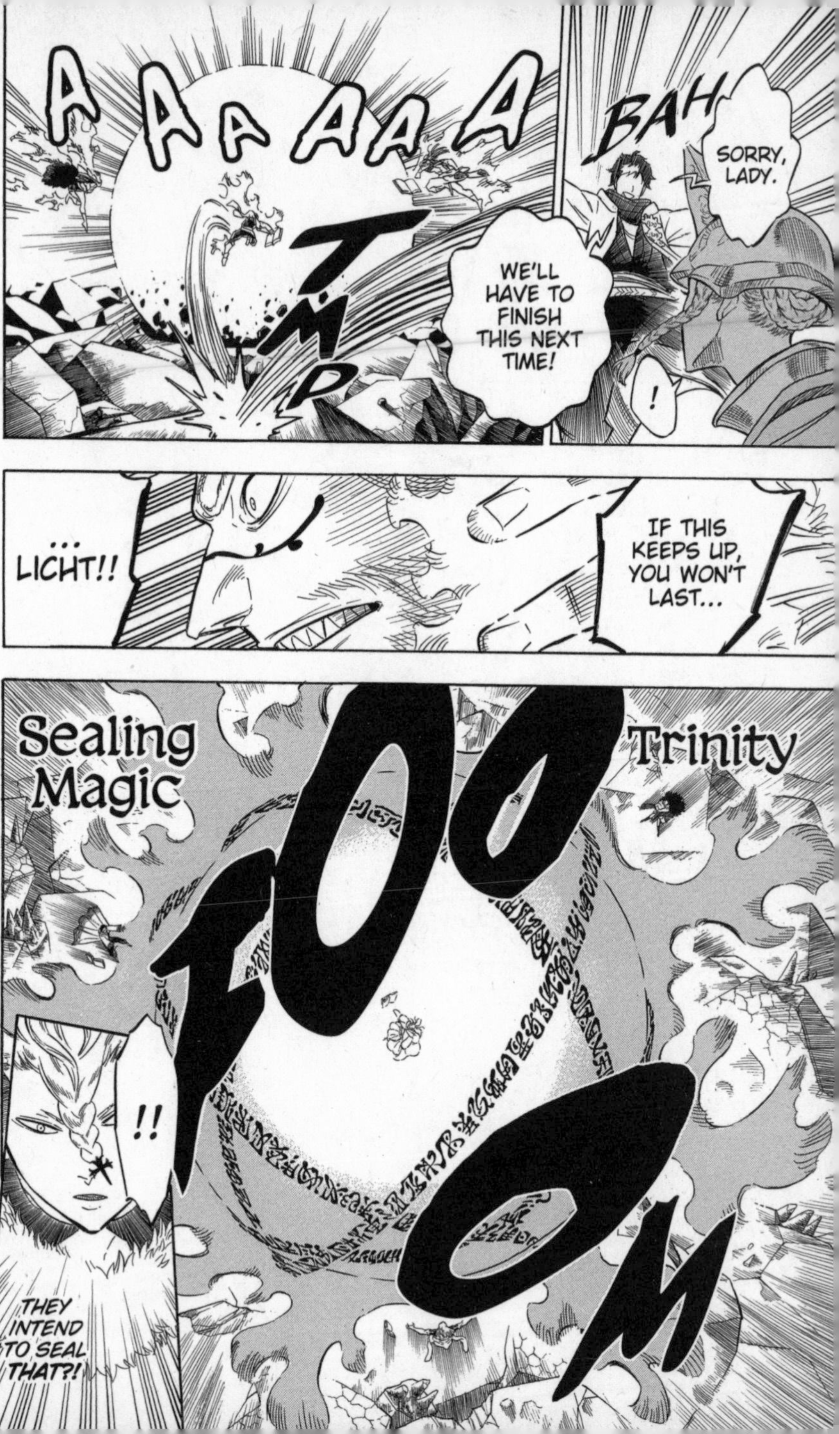
BAH
SORRY, LADY.
WE'LL HAVE TO FINISH THIS NEXT TIME!
!
AAAAAA
TMP
IF THIS KEEPS UP, YOU WON'T LAST...
...LICHT!!
Sealing Magic
Trinity
FOOOM
!!
THEY INTEND TO SEAL THAT?!

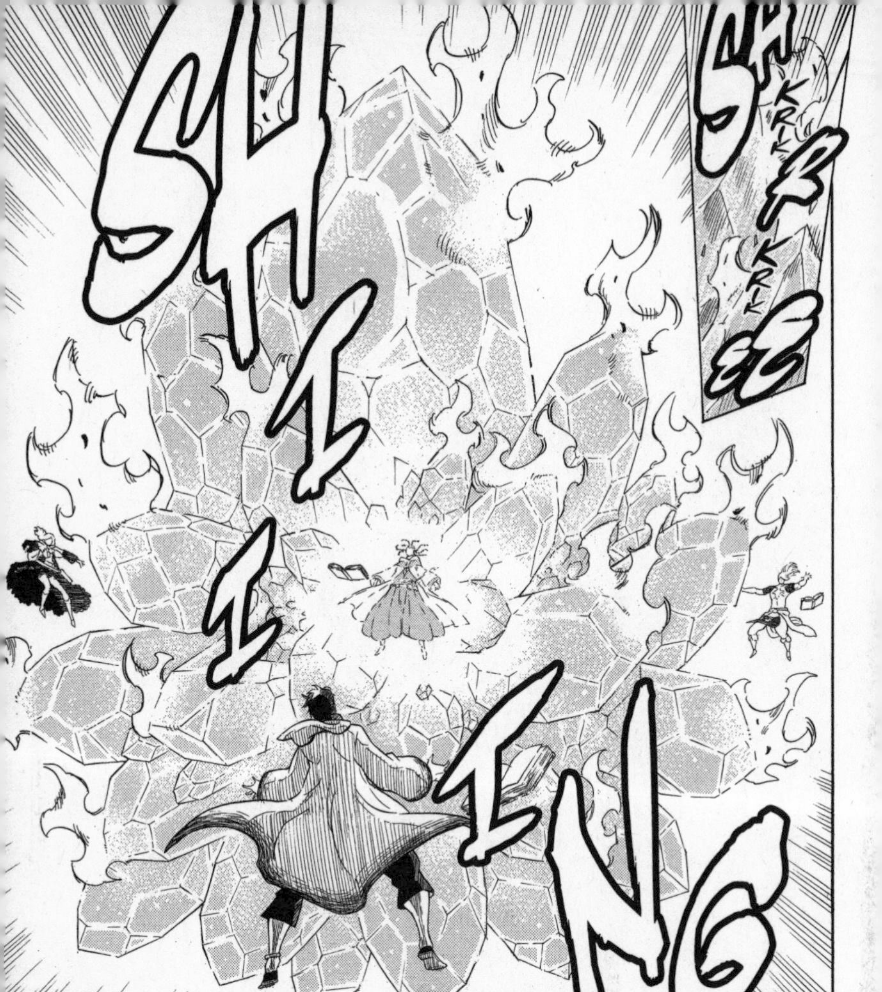
SHREE
KRIK
KRIK
SHIIING
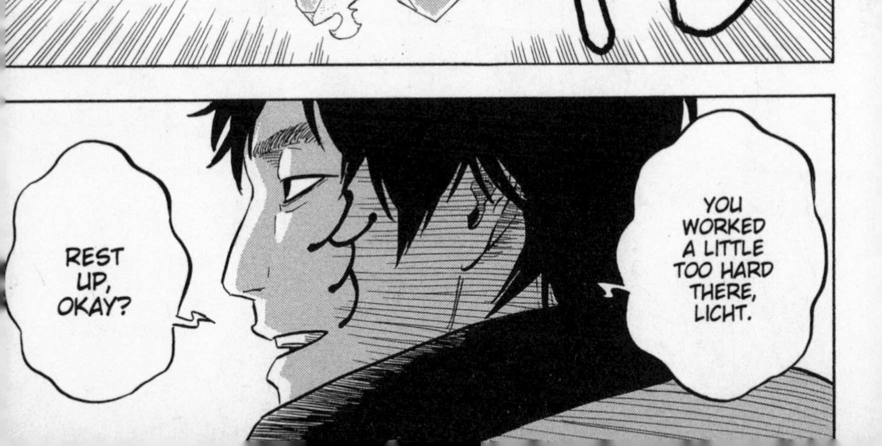
YOU WORKED A LITTLE TOO HARD THERE, LICHT.
REST UP, OKAY?

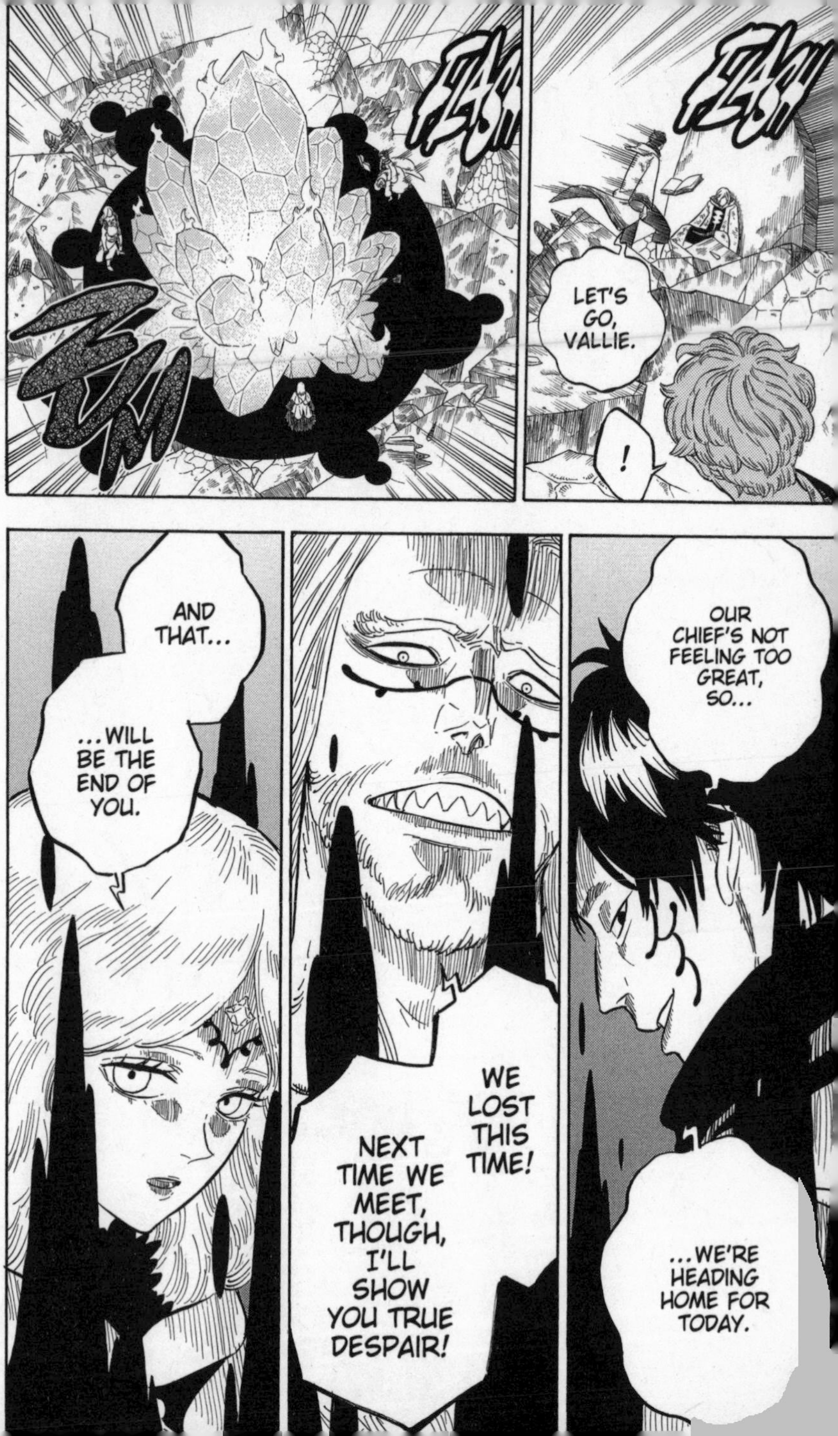
LET'S GO, VALLIE.
!
OUR CHIEF'S NOT FEELING TOO GREAT, SO...
...WE'RE HEADING HOME FOR TODAY.
WE LOST THIS TIME!
NEXT TIME WE MEET, THOUGH, I'LL SHOW YOU TRUE DESPAIR!
AND THAT...
...WILL BE THE END OF YOU.

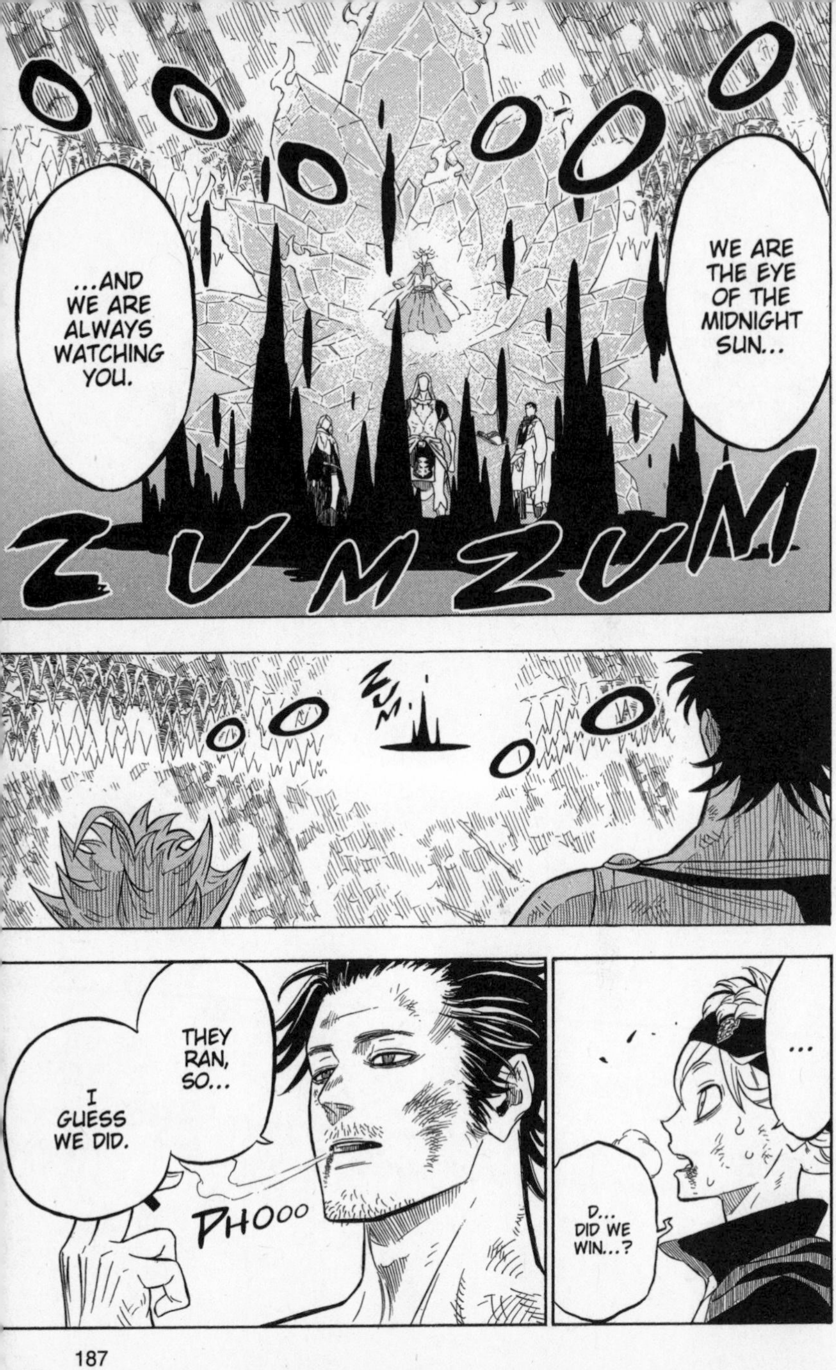
WE ARE THE EYE OF THE MIDNIGHT SUN...
...AND WE ARE ALWAYS WATCHING YOU.
ZUM ZUM
...
D... DID WE WIN...?
THEY RAN, SO...
I GUESS WE DID.
PHOOO

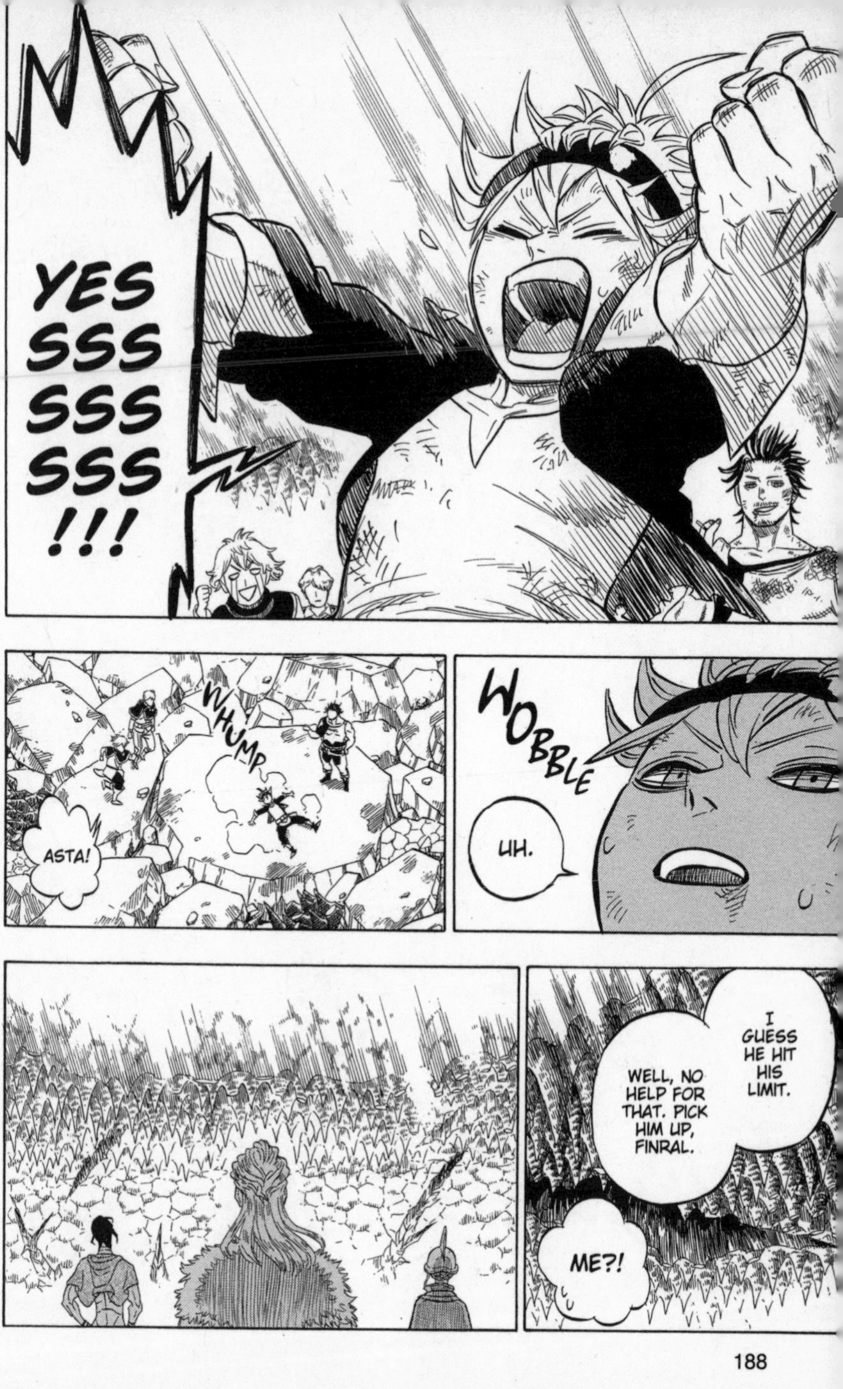
YES
SSS
SSS
SSS
!!!
WOBBLE
UH.
WHUMP
ASTA!
I GUESS HE HIT HIS LIMIT.
WELL, NO HELP FOR THAT. PICK HIM UP, FINRAL.
ME?!

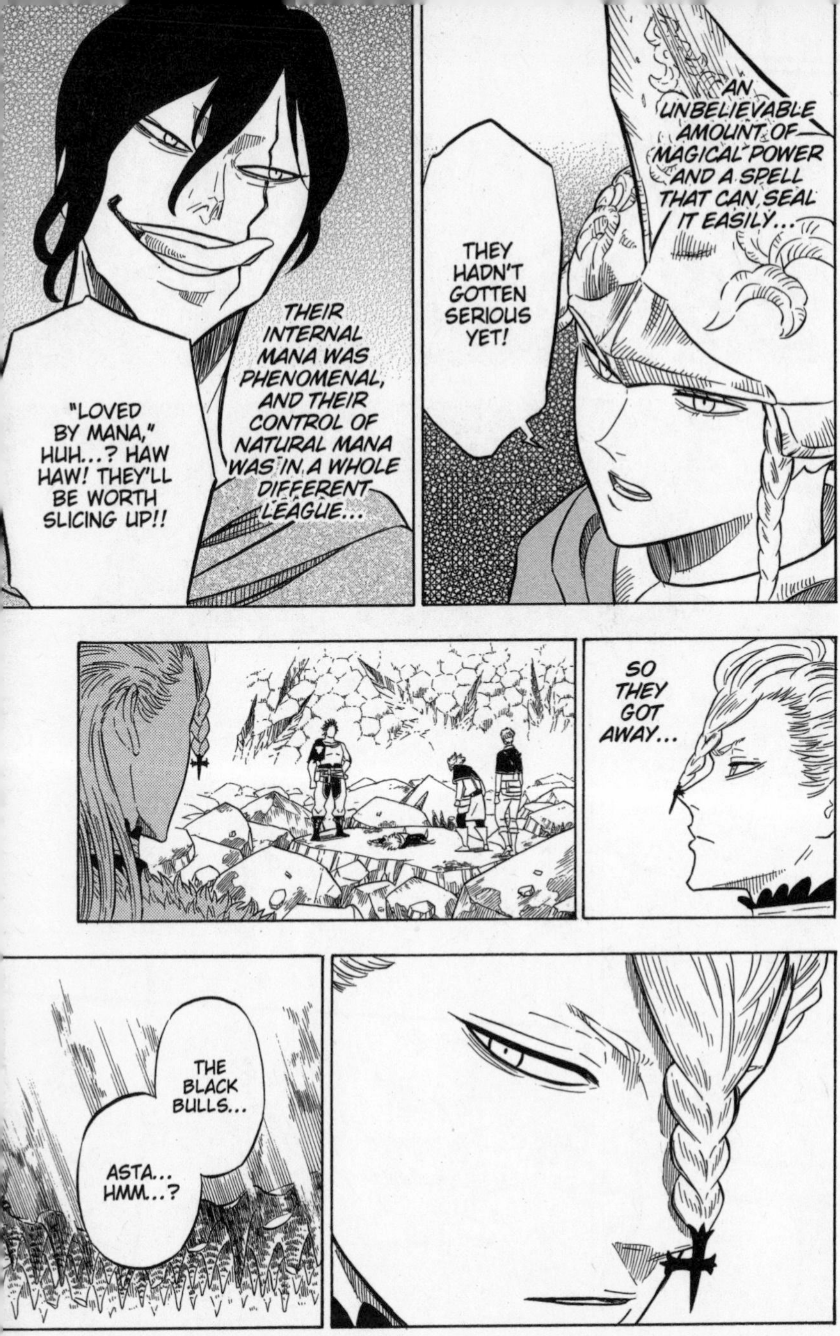
AN UNBELIEVABLE AMOUNT OF MAGICAL POWER AND A SPELL THAT CAN SEAL IT EASILY...
THEY HADN'T GOTTEN SERIOUS YET!
THEIR INTERNAL MANA WAS PHENOMENAL, AND THEIR CONTROL OF NATURAL MANA WAS IN A WHOLE DIFFERENT LEAGUE...
"LOVED BY MANA," HUH...? HAW HAW! THEY'LL BE WORTH SLICING UP!!
SO THEY GOT AWAY...
THE BLACK BULLS...
ASTA... HMM...?

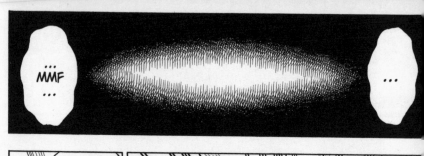

...
MMF
...

...

THIS IS
MAGIC
KNIGHT
HEAD-
QUARTERS.

HUH
?!

WELL
DONE,
ASTA.

SHUP

WHERE
AM
I?!!

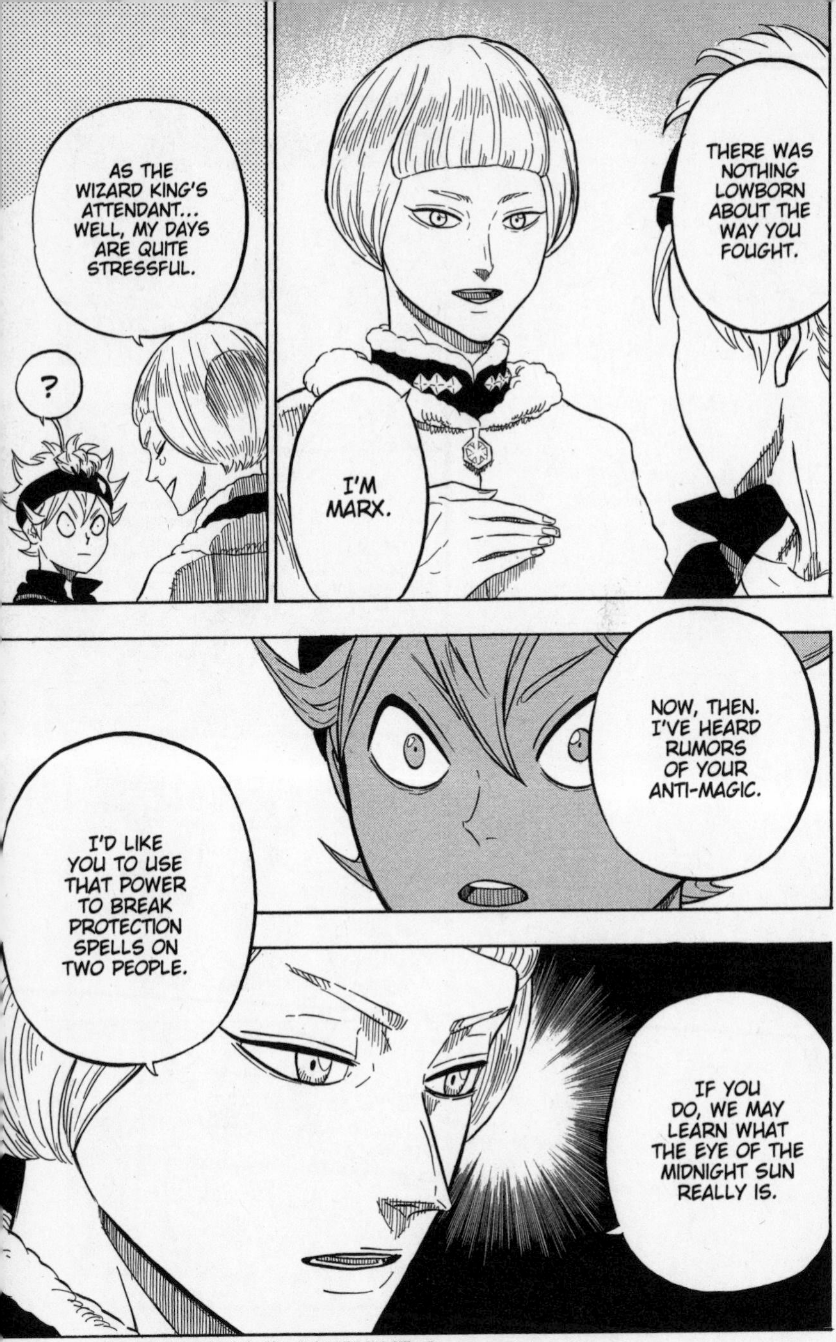
THERE WAS NOTHING LOWBORN ABOUT THE WAY YOU FOUGHT.
I'M MARX.
AS THE WIZARD KING'S ATTENDANT... WELL, MY DAYS ARE QUITE STRESSFUL.
?
NOW, THEN. I'VE HEARD RUMORS OF YOUR ANTI-MAGIC.
I'D LIKE YOU TO USE THAT POWER TO BREAK PROTECTION SPELLS ON TWO PEOPLE.
IF YOU DO, WE MAY LEARN WHAT THE EYE OF THE MIDNIGHT SUN REALLY IS.

TO BE CONTINUED IN VOLUME 7!

Little Sister Love

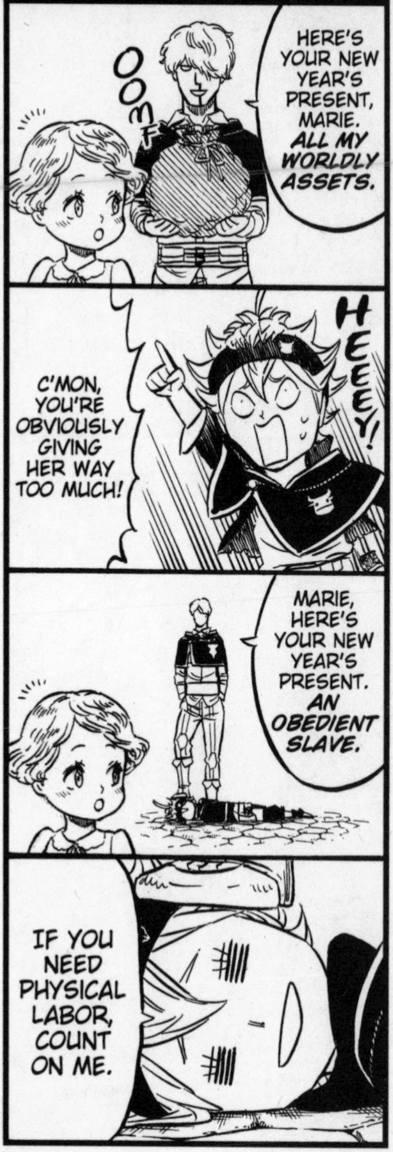
HERE'S YOUR NEW YEAR'S PRESENT, MARIE. ALL MY WORLDLY ASSETS.
OOMF
HEEEEY!
C'MON, YOU'RE OBVIOUSLY GIVING HER WAY TOO MUCH!
MARIE, HERE'S YOUR NEW YEAR'S PRESENT. AN OBEDIENT SLAVE.
IF YOU NEED PHYSICAL LABOR, COUNT ON ME.

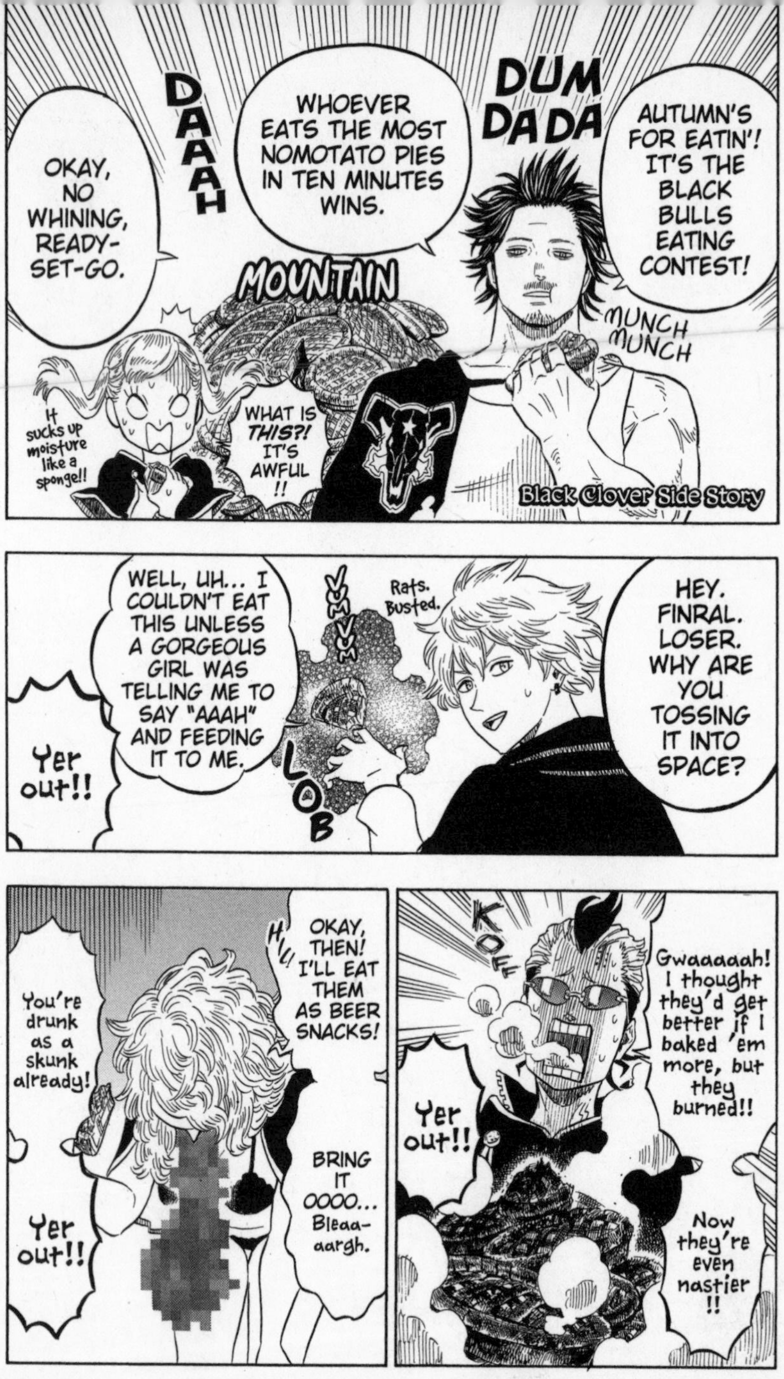
DUM DADA
AUTUMN'S FOR EATIN'! IT'S THE BLACK BULLS EATING CONTEST!
MUNCH MUNCH
WHOEVER EATS THE MOST NOMOTATO PIES IN TEN MINUTES WINS.
DAAAAH
OKAY, NO WHINING, READY-SET-GO.
MOUNTAIN
WHAT IS THIS?! IT'S AWFUL!!
It sucks up moisture like a sponge!!
Black Clover Side Story
HEY. FINRAL. LOSER. WHY ARE YOU TOSSING IT INTO SPACE?
Rats. Busted.
VUMVUM
WELL, UH... I COULDN'T EAT THIS UNLESS A GORGEOUS GIRL WAS TELLING ME TO SAY "AAAH" AND FEEDING IT TO ME.
LOB
Yer out!!
KOFF
Gwaaaaah! I thought they'd get better if I baked 'em more, but they burned!!
Yer out!!
Now they're even nastier!!
HIC
OKAY, THEN! I'LL EAT THEM AS BEER SNACKS!
You're drunk as a skunk already!
BRING IT OOOO... Bleaa-aargh.
Yer out!!

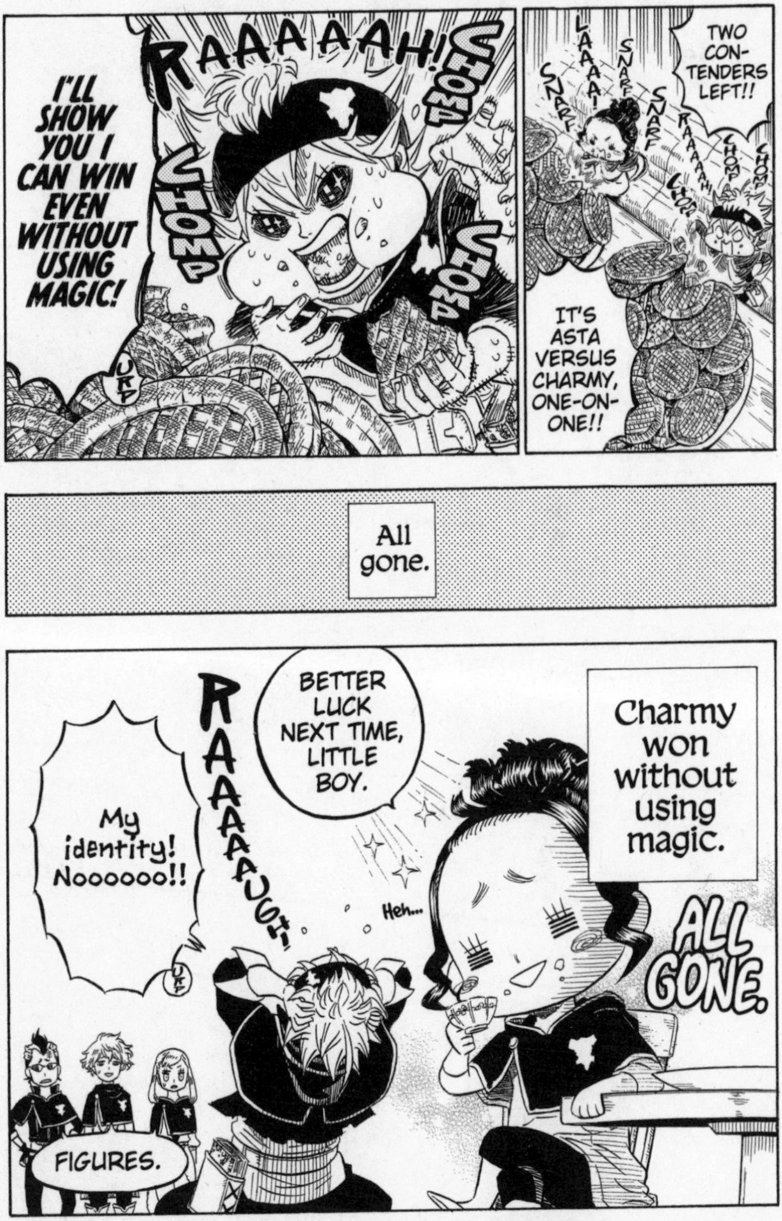
TWO CON-TENDERS LEFT!!
LAAAAA!
SNARF
SNARF
SNARF
SNARF
RAAAAAAH!
CHOMP
CHOMP
CHOMP
IT'S ASTA VERSUS CHARMY, ONE-ON-ONE!!
RAAAAAAH!
CHOMP
I'LL SHOW YOU I CAN WIN EVEN WITHOUT USING MAGIC!
CHOMP
CHOMP
URP
All gone.
Charmy won without using magic.
ALL GONE.
BETTER LUCK NEXT TIME, LITTLE BOY.
Heh...
RAAAAAAUGH!
My identity! Noooooo!!
URP
FIGURES.

Black Clover Side Story...The End

The Blank Page Brigade

This volume's topic: What's your phobia?

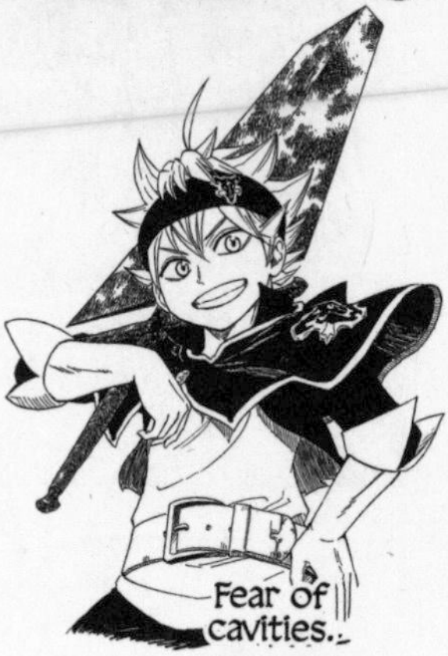

Fear of cavities.

Teruaki Mizuno

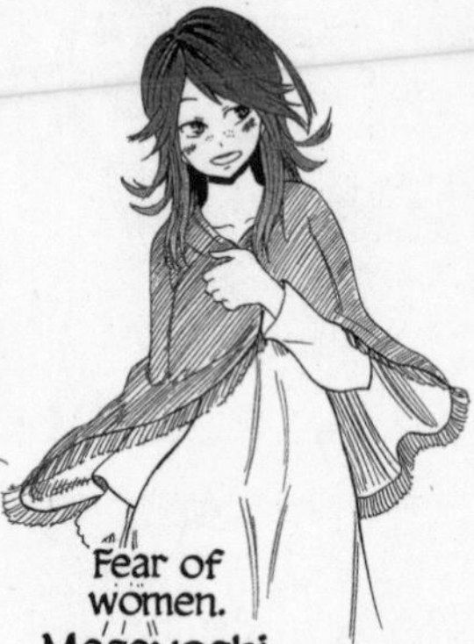

Fear of women.

Masayoshi Satoshō

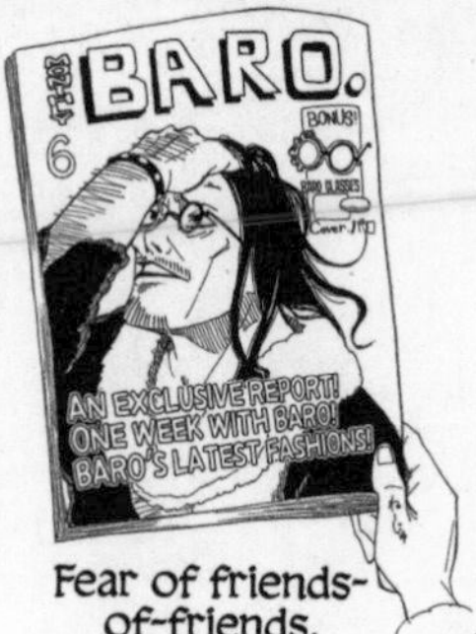
BARO.
6
BONUS!
AN EXCLUSIVE REPORT!
ONE WEEK WITH BARO!
BARO'S LATEST FASHIONS!

Fear of friends-of-friends.

Koki Ishikawa

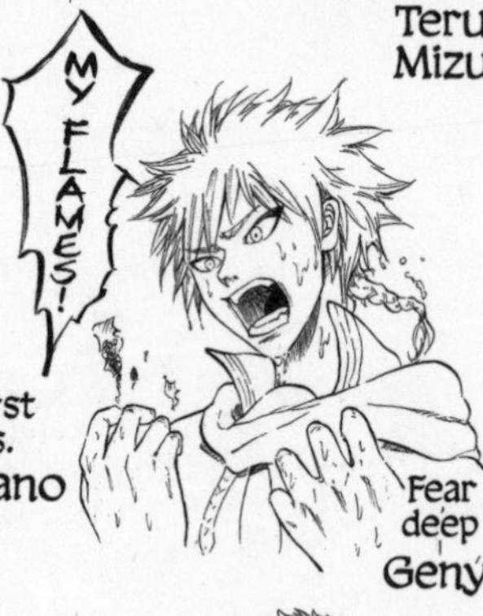
MY FLAMES!

Fear of the deep ocean.

Genya Hori

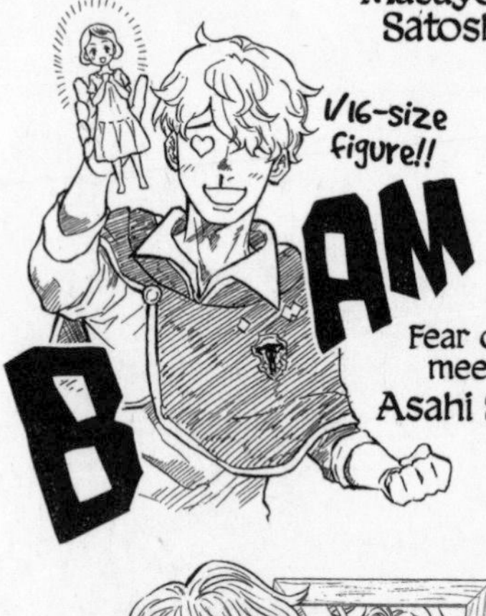
1/16-size figure!!
BAM

Fear of first meetings.

Asahi Sakano

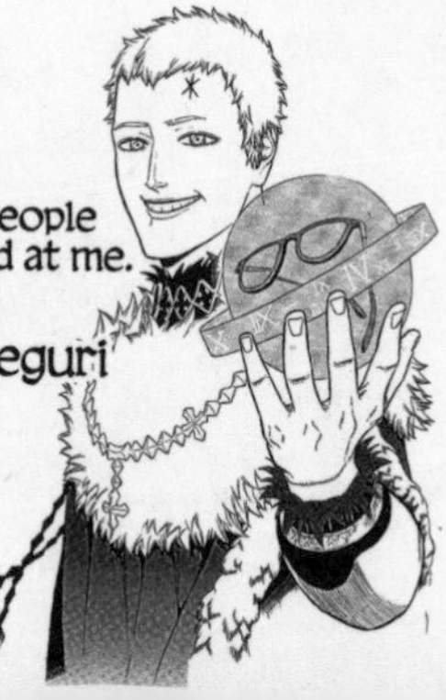

Fear of people getting mad at me.

Ko Shimameguri

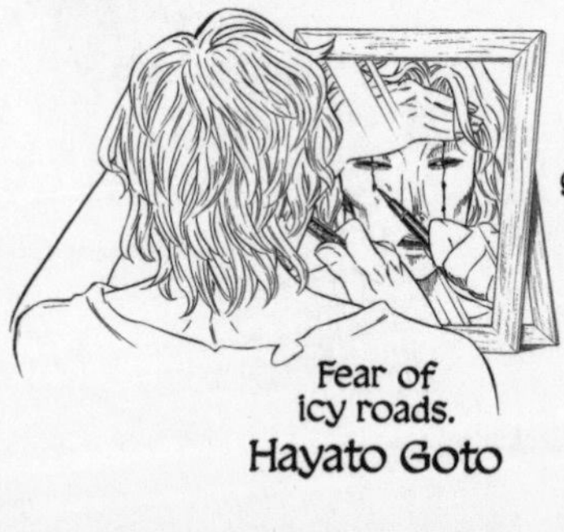

Fear of icy roads.

Hayato Goto

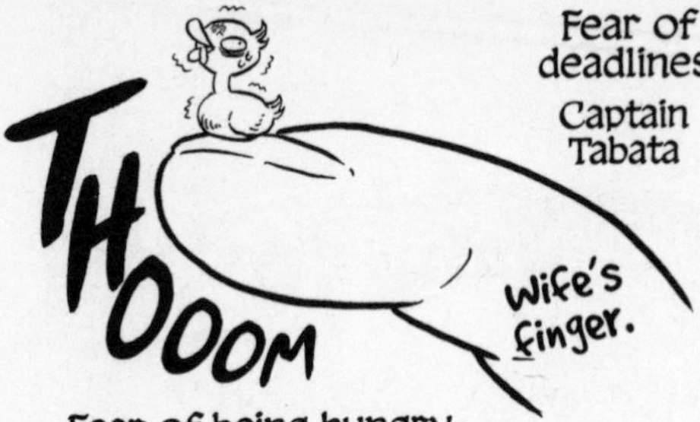
THOOOM
Wife's finger.

Fear of deadlines.
Captain Tabata

Fear of being hungry.
©

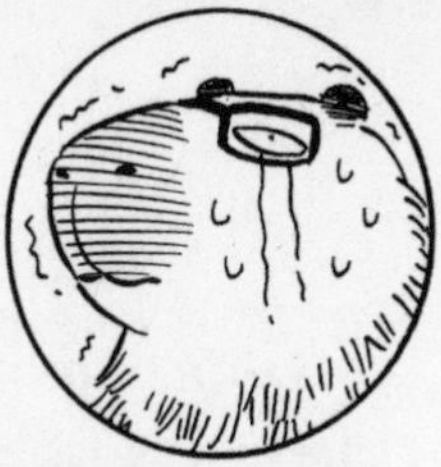

Fear of the clock on the last day of a deadline. (Please stop moving...)
Editor Katayama

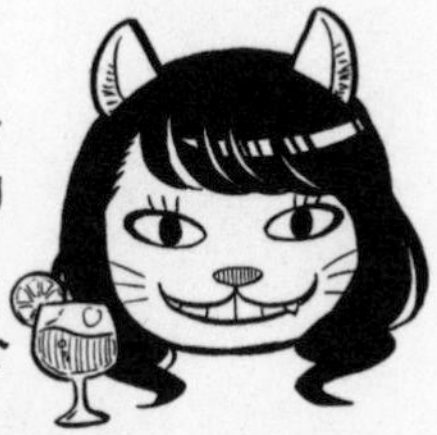

Fear of running out of ideas.
Designer Iwai

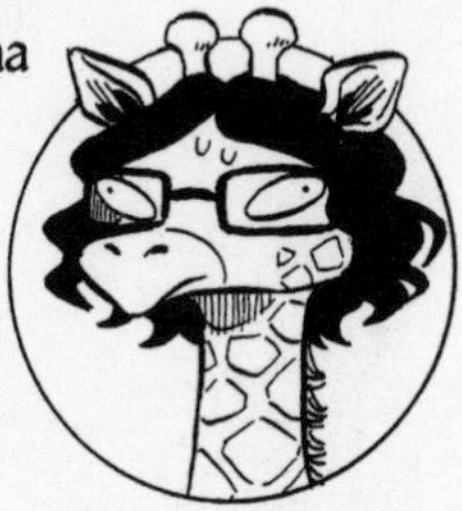

Fear of my one-year-old daughter's cold gaze...
Comics Editor Tomiyama

AFTERWORD

Guess what?!

For this volume, Hirofumi Arai–an actor who's all over the movies and television–provided a blurb! Thank you so much!

When my workplace was introduced on the TV show *Special Research Police JUMPolice*, Arai came by in person for a tour! Wow... I was so incredibly nervous.

Arai was a great guy though, and I had fun!

Due to this and that, a character who's modeled on Arai joins the series in this volume.

What the heck is this manga, anyway?!

I'll keep doing my best so that Raia gets to do a lot too.

Special Bonus Materials

Presenting early sketches of the Third Eye! Raia is actually modeled on actor and *Jump* fan Hirofumi Arai!

Raia

In response to Mr. Arai's request during a project for the TV show *Special Research Police JUMPolice*, Tabata Sensei made him into a character.

Vetto

Fana

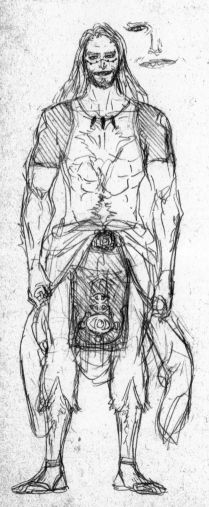

Stop

YOU'RE READING
THE WRONG WAY!

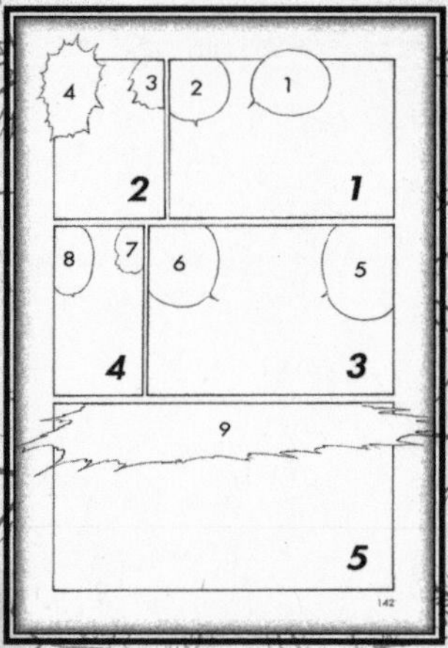

BLACK CLOVER

reads from right to left, starting
in the upper-right corner. Japanese
is read from right to left, meaning
that action, sound effects, and
word-balloon order are completely
reversed from English order.